Early reviews for *Sea Trials*:

"...The author's expressive writing captures the wonder of being at sea in all its glory... her engaging narrative succeeds in capturing the thrills and frustrations of this intrepid family. Taking in remarkably far-flung destinations such as Christmas Island and the New Hebrides, this exhilarating book should appeal to any would-be explorer who has stood at the prow of a ship and dreamed of the possibilities. Highly readable and sufficiently evocative to sense the scent of sea air in the pages.—*Kirkus Reviews* (starred review). Selected a Kirkus Book of the Month.

"What a tale! The Wilcox family's epic 'round-tripper had me turning pages at flank speed. Wendy Hinman crafts a true-life adventure story as outlandish and memorable as *The Swiss Family Robinson*, with shipwreck, reefs, dengue fever, gun-toting soldiers, and teenagers who won't do their homework." —Bruce Barcott, author of *Last Flight of the Scarlet Macaw* and Weed the People and a contributor to Outside Magazine

"A modern, swashbuckling adventure, *Sea Trials: Around the World with Duct Tape and Bailing Wire* will quickly transport readers through a fascinating, light read out to sea aboard the *Vela*." —*Seattle Book Review*

"*Sea Trials* is a skillfully told story of perseverance, ingenuity, and grit. Wendy Hinman is back with another gripping sea saga, one that's vivid enough to make you feel you're aboard the 40-foot *Vela*...or shipwrecked on a reef in Fiji. Hinman's pacing keeps the story humming along and her eye for detail helps us savor the voyage. Brief, well-placed excerpts from the family's letters read like gems in a treasure hunt." —Janna Cawrse Esarey, author of *Motion of the Ocean*

"A gripping tale of a family's harrowing journey to sail around the world against seemingly insurmountable and deadly odds." —Robert Dugoni, the #1 Amazon and #1 Wall Street Journal bestselling author of the *Tracy Crosswhite* **series**

"This true story of the Wilcox family is completely riveting and simultaneously insanely frustrating – which means it's a great book! Hinman's attention to little details like family squabbles and disagreements or stop-gap repairs make the whole trip vivid and real and their concerns intense... you are intensely caught up in the family's decisions and dilemmas while they are facing them and can sympathize with their recurrent optimism and desire to achieve their goal. *Sea Trials* immerses you in the Wilcox's world as you share their great adventure, for good and ill. It is an adventure that, for readers, is well worth the trip." —*San Francisco Book Review*

"In a time before cell phones and laptops, the Wilcox family set out to sail around the world, but after a shipwreck, their adventure takes a dramatic detour. Thrilling, poignant, and hilarious moments surface as this family struggles to cope with each other, repair the wreck and most of all, to keep going. The only thing missing are recipes for their extreme-budget meals!" —Debra Daniels-Zeller author of *The Northwest Vegetarian Cookbook*

"A satisfying read about the costs and rewards of human endeavor and the effects they have on a family." —Jan Burak Schwert, author of *Geezers' Guide to the Galaxy: A Lifetime of Travel Encounters*

"A nail-biting adventure story with thought-provoking lessons for today's sailors."—Elsie Hulsizer, author of *Voyages to Windward* and *Glaciers, Bears and Totems*

"Hinman has written a compelling story of a family's quest to sail around the world, a trip that starts with equal parts of hope and hubris and becomes a survival tale as the family surmounts one obstacle after another to keep their ship afloat." —Sharon L. Morris, Adventure Travel Writer

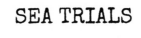

SEA TRIALS

SEA TRIALS

Around the World with Duct Tape and Bailing Wire

Wendy Hinman

Salsa Press, Seattle, WA

Sea Trials: Around the World with Duct Tape and Bailing Wire
Published by
Salsa Press, Seattle, WA

Printed in the United States of America.
978-09848350-3-4 Sea Trials, paperback
978-0-984350-4-1 Sea Trials, eBook

ISBN: 0984835032
ISBN-13: 9780984835034 (Salsa Press)

Library of Congress Control Number Cataloging-in-Publication Data (LCCN)

Hinman, Wendy Elizabeth
Sea Trials: Around the World with Duct Tape and Bailing Wire / Wendy Hinman
Description: First Edition: Seattle: Salsa Press 2017
Identifiers: LCCN 2016920591: ISBN 978-09848350-3-4
Subjects: Travel, Family, Adventure and Adventurers, Biography, Ocean Travel, Sailing
Classification: 2016920591
LC record locator at http://lccn.loc.gov/ 2016920591

Salsa Press, Seattle, WA

Cover designed by Lyssa Danehy deHart
photo frame: euroshot/123rf.com
duct tape: Stu101/bigstockphoto.com

Photos are from the Wilcox family collection
Route Map by Garth Wilcox

A Note from the Author

For years, my husband and his family have shared snippets from their epic voyage around the world. Intrigued to learn more, I delved into the details and discovered a richer tale than I'd imagined, one that deserved to be shared with a wider audience.

Sea Trials highlights major events from the around-the-world journey the Wilcox family took aboard *Vela*, their 40-foot Maine Pinky, from 1973 to 1978. Their voyage occurred during the relative dark ages of sailing when people navigated using a sextant, long before the days of instant communication. Few undertook such a journey, and limited information was available about outfitting a boat for ocean voyaging or ports along the way. Yet, despite unbelievable obstacles, this pioneering family survived a shipwreck and made it all the way around the world. No small feat.

To tell this story, I drew upon:

- Personal interviews with my husband, Garth Wilcox; his mother, Dawn Wilcox; and his father, Chuck Wilcox;
- An unpublished manuscript by Garth's sister, Linda Wilcox, which she wrote when she was sixteen, registered with the Library of Congress, and later shared with us;
- An unpublished partial manuscript by Erika Hublitz, the University of California schoolwork administrator with whom the family corresponded during the voyage;

- The ship's log and related notes from Dawn Wilcox;
- News articles about the shipwreck and the family upon their return by local as well as AP and UPI reporters that appeared in publications around the world; and a TV interview with talk-show host Maury Povich;
- Hundreds of detailed letters handwritten by family members during the voyage;
- Photos and scrapbooks;
- Recordings of family members sharing their story before a live audience;
- Resources the family relied upon for information, including *National Geographic* publications, newspaper and magazine articles, sailing directions and then-available guidebooks, plus modern-day guides and books;
- Weather, tides, currents, and charts of the areas when the family sailed there;
- News stories, events, and popular culture of the day.

In addition I relied upon my own experience undertaking a comparable sailing voyage and visits to some of these locations. Dialogue is based upon recollections and my knowledge of the personalities involved.

My aim was to depict events as accurately as I could. When reading, please keep in mind that even shortly after living it, family members had different perspectives on what happened, and no one's memory is 100 percent accurate, especially after so many years—and I was not there.

I am excited to share this compelling story and hope you enjoy it.

Wendy Hinman

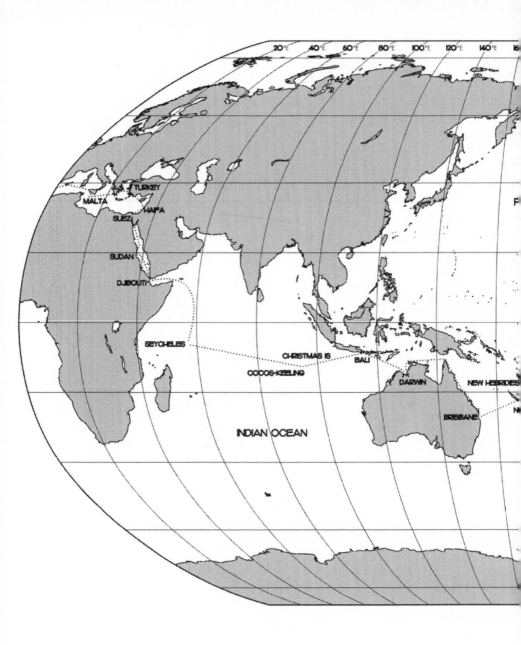

Vela's ro

he world

Prologue

Vela rocked gently, lines creaking with the steady motion of following seas. City lights glowed on the distant horizon like a beacon marking their destination: Suva, the capital of Fiji. After five days of sailing from the tiny island nation of Tonga with little but the change of watch to mark the passage of time, everyone in the Wilcox family eagerly anticipated landfall.

Fiji would be the fifth South Pacific island nation they visited in the exciting year since they'd sailed away from San Francisco's Bay Area, a year filled with fascinating cultures and geography so different from their home in California. With an overcast sky, getting star sights had been a challenge the last few days, but conservative calculations projected they'd arrive at the harbor entrance later in the day. Still, everyone slept fitfully the night before landfall.

Dawn Wilcox blinked away sleepiness as she began her watch duties. She made a careful scan of the horizon before settling into the cockpit with the woolen army blanket the four of them used during night watches. One light stood out against the hazy glow on an otherwise featureless horizon. She found it hard to tell how far away it was since depth perception at night is a challenge, especially when a light is blinking on and off. Besides, she couldn't always trust her vision. She rubbed her eyes and adjusted her glasses, then decided to consult the charts.

Below deck, she fumbled for a flashlight, switched it on and rifled through the charts on the navigation table. Her husband, Chuck, heard an urgency in the rustling paper inches from where he lay.

"What's wrong?" he asked, squinting into the light beam.

Dawn didn't answer immediately. She scoured first one chart of the area, then another. She flipped back to the first. *Hmmm*. Neither showed a lighthouse or a lighted buoy with those characteristics. What was she seeing? Feeling the weight of Chuck's eyes on her and the question that hung in the air, she felt her face flush. Prickles of sweat beaded up on her nose and her glasses began to fog.

"There's a light on the horizon that I can't find on the chart." As she said those words, their implication became clear: They weren't where they thought they were. Just how big a danger that posed was uncertain, but she felt a rising anxiety and a quickening in her chest.

Chuck sat up and rubbed his eyes. "OK, I'll take a look." He climbed out of his bunk and bent over the chart as Dawn returned to the cockpit. With the commotion around him, fourteen-year-old Garth stirred. Something was happening. He might as well get up in case he could help. His younger sister, Linda, lay awake a few feet away in the quarter berth, feeling the alternating pull of gravity and buffeting waves, steady as ever.

What Dawn saw when she returned to the cockpit was far more serious than an uncharted light. An ominous line of froth stretched from one end of the horizon to the other. Whitecaps crashed where water piled against a rocky barrier that lurked beneath the surface. A roar filled her ears. Panic shot through her. *Reef!*

"Breakers!" she yelled through the open hatchway, her voice high and pinched as fear constricted her throat.

"Turn the boat! Start the engine!" Chuck yelled back.

His words from a few days earlier mocked him. "This celestial-navigation stuff is a piece of cake," he'd said. So far on this cruise their navigation had been flawless, but in life there are no guarantees. He hoped they'd have time to alter course.

Dawn twisted the key to start the motor. It came on in gear, propelling the boat forward even faster. It fueled her sense of urgency and quickened her heart rate. She fumbled to release the self-steering wind vane to alter course, her dexterity slowed by rising panic. Time was critical, yet her hands betrayed her.

Garth and his father lunged for the companionway, leaving eleven-year-old Linda stirring below. "We need to get the sails down!" Chuck shouted as he pulled himself into the cockpit, Garth following. With the wind behind them and the boom all the way out, they'd been making good time all night. Now that same wind was hurtling them toward the reef. Rollers surged from behind, adding to their momentum.

Garth grabbed the wood frame around the hatch and pulled himself up. He'd just reached the top behind his father when *Vela* lurched violently, throwing him into the sharp edge of the hatch.

Too late.

In an instant, *Vela* smashed headfirst into fangs of coral. The boat paused for a millisecond. The bow dipped sharply, then ground forward with a groan. An abrupt halt to their forward momentum shoved Dawn into Chuck. Then, just as quickly, Chuck crashed back onto Dawn with the full force of his weight as *Vela* lurched again. Before they could scramble up, a line of waves lifted the hull and tossed it onto the reef as though it were a child's plastic toy. In a single motion the hull pivoted ninety degrees and *Vela* rolled on her side.

A wave swept the now-sideways *Vela* over dramatically, dipping the boom into the swirling froth and smashing it onto the reef. A crack like a shot rang through the air. The wooden boom ripped from the mast. White fabric billowed for a second on the water surface. A wave cascaded over the hull and filled the submerged sail, adding to the force that drove them farther onto the reef.

Dawn grabbed for the now-useless wheel to pull herself up. "Hang on, Linda!" she yelled—a little late. Linda screamed from below.

Garth and Chuck rushed forward. They crabbed their way across the angled deck, grabbing for cleats, line or blocks—anything to pull themselves along on the uneven and violently shifting surface. The deck was slick with water, flowing in a tumble of directions all at once. Garth moved at lightning speed, surging past his father to the bow. In a flash of adrenaline, he let go of the jib halyard and yanked sailcloth into the bow netting, riding the bowsprit like an out-of-control bronco. Then he crawled aft to help his father get the main down.

Crouched at the mast, Chuck struggled to hang on as he untied the main halyard. He and Garth pulled against the force on the sail while the boat careened wildly. Deafening surf thundered over and around them. Water rushed against their bare skin and tugged at their clothing, threatening to wash them into the churning mass of water that tumbled around them and the sharp coral hidden beneath. Garth blinked away blinding saltwater. Chuck gulped, then coughed briny water from his mouth and nose. His water-shriveled fingers tenuously grasped for purchase against the slick surface and the pull of gravity.

An army of waves marched relentlessly against the hull, picking up the boat and driving it farther onto the jagged coral. Each barrage sent menacing plumes of foam flying. *Vela* lay at a fifty-degree angle, shifting and shuddering with each successive wave and moaning in protest as the reef tore at her wooden planks. The twenty-ton vessel could not withstand the powerful, conflicting forces—immutable reef against a perpetual onslaught of waves.

Thirteen months into their long-planned circumnavigation, the world of the Wilcox family was ripping apart around them.

Part I

1

On August 20, 1973, Chuck Wilcox, his wife Dawn and their two children, Garth and Linda, sailed *Vela* through San Francisco's Golden Gate with a plan to travel around the world in four years.

Not all of them embarked on this voyage with equal enthusiasm. Garth, at thirteen, could hardly wait to begin a real adventure, like Horatio Hornblower. The scent of salt air sent a surge of adrenaline through him. His family had prepared for what seemed like his entire life and the day had finally come. He loved the way the wind buffeted his face and loved figuring out how to make the boat go faster. He'd enjoyed racing the family's twenty-six-foot Thunderbird in "beer can" races at their yacht club and weekend cruises around the Bay. In fact, he loved nearly everything about sailing—except for seasickness. And now, on this bigger boat, the family would sail around the world. He couldn't imagine anything he'd rather be doing. He couldn't understand why his sister dreaded the voyage. Life at home was predictable, but that seemed to appeal to his sister.

Garth took a last glimpse over his shoulder at San Francisco Bay, which he'd explored so thoroughly on cruises with his family, and noticed that his mother seemed unusually subdued. Normally she was perpetually in motion, diligently tackling whatever needed to be done without hesitating. Today she seemed tense, squinting through her cat-eye glasses at the hazy features of the San Francisco skyline, as though she'd never seen them before.

Dawn's stomach churned with the cinnamon roll and cup of Nescafé she'd downed at six a.m., before they left Ballena Bay. Some of that surely came from the jitters she felt about embarking on the journey. She studied the city skyline behind them, committing its details to memory. It would be a long time before she might see it again.

Early morning light revealed the TransAmerica building shrouded in fog. She could hear the steady bleating of the foghorns scattered around the Bay, from boats hidden in the murk. She was excited for the voyage and yet her enthusiasm was tinged with sadness and anxiety. Tears pooled in the corners of her eyes and she fought back an urge to let them flow. She'd worked so hard toward this day, and now that it was finally here the swirl of conflicting emotions caught her by surprise.

She still worried whether undertaking this voyage was the right decision. *Were they ready? Would they have enough food, water, and medications? Would her nurse's training prove adequate to address any medical issues they might face? Could her children thrive in a floating world, growing up away from their cousins and friends, doing schoolwork through correspondence school? Would the knowledge they gained about the world offset the dangers they might encounter?*

The thought of leaving her mother and sister for years tugged at her. So did the memory of saying goodbye to Chuck's mother and ailing father, who seemed surprised at their departure despite years of preparation. After her father-in-law's second heart attack and quadruple-bypass surgery, she wondered if they would ever see him again. She dabbed at the corners of her eyes and wiped her runny nose with the edge of her sleeve, resisting the emotions that threatened to pull her under. Not wanting the children to see her conflicted, she turned to look forward. Out to sea. Toward Hawaii and the exciting future they had planned.

After so many years devouring *National Geographic* magazines, Dawn longed to see the world they brought to her doorstep and to share it with her children. Maybe sailing around the world wouldn't be the easiest way, but it appealed to Chuck, and if that was what he wanted, she would do everything in her power to reach his goal. She hoped she could do this and still be a good mother. Garth was fully on board, but Linda didn't want to leave her friends and role as captain of the fourth-grade football team. Still every ten-year-old needs periodic convincing to do things that might be in her best interest. Surely, she'd grow into it.

The wind freshened and the boat heeled. Waves danced on the water in front of them. The occasional whitecap surged forward with a noisy *pffftt*, then vanished. Chuck steadied the wheel to keep *Vela* on track. His job was to keep the boat going. He hoped the boat was prepared for the challenge of sailing around the world. He'd done everything he could imagine to get ready.

But it wasn't possible to anticipate everything, was it?

He remembered their two failed attempts to test the life raft and wondered what other surprises awaited them. The first life raft sank to the bottom of the pool—never inflating because it came equipped with air canisters dating from World War II. A second had inflated, but promptly deflated when holes in the buoyancy tubes leaked air. After salvaging enough parts from both to make a single, hopefully useable life raft, he'd mailed back the leftover "junk," freight collect.

Chuck shook his head at the memory. Isn't that just so typical? You prepare as much as you can, read everything you can get your hands on, study and follow all the advice available, install systems and backup systems, test and retest. Still it might all come down to placing your life in the hands of some stupid life-raft company that can't be bothered to test its own equipment. *I guess no one ever comes back to complain if a life raft doesn't work, do they?* He tried to shake the thought. He hoped they'd never have to use it.

Chuck conceived the idea of sailing around the world from reading *An Island to Oneself* by Tom Neale. The idea of being self-sufficient on a remote island in the Pacific appealed to him. He had begun sailing his freshman year at University of California at Berkeley and spent so much time doing it that Dawn worried he might flunk out of school. He loved the freedom and independence sailing offered and the opportunity to live or die by his own wits.

As their children grew, the idea of sailing around the world took hold. Once Chuck convinced Dawn he was serious, they began to prepare in earnest, first by saving every other paycheck from his job as an electronics engineer. Having both been raised during the Depression, the two shared a natural inclination toward frugality. Scrimping and saving was second nature to Dawn, the daughter of a divorced schoolteacher at a time when divorce was rare. With funds tight throughout her childhood, Dawn, the eldest, strove to help her mother stretch limited resources. Such training would prove excellent preparation for world voyaging.

Fiercely independent and stubborn, Chuck railed against runaway consumerism and chided others for trying to "keep up with the Joneses." He'd never wanted what the Joneses had anyway. "What do they need all that stuff for?" he would say with a laugh. When his parents lavished gifts on Garth, their firstborn grandson, Chuck admonished their excess and demanded they return all but a single gift. The engineer in Chuck garnered satisfaction out of squeezing a few more years out of a tired old tool, a skill that would prove essential for taking a boat around the globe. Though he didn't relate to the hippies in nearby Haight-Ashbury, their philosophy of a simpler life appealed to him.

When Garth entered sixth grade and the family savings had grown to a modest amount, the Wilcoxes began to search for a suitable vessel. In the early '70s, amid antiwar protests, living off the grid was becoming more common, though sailing around the world was still rare. Few boats capable of ocean voyaging existed at any price. The family drove the California coast to look at prospects. Although the kids relished trips to Southern California and Disneyland along the way, the family returned home boatless each time.

In the fall of 1971, sailors in their Palo Alto neighborhood heard of their plans and contacted them. This other family held similar aspirations and had purchased a sailboat, but decided to sell the boat because their high-school-aged daughter refused to go.

The boat was a heavily built, wooden forty-foot Maine Pinky. It was stout and roomy enough to fit a family of four, had already been offshore, and came with hot and cold running water, electric lights, two toilets, a shower, oven, fridge, short-wave radio, and a forty-horsepower diesel engine. It was as well appointed a boat as money could buy. Fancier than the Wilcoxes wanted, but suitable. They paid $33,000 and named the boat *Vela*, after the constellation and the Spanish word for *sail*.

By the age of five Linda had decided that sailing wasn't for her but that didn't deter her family from proceeding. Over the next year and a half, Chuck, with Dawn's help and some assistance from an eager Garth, refitted the boat for the voyage. Despite Linda's hopes that the voyage would never materialize, a month before they departed, the family moved aboard. That last month had been a frenzy of preparations, but they'd finally pulled away from the dock shortly after daybreak that morning, with the kids still groggy.

Though the engine had protested shortly after they untied the lines and raised the sails, they had enough wind to sail. Chuck would have to figure it out along the way. After all, *Vela* was a *sailboat* and they were leaving to *sail* around the world, right? He glanced back at the waterfront. Seeing the breakwater with the city mostly blanketed in fog strengthened his resolve.

We've prepared as much as we can and it's time to just go, he decided.

The day the family sailed through the Golden Gate, no one would have imagined what lay ahead of them. Chuck could never have anticipated the physical and emotional demands they would endure in pursuit of this goal.

2

Within a few hours of leaving the protection of San Francisco Bay, everyone was seasick. The wind was strong and the motion unpredictable compared with the usual wind-stirred chop of the bay. Dawn and Chuck slogged their way through that first night at sea, zombies alternating the watch schedule. The kids were no help at all. Thanks to a fifth crew member, a wind vane they'd named George doing the steering, they sailed an impressive one hundred and eighty-one miles during that first twenty-four hours.

As they sailed away from the coast, the wind continued to rise. By five p.m. on the second day, Chuck and Dawn decided to take down the mainsail to slow the boat and dampen the motion, a decision they would regret. Slowing the boat had the opposite effect, making the motion even more unpleasant. Their years of sailing in the protected waters of San Francisco Bay had not prepared them for ocean swells and other peculiarities of offshore voyaging.

When the children had turned six and three, Chuck bought a Thunderbird, a twenty-six-foot plywood sailboat. In the seven years since then, the family had spent most weekends racing or cruising San

Francisco Bay. Family vacations took them up the bay to the Delta, the confluence of the Sacramento and San Joaquin rivers, which offered countless waterways to explore. Garth developed a strong interest in sailing. Linda did not, though she was better at steering. Everyone assumed that once they bought *Vela*, she'd adjust to life at sea.

Besides pinching pennies to buy and prepare a capable vessel, Chuck and Dawn learned everything they could to prepare for voyaging offshore. They devoured every book and article about the topic available, from Joshua Slocum's classic *Sailing Alone Around the World* to the Hal Roth, Moitessier, and Hiscock books about bluewater sailing. They joined the U.S. Power Squadron and studied seamanship, navigation, and celestial navigation. He and Dawn became certified SCUBA divers so they'd be equipped to handle underwater tasks as needed, though Dawn had to retake the final dive after she'd panicked when she had trouble seeing though her mask. The two learned Morse code and secured ham-radio licenses. Weekends that weren't filled with sailing or classes were spent building radio antennas, transmitters, and receivers, and manipulating a sextant to measure the angle of the stars, and mathematically calculate their position with tables. Dawn carefully tracked family usage of toilet paper and paper towels, peanut butter and oleo, and learned about food-storage techniques. She endured Tupperware parties and diagrammed onboard storage locations where she could squirrel away provisions to feed her family. Despite their efforts, there was much they still didn't know.

When Chuck pulled down the main, he left the metal shackle attached to the sail. This wouldn't pose trouble in San Francisco Bay, but it proved costly at sea. The motion of the flogging halyard worked the shackle loose, sending the unattached halyard up the mast. By midday on day three, they'd lost use of the mainsail because the shackle was tangled around the rigging just beyond reach. There it remained for the next two weeks. They made several attempts to retrieve it—hoisting first Dawn and then Garth up the mast. Ever since Chuck suffered a panic attack while aloft on the T-bird, the thought of climbing the mast produced waves of anxiety. Dawn, it turned out, had a similar reaction. Garth didn't mind, but the violent motion rendered their efforts fruitless. Without a mainsail, their progress slowed as the wind lightened. Yet the swell did not vanish, leaving *Vela* pitching and rolling like a harpooned whale.

On day four, Chuck discovered that fuel had leaked into the bilge from their overfilled diesel tanks. Due to the emerging oil crisis, Chuck had stocked up, securing a generous tax-free delivery of one hundred and fifty gallons of home heating oil for his floating house. Tiny vents drilled into the top of the full tanks had spilled fuel as the boat heeled and lurched in the uneven waves and diesel vapor now permeated everything aboard, adding to their nausea. Addressing this problem after the fact wouldn't be easy, especially given the boat's aggressive motion. It took weeks for the boat to cease smelling like a gas station.

Then a problem arose with the steering. During their first week offshore, the chain linking the rudder to the wheel worked loose and began jumping the sprockets. Chuck feared the chain would fall off completely, causing them to lose steering control. So he set about trying to address the problem. First he retrieved the emergency tiller from the lazarette to steer while he worked on the connection with the wheel, but as he shoved the four-foot-long heavy wooden beast into the rudder fitting, he realized that the backstay was in the way, rendering the emergency tiller useless. Unless the person steering held it in the air, it wouldn't clear the backstay, which meant that it offered little to no leverage to steer a twenty-ton vessel. Since he hadn't looked at it carefully before, he hadn't noticed the problem. Without a decent emergency tiller, the need to fix the cable linkage to the wheel became even more urgent.

Like all Maine Pinkies, *Vela* had a large deck overhang over a narrow stern. This meant that the lazarette was what anyone might call confined. When Chuck proposed to venture inside it and tighten the chain, Garth volunteered, saying he could fit more easily into the tiny space. There was no way Dawn would let her son do that. So six-foot-three-inch Chuck slithered into position, within inches of all those moving chains and sprockets, while his petite wife struggled to hold the tiller straight. Her assignment was to hang on, and that's what she did. Garth watched the operation with interest, periodically pausing to retrieve tools for his father.

The motion of the ocean, of course, was not as benign as it seemed before they began this delicate operation. Waves crashed from behind, slamming up under the overhang and sending a geyser through the hole where the rudder stock poked through the deck, drenching Chuck and reverberating through the boat. *Bam! Bam! Bam!* Dawn wrestled with the tiller to keep it from moving.

"Isn't this kind of dangerous?" Garth asked innocently.

"Uh, yeah…," his mother replied, her tone indicating that he had just voiced the very thought that had crept into her mind: the potential casualties if Dawn let go: to the backstay, the rudder…Chuck's fingers ….

It dawned on Garth at that moment that his parents didn't know everything. They needed him.

Chuck hurried to finish and wriggled out as carefully as he could. Fortunately nothing bad happened—no fingers were severed in the process, but the incident left a strong impression on young Garth. A lesson in what *not* to do.

More sail-handling problems—an inability to sail downwind with the jib poled out because the pole was too short, plus a couple of accidental jibes—frustrated them but taught them other valuable lessons.

If the family had spent more time learning the strengths and weaknesses of their boat before departure, they might have avoided some of these troubles. Instead they had spent weekends rebuilding the pressure-water system, installing an electronic autopilot Chuck had designed, working on the refrigeration system, and rebuilding the fireplace which would never be of use in the tropics. By sailing the boat more before their departure, they might have learned how much weather-helm *Vela* had and anticipated the strain that would put on the steering system.

These struggles slowed their progress and extended their first passage far beyond their original estimate. With the help of their ham-radio and radio-operator friends, Chuck contacted his father and explained the delays so no one would worry.

Eventually the Wilcoxes adjusted to the constant motion and noise. They shook the seasickness that plagued them. Chuck offered Linda five cents for each day she wasn't seasick, and she seemed to improve soon after. The family found a way to sleep through continual jostling and settle into a routine of life at sea. Dawn was able to do more than heat a can of stew for meals. Taking star sights using the sextant no longer felt impossible, nor did the calculations that helped them triangulate their position relative to the stars and thereby estimate their current position. Even the kids resumed correspondence schoolwork at the table below, though at a handicapped pace. As he bounced on the end of the bowsprit, Garth practiced reciting the poem "Paul Revere and the Riders," which he'd memorized for an English assignment. How many of his peers could say that? Then again, it was still August and he was doing schoolwork already.

Now better rested, the family began to appreciate their environment: the ocean dappled with sunlight and the way the sea changed from blue to gray when a cloud passed overhead and from gray to crimson when the sun flamed toward the horizon at the end of the day. They were captivated by entrancing patterns of the waves and abundant sea life: tropicbirds soaring overhead, dolphins gliding along in *Vela*'s bow wave, and three undoubtedly hungry leopard sharks tracking a school of fish.

Initially the family was unsuccessful at catching a dinner-sized fish, though they sampled tiny bites of a flying fish that surrendered by leaping aboard. When a twenty-pound yellowfin tuna finally bit on their pink-lady lure, they discovered that attempts to kill it with a hammer posed more danger to the cockpit than it did to the fish. Over time, the Wilcoxes would develop a more systematic approach to the shout, "Fish on!"

Days and miles passed as they sped along with the lusciously warm tradewinds. On the twenty-fifth day, their navigation indicated they were nearing Hawaii. Standing on the overturned dinghy strapped to the deck, Garth studied the horizon until he spotted the snow-capped cone of Mauna Loa volcano. The Hawaiian Islands were on the horizon, right where Chuck and Dawn calculated them to be. Despite troubles with seasickness, the sails, the steering problem and the fuel leak, at least the navigation had been flawless.

After so many days of seeing nothing but sea and sky, it was a marvel how the island's lush green cliffs rose abruptly from the ocean depths. The view captivated them as they drew closer to the island and the overpowering scent of soil and vegetation confirmed what their eyes were seeing.

By the time they anchored near Hilo, the sun had vanished over the horizon.

"Are you sure we can anchor here?" Dawn questioned.

"If they don't want us to anchor here, someone will tell us," Chuck replied.

Sure enough, in the morning the Harbor Police asked them to move. Soon they were settled in a spot that wasn't in the channel.

This first landfall—and their first foray beyond the borders of California—exposed the family to a rich mix of cultures and dense tropical scenery vastly different from the dry California coast. The moist fragrant air carried the scent of plumeria and ripe fruit. They heard the lilting melodies of Polynesian music, and rustling of towering palms. The bright floral fabrics, blooming flowers and waxy tropical foliage contrasted with the gleaming white sandy beaches, black volcanic rock and water as inviting as a swimming pool.

Books they had all read on the passage about Hawaiian history and culture came alive when they visited the Bishop Museum, the Polynesian Cultural Center, the City of Refuge and the place where Captain Cook gasped his last breath. The natural world offered countless wonders: the museum-quality shells that sprinkled the beach were free for the taking, as were fresh sweet papaya, guava, passion fruit, and hibiscus flowers. Neon-hued tropical fish zipped past their masks in aquamarine water.

The Wilcoxes planned to spend the winter wandering around the islands, and doing so felt like an extended family vacation. In the evenings they played Dictionary; they listened to the local morning radio show featuring Melvin the Mynah Bird, broadcasting from the Hawaiian Land Corporation Building and reminding them to "change the paper under the radio;" Linda would entertain the family with her imaginary friend, Henrietta Smith, who spoke with a funny accent. Even Linda had to admit she enjoyed it, just not the sailing part.

Forays across the windy channels between Hawaiian islands stretched the family's skills at seamanship in new ways: in the notoriously rough Alenuihaha Channel, with wind blowing fifty knots and seas reaching thirty feet, a tug with a tow surprised them in the darkness; sudden tropical squalls and losing the wind-vane paddle forced them into quick action, to get sails down and retrieve the paddle from the water before it disappeared.

Over time the kids participated more fully in boat handling. One day when Linda was steering, Chuck tossed a cushion overboard, saying, "Let's practice a man-overboard drill. Pretend that's me." When Linda missed getting close enough to reach it on the first try, she quipped, "Ah, we don't need that old thing anymore."

Off Lahaina the *Shimmi Maru No. 2*, a mid-sized wooden fishing boat, dragged into them, prompting them to move. It was just after dark and they needed to reanchor safely for the night. The power windlass chose to stop working just then. That forced Garth and Dawn to haul one hundred and fifty feet of three-eights-of-an-inch chain hand over hand. They were breathing heavily from their exertions and fearful they would lose control of the chain—that everything they had hauled in so far would break free and leap over the side, possibly taking fingers and other limbs with it. Then they heard Chuck exclaim from the cockpit.

"Look at the sea snakes!" Until that moment they had been under the mistaken impression that he was doing something important back there at the steering station. The snakes must have been attracted to the refracted light on the water from the stern light.

"Evidently Dad doesn't have enough to do," Garth said.

"Uh, we could use a little help up here," Dawn said with a pointed gaze at Chuck.

As for chores, Chuck would handle most repairs. Nearly all other chores fell to Dawn, from buying groceries and cooking to laundry and sewing. Linda was tasked with doing the dishes and helping Dawn with the laundry. Garth was to fill the water and take out the garbage, easy enough with facilities nearby but a challenge once they left the convenience of major ports. A family of four could consume many gallons per week. In port, Garth might haul six five-gallon jugs each day. Getting water usually entailed rowing ashore, finding a water source—which sometimes required a bit of subterfuge—then hauling it all, two jugs at a time, the half mile to the dinghy or however far it was in that particular port. What made it worse for him was watching Linda waste water while washing the dishes or hogging it to wash her hair. It led to predictable squabbles.

Garth had a lazy streak that tested his parents' patience. Taking out the garbage was the chore he despised most. Like fetching water, he'd have to row ashore and then find an appropriate place to get rid of it—which often involved more deception or creativity. In tropical heat, it didn't take long for the garbage to get ripe and, given the smell, it wasn't something he could put off. But he tried. Sometimes taking it out "that day" meant hauling it off the boat minutes before midnight. Now a full-fledged teenager, Garth never wanted to get out of bed in the morning. The problem was, with him sleeping on the settee cushions in the main salon, no one could have breakfast until he did.

Garth and Linda argued over all sorts of innocuous things: who got to read Grandma's letter first, who used the last square of toilet paper without changing the roll, or who got the bigger piece of cake. Garth had devious methods for provoking Linda's short fuse while appearing blameless, his favorite being to whistle an unflattering tune he'd made up about Linda. Chuck and Dawn would look at each other, bewildered by the sudden explosion that appeared out of thin air.

"What?" Garth would raise his hands in a show of bafflement. "I was just whistling!"

With all the time the family spent together in such a tight space, a sense of humor helped. Garth had always been inclined to take things apart and reassemble them in surprising ways for his own amusement. This annoyed Linda endlessly, particularly the time he took apart her tricycle, removing the large front wheel and placing it where the handlebars used to be. In retaliation, she nicknamed him "Girch." This evolved into the verb "to Girch," meaning to mess something up in a clever "gotcha." He did it to everyone, though Chuck and Dawn were more inclined to laugh about it. On the boat, this practice became more challenging because most things aboard were needed to keep the boat running. Still, he might swap the covers of Linda's hardback books so that what appeared to be *Anne of Green Gables* might actually be *Pippi Longstocking*. Garth dubbed Linda "Lynch," short for "Lynch Mob." It seemed fitting for everyone to have a nickname. So their cheap father became "Dutch"; their mother, a constant nibbler, became "Munch." The nicknames stuck.

Being able to get off the boat also helped defuse some of the tension. Over the next couple months at the Hawaii Yacht Club, Chuck enjoyed the company of other voyagers and the camaraderie and information that had been sorely lacking before their departure. The community of sailors worked together to problem-solve. Chuck sought help diagnosing *Vela*'s engine problem. In turn, he helped others with their electronics and taught celestial navigation to several sailors who were anxious to learn the skill themselves so they could be free from irksome extra crew. It was a tight space, even for people who knew and loved each other.

Like other voyagers, Chuck decided to change *Vela*'s homeport to Honolulu to avoid paying annual California state taxes.

Chuck found that no one would cash their traveler's checks without a Hawaii driver's license. He asked if he could cash a personal check and learned he would incur a one-percent fee unless he had a local account.

So he opened a Bank of Hawaii account, deposited the checks and withdrew all but ten cents to avoid the fee. He reported this with pride to his folks in a letter and added:

> One of the goals of this cruise is being accomplished. I am finding out how little is needed to enjoy life. Also time is not rushing by quite so fast as it was before I left. I am enjoying walking around looking at nature, talking to people and reading good books. Sometimes it's necessary to do a little maintenance work on the boat. I have adopted the following rule: If a particular item's benefit doesn't justify the maintenance required, out it goes.

His parents didn't understand their decision to go voyaging, or the details of their strange lifestyle, though Chuck and Dawn tried to explain. Once Dawn mentioned she couldn't wash her hair as frequently because they had to be careful about their consumption of fresh water. Her sister mailed her a wig. The idea of wearing the equivalent of a fur hat in the tropics horrified Dawn. Clearly her sister failed to grasp the realities of life at sea. After the family had a good laugh about it, Dawn sent it back in the Christmas box.

Originally the Wilcoxes planned to sail directly to Tahiti, the capital of French Polynesia. From other sailors they learned about the lush Marquesan Islands, approximately two thousand miles south. Sailors suggested that if they departed Hawaii during a Kona storm, they'd be able to make enough mileage to the east to first visit this easternmost group of intriguing islands in French Polynesia. Chuck and Dawn bought charts and decided they would give it a try.

One afternoon in mid-February, Dawn was kneading dough for a couple of sourdough multigrain bread loaves while the kids finished the day's schoolwork. Dawn placed the loaves in the pan, gave them a final pat and looked up.

"When you finish I have a special Valentine's Day treat for you." Dawn said, washing her hands.

"What, a one-way airplane ticket home?" Linda quipped. Her opinion about the voyage hadn't changed any.

Despite Linda's reluctance, the family carried on preparing the boat for the next leg of the journey anyway. This next passage would be even longer than the one to Hawaii. They waited for the next Kona storm. In the meantime, they did a quick haul-out to repaint the bottom at the smelly "Tuna Packers" boat yard, aptly named for the pervasive stench of the tuna boats it primarily served.

On March 11, 1974, after six pleasant months in Hawaii, the family set sail for the South Pacific.

3

By the time the Wilcoxes were en route to the Marquesas, everyone felt more confident about their offshore seafaring skills. Still, they were seasick. The first time Chuck went forward to adjust the jib, he lay heaving on the bowsprit for nearly an hour. But this time—*with* the benefit of experience and *without* the pervasive stench of spilled diesel fuel—they recovered more quickly.

Still, beating against wind and current took its toll on both boat and crew. As the boat slogged south toward the equator, temperatures climbed. Frequent squalls were interrupted by long stretches of bright sunshine when the equatorial sun beat down on them mercilessly. Without a decent awning, they rushed to get out of the hot sun at the end of their watches.

Garth and Linda began to stand night watches. And it was a good thing, too, because Chuck grew lethargic, uninterested in doing anything more than standing watch and taking star sights. It wasn't until later that "Nurse Dawn" realized he was suffering from heat exhaustion. A quick batch of salty lemonade eventually restored Chuck into a functioning captain but not before Dawn nearly reached wit's end with all that she was attempting to juggle. Besides cooking and cleaning after meals, sewing a French courtesy flag, and calculating their position, Dawn carried most of the burden of running the boat, with help from Garth.

A series of squalls kept them busy and stressed the sails beyond their capability. It was one trial after another. On a single unlucky day, the masthead light fell off, the wind-vane paddle broke, and the mainsail ripped. The next day—April 1—Dawn and Garth slowly re-sewed the mainsail "in situ," with Dawn feeling very much like an April fool.

At one point in the doldrums, a belt of calm winds near the equator, the only functioning sail was the storm jib. All the slides and hanks came off the cheap sails that Chuck—*Dutch*—had mail-ordered from Lee Sails. Even the clew ripped out of the staysail. To Dawn it felt like triage.

After twenty-nine days, Chuck's navigation again proved precise. Though overcast skies proved too hazy to see the Marquesan Islands, position calculations plotted them within ten miles the afternoon before they arrived. That evening, as skies cleared, Chuck took a set of star sights and set a course for Taiohae Bay.

The first morning rays of sunlight illuminated the sharp saw-toothed summits, crenulated with deep ravines that make the Marquesan islands so striking. As the sun rose higher, the entrance to the largest bay on Nuku Hiva was right there. By seven-thirty a.m., *Vela* was anchored beneath the serrated peaks of Mount Muake in a volcanic crater that was now open to the sea.

Frustrations of the passage were quickly forgotten as they took in the lush tropical vegetation and volcanic mountain peaks, valleys and waterfalls of the Marquesas and the intriguing culture of Polynesia that Herman Melville had described in *Typee*.

4

Ten days after arriving, anchored in the lush valley of Baie de Taioa ten miles west of the capital of Nuku Hiva, Dawn was entranced by its natural beauty, with steep cliffs that dropped abruptly to the water's edge. Intense heat and heavy, sudden showers fed this verdant valley, which reminded them of Kauai. Yet the islands were nearly uninhabited. Only an ancient stone road and an abandoned church hinted of its former population, which had been decimated by sailors bringing disease.

A young Marquesan couple, Daniel and Antoinette, appeared to be the only people living in this rugged cathedral-like setting. The family visited the couple's tiny open-windowed house, bearing Dawn's home-made multi-grain bread, which they traded for two stalks of bananas, eggs and pamplemousse (a plump sweet green grapefruit Garth adored). Chickens strutted across the garden as they chatted over steaming cups of tea and watched Daniel carve a war club, his chisel slowly cutting into the fiber and sending curly ribbons of wood into a pile of shavings around his bare feet. Though Dawn longed to take the carving home for a souvenir, Daniel told them its price: 9,000 francs (eighty-two dollars). *Maybe not.*

The family's attempt at navigating through the jungle to a waterfall Daniel described proved less successful. Garth noticed, more quickly than the others, the tiny, nearly invisible bugs that pestered him. As Dawn stopped to pick taro from the river to add to her collection of coconuts and breadfruit, Garth slapped at his arm and told his mother, "These bugs are driving me crazy. I'm going back to the boat." The others carried on until they too realized how pesky the bugs were, but it was too late. They later learned these bugs were called No-See-Ums, and unlike the laser-point, penetrating bite of a mosquito, No-See-Ums tear out chunks of flesh, leaving welts that take forever to heal. For the next several days, while Garth worked on his model boat, the rest of the family scratched until they bled. Nurse Dawn dug into her medical potions in search of an ointment to sooth the agony.

Swimming in the cool water of the bay offered some relief. A steady runoff from the steep cliffs and gushing rain-fed rivers lent the Marquesan bays a murky green hue. This bay was no exception. Since it was not ideal for snorkeling, Garth rigged a twin-boom arrangement they could use to swing out over the water. He and Linda could easily spend hours zipping out over the glassy surface testing to see how far they could travel, sending a cascade of water droplets across its smooth surface before plunging into the still water.

One afternoon the Wilcoxes splashed around the boat, lathering shampoo in the dinghy, then diving into the surrounding water to rinse away the suds. When they finished, one by one, they clambered aboard *Vela*. While the others toweled off and combed their hair in the cockpit, Garth lingered in the bathtub-warm water, glad for a few precious moments of quiet time. When he noticed his shriveled fingers, he reluctantly paddled toward the dinghy and hauled himself over its inflated bulge. As his torso cleared the hump, he felt a rush of water against his feet and heard a perplexing splash. He cast a casual glance at the water where his feet had just been. There, where he'd swum only moments ago, lurked a vertical dorsal fin.

Shark! His eyes shot open, his pulse spiked, and blood thudded in his ears...*But for a few seconds, he could have been lunch!* Between him and this predator was two millimeters of rubber-coated fabric...filled with air. Rubber that could easily puncture if it encountered something sharp. Like the teeth of a shark.

Garth couldn't fling his body into the cockpit of *Vela* fast enough.

"Ow, watch out!" his sister yelled as he barreled into her. His mother gave him a questioning look.

"What's wrong?" his dad asked, peering up at him as he dabbed his neck with a towel.

"Nothing." Garth shrugged, regaining his cool. He didn't want to tell them he'd just had the fright of his life. They would tease him mercilessly and might not believe him anyway. They quickly forgot all about it, but Garth would not swim for a year.

Over the next month, days sped past as the family explored Marquesan culture and geography. As they sailed between the bays, they often ferried native Marquesans—Antoinette into the main town of Taiohae so she could shop without having to hike a whole day over the pass between the valleys, and three men back to Ua Pu after getting TB shots. Anchored beneath striking conical black basalt rocks, the family hosted cockpit parties at all hours for curious villagers who developed a taste for cookies and Grape-Aid. Few locals spoke English, or even much French. To enjoy each other's company, they communicated through pantomime and music, using Dawn's clarinet and a ukulele she had purchased from a carver in Taiohae. Much as Dawn appreciated these interactions with local people, she fretted about the threat they posed to the kids' schoolwork.

Vela left the Marquesas in mid-May, bound for Tahiti. The second of the three main island groups that make up French Polynesia, the Tuamotus, have earned the nickname "Dangerous Archipelago" because of the atolls' low-lying reefs and swirling currents. Chuck concluded they would be too difficult to navigate using celestial navigation, so he decided it would be safer to skip them. He did not want to risk hitting a reef.

After an eight-day sail, the Wilcoxes settled along the quay in front of Tahiti's capital, Papeete. They spent their first few weeks tackling schoolwork and boat fixes and upgrades. The primary projects were to repair the wind vane, sew a sailing awning so they'd have shade from the blistering tropical sun while underway, and to fix the toilet, again. Their Groco brand "head" had spent more time as a project than a functioning toilet. Stern-tied alongside the quay near them was a thirty-six-foot ketch named *Sea Foam*. Its owner, Herb Payson, just happened to have a Groco for sale. Chuck thought it might be useful for parts. Herb had concluded what Chuck had only begun to suspect: this model wasn't worth the trouble.

Starbound, from Annapolis, another boat already tied along the quay, was a larger replica of the boat *Spray* that Joshua Slocum had sailed alone around the world, a story Garth had loved. Aboard *Starbound* was a man named Gordon who designed boats for a living.

Garth, whose earliest drawings adorning their Palo Alto refrigerator had been of boats, was intrigued. As a child Garth overturned the back-yard picnic table and directed his "crew" of Linda and neighbor Patrice to "hike out" like he'd seen his parents do when they were racing the T-bird. Garth would "captain" them across the yard; he even rigged the umbrella pole with halyards and raised bedsheets hanked on with paper clips.

Here in Papeete was a person who had trained and earned a living doing something Garth had fantasized about since he first laid eyes on a sailboat at age three. From Gordon, Garth learned that boat designers were called naval architects and college programs offered this training. Though Garth was not quite fourteen, Dawn was happy to discover a college existed that offered a full scholarship where Garth might follow his interests. Now if she could only get him to finish his eighth-grade schoolwork.

Once the Wilcoxes made adequate progress on their project list and the kids completed most of their coursework, Chuck relented and the family explored more than just the machine shops, the post office, and the inside of their school books.

Dawn's letter from Papeete to her mother describes one of their first forays around Tahiti in June:

We went on the bus-LeTruck-to Gaugin's [sic] museum. The best part was the ride. We shared the bus with a refrigerator, 15 sacks of copra, several Tahitians with their baskets and boxes of groceries, an old French couple who were eating all the way, a dog who examined everyone's ankles and then went to sleep on the back step. (There are no doors.) We started off, then stopped off at a gas station and 2 natives jumped out with their jerry cans to be filled and then filled the bus, too. Then we had a scenic and bouncy ride, on wooden seats naturally. Later we stopped at a grocery store so everyone could go buy beer and French bread. . . The Le Truck was difficult to climb into on the way home because it was filled with 6 banana trees and a pile of taro leaves. The bus stopped several times for passengers and the driver to tie their bundles to the top of the bus. He also stopped once to wipe his son's nose, as his baby rode with him up front. It only cost $.50 for the ride and all that entertainment.

As a colony of France, French Polynesia and Tahiti in particular celebrated the storming of the Bastille prison each July with a lively multi-week festival called Fête. The Wilcoxes joined the other boats along the quay in raising their signal flags to commemorate the celebration and watched outrigger-canoe races from *Vela*'s bowsprit even before they ventured ashore to take in the fruit carrier's race, coconut-cracking contests, and basket-making competitions. The cotton candy and sno-cones were a hit with Garth and Linda. Dawn loved the military bands; she'd played in bands all her life. But the three loved the dance competitions most.

Buying tickets was an experience. The crowd waited patiently for the ticket booth to open, but when it did, the throngs rushed forward. Dawn made no progress, until Linda, employing skills she learned playing football, teamed with Garth—by now a good-sized boy—to form a V-wedge that drove Dawn toward the ticket counter. Later, they watched locals climb through the palm-frond fence. Eventually the Wilcoxes learned they could watch for free from the bleachers. They sat with rambunctious locals, who were as fascinating as the performers. Together they watched dancers in grass skirts swinging their hips to a staccato drumbeat, leaping through flames and twirling lit torches. Less exciting were the stout ladies in shapeless bright floral shifts, known as "Mother Hubbard" dresses, singing endless rounds of church hymns called *himeni*, which appeared to bore the locals just as much.

Between festivities, Dawn replenished their dwindling food supplies. After visiting three stores in the Marquesas without locating a single tomato, cucumber, or piece of fresh meat, Dawn was thrilled with the expansive open market in Papeete. It was filled with tables piled with fresh produce, meat and dairy, along with baskets, shells, and flowers. After she carried her first fish home by the tail, she brought her own bags.

Dawn was proud of her ability to find what they needed despite her limited success with French once she realized that she made more progress pointing and smiling than she did by trying to pronounce the word *oeuf* (egg). Chuck, with the aid of engineering drawings and a French-English dictionary, had better luck at machine shops in reinforcing the wind-vane paddle.

Dawn loved exploring the shops to see what they carried, especially the Chinese stores, which reminded her of the old-time general stores from her small-town Chowchilla childhood. She still searched in vain for many specialty food products, like Egglo, some of which her family mailed from the States for pickup at General Delivery. But she was delighted to find powdered milk and dried potato flakes to replenish her supplies. She found fabric for Fijian and New Zealand courtesy flags and to make Linda a pair of shorts, all of which she sewed by hand until she could locate a place to repair her Necchi sewing machine. The sewing-machine dealer she found had never seen one as antique as hers. Though it had been difficult to haul her machine over the rocks to shore, the man fixed it without any drama for $2.20.

Dawn was thrilled to find the plastic sandals for reef walking that she saw some Marquesans wearing. She bought pairs for the entire family. The clear plastic resembled jellyfish and made their feet sweat, but few options existed at the time. Their salt-encrusted sneakers refused to dry and, when it came to hiking, flip-flops "just didn't cut it," as Garth would say—especially in mud. At the rate the kids' feet were growing, Dawn loved the price. She could never have imagined how critical those reef shoes would become in only a few months' time.

Days passed quickly. Dawn ran errands in town. After school hours officially ended, Garth helped Chuck with boat projects—replacing the backstay so they could actually *use* the emergency tiller, rigging ratlines for climbing the mast to watch for coral heads, painting and varnishing. Otherwise he was sailing his dinghy, repairing it or building model boats. After finishing her daily schoolwork—often early—Linda would spend hours snorkeling in the crystal-clear aquamarine water and adding to her array of shells. On board, she organized her stamp collection or read *The Lion, the Witch and the Wardrobe*, which Grandma had mailed to her, and *Bedknobs and Broomsticks*, which she'd gotten in trade from another girl cruising with her family. Each evening the sun slipped over the horizon, silhouetting the island of Moorea—eight miles away—in crimson, magenta and orange. On Sundays the family heard melodic voices drifting over the water from the church across the street. Dawn imagined the ladies inside, dressed in white with crowns of flowers adorning their hair, belting out hymn after hymn at top volume. She could almost smell the fragrant plumeria in their headdresses.

Papeete offered plenty of distractions to help keep the peace aboard. It was an ideal, vacation-like existence, except for the boat projects and schoolwork that gave shape to their days. Or sometimes hung over their heads, like when Garth's teacher returned his history and science tests for "insufficient information," forcing him to retake them and delaying the family's departure as they waited for materials for the new school year.

By late July, projects done and school materials finally in hand, the family was free to leave French Polynesia and sail on.

Dawn with Daniel and Antoinette in the Marquesas

5

When Chuck read Tom Neale's inspiring story of carving out an existence on a remote island atoll in *An Island to Oneself*, he never imagined he'd have the opportunity to meet the author. At the end of the book, Tom leaves the island. But fellow cruisers told Chuck that Tom had returned to Suwarrow, an outpost in the Cook Islands chain. The family's voyage westward passed through the Cook Islands.

Though Suwarrow was spelled four different ways on the charts, Chuck was sure this was the place he'd read about so many years earlier in Tom Neale's book. According to the chart, the only navigational aid was a tall palm tree. Sailing from Bora Bora, the most western of the Society Islands in French Polynesia, the Wilcoxes reached Suwarrow, a low, flat island so different from the green-shrouded high volcanic islands of Hawaii, the Marquesas, and the Society Islands. After a brief but intense squall, the sun emerged. They ventured slowly through the entrance, steering carefully to align their heading with the palm tree to avoid coral heads, as the chart indicated.

The beauty of the atoll captivated them. It stretched six miles long and was made up of Anchorage Island—where Mr. Neale reportedly

30

lived—plus several tiny islets on an outer reef surrounding a lagoon of varying shades of brilliant aquamarine water.

Inside the reef pass, they dropped anchor into translucent blue water. For as far as the eye could see, there was nothing but sand, sea, and sky, interrupted by the occasional islet, palm tree and low-lying scrub that could withstand a steady diet of salt air and blasting wind. They immediately spotted the modest enclave of buildings that Tom Neale had created for himself. Curious, the family rowed ashore—minus Garth, who was restricted to the boat for "fourteen-year-old behavior" (backtalking).

Tom Neale, still the island's only resident, greeted them as they stepped out of the dinghy. He was lean, yet muscular, and deeply tanned. Dawn guessed him to be about seventy years old. As they stood in a circle on the sandy beach near the Avon, with the sun warming their backs, Mr. Neale picked a young coconut and cut into it, urging them to drink its sweet juice. The family had discovered Poisson Cru, a Polynesian salad that uses coconut milk, in the Marquesas and adored the raw fish pickled in lime juice and coconut milk, but they'd not yet sampled the refreshing raw taste of a young coconut. It was a revelation.

As they sucked the sweet nectar, Mr. Neale told them he was the official caretaker and postmaster, earning a salary of fifty dollars per year from the New Zealand government, yet his only interactions with the outside world were with yachts that passed infrequently. He'd first come in the 1950s from New Zealand, periodically leaving to work or recover from illness in Rarotonga. This time he'd been on the island since 1967—six years—and currently shared it with two cats he'd brought with him. He seemed a simple, honest man, with few requirements. Clearly he worked hard to keep up with the maintenance that a relentless tropical sun and abrasive salty breeze demanded, and to grow vegetables in the sandy soil.

Mr. Neale steered them around his one-man compound, as chickens squawked and flitted around their feet. His grounds consisted of a wooden house with a tin roof left behind by occupying forces after World War II that he used for sleeping, plus several outbuildings. He'd added a cook house, a shower house, and work and storage sheds—each equipped with a water catchment system—plus a fenced-in area enclosing his vegetable garden and chicken pen. His industry was evident. His survival depended upon it. The man was keen to trade his freshly grown tomatoes, green peppers, and cucumbers for New Zealand canned butter and canned meat of any kind. Linda yearned for a set of Cook Island stamps from this remote postal station and even bought a set for her quarantined brother.

Mr. Neale explained that he still had work to do that day. He showed them where they could collect clams for dinner and returned to his tasks. Dawn and Linda floated in soothing tropical water, watching giant clams slowly open and close brilliant teal, jade, and magenta mantles. What a revelation to think that these spellbinding creatures could be harvested for food. They might make a nice clam spaghetti.

After the two spent hours hacking clams from the reef and then painstakingly removing the meat from the shells, they'd amassed the equivalent of a thirty-nine-cent can of clams as chewy as a pile of rubber bands. Dawn developed a respect for this man, who fed himself daily from nature.

Just after breakfast the morning following the family's arrival, on August 8, 1974, Chuck noticed Mr. Neale rowing out to their boat. He was surprised to see the man paddling out to *Vela*, since the boats he'd seen on the beach were in various states of disrepair; it appeared that Mr. Neale rarely used them to visit the outer islands as he once did. The man struck him as someone who kept to himself as much as possible, which Chuck could understand, so no one expected his visit as they cleared the breakfast dishes.

As Mr. Neale pulled alongside *Vela*, everyone headed up to the cockpit to chat with him.

"Your president has resigned," he announced as he pulled an oar from the oar lock and reached for *Vela*'s toe rail. "I just heard it on the HF radio."

For years before the Wilcoxes left California, they'd heard about the Watergate break-in and followed the associated revelations that slowly traced a connection between the burglary and the Nixon campaign all the way to White House. The family had watched the hearings on TV. But since they'd left the States, they had lost track of the details, thanks to poor reception on the HF radio along the quay in Tahiti and the fact that English broadcasts were limited to ten minutes per day on the local FM station.

"Huh," Dawn said in reaction, not quite sure what to say. The family hadn't realized that events had reached a crisis point. Chuck remained silent.

"I just thought you might want to know," Mr. Neale added. Almost as quickly as he'd come, he let go of Vela's toe rail and shoved an oar into the oarlock. Within a few moments he was splashing his way back to shore.

Garth dived for the HF radio, flipping the dial to see what he could tune in. Radio Australia had the best reception that day. The family spent the rest of the morning listening to the details, shocked by the development, yet feeling strangely disconnected.

It was a monumental event in their country, though in the context of their floating lives it now seemed strangely irrelevant. The Wilcoxes had been voyaging less than a year, but already felt as if they'd been away a lifetime.

That afternoon, Chuck snagged four fish in the lagoon with the pole from the *Vela*, using the rubbery clam meat for bait. He was quite pleased with himself and rowed ashore to invite Mr. Neale to dinner that evening. Imagine Chuck's surprise when Mr. Neale told him he couldn't come for dinner until six p.m. *Office hours in the tropics?*

Chuck shrugged and agreed to pick him up at six.

A few minutes before six, Chuck rowed ashore to fetch Mr. Neale. The sun hung low on the horizon, casting a golden glow on the sandy ground.

"Just a moment," Mr. Neale said, standing idly near the pen. Chuck looked around, perplexed by the delay. *I suppose someone who spends this much time on his own has earned an oddity or two.* Just then Chuck heard the clucking of tiny voices. Coming around the corner of the hen yard was a scraggly line of chickens rushing towards the fenced-in yard. Mr. Neale unlocked the gate and stood aside, as one by one they marched into the enclosure. Chuck laughed. *I guess chickens have learned how to tell time.* When the last little chick cleared the gate, Mr. Neale swung it closed and locked it. He looked up at Chuck and nodded.

"OK, now we can go," he said with authority. *A man lives on a remote island, and even he has a boss.*

The two climbed into the dinghy and gave it a gentle shove. Chuck slid the oars into the rubber oar locks on the Avon and began to pull. The sun slipped quietly over the horizon. By the time they reached *Vela*, darkness had descended.

Mr. Neale stepped aboard, ducked below and gave a cursory glance around the cabin. Places had been laid at the table and Dawn had made a fish curry. She served it with a salad of tomatoes and cucumbers and set a plate before each of them. Mr. Neale looked at his.

Garth spotted movement behind the man's head. His eyes tracked it for a moment and it occurred to him that he was seeing a cockroach, hints that the infestation they suspected was worsening. He tried to ignore it so their guest wouldn't notice.

"This is the kind of fish I usually throw back," Mr. Neale said, as he picked up his fork. "The flavor isn't good."

Dawn looked at him in stunned silence.

"You should try fishing in the pass," he continued, oblivious. "That's where the good ones are—a type of grouper that's especially delicious." That would soon prove to be excellent advice, for they caught a red grouper with striking blue spots on their next attempt.

Mr. Neale poked at the salad and looked up with raised eyebrows. "You've wasted the most nutritious part of the cucumber," he said, noticing Dawn had peeled them as usual. "Here's how you score the skin to soften it," he said, pantomiming the technique with his knife. Admonished by her guest twice within five minutes, Dawn began to suspect why he lived alone.

As the evening wore on, Mr. Neale loosened up and shared engaging tales from his unusual life. Soon this gifted storyteller had them in stitches as he recounted the story of how a shipwrecked yacht quadrupled the island population, suddenly saddling a horrified Mr. Neale with a man, his wife, and their fourteen-year-old daughter as roommates.

Tom Neale in Suwarrow, Cook Islands

6

The family's visit to Suwarrow was brief. It was already mid-August, and they planned to stop in Samoa, Tonga and Fiji before sailing to New Zealand, where they could safely wait out cyclone season. The season started in November, and they couldn't linger in any of these places, much as they might enjoy longer visits.

After five days of sailing, they entered the lush, spacious, crater-like Pago Pago Bay in American Samoa. As they drew into the bay, their eyes settled upon the fifty or so Korean tuna boats at anchor with full cargo to unload at the fish-processing plants that detracted from an otherwise attractive natural setting.

While the family waited to clear customs, they met the owners of *Vela*'s sister ship, *Chanson*, also anchored in the harbor. Built alongside *Vela* in southern California, *Chanson*'s design was almost the same as *Vela* but with a different interior. *Chanson*'s layout was superior in two respects: the navigation station had a useable seat so that when consulting the chart one could sit down instead of falling against the off-watch person who was attempting to sleep in the quarter berth behind it; and the dining table didn't require stowing and therefore manhandling two large table leaves in a cramped and unstable environment—a feature on *Vela* that discouraged the Wilcoxes from using it.

The day after their arrival, August 20, marked the one-year anniversary of their departure. The family—all but Linda, anyway—was enamored with this carefree lifestyle and the fascinating change of scenery and cultures that accompanied it. "First chance I get I'm going to run this boat on a reef so we can go home," Linda still swore. The others tried to ignore her rants.

To celebrate the anniversary, Dawn invited the people from *Chanson* aboard to celebrate with special cocktails for the adults and Tang for the kids.

With the fresh paint they'd applied to the cockpit and boom in Papeete, and the newly varnished interior, *Vela* looked dapper and compared favorably—at least visually—to her sister ship. Still the Wilcoxes were beginning to realize their boat's limitations. As fancy as *Vela* was, many of her basic features hadn't been designed to meet the rigors of offshore sailing. During the course of their dinner, the Wilcoxes were astounded to hear how much better *Chanson* sailed than the nearly identical *Vela*—which in their opinion "sailed like a dog "—until Chuck began to question whether the owners' perspective might have influenced the "facts."

Once Chuck had completed the usual clearance procedures, he expressed no interest in venturing ashore. On the third morning Dawn was gathering her shoes and purse and urging the kids to get ready for a trip ashore. Chuck lay on the bunk reading a book.

"Ready to go?" Dawn asked him. He looked over at her blankly. She waited, tapping her fingers impatiently.

"No," he answered. She peered intently at Chuck, unsure whether he might be joking. She couldn't always tell. His silence confirmed he was serious.

"But I've been itching to go all morning!"

"So?" he said calmly. She sighed. Wasn't it obvious? It was so maddening.

"I waited all day for you to finish working on the engine yesterday." A hint of a whine crept into her voice.

"I'm not going," he told her, flatly, holding her gaze.

"Why not?" Her voice rose. Heat rushed to her face and her pulse jumped.

"I've been ashore once," he said. "I've seen everything I need to see." Dawn looked at him in stunned silence. For years she'd dreamed of this voyage and exploring different cultures as they sailed from place to place. Ever since she was a little girl, after her mother gave her a copy of H.G. Wells's *A Short History of the World* and Richard Halliburton's *Book of Marvels*, she'd been keen to experience the vast universe beyond her small town that they had revealed to her. Though Chuck had never been fond of travel and had always hated hotels, when he suggested this voyage, she considered it her chance to see the world. She assumed Chuck would be right beside her sharing the discoveries, but he seemed less interested in the destinations than in the challenge of getting there.

Pent-up anger bubbled up inside her. All the chores and the sacrifices she'd made to get here and the times she'd had to cajole him to go ashore collided with her crushed hopes.

"But we've sailed all this way!" she yelled. "And all you want to do is sit on the boat? Why can't we enjoy these places?" This was her reward. How could he deny her this? Her bitter feelings flooded forth.

Garth and Linda looked on in bewilderment at this sudden display of emotion, like a volcano erupting without prior warning. Their normally acquiescent mother had transformed into a raving maniac.

Dawn noticed her kids' shock and quickly recovered herself, but not before resolving that she would no longer miss exploring just because Chuck didn't want to go. She grabbed her purse.

"Come on, kids, let's go." Garth and Linda hopped in the dinghy, happy to forget what they'd witnessed.

Though American Samoa possessed some of the same natural assets as the Hawaiian and Society Islands, Dawn later admitted in a letter that Pago Pago was a "dumpy town that looked like a slum." It was hot and dusty, with litter sprinkled in the streets; alongside candy wrappers and cans, she spotted an abandoned bra on the side of the road. It lacked the pride of French Polynesia and women in long skirts and dresses didn't appear as carefree as the half-dressed Tahitians.

Besides searching for provisions, Nurse Dawn always went in search of medical facilities to gauge life in each port. Impressed by the modern facilities at LBJ Hospital in Pago Pago, she was amused to note that the number of hospital staff exceeded the number of patients, though the outpatient clinic was jammed. She learned both the chief surgeon and the head of physical therapy lived aboard boats anchored in the harbor.

Dawn stocked up on New Zealand frozen meat she found there, a boon after so many frustrating attempts to buy meat throughout the Marquesas and Polynesia. She was always in search of hearty foods to satisfy her family, especially her perpetually ravenous fourteen-year-old son. Feeding him was like stoking a coal-fired furnace; he seemed to shovel morsels in as fast as she could produce them. Dawn scooped up American products like peanut butter, which both kids consumed at an alarming rate. She picked up canned tuna from the nearby Star-Kist and Van de Camp canneries; the factories were eyesores that dominated the landscape and lent a pervasively pungent odor to the bay.

The Wilcoxes appreciated finding American brands they hadn't seen for months and being able to mail letters and souvenirs home via the U.S. postal service. They could use American dollars to buy *Newsweek* and *Time* magazines to learn more about events leading up to President Nixon's resignation. Mostly they thought little of the country they left behind, except for long, chatty letters from relatives. Linda still keenly missed her friends and wrote them often; she cherished their occasional replies, but they came far less often than she hoped. Aboard *Vela*, the family floated in a timeless world, so different from their lives at home. She worried about losing touch with her community back home, of becoming ignorant of what her peers considered normal.

No one in the family was sad to bid adieu to American Samoa after six days. More interesting places lay over the horizon.

7

What the Wilcoxes found at their next landfall was indeed interesting—though not nearly as surprising as the one that followed.

The next country they visited was Tonga, the last Polynesian kingdom, and the only South Pacific country that has always been independent. After a four-day passage from American Samoa, through a mixture of no wind, then too much wind and heavy rain, they sailed past islands thick with brilliant green foliage; past scattered undercut islets that resembled mushrooms jutting from still, jade water; past the occasional reef and cave; and into the cavernous bay of Neiafu in Tonga's northern island group, Vava'u. Mid-afternoon sun glinted off the water's surface as they dropped anchor near the town pier. It was the first of September.

Two men greeted them, boarding *Vela* with a boldness that led the Wilcoxes to think they were Customs and Immigration officials. In these remote islands, where uniforms and other resources were scarce, it could be hard to tell. But no, they were just a couple of residents who were eager to trade. One introduced himself as William. The family quickly forgot the name of William's companion, but the man's distinct outfit of hand-me-down clothes earned him the nickname of "Blue Skirt."

The two came bearing coconuts, papaya, pineapples and bananas to exchange for a batch of clothes Garth and Linda had outgrown. This was the first of daily visits. Sometimes the men would bring a cowrie shell or baskets, but often they came empty-handed. They requested blankets—failing to grasp why these sailors had none to spare in ninety-degree heat—and even money, because the Wilcoxes came from "a rich country with many factories." During his visits, William developed a taste for dried peanut butter, which the kids abhorred and were happy to share. He ingested copious amounts of the despised chalky substance with tea and bread as he shared stories about his family and his village. William urged the Wilcoxes to visit his village. "You come my island. Put your anchor on number five," he said, referring to a sounding on the chart. It was a refrain he revisited each time there was a pause in the conversation. He made himself a pest, though the family didn't mind that first afternoon when William and Blue Skirt lingered for hours.

The Wilcoxes were a captive audience until they cleared into the country, which didn't occur until six p.m. that evening. They learned from William that Tonga's king was visiting the island group; evidently officials were too busy administering to the king and his entourage to bother with a visiting yacht.

• • •

In the morning the Wilcoxes rowed ashore to explore the town of Neiafu. Clapboard storefronts lined the dusty streets and reminded them of California Gold Rush photos. There the resemblance ended. The sidewalks were teaming with dark men, women, and children, all wearing bulky woven mats wrapped around their middles, belted with twine. From *National Geographic* the Wilcoxes had learned that the woven waist wrap, called a *ta'ovala*, was worn as a sign of respect and status. The *ta'ovala* were family heirlooms, handed down from generation to generation, the older and thicker the layers, the better. Dawn noticed many were tattered. According to *National Geographic*, King Taufa'ahau Tupou IV could trace his ancestry back a thousand years.

The family wove a path among women in plain dark dresses carrying black umbrellas and men in skirts called *lava lavas*, all wrapped in the obligatory *ta'ovala*. No one else seemed to notice the soaring temperatures that made Dawn feel faint. Dawn, Garth and Linda made their way past the Morris Hedstrom and Burns Philp stores to the Treasury, to exchange Western Samoan *tala* bills and *seni* coins for Tongan *pa'anga* and *seniti*.

Flush with cash, they went in search of Tonga's famed, unusual stamps for the budding philatelists. And to mail Garth's first Algebra lesson. (The *"Vela* School District" had resumed classes for the new school year.) After parting with as much Tongan *seniti* as their meager allowances made possible, Garth and Linda clutched their bounty: stamps cut to the curve of a banana or a colorful parrot-like local bird or a heart commemorating Queen Sālote, who had died in 1965. Garth's favorites were ones in the shape of a wrist watch that read WHERE TIME BEGINS to celebrate Tonga's unique location as the first country across a gerrymandered international dateline. Linda regretted spending so much of her allowance money on ice cream in Hawaii and Samoa.

The streets buzzed with an energy rare in most islands, perhaps because of the king's visit. Arches of palm fronds and woven mats decorated every intersection, constructed to honor visiting dignitaries.

Dawn was in search of provisions that William and Blue Skirt couldn't offer (i.e., not coconuts). She bought a loaf of bread for twenty *seniti*, then attempted to purchase cheese. As she recounted in one of her letters home: *The girl got out a 5-lb hunk and tried to cut off a section with a cheese wire—much laughter ensued. She got two people to help her, but no go. She told me it couldn't be cut. I suggested a knife but, no, I'm to come back this afternoon when the cheese will be softer!*

Back on the busy streets, they happened upon a parade of women carrying chocolate cakes followed by fifty students carrying three tapa cloths the size of a room and several mats. Intrigued, the Wilcoxes followed the procession up the hill. To their surprise, at the top of the rise, the entourage stopped and reversed direction, back the way they came before dispersing. It was comical how disorganized the spectacle seemed.

Dawn urged her family toward the pier, where she could hear music. There the king's ship was tied alongside the pier, where dozens of Tongan flags fluttered in the breeze—a flash of red bearing the Christian cross on a field of white in the upper left corner. A line of men and women dancers and singers performed, all in normal dress topped with a *lava lava*, a mat belt, and a sparse grass skirt. The women, wearing simple headdresses of feathers and flowers, waved their arms while keeping their feet firmly in place as male dancers leapt around them. To Dawn this dancing paled in comparison to the passionate hip thrusting they saw in Tahiti.

A brass-and-drum band dressed in black *lava lavas* with white shirts and mat belts then played their own renditions of various American marches and "Waltzing Mathilda," which prompted students in uniforms to burst out dancing in Western style as if they were on *American Bandstand*. One gray-haired woman from the king's entourage, who couldn't have been a day under seventy-five, stepped off the king's ship and threw herself into the dancing while a man pinned money to her hair.

Eventually the king arrived in a shiny black Mercedes and the band struck up the Tongan national anthem. His Majesty resembled a sumo wrestler, but one wearing a lava lava mat with a thick but tattered *ta'ovala* over street clothes. He made his way down the dock with his head held high, stepped aboard his ship and stood in the shade waving as a captain dressed in a white uniform directed the departure. After the last crescendo, the king's hundred-foot vessel toured the harbor, escorted by another boat decorated with flags and palm fronds. They traced several loops around the anchored *Vela* before a politely cheering crowd, then motored out of the bay.

A much less restrained revelry lasted long after the king's departure, deep into the wee hours with dancing, drums and electric guitars that led

Chuck to joke that it sounded more like a *Thank God, he's gone* party than anything else.

. . .

At about ten p.m. that night, Garth heard a noise on deck and discovered a boy who said he'd come to offer taro.

"We don't need any taro," Garth said.

"Oh," the boy said and paddled away before Garth could wonder why anyone would be trading at that hour.

At midnight, Chuck and Dawn saw a dark figure step over the life lines. Chuck surprised him by shining a spotlight in his face. To Chuck, he said, "Lady, you want to buy a coconut?" Except that he didn't have any. The man disappeared quickly over the side, not pausing to hear the reply.

That brought an end to the nocturnal visits.

. . .

Early the following day, the Wilcoxes' new best friend William reported that the Tongans had caught a whale. If the Wilcoxes wanted meat, they needed to head ashore without delay. And so, equipped with a plastic bag, Dawn and her modest entourage (Garth) dinghied ashore.

The family had read that Tongan men still chased whales with sailboats. Once they harpoon one, they hang onto the four harpoon lines while the whale races around until he tires. Sometimes it takes four hours, sometimes most of the night. When the exhausted whale stops fighting, men thrust lances to finish him off, then jump into the bloody, shark-infested seas to sew up the dead whale's mouth so it wouldn't fill with water as they tow it into port. Garth remembered his close call with a shark and cringed at the thought.

On the beach, hordes of people milled about to witness an epic event in village life. Whale meat was an important source of protein in

Tonga, especially since the king's visit left Vava'u villages with little to no livestock.

This whale was thirty-five feet long and only the second catch since the season began in June, and possibly the last before the season ended in October. Men stood in the shallows, carving the carcass and tossing hunks of meat to waiting customers. Ladies rinsed the intestines in the water, with their long dresses tucked into their *ta'ovala* waist mats to raise the hems above their submerged ankles. Children wandered about, chewing on blubber.

Dawn and Garth wormed their way into the fray. Dawn struggled to catch the attention of a man who seemed to be coordinating sales between people on the rickety pier and men carving off hunks from the carcass. Eventually the man nodded at her and she handed him two *seniti* coins. He shouted at the men in Tongan, tossed down her coins and a plastic shopping bag. A man next to the carcass pocketed the coins, whacked off a large chunk—about five pounds—and stuffed it into the bag, then tossed the meat in Dawn's direction. Seeing this hunk of meat flying at her, Dawn ducked. Garth reached around his mother and caught the package in mid-air.

By late afternoon, little was left of the enormous beast. By law, the carcass must be towed out to sea within twenty-four hours to avoid attracting sharks. By the next morning there would be no sign of the creature that had fed hundreds of people, including the Wilcoxes. For dinner that night, Dawn planned a flavorful stew using her trusty pressure cooker.

After seeing kids chewing on whale blubber, Garth decided to give it a try. Once his mother trimmed the meat for the evening's stew, he grabbed a couple of slices from the cutting board and handed a piece to his father, who was also game to try it. He gnawed at it with purposeful intent, knitting his brows in concentration.

"Blecch!" Garth said after a minute. He pulled the piece from his mouth and scrunched up his nose as he gave the piece a thorough inspection. "How can they eat this? It's awful!"

"It tastes like pure fat!" Chuck grimaced, agreeing with his son's assessment.

"Well, that's what it is," Dawn said, shrugging with an amused smile.

• • •

On Sunday morning, church bells started clanging at five a.m.

"Ugghhh!" Dawn groaned, pulling the pillow over her head. Devout Christians, Tongans took pride in being the first country in the world to worship the Lord each day. *For God's sake, it's only five a.m.!* Time to escape the noise of Neiafu.

After so many visits from William, the four decided they had no need to "put their anchor down on number five" to see his village. Instead, the Wilcoxes motored around the back of Mala Island to Malafakulava Island, which appeared uninhabited. They dropped the anchor into water the color of a swimming pool within sight of a sandy beach. The sun's rays sparkled off the surface. Paradise. Dawn and Linda splashed their way toward shore, taking in neon-colored tropical fish in the shallows, then hunted for shells along the blindingly white sand.

Just beyond the beach, Dawn noticed a lovely garden where someone evidently cultivated taro, manioc (tapioca), banana and papayas. Soon the owner of the garden and the island called down from above and introduced himself as Telenoti. With a big smile, he showed them around his small farm. He broke off a stalk of sugar cane, which they nibbled on as they wandered about. He stooped to pick his best pineapple and presented it to them. Dawn was thrilled to see this heavenly fruit emerging from a nestle of leaves. Garth adored pineapple and would treasure this prize, freshly picked just for them. Telenoti described how he foraged papaya and coconut twice a day to feed his family of eight kids and his three pigs. He told them what a strain it had been for the villages to feed the three hundred and fifty-pound king and his retinue of one hundred and fifty attendants. His own family had sacrificed two of his three chickens for the king and his entourage.

The next day Telenoti and his son John (pronounced Shione) paddled out to *Vela* in an outrigger canoe, bringing papaya, baskets and a number of large pink Murex shells, which they traded for old clothes. When the family saw Telenoti's fifteen-year-old son the following day, he was wearing Linda's jeans and one of her shirts.

On another visit, Telenoti strung a net near *Vela* to catch fish, then gave the family the fish it trapped. He asked to take home the fish heads for soup once he realized the Wilcoxes would only throw them overboard.

At seven thirty one morning, Telenoti brought his wife, an enormous woman he introduced as "Bivalve," though they found out later her real name was Anna. At that hour, the Wilcoxes invited them to share breakfast, which Dawn had just begun to cook.

Getting Bivalve's tremendous girth aboard *Vela* proved a challenge. Linda wondered how she'd ever gotten into the outrigger canoe in the first place, while Dawn wondered how they would ever get her back aboard without sinking it. Chuck reached over and grabbed her beefy arms to help pull her aboard *Vela*. Garth stepped in to help pull. With a hand on her corpulent bottom, Telenoti pushed from behind. Noticing the strain on Chuck's face and Dawn's look of concern, Telenoti joked, "Eat too much, talk too much." At that moment, they gained insight into her strange nickname—no doubt inspired by the open mouths of the giant clams they'd seen snorkeling along the nearby reef. Telenoti was only half joking. The woman hardly paused for a breath the entire time she was aboard, though no one knew what she talked about; Telenoti soon grew tired of translating. What needed no translating was her amusing reaction to shampoo. After spotting a bottle, Anna wanted to smell it. She wondered what it was for, and they told her for washing. She poured some out and patted it under her arms and exclaimed, "Beautiful! Beautiful!" Her favorite word, it seemed. To her delight, along with some old clothes, Dawn sent her home with a souvenir cup of the thick yellow liquid.

• • •

After several days, Telenoti invited the Wilcoxes to a picnic and urged them to move *Vela* to the other side of the island, closer to his village. He guided them directly over a narrow coral pass between islands, so shallow that *Vela* nearly ran aground. Chuck flinched to think of the consequences if they'd struck the reef, but a man experienced with out-riggers could hardly be expected to understand the depths required to accommodate a sailboat keel.

Moving nearer to the village brought many more visitors out to the boat. Telehau, they discovered to their dismay, housed two thousand people.

The picnic was in honor of a wedding. To prepare for the big feast, a number of villagers were busy cutting up pig and horse meat, which they would wrap in banana leaves and roast overnight with hot stones in an underground earth oven, or *umu*. After dark, Telenoti paddled out to the boat and invited them ashore. The family was already in bed and decided not to go. Later they discovered they'd missed the dance ceremonies for the wedding couple.

At six a.m. the next morning, Telenoti again paddled out to the boat and urged them to come for the feast. Barely awake, the family finished breakfast, then rowed ashore. They arrived after festivities had already begun. The wedding party sat cross-legged on a tapa cloth under palm fronds that were stretched across a light framework of sticks. The gathering resembled the luau they'd witnessed at the Polynesian Cultural Center in the Hawaiian Islands. Each Wilcox was given a lei and led to a place at the side of the dining area, except for Dawn, who was seated at a place of honor at the head of the table, perhaps because she was holding the camera.

Before them lay a long line of banana leaves on the ground with various lumps of brown goo. As everyone dug into the piles with their hands, so did the Wilcoxes, each wondering what they would discover. Dawn concluded it must be roasted horse and pig meat, squash and sweet potato, flavored with coconut milk and cooked in an underground oven, or *emu*, like she'd read about. Once everyone finished eating, the grandmother pulled out a fancy white cloth handkerchief, gently wiped her fingertips and her lips, then passed it with reverence on to the person beside her. One by one, each repeated the act and passed on the coveted communal napkin until all had used it. An amused Dawn snapped photos of the wedding couple, dressed in bright floral clothing buried under thick layers of ta'ovala mats, while one man after another, including Telenoti, made a series of long speeches in Tongan. A few people danced, much as they had for the king. After the meal, leftovers were divided evenly among the guests. Even the Wilcoxes were handed a share wrapped in banana leaves. Following the festivities, Telenoti asked if the Wilcoxes could take the wedding party to Neiafu to register the wedding with the church. Chuck agreed.

At seven a.m. the next morning, Telenoti arrived with a canoe full of people. The Wilcoxes soon learned it was only the first load. It seemed the whole village planned to join the trip to Neiafu. With forty people aboard, Chuck finally said, "We can't take any more." Bodies were scattered all over the deck and more filled the settee cushions below decks. There was no way the family could raise the sails with this many people in the way, so they motored the five miles into town. In the crowd Linda recognized Blue Skirt, though he was now incognito in Dawn's old sleeveless floral blouse and a pair of blue gym shorts that no longer fit Garth.

When *Vela* reached Neiafu, only the wedding couple, their parents and a few others ventured ashore. That left about thirty still aboard—at lunch time. Dawn assembled countless peanut butter sandwiches from the dried peanut butter they still had aboard. Their guests had no interest in coffee or tea, but drank through the family's remaining supplies of cocoa. Bivalve kept up a steady commentary to no one in particular while one man played guitar, another played ukulele, and many sang along until the wedding party returned to the boat. Telenoti's son, who'd taken over shuttling duty after the third trip, gave Chuck a sheepish look as they tied the Avon alongside; their dinghy was now half deflated, the victim of a cigarette burn.

Once everyone was back onboard the Wilcoxes and their merry crew made their way back to Mala. When Bivalve announced she was going below to take a nap, everyone looked relieved. As she disappeared below, Telenoti shook his head and said, "Talk too much." Titters spread across the deck as one after another recounted the joke.

• • •

For a few more days the Wilcoxes enjoyed the bay and the hospitality of Telenoti, his family, and the friendly village. In Telenoti's home, a hut with mats covering the dirt floor, the family's last remaining chicken and her chicks squawked under a bed in the back room, while Chuck joined the men drinking kava, a mild narcotic made of pepper root that numbed the lips and the minds of those who imbibed. Enjoyable though their visit was, once Chuck patched the dinghy, the family needed to move on if they wanted to reach New Zealand before cyclone season.

Just before they started the engine and raised the anchor, Telenoti pressed a bundle into Dawn's hands. It was a coarse fiber mat festively accented with red yarn tassels. The family waved goodbye with a promise to mail photos of the wedding once they reached Fiji. *Vela* motored back to the town of Neiafu to check out of the country and top up on food and water.

On September 14th, the family set sail for Fiji. With a fresh glow from their rich experiences in Tonga, the Wilcoxes had nothing but high hopes for their next landfall.

Bringing in a captured whale in Neiafu, Tonga; *Vela* in the background

8

Shortly after the family left Tonga for Fiji, the weather turned miserable. Heavy rains and clouds made getting star sights difficult. To compensate, Chuck and Dawn kept careful track of their course and speed to estimate their current location, a method known as a DR, or "Dead Reckoning." But, of course, a DR is only a "guesstimate." As Chuck liked to joke, "It's called dead reckoning because we are either right *here*, on course, or we're dead." It's actually a deduced reckoning, using the formula of estimating distance traveled by multiplying the rate of travel by the time traveled—elementary arithmetic, except when other factors are involved, like variations in course or currents.

In the days before GPS could immediately tell a sailor where he was, "getting a fix" seemed nearly as critical as it was for a junkie. The longer it had been since the last fix, the more urgent it felt. Errors had a way of compounding, and only a fix—triangulating the known position of the stars relative to your current position—could confirm if you were indeed where you *thought* you were.

Usually at sunrise or sunset, when both the stars and the horizon were visible, Chuck would take star sights with a sextant. Stars offered the most reliable sight for navigating, because there were so many to reference at a given time. The sextant would let Chuck measure the angle between the current location of a star and the horizon while Dawn noted the exact time down to the second. To insure accuracy, her watch was synchronized with time signals transmitted on the Zenith Trans-Oceanic radio. Dawn would reference tables that indicated the daily movement of each star and then calculate *Vela*'s relative position using worksheets that accounted for potential errors caused by light refraction or the height of one's eye. Once Dawn finished her complex calculations, which could take twenty minutes, Chuck would mark each star's location on a plotting sheet. Through triangulation he could estimate *Vela*'s location to be within a certain small area. When he finally marked their calculated position onto the chart, his family would hover over him, curious to see how far they'd sailed that day. It's a complex process, and by no means foolproof. But Chuck and Dawn's teamwork had proved reliable. For each landfall they'd been remarkably accurate, with land appearing right on schedule just where they expected it to be.

It had been days since Chuck had gotten a decent star sight, but just before nightfall on September 16th, a star barely poked through the clouds long enough for Chuck to grab useable readings on the sextant. Once Dawn finished her calculations, Chuck discovered *Vela* was further north than their DR positioned them. He concluded a current was pushing them northward and made a course correction to compensate.

On the morning of the 17th, the clouds lifted and Ogea Levu island was dead ahead. The sighting confirmed that the fix had been accurate and that altering course had been the right thing to do. The weather, though still cloudy, improved, making the sailing more pleasant, and "George," the wind vane, was steering well downwind. By this time, the kids were standing regular watches, three two-hour stretches for a total of six hours a day.

On the 18th, as Linda stood watch, *Vela* sailed around what they thought was Matuku. Chuck had nagging doubts about whether the island was indeed Matuku; with so many islands in this vicinity it was hard to know with certainty. But as it grew dark, the family could see the lights of Suva, like a beacon marking their destination.

Chuck stood watch between ten p.m. and midnight. Because the night was so pleasant, Chuck stayed on deck after Garth took over for him, riding the bowsprit and watching the city lights in the distance. But shortly before Linda came on watch to relieve Garth at two a.m., Chuck went down to bed, anxious to get a little sleep before they made landfall.

When Dawn awoke to relieve Linda at four a.m., she donned her yellow spray suit as usual and clipped into her harness. When she arrived on deck, a perplexing light blinked at her.

This was her first indication of the threat that lay before them, though she did not yet grasp its significance or have time to heed its warning.

Part II

Shipwreck

9

*V*ela lay on the reef with her starboard side facing the sky. Waves crashed over the hull and deck, as though she were on the edge of a waterfall. Tons of water pushed against the hull, splintering the wood as it ground over raw coral. The boat shuddered and vibrated. The air was filled with the noise of cracking wood and the thundering sounds of cascading water.

Chuck's muscles screamed in agony as he gripped the wooden mast to brace himself against the violent motion. In the darkness he could barely see his clenched fingers. All around him white foamy water tugged at his body and clothes. Garth tightened his grip around the stay, trying to hang on. Surrounded by tumbling seas, he felt as though he were caught in a vortex of converging hydraulic forces. Suction held *Vela* onto the reef and trapped her in roller backwash in the path of a chain of breakers. Waves pummeled them one after another in rapid succession, crashing down in a tumult of foam and spray.

During a lull between waves, Garth and Chuck picked their way aft on all fours, water thrashing against their bodies. Garth's shriveled fingers seemed no match against the hard metal fittings he used to pull himself along the angled deck. For a brief moment a flash of the beacon lit the deck.

Dawn tried to slow her breathing. Movement from below deck reminded her of Linda's haunting scream. She loosened her grip on the wheel to crawl forward and see if Linda was all right.

Below deck, Linda's world had turned sideways. The screech of grinding timber and the roar of surf outside were amplified in the cavernous interior. Would she be buried alive in this wooden tomb?

In the dark, Linda picked her way across the cabin, which now sat at a disturbing angle and was littered with their belongings. Disoriented, she couldn't find the steps to the cockpit. In a panic, she grabbed the edge of the companionway and pulled herself through the opening, sliding into the cockpit next to Garth as a wave cascaded over them and smacked her in the face. She screamed again.

Dawn fished for the lifejackets and made everyone put one on. With the deck slick with water and surfaces they normally used to brace themselves now vertical, at any moment one of them could be hurled overboard or become injured if they lost their grip and went flying. Waves slammed at the hull and splashed onto their faces. Fortunately they were together and uninjured—at least for the moment. The periodic strobe of the beacon—now closer—flashed on their frightened, strained faces. The useless engine throbbed softly. Chuck reached down and turned it off.

The incoming waves threw up steep mounds of water, which shoved them this way and that. In the battle of powerful opposing forces, something had to give. Either *Vela* would tear open on the reef or skip over it and sink in deeper water on the other side. Likely both. Either option would put them at great peril. How long would it be until they were dashed to pieces?

In that moment, Chuck felt the full weight of his responsibility as captain and instigator of this doomed voyage. He prided himself on being self-sufficient, but he had few options at this point. He, his wife, fourteen-year-old son and eleven-year-old daughter clung to a boat filling with water and grinding into shards atop a reef in the South Pacific. An ache reached up through the base of his skull.

Chuck went below. He turned on the radio and reached for the microphone. He spoke words no sailor imagines ever having to say aloud.

"Mayday, Mayday." He took a deep breath. "This is the sailing vessel *Vela*. We are hard aground, southeast of Suva." It was a bitter pill to swallow. He waited. No reply.

He repeated his distress call. Again, no reply. The only sounds were radio static and the protesting hull as waves battered it against the coral.

With flare gun in hand, Chuck climbed back on deck. Bracing himself against the dodger, he loaded the cartridge and shot off first one flare, then another. In the pre-dawn light, a rocket of light zoomed high into the sky, arched and hung in the air then returned to Earth. Their eyes traced the trajectory of each flare until its flame sputtered out in the water. Once it disappeared, darkness enveloped them again. Would anyone see their signal?

The more urgent question was how much longer could *Vela* withstand the pressure of the waves before she sank. Or would the hull roll, trapping them underneath? Prudent advice suggested staying with the ship for as long as it seemed safe. But how much time did they have?

The grinding, cracking, and crunching continued unabated.

The sudden flash of the beacon blinded them. Its steady insistence seemed obnoxious, tormenting them with its impassive regularity. How could they have missed seeing this aid to navigation sooner? Their folly mocked them in the form of that blasted beacon, every sixty seconds. Chuck set down the flare gun and they sat numbly, pondering their fate.

Then an ominous groan of the hull sparked a discussion of options.

"If we get pushed over the reef, the boat will probably sink in the lagoon." Chuck had to shout to be heard over the noise of the thundering water. "I think we need to be ready to abandon ship." Garth nodded.

Dawn shouted, "Maybe we should wait until it gets light. It's only a couple of hours."

"Let's at least get ready," Chuck said. "In case we have to go before then."

"I'll fetch the passports, money and documents," Dawn said, heading below.

"Garth," Chuck shouted over his shoulder, moving toward the cabin top where the hard dinghy and life raft were lashed. His son was right behind him. Linda shivered in the cockpit. In her waterlogged clothing, the oppressive heat and humidity of the cabin was forgotten.

Chuck had two options: the hard dinghy or the life raft. He chose the sure thing. Garth and Chuck untied the dinghy that Garth had sailed around the cerulean lagoon in Bora Bora only two months earlier. He could never have imagined using it to abandon ship. He and his father carefully lowered it into the water. Chuck grabbed the painter and pulled the boat aft toward the cockpit. The next breaker ripped the line out of his hands. In an instant, the dinghy was gone.

They heard Dawn's muffled cry from below.

Inside, cabinets had flown open and disgorged canisters of rice and flour, t-shirts, sea boots, and books into the saltwater sloshing across the cabin sole. Dawn's beloved clarinet had lodged itself against the wooden mast that rose from the settee, where the family had spent tropical evenings drinking tea. The kerosene lamp hung at an odd angle. Dawn had worked her way across the debris to retrieve her purse that held their money and passports, which they would need—if they survived.

Without thinking, she opened the hanging locker door, forgetting that, being above her head, it was likely to disgorge its entire contents on top of her. Pinned beneath two forty-pound scuba tanks and two tailormade wet suits—never used—and a closetful of clothing, she lost her calm. "Help! Help!" she cried. She tried to rein in her panic, but she was trapped inside a boat smashing against a reef and rapidly taking on water. Garth rushed below to free her. Fueled by adrenaline, he bent the door to pull her from under the pile. He checked to make sure she had the purse.

"Maybe we should take the plastic French sandals," Garth said, collecting a pair for each of them from the forward berth. "We'll need them so we don't cut our feet on the reef."

While Garth rescued Dawn, Chuck moved toward the life-raft canister for attempt number two. He was glad he'd tested the life raft before they'd left, but finding two life rafts with problems didn't bring him much confidence that the third would be any better. Either it worked or it didn't. This time their lives depended on it.

Chuck unbuckled the straps that held the life raft on deck. He opened the lid and tied the painter to the boat. He sucked in a breath, then pulled the cord to launch the CO_2 cartridges, hoping this set actually had CO_2 in them. To his relief, he heard a rush of gas and a wrinkled mass of orange and yellow rubber billowed out of the canister, unfolding like a lumbering giant awakening. It grew to epic proportions in moments. To Chuck's relief it didn't immediately deflate like the second life raft they'd tested. Except...

As it inflated the raft hit the water upside down. Just as it settled alongside the boat, a wave surged under *Vela* and lifted the hull. In a split second, the life raft was sucked under the boat, trapped between their sinking vessel and the sharp spikes of the reef below. It was hardly in a position to save them now. The raft seemed more likely to puncture on the sharp edges than keep them afloat until help arrived.

Waves continued to pummel the hull. Worried the boat would turn over and they would be trapped, Chuck had no choice but to try to salvage the life raft. He strapped on his plastic sandals and tightened the strap on his life vest.

By five thirty, enough light filled the horizon that, when he looked up again, he could see the outline of an island. The silhouette gave Chuck hope. Finally a break. They might be able to swim for it, though he worried about his eleven-year-old daughter.

Linda shivered in the cockpit with fear, overwhelmed by the smell of diesel mixed with saltwater, the sound of splintering wood, and the power of the waves that crashed over them and sent the hull shuddering. She was only eleven; she was too young to die.

Chuck eased over the side, feet first. As his feet plunged into the water, he discovered it was only three feet deep. He gently tugged on the line for the life raft, watching the waves and the shifting of *Vela's* hull for the best moment to give it a yank. He got the timing right and the life raft slid out easily from under the hull. He flipped it over and examined the raft. It looked intact except for a small tear in the canopy.

"Come on, Linda," he said, nodding at the life raft.

"There might be sharks!" she cried, her face contorted in fear. A wave smacked against the hull.

"COME ON!" he yelled.

Still trembling, Linda climbed into the life raft as her father steadied it.

Dawn and Garth put on their reef shoes and Dawn handed the last pair to Linda. Garth tossed the abandon-ship bag, a bucket, and the old cockpit army blanket into the life raft. Then they stepped gingerly onto the reef.

Chuck and Garth moved slowly across the sharp surface toward the island, pulling the life raft with Linda and their emergency supplies. Chuck, who'd stuffed the camera into his coat, paused for a moment to take one last photo of *Vela* before it sank. It represented years of work, the embodiment of their hopes and dreams.

Dawn trailed behind, picking her way around peaks of coral through waist-high water. A wave swept her off her feet.

"Ahh!" She tumbled in the surf, aware that the jagged coral below the surface could slice her skin. It happened so fast no one saw her fall. Struggling to regain her footing, she worked her way back to where the rest of her family labored toward shore.

As Garth tromped across the reef he could feel the jagged edges of the coral through his plastic shoes, suddenly grateful for the ugly things. He thought, how ironic that so soon after reading about Robinson Crusoe, at fourteen he, too, was shipwrecked on a remote island.

On the way into shore, Garth spotted the dinghy that had been ripped from his father's hands, battered and nearly sunk. He freed it from a coral head and emptied most of the water, then rejoined the bedraggled procession shoreward, trailing it behind him. There didn't appear to be an inner lagoon and they were able to walk all the way in.

It was daylight by the time the family reached the sandy shore of the tiny island. They sat dripping on the soft sandy beach, before a line of scrubby bushes. A soft breeze played on their cheeks as they munched on life-raft rations, pemmican, crackers and glucose candy and stared at the hulk that had once been their home.

The day was just beginning but they were exhausted.

10

"Well, we all lived." Dawn broke the silence. The others were numb with cold and shock. Dawn chattered with nervous energy. "We still have all our fingers and toes and we haven't starved to death yet," she noted, trying to lighten the moment. When no one said anything, she added, "But I don't think we'll be going anywhere on the *Vela* anytime soon," in a playfully serious voice. The kids paid no attention, continuing to chew and stare in disbelief at *Vela*, lying at that strange angle. Water dripped from their clothing onto the sand. Scattered around them were the contents of an enormous tin: mini cans of pemmican—two now empty, their pull tabs discarded, some foil-wrapped brick-like things, and World War II army-style gray cans marked WATER. The kids leaned against the inflated tubes of the life raft, the army blanket wrapped loosely around their wet shoulders. They were tired, yet too hyped to consider sleep.

"You know, this could be an ideal spot for a vacation," Dawn couldn't help saying as she gave an appraising look around them. Chuck gave her a dark look and she stopped speaking. Garth glanced at what was mostly a sand spit, backed by short scrub and a few sparse trees. At best, it stretched a quarter mile and was only one hundred feet wide.

Dawn knew everyone would soon be hungry again and began to calculate how long the supplies would last. For the kids, the rich, sweet suet-like pemmican was a treat—the combination of nuts, berries and fat was filling and had boosted their morale. But glucose candy, high-carb cookies and crackers, and the few sea rations from the life raft wouldn't get them far. They'd already drunk half the water they had brought from the boat. As soon as the heat of the day hit them, they'd need far more water just to stay hydrated. Obviously no one had heard their distress call or seen their flares. Who knew when someone might come? They could be on this uninhabited island for weeks. Keeping a family of four healthy could be a challenge. Her nurse's training had taught her to anticipate problems, but it hadn't prepared her for this. Life was reduced to the basic necessities: food, water, shelter.

Chuck pulled at his lip, staring at his shipwrecked vessel, his face grave. Their boat sat at a crazy angle, lying on its port side, water crashing around it. *Vela's* mast pointed directly toward them. From low on the beach, he could see the entire surface of the deck. Looking out on the wreckage of his dreams, he tried not to let emotions creep into his thoughts. They needed to get out of this predicament and they didn't have the luxury of feeling sorry for themselves.

Chuck realized that the hull hadn't shifted much since they'd abandoned the boat. The motion seemed less violent, although that might boil down to a difference in perspective. Since they'd been able to walk ashore, his fear of the boat sinking in an inner lagoon seemed unfounded. Maybe they could return to *Vela* when conditions calmed and pull off food and water.

Chuck voiced his thoughts, which sparked a discussion of possible options. One idea was to sail the dinghy to Suva to seek help, but not everyone could fit into the hard dinghy. Staying together seemed safer for the moment, since they didn't know how far they'd have to sail or what they might find. They dismissed the idea for now, but if no one came to rescue them, they'd reconsider. One thing was clear: getting more supplies off *Vela* was a priority.

Their debate was interrupted when Garth spotted a fishing boat in the distance. Grabbing the signaling mirror from their "abandon-ship" bag, Chuck caught the early morning sun's weak rays against its shiny surface and deflected the beam toward the fishing boat. But the vessel kept moving away, growing smaller until it vanished from view.

A wave crashed against the beach, sending threatening tendrils of water up the sand toward them. They were perched on the windward side of the island on a narrow stretch of sand not far from the water's edge.

"Maybe we should move to the protected side of the island," Chuck suggested.

A breeze blew across the island, keeping the temperature comfortable for the moment, but bright sunshine in the topics could be brutal. Once the clouds burned off they would need shade, though there was little to be found among the scrub and few skinny palm and paw paw trees. Garth and Linda set off to scout the island. Sand clung to their damp bodies and clothing.

Dawn picked up the blanket, shook out the sand, folded it and set it in the life raft, their new home. After everything was back in the craft, Dawn and Chuck moved it back into the water where it would be easier to haul. They towed their scarce supplies around to the opposite side of the island and nestled the life raft under two scrawny paw paw trees. Dawn designated an area for a galley and another for a latrine, imposing the order of a more permanent settlement in case they found themselves stranded for weeks.

Anxious to salvage as much as possible, their thoughts immediately shifted toward returning to *Vela*. Unfortunately their new campsite would no longer be within sight of the boat.

Chuck, Dawn and Garth headed for the wreck, trailing the hard dinghy behind them. The tide had receded, which made it easier to walk to the boat. They retraced their path across the coral to where *Vela* lay a half mile from shore, leaving Linda behind to look after their modest camp.

At a distance the sight of the *Vela* lying on the reef was disturbing. Close up, it was heartbreaking. All the money they'd saved, everything they'd worked for, their dreams, lay in shambles. Dawn fought back a flash of regret that she had been unable to avert this disaster.

The force of the waves against the hull was far less intense than when they'd abandoned ship, but couldn't be ignored. The hull still shifted and shuddered, creaking and crunching depending on the force of the wave-train that rushed against it. The boat had settled lower onto the reef where the coral had chewed away at beams on the port side. They would have to work fast before the tide came in again and the motion became untenable.

Garth pulled himself aboard, Chuck right behind him. Garth turned around and extended his hand to help his mother aboard. The steep deck was slippery and they had to crab-walk across the angled surface, grabbing onto fittings to keep from slipping off.

They ducked around the blue Sunbrella dodger to the companionway. As they looked below, their eyes took a moment to adjust to the gloom of the interior. Inside, saltwater sloshed back and forth, an oily brine littered with bits of paper and clothing. Linda's most recent issue of *Tiger Beat* magazine that Grandma had sent to Papeete for her birthday lay waterlogged on the floor. So was her recently completed schoolwork they planned to send to Calvert School from Suva. Everything they had assumed only yesterday now seemed blissfully naive. Everything had changed. Dawn was sickened by the sight and temporarily overcome with a sense of futility.

Garth was shocked to see his home in such a state. It seemed familiar, yet not. There were the shells impregnated in the resin tabletop of the dinette and the fireplace that had so impressed them when they'd first bought the boat—the fireplace he and his dad had rebuilt when the new compressor for the refrigerator demanded more space. They had never used it, and soon realized it was a romantic notion absurdly inappropriate in the tropics. The gimballed kerosene lamp hung sideways as though caught in a strong wind. The bunk where he'd been laying only six hours earlier was now above his head. The port settee, now on the low side, compressed strangely inward.

Garth's eyes took in the shelves lined with books and the tiny, framed California poppy watercolor his grandmother had painted—still dry, but for how much longer? They were in a race against the deteriorating effects of saltwater to salvage as much as they could of their shipboard life. He scrambled forward to grab the Avon Redcrest inflatable dinghy to help carry some of the load. He handed the heavy dinghy bag to his father, who hauled it through the forward hatch. On the foredeck, Chuck began to unroll the rubberized gray fabric and get it ready to inflate.

Garth grabbed his schoolwork from its locker, then searched for their beloved stamp collections, which had been so much fun to collect. He was glad to discover them still intact.

At first Dawn had assumed they'd lost everything, but now saw much could be salvaged. Food and water were critical. Perhaps later they could save more. She braced herself against the low side and stuffed canned goods into a pillowcase. Cans on the low side would be the first to rust, even though before they'd left, she and Linda had spent weeks carefully removing paper labels, varnishing and marking each can with its contents. There was no time to pick through them—God knew what combination of food she'd come up with to feed her family, but they couldn't afford to be choosy. When she could barely lift the sack, she set it aside and sought the next key item: water. Together, Garth and Dawn worked steadily, struggling against gravity to collect the full water jugs she had amassed for an emergency. She'd prepared in theory, but had never pictured using them under such conditions.

Chuck had his own struggle with gravity on the foredeck, where he was pulling out the hoses to fill the Avon dinghy with air. Inflating the rubber dinghy at a fifty-degree angle wouldn't be easy, but the Avon would let them haul twice as much. They would be limited by the tide cycle. The hard dinghy bumped against the hull, gently reminding them that the tide was rising.

They stepped on the side of the oven to get through the hatchway as Garth hauled load after load up and out to the cockpit. He had to brace items on the sides of the foot well rather than floor, since the floor was now vertical.

"Garth," his father called. Chuck was ready to inflate the Avon. Garth held it steady while Chuck forced air into its rubber tubes. Garth had to rest his weight on the narrow bulwarks on the steeply angled deck and wedge his body against the stay, while Chuck braced himself against the mast, which was now horizontal. Chuck compressed the foot pump over and over until the gray rubber material took shape and grew firm.

As the tide came up, waves slammed into them and sent spray flying. Every maneuver became more difficult, their situation more tenuous. They'd gathered nearly all they could for now and needed to load it and get off while they still could do so safely. They hoped to make a return trip before everything was ruined, but there were no guarantees. Water came first, then the heavy cans of food. All else would have to wait. That is, *if* they could salvage more.

Dawn quickly located utensils, dry matches and Sterno for cooking. She passed them through the open hatchway, where Chuck and Garth were wrestling the heavy water jugs into the hard dinghy next to the sack of canned goods. The weight drove the dinghy lower in the water until its freeboard was nearly submerged by the surrounding waves.

When they could fit no more, Chuck eased the inflatable into the water. As soon as the empty Avon settled next to the loaded hard dinghy, Chuck told Garth, "OK, go ahead and take that load in. This is as much as we can do." Garth grabbed hold of the painter and towed the loaded dinghy ashore, kicking up waves with each step through knee-high water.

Chuck shouted, "Come on, Dawn. We've got to go. The tide is rising." She grabbed a bunch of dry clothes and stuffed them into a roll of blankets and shoved them into the cockpit, and gave a wistful glance at her floating clarinet. It wasn't critical to their survival but she was sad to abandon it.

She pulled herself through the companionway and worked with Chuck to load the lighter items that remained: clothes and blankets, cooking items, the stamp collection, the kids' schoolwork, a radio, and Linda's new camera that Chuck's parents had sent to Papeete for her birthday. Dawn was grateful that she'd mailed home nearly all the photos they'd taken of their voyage so far. At least if they couldn't finish the voyage, they would have some great memories. As she and Chuck pulled the Avon slowly behind them, Dawn kept peering over her shoulder, worried the waves would ruin these dry items before they could get them to shore.

As they made their way to the beach a short distance behind Garth and the hard dinghy, Chuck noticed a skiff with two men approaching the island. He picked up his pace. After a moment of surprise, Dawn saw why.

11

As soon as Chuck reached the beach, he dropped the line to the Avon, grabbed the signal mirror and flashed a beam of light in the direction of the skiff. The men looked up, revved the engine and brought the boat into shore. Chuck met them at the water's edge. Dawn, Garth and Linda strained to hear but couldn't make out the words.

The men told Chuck he needed to take their passports and ship's papers to clear into the country and offered to take him to a nearby island, where he could radio the authorities to report the shipwreck. Only yesterday Chuck had imagined checking into Fiji, filling in requisite forms followed by the satisfying thud of rubber stamps—a cursory step before his family was free to explore the wonders of a new country, address equipment issues and resupply. Now none of that mattered. He'd forgotten about the usual bureaucratic procedure in the drama of their shipwreck. Was it only this morning that a fury of waves threatened to wash them overboard and they'd feared for their lives?

Right now, official procedures seemed irrelevant, but he was in no position to argue. Chuck fished for the requisite paperwork from Dawn's purse. Dawn glanced at the stack of passports and immunization records he held, which represented who they were, where they came from, where they'd been. Her stomach clenched.

"Now, you *will* come back for us, right?" Dawn joked, a catch in her voice betraying her worry.

"Sure," Chuck said with more confidence than he felt. They held each other's gaze for a moment; then he joined the men alongside their boat. Dawn swallowed hard.

Chuck climbed into the skiff and they shoved away from the beach. When the skiff driver hit the throttle, Chuck looked back at his family standing on the beach, looking like the forlorn castaways they were. Soon each became a tiny dot on an empty beach.

As they pulled away from the island, Chuck could see the beleaguered *Vela*, high and dry on the reef. He was the "captain" of this "vessel," which now looked more like a hulk from World War II than the home he'd carefully prepared and sailed to Hawaii, French Polynesia, Tonga, and other delights of the South Pacific. Their voyage was over too soon.

For a time all he could see was the bright orange canopy of the life raft. Soon it became no more than a dot of color and was gone. At that moment their insignificance in the world could not have been more clear.

He hoped to return to his family within a few hours, but was apprehensive, given how little control he had over his life at that moment.

12

Dawn's anxiety rose as Chuck and the men motored away with their passports, the ship's papers and all their cash, leaving her alone on an uninhabited island with two children. When the skiff was no longer visible, she shifted into action, putting on a brave face for her kids.

The three kept busy for several hours, unloading the two dinghies and organizing their land supplies. They shed their damp clothes for dry ones they'd salvaged from the wreck. Then they laid the soggy items in the sun to dry. With their belongings scattered around the area, the island looked like a giant garage sale. Saltwater-drenched items have a stubborn tendency to remain wet and develop mildew. Their only hope was a rain squall followed by bright sunshine, to rinse and then bake the moisture out. But the sun eased toward the horizon with little sign of either.

At the end of the day, everyone was physically spent and emotionally numb. They knew that when the sun set there'd be nothing more to do until sunrise. As the sun dipped over the horizon, Chuck still hadn't returned. Dawn dreaded the night. All they could do was wait in helpless uncertainty until morning. Sentenced to hours of inactivity by darkness, her mind would turn over the events of the day and mull over the what-ifs and might-have-beens, and relive the moment in which one of her worst fears had come true.

When the warm tropical sun vanished, the temperature dropped, and everyone shivered. Building a bonfire offered a distraction. They picked among the driftwood for firewood and scavenged a log to sit upon. Dawn reached for the Zenith radio they'd grabbed from the boat. She flipped it on and—miraculously—it still worked. She wound the tuning knob up and down the spectrum until she came across three stations—one of them in English. The familiar words brought them comfort and distracted them from their plight. The three settled atop their new "living room couch," watching flames leap into the air, and listened to a Nevil Shute radio serial until the station went off the air. They doused the fire and climbed under the orange canopy of the life raft for one of the most miserable nights of their lives.

Although it had been billed as a six-person life raft, three could barely fit inside. Their legs crossed one another, making for a crowded and humid, claustrophobic environment. It smelled of damp wool and rubber.

They'd forgotten about the slope of the beach, so the raft sat cocked at an angle that felt unsettlingly odd from the inside. Every time one of them shifted, his or her weight deflected air in the pressurized tubes, disturbing the delicate balance and a fragile truce. Even worse, the rubber floor of the life raft was suspended between the side-tubes, so the middle sagged, drawing each person toward the center. Bracing their legs kept them from falling into the center, but it also kept them from relaxing—a necessary ingredient when it comes to sleeping. A moment of neglected vigilance would send them into a pile in the middle of the raft.

And that was *before* the rain.

It was the freshwater rinse they'd craved, and then some.

Tropical showers are not the gentle rains of California. *Torrential* was the word that sprang to Garth's mind. Once water flowed freely from the skies, they discovered the striking effectiveness of the life raft's freshwater-catchment system. Water pelted the canopy like a barrage and funneled down the catchment chute directly into the raft. Fresh water—so precious and welcome under survival conditions—is less welcome in bed. Surrounded by jugs of fresh water they'd salvaged from the boat, they were now trying to sleep beneath an open water main. Streams gushed down their necks, soaked their clothing and collected under each of their bottoms where their weight depressed the fabric, forming a lake in the center. The pool of water only magnified the pull inwards. They slept fitfully, if at all.

During the night, Dawn heard a motor approaching their camp. She felt powerless, acutely aware of their vulnerability in the darkness, like a mother hen clutching her brood close while wolves prowled outside the hen house. To protect her meager nest, she shined a flashlight beam in the direction of the noise. She held her breath and listened until the sound of the engine died away. Afterward her attention returned to the stifling humidity of the life raft and her restless charges.

Morning finally arrived. The suffocating moisture inside the water-filled life raft made them eager to get an early start. Dawn worried but tried to keep her thoughts in check as she dug through the provisions to find something for breakfast. Biscuits, glucose tablets, canned chocolate milk, and cold canned tuna started their day.

As the sun rose higher, the clouds cleared and the temperature rose. Garth and Linda wandered the island while Dawn sorted through the food. Garth found a ten foot-by-ten foot cinderblock and concrete hut in the center of the island, in an even shadier spot than they'd found. Relieved that he wouldn't have to spend another night in that godforsaken life raft, Garth rushed back to tell the others.

Then he heard Linda scream. He and Dawn nearly collided trying to reach where Linda stood.

"Stand back!" Linda shouted, poking a long stick in front of her. "There's a huge snake!" A six-foot-long, five-inch-thick black-and-white striped snake formed an S shape on the sandy ground in front of her. It was the deadly poisonous kind that they'd read about in *Dangerous Marine Animals*. With no antidote. In the middle of their campsite.

This specimen was broader than Linda's leg. Visions of snake bites and medical trauma swirled in Dawn's mind. After surviving a shipwreck, one of them could die a slow and painful death from the venom of an enormous sea snake.

Searching for a weapon, Garth grabbed an oar. It was heavy and long and at hand. Inspired by fear and adrenaline, he brutally beat the snake until he was sure it would never slither again. All his frustration surged into that oar, and he gave it everything he had. *Thump, thump, thump.* When the carnage was complete, Garth picked up the snake carcass and flung it into the sea. All were vastly relieved. As though it were the only snake on the island.

As soon as the tide was right, Garth and Dawn returned to the wreck with both dinghies. Linda remained on the island to guard their camp and the sordid array of salvaged items drying in the sun. When they reached the boat, Dawn and Garth realized how fortunate they'd been to salvage that first load with Chuck before the tide had risen. Now the boat was half filled with water. Just over twenty-four hours after impact, many things were beyond saving, especially on the port side. Few items aboard could withstand submersion in saltwater. Spaghetti noodles had long since solidified into an enormous clump. Dawn's clarinet already showed signs of rust. Still, much remained intact—though for how much longer was anyone's guess. Moisture in the air could easily destroy whatever the water didn't touch; the humidity inside was already like a sauna, an atmosphere ideal for harboring bacteria and mold.

Dawn held the rubber dinghy in place while Garth climbed in and out of the hull, first rescuing anything electronic before it corroded. Now that they'd found the cement hut, boat cushions moved to the top of the salvage list. Clothing, memorabilia and personal items also took priority, once they grabbed pots and other items for cooking. Garth stuffed smaller items into a pillow case to lower to his mother.

Dawn was especially keen to save the six-inch-thick Columbia encyclopedia that Grandma had loaned them. She'd tried to wrestle it out on the last trip but couldn't get it out of the locker. After retrieving this universally despised tome, Garth dropped the heavy book toward his mother with a shout—"Catch!"—but at that moment a breaker knocked her off balance. She caught it as it touched the water, but not before it got wet. Back in camp later, salvaging the encyclopedia would become a pet project, requiring the careful periodic turning of each page so that it could dry in the sun. Garth and Dawn kiddingly assigned the project to Linda, reasoning that, after all, Linda had nothing but time as she guarded their belongings. But Linda kept busy sorting and drying items once they reached her beach kingdom of boat detritus.

As they finished loading the dinghies that morning, Garth saw a skiff with two men approaching the island. He was glad someone was ashore to guard their things, but they hurried back anyway.

Linda saw the two fishermen before they saw her, but she was still apprehensive. They wore torn t-shirts and dirty shorts. When they spoke to her, she discovered the men spoke English. They'd seen the orange canopy of the life raft. She answered questions about the shipwreck and pointed to her family on the boat.

The men explained that they were fishing for turtles and that this island, named Makaluva, was their fish camp. Linda looked at the nothingness around her and wondered about the word "camp." Then she remembered the cement hut they'd been so excited to find. The men told her it had been the only building to survive Cyclone Bebe a few years earlier. With a third set of visitors in less than thirty-six hours, it was clear how much curiosity the wreck had elicited. And she'd thought they'd be stranded without human contact for weeks.

A pause followed and one of the men shimmied up a palm tree and hauled down a coconut, as fast as she'd seen at the Polynesian Cultural Center show in Hawaii. He wrenched open the nut and offered her a drink of its sweet milk. It helped ease the tension, but she wondered how long she'd have to "entertain" these two. When Garth and Dawn returned to shore, the men seemed to lose interest and motored off.

Dawn, Garth and Linda spent the intervening tide cycle unloading and sorting once again, while Linda shared her story of the turtle fishermen. When the tide was right in the afternoon, Garth and Dawn made another trip to the boat. They learned to turn off their minds and move as quickly as possible. The work was physically demanding, but it helped them steer clear of the emotional baggage that came with dismantling their waterlogged home piece by piece. They loaded and then unloaded another batch of items, some drenched some still remarkably dry. Steady work kept their minds and bodies occupied while they waited for Chuck to return.

In the late afternoon sun Dawn grew uneasy, thinking she would have to spend a second night or more alone with the children. Could checking into the country really have taken Chuck more than twenty-four hours? She imagined the worst of horrors that might have befallen him. Her jaw ached from clenching it and grinding her teeth, an old habit in times of stress.

So far, she'd relied on her instincts for survival. Addressing their most immediate needs made decisions easy. Working to haul items off the wreck seemed logical to save them from water damage. But the future loomed with so many unanswered questions, especially if something had happened to Chuck. Her stomach twisted in knots with worry.

13

An hour later, Dawn stood up to stretch her aching back. She'd been stooped over the dinghy, loading and unloading items all day. A flash off the beach caught her eye. Another open skiff. Yet another "looky-loo" to gawk at their misfortune? She didn't want to hope that it was Chuck, but the thought crept in all the same. As the boat drew closer, she shielded her eyes and peered at it intently, trying to make out the tiny dark figures inside. Her eyesight—never good under the best of circumstances—was compromised by late afternoon sun glinting off her glasses. She thought she could make out Chuck's floppy hat, sitting taller than the dark heads in the boat, but it was still too far away to be sure. Garth noticed she'd stopped working and looked up. Linda heard the engine and stopped sorting their wet belongings on the other side of camp.

"Dad's back!" Garth shouted. Dawn felt tears prickle the corners of her eyes. Relief swept through her. She'd never been so happy to see anyone. She no longer had to face it alone. The return of Chuck, the money, and their paperwork was reassuring.

Everyone burned with curiosity to know what had happened while he was away, but that would have to wait. After quick hugs, Chuck took the men out to the wreck to assess the salvage job. They were there for a half hour tromping around onboard. Before the men left they gave Chuck an estimate of how much they would charge to help salvage items off the boat and to haul them and their belongings to Suva. Chuck immediately agreed to the price—cheap for such a daunting job. The men promised to return in the morning to begin work.

After the men left, darkness descended quickly and the family settled in for mystery-meal-in-a-can. Dawn's new island galley took cooking to a new level of austerity. She thought back to Tom Neale and how far he'd come from where he started on an island like this one. Over a single can of Sterno, she heated green beans and tuna. After "dinner," Dawn boiled hot water for tea while Garth and Linda collected driftwood—gnarled and bleached white as bone. They piled it high to make a bonfire. Once they fanned the flame into a moderate blaze, they settled atop their new "living room couch" with mugs of steaming tea. They watched flames leap into the air and dance as Chuck told them how he'd spent the last two days.

After he and the other men had motored off, they'd stopped at the island park on nearby Nukulau Island, where one of the men was the captain of an excursion boat. There, Chuck radioed Suva Harbor and officials sent a pilot boat to bring him to Suva to clear Customs and Immigration. Usually when a shipwreck occurs in Fiji, Customs impounds everything until they determine what should be done with it. Inside a sticky, airless office, Chuck argued that, with any delay, everything aboard would be completely destroyed. The Customs official relented, giving Chuck permission to remove and inventory all items under his control.

By the time Chuck finished with "officialdom," it was too late to hire anyone to take him back to the island. He figured he might be able to organize resources to help with the salvage operation. So he booked a night in a modest hotel.

"Exhausted as I was, I could not fall asleep. I kept tossing and turning. I just couldn't get comfortable," Chuck said. "The bed was too soft!" Garth looked at his mother and cracked a smile.

"Oh, poor Dutch!" Linda teased, rolling her eyes. "The bed was too soft!"

Chuck went on: "So I pulled the mattress onto the floor. As soon as I did that I promptly fell asleep." He cracked a smile.

"Good for you," Garth said. "We spent the night crouched in the life raft with water raining in."

"It was great fun," Dawn agreed with a wry laugh.

While sympathy was sorely lacking, Chuck went on without missing a beat. "Wait, I'm not finished yet … I talked with several salvage crews and rented a house in Suva where we can live while we figure out what to do next. The crew you saw today will be back in the morning to help us pull off our gear."

It was a plan—at least for the short term.

After nearly forty-eight hours without much rest, everyone was eager to get some sleep. After laying out the boat cushions on the floor of the cement hut, they were soon fast asleep, dreaming of happier times.

14

For the next three days the family worked with the Fijian laborers, who came each morning to remove items from the wreck and row them to the island. The rest of them would trudge back and forth, back and forth across the sand all day, carrying as much as they could fit into the cement hut. Six months' worth of wet toilet paper, a dripping sewing machine, damp clothing, books, canned goods, radios, cassette tapes, sails, medical kit ... the list went on and on.

They toiled from dawn to dusk. At the end of every day they were bone-tired. When the sun went down, they huddled around a bonfire for dinner and tea and listened to radio stories and ten-minute news broadcasts on Radio Fiji. Soon after nightfall they fell asleep on the boat cushions in the hut, surrounded by the soggy remains of their voyage. Preoccupied with getting their belongings off *Vela* before they were completely ruined, they had little time to think of their future.

Dawn spent days cooking over a can of Sterno under a papaya tree and a sail they'd rigged for shelter. Meals were still simple combinations of canned meats and vegetables or fruit, but they were warm and filling, exactly what they needed after a hard day's work. Dawn got better at remembering to sort through the varnished cans and read their hand markings during daylight so that they would end up with a balance of fruit, vegetable and meat instead of all vegetables as they had the first couple of dinners.

Day by day, the island was covered with more of their belongings. Chuck complained of a sore ankle, and coral cuts on his legs grew infected. Dawn's hip threatened to give out. They had no choice but to carry on as best they could. Dawn organized items by categories and gave clothing and boots to the work crew, since she figured they would have to abandon the voyage. Still the family was shocked at the mass of material they'd stored aboard the boat.

After the *Fiji Times* had printed a story about the wreck on Makaluva, the family became the local entertainment, especially on Sunday. The island was only ten miles from Suva, and people came with picnic lunches and settled down to watch the family work. Shipwrecks were so common in Fiji that locals failed to grasp the magnitude of loss for the victims. Picnickers joked amongst themselves, but none offered food or made kind gestures toward the family. Dawn felt the strain of nonstop backbreaking work, with the added burden of keeping her family fed with so few resources. What she wouldn't give for a piece of fresh fruit or a vegetable like the picnickers enjoyed—something *not* out of a can. She burned with resentment until the fourth morning when Roden, the crew boss, arrived with a loaf of fresh bread from Suva.

Roden and his crew earned their money. Each day they removed hundreds of pounds of gear from the hull, yet more remained. When Roden realized the magnitude of the project, his salvage estimate doubled. Still the total cost to get all their belongings off the boat and into town would only total six hundred and eighty dollars Fijian, less than what Chuck had paid for the Aries wind vane.

When the crew finally uncovered the damaged hull, they discovered that, instead of a small hole in the planking, the planks and frames had been ripped away, leaving a hole five feet by eight feet. Big enough to drive a car through.

Roden told Chuck that he and his crew could not save the boat. His words hit hard. Until that moment, Chuck had been hopeful that they could repair the boat and continue their voyage. But with such a sizable hole, a boat yard repair would cost more than the family could afford. And Chuck didn't think he had the skills or the tools to repair it himself.

He wrestled with the idea of giving up the cruise, which haunted him as he worked to pull everything off *Vela*. He mentally weighed what might be worth saving and shipping home for another attempted cruise and what might have to be sold locally.

By their fifth day on the island, the Wilcoxes had removed nearly everything that wasn't bolted to the boat. Garth and Chuck had worked together to remove the wind vane and lay out all the anchors and chain to hold the boat in its current location. Chuck hoped to be able to sell the hull for something. Anything he could get might help pay for the next voyage.

Early the last morning, as everyone else prepared to vacate the island when the salvage crew arrived, Garth grabbed some tools and headed out to the wreck one last time. He had read of shipwreck looting and knew the value of the equipment that remained. He knew enough about the cost of winches and the cast-bronze fittings to try getting it all off. The number of visitors to the island had convinced him that people would strip *Vela* where she lay on the reef.

Using the largest screwdriver and wrench they owned, along with a hammer, Garth spent hours methodically unscrewing winches and cleats from the wrecked wooden hull. Not easy to do at that angle, with screws that were seven inches long and corroded into place. Though he wasn't completely sure what he'd do with them once he pulled them off the boat, it was a matter of principle. He knew their value. That was motivation enough.

This small act would play a crucial role in determining their future.

On September 24, 1974, five days after the shipwreck, the salvage men returned with two copra boats to load all the gear for the trip to Suva.

Little by little, they and the family emptied the concrete hut of their belongings and lugged them to the waiting "barge," a twenty-five-foot-long open wooden boat, reversing the process they'd so laboriously undertaken the last few days.

While clearing the last few items from the hut, Garth pulled up the boat cushions they'd been sleeping on. There, nestled in a crack between them, was a poisonous snake identical to the one he'd so savagely killed. Garth leapt back. Roden, who'd been standing near the doorway to the hut, let loose a hearty laugh. "What?" Garth said from where he'd leapt away from the snake. "Those things are deadly!"

"No problem," Roden said as he came in the door. Pushing past Garth, he leaned down and picked up the enormous snake. Its black and white tail curled around his thin brown arm, its scaly skin glistening in the dim light. Roden grabbed its tail and swung it in a circle, saying "See? Harmless!" Garth and Dawn recoiled in horror. They gave him a wide berth as he carried the creature outside and into the bushes. Despite Roden's casual attitude, no one wanted to see what might anger a gargantuan reptile that possessed a toxin for which there was no antidote.

Garth could not shake the thought that he'd spent days sleeping with this deadly creature.

15

A fter days of unloading *Vela*—wading with every single item from wreck to beach to boat—the Wilcoxes were finally ready to leave their castaway island, with the soggy remnants of their seagoing life stuffed to the gunwales of an open boat. The island that had been their home—every inch intimately known to them—now looked as remote as it had that first desolate morning when they'd trudged ashore in a daze. All they left behind were hundreds of footprints snaking across the sand where they'd lugged load after load, footprints that would be washed away with the next storm surge.

And *Vela*, a sad monument to their broken dream.

Once the tow line was secure, the family boarded the lead boat. As Roden pumped the throttle, the line slowly straightened. The "barge" spun and began to follow. The procession weaved its way through the reef to open water, a hint of ocean swell reminding them of their last innocent hours under sail before impact.

They looked back at *Vela*, each wondering if it were for the last time. Once underway, Dawn felt the tension of the nonstop work slip from her shoulders. She no longer had to worry about survival. As a rescued passenger, she could relinquish control, let her mind float free and notice her surroundings. Memories of the thoughtless picnickers faded—in every culture, some people gawk inappropriately at the misfortune of others. Her innate curiosity about other cultures came to the fore for the first time since they'd left Tonga ten days earlier. Unlike the Polynesians and Tongans with their long wavy hair, indigenous Fijians had closely-cropped, nappy hair. The hardworking young men whom they'd worked alongside for days had easy smiles, with bright white teeth that gleamed in their dark faces.

With confidence, these men navigated the murky waters that made reef-spotting impossible. Instead of heading directly toward the city, they steered a wide berth around invisible obstacles. No wonder navigating had presented such a challenge, especially under overcast skies. In the distance, Dawn could see far less hospitable places where they could have run aground, where waves crashed against rocky ledges miles from land. She was grateful for their relative good fortune. With a minor shift in location, a navigational error like theirs might have cost them their lives.

A half hour into their journey to Suva, the Indian-Fijian crew made themselves a lunch of scrambled eggs and peppers rolled in roti—almost like an Indian burrito, with spices that Indian indentured servants had carried with them when the British brought them in to work the colonial sugar cane plantations three or four generations ago. After days of eating nothing but canned goods, the famished Wilcoxes salivated. Roden offered them a taste and they each had a memorable bite.

The tow boat with the beleaguered family and their trailing cargo neared the city. A typical day's work for the men, but for the Wilcoxes, this was their introduction to Fiji. With wide eyes they took in the head-spinning flurry of urban activity, a stark contrast to the gentle creak of lines in the blocks aboard *Vela* or the sweep of waves lapping against the sandy shore of Makaluva. Suva harbor was large, with fishing seiners and long liners from Taiwan and Korea tied to wharves nearby.

Traffic in Suva harbor zipped around them that Tuesday afternoon. Open skiffs and inter-island ferries zoomed back and forth across the water. The occasional Fijian sailing canoe emerged from mangroves, presumably headed for fishing grounds along the fringing reef. The activity was dizzying.

Their eyes took in the low concrete and wood buildings and brightly painted signs dotting the rest of the shoreline, built on land reclaimed from mangrove swamps. Beyond the lowlands, lush green hills rose into the mountains that divided Fiji's main island of Viti Levu into two micro-climates: the drier leeward side and the (unfortunately) wetter, windward side where Suva sat. The family had already experienced its sudden torrential rains but had given them no more than a passing thought.

The boats eased into the landing at Princess Wharf, a public pier that headquartered the city's waterborne traffic. In the late afternoon, the pier was a swirl of action, with passengers and their cargo loading and unloading: slender Indian ladies in saris; stout Afroed women in bright floral dresses carrying burlap sacks on their heads; bearded Sikhs in turbans and button-down shirts with slacks; dock workers in faded, torn t-shirts and shorts hoisting stalks of bananas from the boats; young girls in crisp blue school uniforms clutching textbooks. Light blue Fijian flags with Union Jacks flapped frantically from larger vessels as they picked up speed with a punch of the throttle.

The Wilcoxes' arrival in Suva was so different from what they had envisioned. Dawn had sewn the Fijian courtesy flag with the assumption that it would hang below *Vela*'s starboard spreader while they explored the country and resupplied before sailing on to New Zealand. Now their future was uncertain and they were essentially homeless.

Once the men secured the boats, the unloading process began all over again—with an audience. Within an hour the boats were empty and the workmen had gone home to dinner and their families. The Wilcoxes stood in a daze before their belongings: a rusted bicycle, Garth's chemistry set, Bunsen burner, drafting tools and art supplies, ships models he'd carved from scraps of wood, the Honda generator, fabric Dawn used to make flags, the spare Groco toilet ... now a waterlogged pile of junk. This enormous pile of items had been relatively new and in good condition, until five days ago. A crowd of Fijians looked on at the spectacle, while others jostled past, crinkling their noses at the odor.

Dawn's respite had been all too brief. She sighed out loud.

"Well, I guess I'll go hire a truck to get it all to the house," Chuck said and ran off, leaving the rest of the family standing on the pier in the full sun. The stench of mildew was as overpowering as the intense heat. After the cool breezes blowing across the island, the still air of the city seemed stifling.

Minutes ticked by. Garth felt as if his life were on display for all the world to see. What had once been his entire world lay in a mess of salt crystals, shredded paper, rust and corrosion. Worthless though it appeared, it contained things they might need, provided they could clean them before corrosion and mildew completely ruined them.

After five days of hard labor, with seven people working, they'd salvaged all but one winch, the anchor windlass, plus the three anchors, line and chain they'd used to hold *Vela*, as well as the mast, engine, stove, galley sink, and holding tank. Everything but what was still attached to *Vela* lay in this gigantic pile. Or so they thought.

Linda sat down on the hard surface, dwarfed by the pile. Cross-legged, with her hands cupping her chin and her dark blonde hair covering her face, she settled in for a long wait, taking in the bustle of the scene around her.

Dawn's hip, aggravated by days of loading and unloading, throbbed as she stood on the stiff wooden planks. She shifted her weight from one leg to the other, trying to ease the strain. The repetitive motion had taken its toll on her thirty-eight-year-old body, though she assumed the pain would pass once she could get off her feet for a while. It had been the longest week of her life, and it wasn't over yet. Dawn wondered how long they'd be standing in the sun. Noticing a Tongan woman wearing a *lava-lava* with a woven mat sash and carrying an umbrella, Dawn's concerns about the potential for sudden heavy rain joined her litany of worries.

"Oh crud and corruption!" Dawn said with exasperation. This was her version of swearing. Though her family knew she only said this when she was upset, her mild-mannered attempt at anger made it hard to keep a straight face. Garth and Linda stifled snickers. The seriousness of their situation and the heat quickly wiped the smiles off their faces.

After what seemed like hours, Chuck returned with a flatbed truck and, item by item, the four of them spent the next hour moving the pile from the pier to the truck bed. Once they were loaded they pulled away. The smell of exhaust and asphalt was overwhelmingly strong after weeks of exposure to nothing but salt air.

From the stake-sided truck bed, Linda peered out at the hodgepodge of colonial two-story structures of wood and concrete with second-floor porches overhanging the sidewalks. As they sped through the streets a flash of color whirled past, a combination of brilliant floral clothing and brightly painted buildings and signs, muted by the blinding brightness of full sun alternating with shadows from the thick foliage of the stately old trees. This was the fastest they'd moved in months, and Linda relished the wind on her face as they zoomed through the city to the house her father had rented. *A house!* She could hardly wait.

Arrival at the house produced yet another opportunity to revisit their soggy belongings in their entirety, and they spent the rest of the day unloading everything into the carport. When they were done, they fell into bed and slept their first deep sleep in ten days.

16

In the ten days since they'd left Tonga, their lives had completely transformed from being seafaring explorers to castaways to residents of Fiji.

Tired as they were, they barely noticed the house and its sparse furnishings the night they arrived. But in the morning light, when they saw the pink plastic metal-legged couches in the living room, they shared their first laugh as a family in what seemed like ages.

The house had three bedrooms—more than they needed, but the plumbing left much to be desired. The sink and shower drained through holes in the walls into a concrete ditch that ran out into the yard. There open water sat brewing a fetid mixture of decomposing waste and vegetation—fertile ground for weeds and mosquito larvae.

For Dawn, the house offered an improvement over cooking aboard and certainly the limited galley facilities—or lack thereof—on Makaluva. In addition to unlimited fresh tap water, Dawn was grateful to have a working refrigerator. The one on *Vela* had never worked properly, freezing everything on port tack and not running at all while on starboard tack. The family joked about this fabulous new invention of cold, transparent white hard things that people called "ice."

Rent was two hundred dollars per month. Chuck had thought it a good deal when he first agreed to the price, but was irritated to find out he was being charged one hundred and fifty dollars more than the standard rate for houses in the area. He thought it might only be for a month or two. Their closest neighbor was the impressively active China Club, which regularly featured cookouts using the most giant wok they'd ever seen and out-of-tune but enthusiastic bands at ear-splitting volume.

One of their first tasks was to contact their families so they wouldn't worry. By this point, it was too late for them to worry in any case.

On September 25th, Chuck wrote to his parents:

Dear Folks: We left Tonga on the 14th and after one of the most difficult trips of our lives we stepped ashore yesterday, the 24th, very tired. We are all well and uninjured and feel very fortunate except for the fact that Vela didn't make it all the way to Suva. On the morning of the 19th we struck a reef off of Makaluva Island. Before we knew what happened the breakers threw us up on the reef 100 feet from deep water.

He described abandoning ship and salvaging their belongings. Despite this terrible setback and public humiliation, Chuck was still determined to circumnavigate the world by sailboat.

We will probably eat all the food, sell the boat equipment that we wouldn't use on our next boat, sell other stuff that is too expensive to ship back. Then we will give some away, throw some away and ship the rest back to the USA, where we will return, go to work to earn another boat and start the trip again. With luck we could leave again in 3-4 more years.

Then he tried to let his father know their immediate plans and what to do about their Palo Alto home (referred to as "810 Wintergreen"), which he had been managing.

I don't know when we will come back but it will be after disposal of the property and the consumption of the food. It costs less to live here than in the USA so since we can't get 810 back for a while there is no hurry, probably 3-4 months. We could live in an apartment until 810 Wintergreen is available again. You asked for me to write so that ought to give you something to talk about. We need absolutely nothing so no CARE packages are necessary. Hope everyone's health is good there and I suppose you will be happy we are coming back. You and Linda who wanted to go back anyway. Love from Chuck

On the same day, Dawn wrote to her mother and sister:

Dear Mom, Our address is now 10 Charlton Avenue, Suva Fiji. You say, that's strange -- it sure is. We moved yesterday after 5 days spent on Makaluva Island living like "American Family Wilcox." Problem was Vela ran onto a reef around said island and she is still there. We were very fortunate all hands saved and no injuries. We planned to be 10 miles off Suva at dawn and we were but must have had a steering error. I came up for my watch and saw a light too close and breakers. I had 1 minute to decide which way to turn and yell for Chuck, then we hit. It was a sickening feeling. I'm afraid I yelled at the boat to no avail.

She told them about the next five grueling days on Makaluva in brief while highlighting how lucky they were and conveying that her plucky sense of humor remained intact.

We picked the greatest place to crash--this island is a very pretty island and we didn't have to swim. We later saw all the other less hospitable reefs we could have picked . . . If it hadn't been for the hard work it would have been a great vacation spot. We had bonfires with our tea & listened to the radio, really a very pleasant uninhabited island.

After she signed off, she added:

P.S. Chuck wrote to his folks. We'll come back to California to earn our next boat -- was a great cruise too short.

So began their post-shipwreck life. They were focused on the immediate future, but from then on, time would always be split between *before* and *after*. Though the details of *how* still eluded them, Chuck and Dawn were intent on voyaging again. So was Garth.

They spent their days going through all they had salvaged from *Vela*, hosing off the saltwater with hundreds of gallons of fresh water and laying it in the sun to dry. The Fijian house looked like a perpetual garage sale. As they cleaned and sorted, they were unable to find sea boots, shoes, and other items they remembered unloading from the wreck.

By the 27th, Dawn and Linda had washed half the clothes and gone through all of the food. Garth and Chuck had washed all the tools in engine oil to save them from rusting. They flushed the outboard engine and washed the larger, more expensive boat equipment. Stretched before them was a seemingly endless task list of urgent needs. Their spirits sagged with the overwhelming amount of work.

Word spread quickly through the community of international sailors that the Wilcoxes had been shipwrecked and were selling used gear. A flood of fellow cruisers, eager to pick up a good deal, descended on the detritus of their voyage like vultures. Overwhelmed by the flood of activity and dazed by their dramatic change in circumstances, the Wilcoxes made many decisions that were not well thought through.

Each day sailors stopped by to haggle over what had once been pricey equipment—equipment that still had tremendous value, or none, depending on one's circumstances. Canned goods, especially cans that had already been protected from rusting with a coat of varnish, were surprisingly popular among sailors. The ham radio and other electronics were of immediate interest, of course, and were the first to sell. Also popular were the Avon inflatable and the little motor, the Honda generator, the SCUBA gear, and the compressor. The boat cushions, too.

So was Garth's hard dinghy. He was sorry to sell it, even to friends from the crew of the boat *Topaz*, a large schooner of young hippies that had sailed with the Wilcoxes from Hawaii to the South Pacific. With his father's guiding hand and encouragement, Garth had done the fiberglass work to build a centerboard trunk and a rudder, built a sailing rig and even sewn a new sail. He'd spent most of his days in Honolulu sailing around the Ala Wai marina and in Tahiti, Moorea, and Bora Bora exploring their shimmering turquoise lagoons. Most recently his dinghy had served heavy duty, helping the family salvage their belongings from *Vela*. Now they had no choice but to take the money and watch it sail away. Most of their fellow sailors were only a few weeks from sailing to New Zealand for cyclone season. The Wilcoxes had planned to do the same, but now everything was different.

Many sailors came with news and advice. Two other boats nearly wrecked on reefs on their way into Fiji and another family battled fish poisoning and life-threatening encephalitis. Dawn took little comfort from hearing they were not alone in their troubles. She knew how lucky her family was, but still ached for her lost life under sail. Some sailors suggested the family buy a new boat in New Zealand, Miami or England. From day to day the family's spirits rose and fell with encouraging rumors and discouraging facts. Their plans changed by the hour.

On September 29th, Dawn wrote to her mother that despite enjoying showers with endless fresh water, she still preferred life onboard a boat. She missed the thrill of the unknown that each landfall offered. She wrote:

Chuck and I are sort of depressed about losing Vela and having to go back to civilization. Garth is upset and says he doesn't see how he can go back to being "normal." He really enjoyed cruising and was great crew. Linda is happy because she always wanted to go back though she seemed adapted. I guess we were just too confident. We are still very thankful we all survived and salvaged so much gear. And we still have 3 years of cruising money left too.

Harsh judgments from other cruisers about what they should have done weighed heavily on Chuck. His overconfidence had cost them dearly.

Next time they would do things differently. If there was a next time.

17

Little by little the family settled into the Suva house and into a new routine. In the midst of hosing and scrubbing off saltwater, laying things to dry in the sun and tossing what couldn't be saved, they decorated the house with Linda's Murex shells and Grandma's poppy watercolor. When the salvageable books were dry, Garth stacked his favorites—*Mutiny on the Bounty*, *The Caine Mutiny*, and *Kon-Tiki*—along with the schoolbooks in the bookshelves that came with the house. They still had plenty of work to do, but Dawn was determined that the children not fall behind in school. So between sorting and disposing of boat equipment to other cruisers, the kids resumed schoolwork.

While the kids studied, Dawn tried to save the large floor mat that Telenoti had given them in thanks for taking the Tongan wedding party to Neiafu to register the marriage. Or maybe for burning a hole in the dinghy. The wet fringe bled crimson on everything it touched, so she carefully cut and unraveled each piece of yarn free before it could cause more damage.

Using the 1953 Royal typewriter they'd carried from California and salvaged from the wreck, Dawn typed an inventory of salvaged and lost items, then scoured the streets of Suva to find someone who could save her Necchi sewing machine from saltwater corrosion. Finally she found someone with the skills and tools to fix it.

After much urging from Nurse Dawn, Chuck visited a doctor about the festering coral infection on his legs. To everyone's delight, he brought home a steak he'd bought for ninety cents. It was the first fresh meat they'd eaten in months—aside from the stewed whale meat in Tonga.

Garth devised a system for salvaging the cassette tapes, setting himself up with a little money-making scheme in the process. For five cents apiece, he offered to crack open each of the cassette tapes so they could clean out the salt—rewinding the tape with a hand drill while wiping it clean with a handkerchief—and then to reassemble them afterward. Tempted though he was, he refrained from "girching" them by swapping the contents. Still, for Linda, he charged a premium of ten cents to clean her universally despised (except by Linda) Donny Osmond tapes. A laborious process at a rate of one per day, but it saved the tapes and Garth had little choice but to work cheaply.

Linda loved living in the house. She took up embroidery, did word puzzles, played jacks, and made friends with two girls, Anna and Ilisapeci, who lived with their grandmother in a hut behind the Wilcoxes' back yard. For everyone else, the predictably-boring routine paled in comparison with explorations under sail.

Chuck tried to find a company to salvage the hull from the reef, but the bids were unreasonable. So *Vela* sat on the reef, filling with sand and water. Periodically Chuck would ride the family's salvaged bicycle out to where he could inspect *Vela* on the reef through binoculars. She looked so vulnerable, high and dry at an awkward angle, her mast like a tombstone marking where she lay. Chuck had hired an agent to figure out how to sell *Vela* in her current state, but so far he hadn't been able to get Customs to assess the value of the hull so they could proceed. There was little he could do. His frustration grew, and he worried that a storm would do her in before he could sell her.

On October 5, eleven days after they reached Suva, Dawn took the kids to explore Fiji for the first time, catching the seven-cent bus downtown. Through the open vinyl flaps of the windowless bus, they gawked at the fascinating mix of elegant Indian ladies in saris and barefooted Fijian men wearing Sulus, a type of skirt that was the basis of many uniforms. Even policemen and prison guards wore what was essentially a skirt and carried only a club, even while supervising work parties of prisoners wielding machetes. Among the saris and Sulus was the occasional Caucasian woman wearing a miniskirt and platform shoes. Suva, one of the largest urban centers in the South Pacific, drew Polynesians and Melanesians from throughout the Pacific. *National Geographic* explained Fiji's multi-ethnic culture and the friction between the land-owning indigenous Fijians and the second- or third-generation Fijian-born Indians, descendants of indentured laborers. The ethnic tension posed challenges to the young democracy, which had gained its independence from Britain only four years earlier.

At Suva's fresh food market, they found the largest selection of foodstuffs they'd seen since they left California fourteen months earlier. The air was thick with the scent of peppers and incense as they passed mounds of crimson and marigold spices. Dawn was thrilled with the variety and low prices: ten-cent pineapples, twenty-cent papayas, and eggs for sixty cents a dozen. In this sugar-producing region, she could buy four pounds for only twenty-four cents. Ten pounds of Sharps brand flour cost only one dollar and twenty-nine cents. Baskets, tapa cloth, hats, shells and more tempted the kids, but they saved their allowance for stamps.

After losing themselves for hours in the market, they headed for the Suva Yacht Club, where they'd told their families to send mail, which would undoubtedly trickle in for weeks. Dawn collected letters from Chuck's parents and from her mother. She sucked in a breath and tore the first envelope open, wondering whether their parents yet knew of their drastic change in circumstances. Ironically, while they were abandoning a wrecked *Vela*, Chuck's father had renewed the lease for their rented Palo Alto home. This development left an opening. Without a home to rush back to, their plans could remain unsettled. It would give them time to think. Dawn quickly dashed off a letter, urging Chuck's father not to undo the lease.

Afterward, they visited friends Geoffrey and Ruth Goodman, an older Australian couple who'd built their thirty-foot boat *Karloo* and had been sailing the South Pacific islands for eight years. The couple couldn't believe that *Vela* was a total loss. Their experience made them confident that she could be rebuilt and they urged the Wilcoxes to reconsider abandoning *Vela*. Geoffrey and Ruth knew of an experienced salvage firm that might have the equipment and expertise to salvage *Vela* from the reef. This was the first positive news Dawn had heard. She still wanted to see the world.

She went home that day hopeful that their voyage could be revived. Garth, too, was encouraged by the discussion. Linda still wanted to go home, but she was outnumbered.

For someone like Chuck who yearned for independence, the waiting and wondering was excruciating. Hoping to spur action, on Friday, October 11, Chuck placed an advertisement in the *Fiji Times*:

BOAT FOR SALE
Forty Foot Yacht on Reef. As is, where is. For details, phone C. Wilcox 25996.

There were three inquiries, but no offers. What if he had no offers at all and then Customs assessed a duty on the shipwrecked hull? Chuck wondered if he could deduct *Vela* from his prior year's taxes as a total loss so they might have the resources to repair and carry on. He dreaded the idea of returning to work in California to earn enough to begin voyaging again, but they didn't have enough money saved to cruise *and* buy another boat.

Chuck was encouraged by what Geoffrey and Ruth Goodman had said. If he could find a company to salvage the hull and tow it to Suva for less than $10,000, he might repair it and continue their voyage. Regardless, he figured that trying to sell the damaged boat in Suva might prove easier than where it lay on the reef, suffering more damage with each passing day. He revisited the salvage agent they mentioned, who had been unavailable when he'd first contacted them.

Chuck's discussions with Marine Pacific Ltd. seemed promising. The Australian manager, Ian Hoskison, seemed knowledgeable and was willing to work on a No Cure/No Pay basis, meaning that if the boat were destroyed in the process or the firm couldn't salvage it, the Wilcoxes would pay nothing. The price was a third of what the other companies had quoted. Most importantly, they seemed more competent. It seemed worth a try. Once the Wilcoxes decided to try to salvage the hull, they made a feeble attempt to buy back the boat equipment they'd sold to other sailors, but unfortunately many of the items they'd sold for a fraction of their value had since been sailed to New Zealand. They'd replace what they could and the rest they would live without as best as possible.

On Monday, October 14th, the *Fiji Times* got wind of the discussions, reporting: NEW SALVAGE BID LIKELY ON YACHT. That report sparked interest from the Associated Press, which was picked up by a number of publications around the globe.

On Tuesday, October 15th, nearly a month after the shipwreck, Chuck signed a contract to pay $4,800 if the firm were successful in bringing *Vela* off the reef and into Suva intact. Unfortunately the firm would be unable to begin salvage work for another week or more, and significant preparatory work needed to be done before they could move the hull. Each day the hull sat on the reef, buffeted by wind and waves, the less likely they'd be able to salvage her.

On October 16th, the Associated Press account of their shipwreck hit the *San Francisco Examiner* under the headline ROUND-WORLD YACHT STALLED ON FIJI REEF. The *Palo Alto Times* reported the same story as PALO ALTO FAMILY'S DREAM RUNS AGROUND ON FIJI REEF. Former colleagues, classmates, neighbors and yacht club members read about their devastating loss. Their families clipped the articles, stuffed them in an envelope and mailed them to the Wilcoxes in Fiji. These error-ridden, tragic stories were not how the family had hoped to be remembered. Reading accounts of their demise rubbed salt into the wound.

In addition, when Chuck and the salvage team returned to *Vela*, he discovered thieves had broken in. He'd left the companionway pad-locked. Since then, someone had smashed the large window-like port lights, broken the companionway doors, and made off with water pumps, faucets, shower, bilge pumps, even the kitchen sink. And they stole the holding tank for the toilet. Too bad it hadn't been full ...

On October 28th, the *Fiji Times* reported the break-in under the head-line THIEVES STRIP STRANDED YACHT. Chuck naively hoped the report would spark the return of the stolen items. No one came forward.

Rebuilding without these essential items would be that much harder. Plus, in the six weeks *Vela* had been out on the reef, storm surge had driven her three hundred feet from deep water. Demoralized once again, Chuck wondered whether they could salvage their dream.

18

Time dragged by as they waited for the salvage crew to begin work. In the interim, Dawn took Garth and Linda to see the movie *Dove*, about Robin Lee Graham, a teenaged boy who'd single-handedly sailed around the world. The entire family had read his book and knew the story of this voyage, which closely resembled their own—at least until they'd hit the reef. In a dark theater, surrounded by Fijians gasping, giggling and pointing whenever they saw a familiar face or location in the Fijian Islands where much of the movie was filmed, the three relived their previous life afloat.

The movie reminded Garth what he loved about voyaging: the challenges of getting the boat moving in light air and navigating through unknown waters, the thrill of exploring new geography and cultures, the mesmerizing pattern of clouds scudding overhead, and seeing flying fish zipping in and out of mountainous watery peaks. More than anyone, he could relate to this young man only a few years older than he was. He came away from the movie more excited than ever to rebuild *Vela* and resume cruising.

Preparing for the family's voyage had consumed most of his young life. He could hardly remember a time before his family began actively turning a voyaging dream into reality, either by saving money, taking classes, shopping for a boat, or readying the house to rent and the boat for sea.

Once they'd set off, the trip had absorbed Garth like nothing else he could remember. He had a clear goal that required learning practical skills, unlike school, which often seemed irrelevant to the real world. Hours in the cockpit studying *The Ashley Book of Knots* could help him produce a lanyard to carry a bottle, a Turk's head to mark the wheel's centerline, a set of lazy jacks, bow-netting, or ratlines for climbing the mast to watch for coral heads. Knowledge he could put to immediate use. Being independent and self-sufficient appealed to him in the way it appealed to his father.

Garth knew that if his parents returned to California to work and save for another boat, he might lose his chance to cruise. He had no interest in returning to the boring predictability of school, where overwhelmed teachers seemed to spend less time teaching than on crowd control. Lessons were unchallenging and pedantic: dates without context, formulas without practical application. Even his homeschooling often seemed like busywork.

He would work hard when it interested him, but he had little interest in doing things because someone else deemed them important. His folks were always cajoling him to finish his assignments so they could mail them in and order the next set. It was so rigid. Lately they'd begun withholding Math to get him to complete English, but that approach could backfire. Meanwhile Linda eagerly pushed ahead, intent on catching up with Garth, three grades ahead. He didn't much care.

When his father signed the contract to salvage *Vela*, Garth expected to help with the effort to pull the boat off the reef, continuing to function as the full crew member he'd become. He could learn so much—this was no model boat. But as he began pulling on his reef shoes to join his dad that first morning, his mother looked at him. "What do you think you're doing?"

"Getting ready to prep *Vela* for salvage."

"You can't go. You need to finish your schoolwork," his mom said, pointing a finger toward the dining-room table where his books sat in a sloppy stack.

"I can do schoolwork anytime! But salvaging the boat?" How could he concentrate on English, World Geography, and Algebra at a time like this? "I can help get the boat off the reef sooner, with less damage." His parents would need all the help they could get. Besides, he'd learned more geography sailing this last year than he had his whole life, and he'd read far more books, too. He was experiencing the school of *life*, which was far more informative and engaging.

For the next fifteen minutes, Garth threw out every argument he could conceive. But his mother crossed her arms and peered at him through her cat's-eye glasses, unconvinced. Linda smirked behind her. His mother's stern look was bad enough, but Linda's taunting was worse. When Chuck entered the room wearing his sun hat and carrying his reef shoes, Garth gave him a pleading look. His father said, "You need to finish your schoolwork." A final pronouncement.

Garth had lost this round. He stalked into his room, grabbed his dog-eared copy of *The Caine Mutiny*, and flumped down on the bed. He opened to some random page and dove into the action. His stubborn streak kept him from his schoolbooks all morning. This wasn't his first standoff with his parents over schoolwork, and it certainly wouldn't be the last. But his procrastination wouldn't change anything. He would still miss getting *Vela* ready to tow into Suva. He seethed with anger and frustration for a time, then quietly retrieved his books from the other room when he heard Linda and Dawn go into the kitchen to make lunch.

On the last day of preparations—after Garth completed an acceptable amount of schoolwork—his parents would let him join the salvage effort.

Chuck and the salvage crew had days of work ahead of them before they could tow *Vela* into Suva. They headed out to the reef on little boats as early as four a.m. to catch the low tide when it was easiest to work. If they just attached a tow line to her in her current state, they'd yank her into deeper water where she would sink. First they needed to patch the eight-foot hole well enough to pull her off the reef and into town. The problem was that she lay on the reef on top of that very hole. She had been scraping against ragged edges of coral, scooping sand and water into her interior, the hole and damage growing with each escalation of wind and waves.

For once Chuck was grateful for how heavily *Vela* had been built. Though she had been difficult to sail in light winds, few boats could have withstood being pounded on jagged coral for six weeks. Few boats could be salvaged after hitting a reef. He was hoping *Vela* would prove the exception.

The crew decided to lay her over onto her intact side on a bed of tires while they created a temporary patch. Gingerly stepping over the sharp, uneven coral, after pumping out the fuel and water that remained in *Vela*'s tanks, the crew spent a day attaching boards and tires to the good side of the hull to protect it. Then they spent another full day pumping out the water and jacking *Vela* over onto her good side before they could even begin patching the hole. They spent another couple of days building new frames with quarter-inch strips of plywood and fiberglass.

Presumably they'd covered the hole well enough to attempt the tow into Suva. High-speed pumps would remove water from the hull and hopefully keep it from refilling—at least for the duration of the salvage attempt. But once the patch was complete, they had a new problem: The patched hull was now buoyant. At high tide the boat would attempt to float and bounce along the jagged coral with every sweep of the waves across its surface. So the crew pumped water back *into* the hull to keep it anchored onto the reef until they were ready to move it.

The crew spent a final day securing a bridle around the hull through her propeller aperture and the Sampson post on the bow for towing. Then they planned and marked the best route off the reef.

After a laborious week of preparations, there was no more they could do but see if it would work. Though Chuck had agreed to pay the firm only if they could successfully get her off the reef and into town, the Wilcoxes still ran the risk that *Vela* would incur more damage in the process. It seemed worth the risk, but Chuck and Dawn still worried they'd be out all that money and be unable to repair her. They spent a sleepless night, tormented by competing thoughts of the innumerable tasks required to rebuild *Vela* and a nagging fear that she couldn't be saved.

On October 29th, a tug was finally scheduled to pull *Vela* off the reef. The *Wallacia* had just returned from the neighboring island country of New Hebrides, but Customs clearance took so long that they missed the high tide. Everyone waited hours in the pouring rain, but in vain.

Deflated, they returned home for another night of worry.

19

The next morning, Wednesday, October 30, 1974, brought oppressively low clouds and heavy rain. Still Chuck, Dawn and Garth boarded *Wallacia*, hopeful they would finally be able to tow *Vela* ashore for repair. Though the world's attention focused on Kinshasa, Zaire, where Mohammed Ali floated like a butterfly and stung his way to victory over George Foreman in the "Rumble in the Jungle," the Wilcoxes were oblivious. Today's outcome might decide their fate.

After six weeks in a house on shore, their primitive life on the island seemed as though they'd imagined it. Yet when they neared the island, its familiar features confirmed their memories. So did the sight of *Vela* in her forlorn state. Dawn's first glimpse at her former home brought back a flush of emotion. It also reminded her of the magnitude of the task to rebuild her.

Half the crew had been on the reef for hours already, pumping *out* the water they'd pumped *into Vela*, trying to ensure the boat would be buoyant by the time the tide was high enough to float her off. On the day before a full moon, the tidal range was greater than usual, which gave them more maneuvering room, but still only a narrow window during which they could pull the boat off.

The weather looked ominous. In a flash rain squall, heavy drops pounded the water white. *Vela* was barely visible from the tug. Conditions were starting to look doubtful. All eyes were on Australian crew boss Ian Hoskison, in a knit jersey and Speedo, hair plastered to his head, water dripping from his nose and thin beard. His decision would dictate whether they would proceed or not. If conditions weren't right, it would be better to wait another day, though another delay would be agony for the family.

Ian inspected the hull patch. He double-checked the bridle they'd stretched around the hull. Then he surveyed the scene carefully, taking in the position of *Vela*, the position of the tug and the wind and wave directions. Everyone observed his every move, hoping the rain would abate, but rain continued to fall heavily. After a few minutes, Ian stepped aboard the tug to discuss salvage strategy with tug captain Rigamoto Nakaora.

Everyone waited anxiously while the men discussed the situation. Chuck, Garth and the crew stood on the jagged reef, waves lapping at their legs. Chuck's soaked hat drooped into his eyes and pointed tips of coral dug into his reef shoes. Next to him, Garth held his hand over his eyes to shield them from the heavy drops, trying to see what was going on aboard the tug. Garth's orange Primo Beer shirt was easy to pick out from the tug and Dawn couldn't help but chuckle. It was the first shirt he'd bought himself in Suva. He had no clue about sizing, so he bought a size 50 and it hung on him like a dress.

After a few minutes the rain tapered off and the sky began to brighten. A moment later might have been too late.

When Ian and the tug captain finished their discussion, Ian gave a nod. It was a go!

His signal sparked a flurry of activity. The crew stretched the tow line between the wreck and the tug, checked the attachment points, and added chafing gear. Then Chuck, Garth, Ian and the men climbed aboard the now-buoyant *Vela* and checked the pumps, which might be all that would keep her afloat during the transit into the city. With hoses protruding from the large cabin port lights and another through the companionway hatch, *Vela* looked like an octopus. Chuck, Garth and the crew climbed off, and all but Ian stepped into one of the chase boats.

Ian directed the operation from the reef using a radio ensconced in thick plastic. Waves slammed against his legs as he communicated with the crew aboard the tug and the chase boat standing by. His Australian accent boomed through the speakers aboard the tugboat, giving Dawn an inside perspective on what was happening on *Vela*. The rumble of the tug's engines and static completed the soundtrack to action that didn't seem real from this distance. She heard the tug captain revving the engine and felt her chest tighten with anticipation. *This is it*, she thought.

At first it seemed like nothing happened and a wave of panic washed over her. Worried that the crew had abandoned the effort, she looked frantically around her. A man from the *Fiji Times* stood nearby, snapping pictures. Fellow cruisers, a father and his son from the boat *Orca*, were taking movie footage. No one else appeared concerned. Of course, it wasn't their futures that hung in the balance. Or their boat that might be destroyed in an effort to save her.

The tow line drooped, then yanked taut again. *Vela* started skipping on the reef. While the hull was technically floating, the seven-foot keel dragged over coral as she rocked in the waves. The mast shook violently. Chuck cringed. Seeing the attempt to save the hull inflict more damage was troubling to watch. He wanted to look away, but couldn't. He had little choice but to trust the expertise of Ian Hoskison and his crew. The tide was still rising, but it wouldn't for much longer. *Vela* needed to be off the reef and on her way into Suva soon. Chuck just hoped the keel wouldn't be ripped away in the process.

The *Wallacia* dragged *Vela* sideways, parallel to the breakers, following the channel markers that the crew had carefully laid through the coral heads. A turtle net someone set near their marked route added another obstacle to an already challenging task. The tug nudged around the net while Dawn watched nervously. She focused her eyes on the tow line, which alternately drooped into the water when it slackened and rose as it drew tight, sending out a spray of water droplets. The sun broke through the clouds. As the tug pulled *Vela* away from the reef where she had thrashed for nearly six weeks and the distance between them grew, Chuck, Garth, Ian and the crew became nearly indistinguishable from the waves around them. Dawn snapped a few photos, but doubted whether they would show anything, so she stopped to watch.

After more than a half hour dragging *Vela* along the reef, the procession finally reached deep water at the reef edge. Everyone watched to see what would happen once the reef dropped from beneath her. When that moment came, all froze with eyes focused on the bouncing *Vela*—as though breathing might affect the delicate operation.

Suddenly *Vela* popped upright and looked like a sailboat once again. A cheer rose from the crew. A smile swept across Dawn's face, and she relaxed her white-knuckled grip on the life rail. *They'd done it!* They'd gotten *Vela* off the reef. Dawn's watch said 4:23, just over an hour before the high tide. Now if they could just get her all the way into Suva without her sinking. She wouldn't be able to relax until *Vela* was tied alongside the wharf in Suva. Then again, they couldn't relax then either with a complete rebuild facing them. Just then a rainbow appeared over *Vela*, which Dawn interpreted as a good sign.

The rumble of the tug engines changed tone, dropping a decibel or two. The procession paused briefly while the chase boat ferried Ian, Chuck, Garth and several crew to *Vela* to start the pumps and monitor her progress underway. Smiles all around, followed by a few back slaps.

Within minutes, they were underway again, making painstakingly slow progress. Still the tug was towing *Vela* faster than she'd ever moved before. Chuck and Garth worried about the strain on the towing line, the hull, and the patch.

"Slow down!" Chuck and Garth both shouted. Their words disappeared into the wind. They shouted again, louder. Garth pressed his palms downward in the universal symbol for "slow." Ian was still looking forward, watching the tug, and the other crew looked at them blankly.

Chuck and Garth rushed below to check on the patch. As they suspected, the front end of the patch was separating from the hull. Water was gushing in. Chuck rushed back on deck, shouting even louder, "The patch is coming off!" That finally elicited a reaction.

Ian grabbed the radio and commanded the tug to slow down. Two of the crew went below to restart *Vela*'s gas-powered pumps, which required priming with buckets of water. After a few tense moments, the pumps rumbled to life and began to pump water from inside.

At a lumbering pace, tug and tow moved toward a channel through the reef into Suva, with everyone wondering whether the patch would hold.

20

The tug pulled *Vela* around markers that identified hidden reefs, past Suva Point and the *China Club* next to their rented house in Nasese. By the time they reached the Government Slipway, sunset was fast approaching. *Vela's* mast cast a long shadow along the concrete pier in the fading light. The patch had held.

The Government Slipway was an industrial marine railway for small ships, fishing vessels of one hundred to one hundred and fifty feet, and large inter-island traders. It wasn't designed for yachts. To lift *Vela* out of the water they'd have to hire a crane. As the sun sank lower in the sky and the horizon turned to pinks, oranges and reds, Marine Pacific agreed to station one of the crew aboard the boat through the night to ensure the pumps kept *Vela* afloat until they could pull her out of the water.

The next day, Thursday, Chuck agreed that getting *Vela* out of the water trumped schoolwork this time and he allowed Garth to help. The patch was leaking and the hull was bashing against the cement pier. So Chuck, Dawn and Garth left the house early for the slipway two miles away, Chuck by bicycle and Dawn and Garth on the seven-cent bus.

As Chuck arranged for a crane to pull *Vela* from the water, he was dismayed to discover that the largest crane in the country was rated for only twenty tons. *Vela* weighed twenty tons. An *estimated* twenty tons. Even if he'd been in a first-world country, Chuck would have been reluctant to test the stress tolerances on the crane. And in Fiji? Well ... When had the crane last been tested? How new was the cable? The slings didn't look so good ...

If Chuck wanted to get his boat out of the water, he had to lighten it. With the hull empty, the only thing left to remove was the ballast that had been built into the boat with no intention of ever being removed. With a groan, he realized what that meant: pulling out the pig iron—now oxidized into a reddish-brown mess—from the bilge. A grueling task he knew would have to be reversed once the rebuilding was complete.

And so the three of them set to work under a blazing Fijian sun.

November 1st went into the history books as a record heat-wave day for Fiji, with temperatures nearly nine degrees above normal. At an air temperature of 91 degrees with 68 percent humidity, it felt easily twenty or thirty degrees hotter on the shadeless concrete pier and in the stagnant air below decks.

With a hammer and a crowbar, Chuck wrestled heavy slabs of pig iron away from the bottom of the bilge, leaving dusty red fingerprints on everything he touched. Sweat dribbled into his eyes and down his spine as he pried the pieces out. He'd hand gnarly chunk after gnarly chunk to Garth, who ferried three-foot-long deformed pig ingots up the steps, then handed them to Dawn across the three-foot gap between the boat and the safest place where she could stand on the rounded edge of the concrete pier without falling in.

Dripping with perspiration, they felt their shirts sticking to their backs and sweat stinging their eyes. Hour after hour passed and still there was more. Hunger gnawed at their stomachs, but they couldn't stop. The sun reached its zenith and the heat grew more intense. They worked beyond what they thought they could endure. Piece by piece, slowly the stack grew bigger on the pier, until finally Chuck pulled out the last of the pig iron in the bilge. All they had to show for hours of manual labor in stifling heat was a four-foot pile of rusty metal on the concrete.

With much of the day gone, Chuck worried that *Vela* would spend another night bashing alongside the pier, pumps running, before they could get her out of the water. But he was relieved to learn the crane could come.

While the crane sat at idle, charging them all the while, more hours passed as Chuck and Garth wrapped the wires, shackles, and spreader bars in old copra sacks made of burlap to protect them and readied the rig to haul *Vela* out of the water.

When the crane lifted *Vela*, Dawn held her breath. She stood transfixed on the blisteringly hot pavement, peering at *Vela* with shielded eyes as the hull rose and loomed overhead. The cloth of her shirt was dark with streaks of sweat, her hair damp and matted on her forehead.

"I hope they don't drop her," she said, voicing everyone's fears. Garth gave a nervous shudder and Chuck pressed his lips together.

After a brief pause, Garth, Chuck and several yard workers scurried to position empty oil barrels and miscellaneous blocks to prop *Vela* upright. Water streamed from the hull, dark splotches dotted the concrete below. Slowly, with a gentle tug on the lines attached to her bow and stern, they eased her down to the "cradle" they'd created. It resembled a Rube Goldberg contraption, but for the moment it served its purpose. Once *Vela* was secured, the tension in their shoulders eased.

Chuck learned they could keep the boat on the Government Slipway for free for as long as they needed. Their first big break. He could stop worrying that a fee for the yard on top of the house rent would add to the drain on their dwindling voyage budget.

It had gone as well as could be expected and everyone was relieved. As soon as the work crew vanished, Chuck, Dawn and Garth collapsed onto the concrete pier, their fingers, faces and clothes tinged with reddish-brown ferrous-oxide dust. They were numb with exhaustion.

Now the real work could begin.

Staring at the hulk that had been their home, the magnitude of the task before them began to sink in.

Shipwreck Damage

21

In Suva's sultry heat, Chuck, Dawn and Garth spent that first week-end pulling off the temporary patch and scraping coral and barnacles from inside the boat. Climbing in and out through the massive hole, the three cleared anything that would hinder rebuilding. While Dawn wiped away mold and swept coral, Chuck and Garth removed the remaining settee furniture and water tanks, and prepared the engine to haul. It was sweaty business.

Once *Vela*'s hole was exposed down to her barnacled ribs, Chuck could solicit estimates on the hull repair. While he had worked as a carpenter in college, he knew that repairing the hull was beyond his abilities. With much of the interior destroyed in the middle of the boat, Chuck and Garth redesigned the galley, living and dining area, incorporating a few details they'd gleaned from sister ship *Chanson*.

Garth had done extra schoolwork so he could help with the salvage efforts. But come Monday, his parents insisted he return to his studies.

Annoyed, Garth procrastinated. Instead of writing a report about Picasso, Cezanne and Rembrandt for art class, Garth completed his model of a Lightning sailboat and reread Michener's *Hawaii*. In one of her frequent letters home, Dawn griped:

> Garth's schoolwork started coming back from the University of California, except for the first lessons, which were all sent by UC to Papeete, despite the addresses on them. He got A's and B's on everything, but he's working so slowly, I think he'll be 82 by the time he graduates.

Dawn initially thought she might work as a nurse to help defray the costs of boat repair. She discovered that unless she were a permanent resident, she couldn't get a work permit. Dawn was briefly disappointed, but she soon realized her time was better spent working on the boat if the family was to leave Fiji before the end of the next sailing season.

Chuck contacted four firms, but only two came to inspect the hull and bid for the job. He hired first one firm, then another after discovering the first company couldn't begin work for a month. This was the beginning of endless months of anguish, trying to rebuild a boat in a sleepy backwater.

With the Diwali festival of lights for Hindus and Prince Charles's birthday, little professional work got done those first few weeks. But even after the holidays passed, frequent delays would chafe at Chuck. Every setback felt like a threat to their dream. He would joke that there were "too many chiefs and not enough Indians," which carried a double meaning in Fiji, where the hardest working crew were usually Fijians of Indian heritage rather than indigenous Fijian villagers led by their chiefs.

By mid-December the carpenters had replaced the frames, planked over the hull and rebuilt the bulkheads. To Chuck's relief, local Vesi and Dakua hardwoods were ideal building materials. Though Carpenter Fiji Ltd.'s original estimate to patch the hull for $1,800 had morphed into a $2,800 bill, Chuck was pleased with their work. He even hired one of the carpenters to rebuild the rudder and arrange the engine overhaul. Yet progress was still distressingly slow.

When Garth finally finished his coursework for the term, his parents let him help. Materials for his new classes were delayed—they'd accidentally been sent to Nasese, *Nigeria*. He was young, strong and eager to get them voyaging once again. And they realized how much they needed his help.

Soon the three of them were working long, hot days, often seven days a week. While the rest of the family labored in the steamy boat yard, eleven-year-old Linda looked after the house. Dawn performed double duty, taking off Thursdays to run to the market and bake bread. She returned home slightly early each day to cook, review Linda's schoolwork and mend their work clothes. Days and weeks passed in uninterrupted toil.

One of Dawn's experiments with local vegetables nearly ended in tragedy. Seeing taro leaves at the market, she decided to give them a try, thinking they resembled chard or spinach. When she served up the steamed leaves, after a few bites, everyone reached for their throats and started coughing. A quick check of her nursing manual revealed they had a strong reaction to oxalic acid from insufficient cooking. Once they recovered, the family gave her no end of grief about nearly poisoning them.

As spring turned to summer in the southern hemisphere, hibiscus and plumeria bloomed and temperatures climbed even higher. Gray clouds hovered over Suva, dumping heavy rain. The Wilcoxes couldn't decide which was worse, the torrential rain and thunderstorms or scorching hot sunshine and energy-sapping humidity.

Christmas 1974 nearly skipped by without notice. A few holiday cards and a package from their families trickled in, along with a letter from Telenoti in response to the photos they'd mailed as promised, despite their ill-fated arrival. Clearly he'd hired a scribe to write on his behalf. In all caps the letter said:

TALIHAU, VAVA'U, 8.12.1974, DEAR WILCOX, I FIRST THANK
YOU FOR THE GOD BECAUSE HE KEEP OUR LIFE FROM
ALL DANGROUS AND THE SECOND I AM THANKING FOR
YOUR REMEMBER ME AND ANNA AND MY POOR ISLAND
MALA. HERE I GOT YOUR LETTER AND I AM THANKYOU
FOR THE PICTURE AND WE ARE VERYVERY GLAD. WE
WISH TO HELP YOU WHEN THE TIME DID YOU LIVE IN
THE REEF FOR 5 DAYS AND WE TRUST THE GOD SAVE
YOU FROM DEAD AND WE ASK FOR HIM TO HELP YOU
EVERY TIME AND RETURN BACK YOU TO YOUR COUNTRY.
NOW WE ARE READY FOR THE CHRISTMAS AND WE
WISH TO HAVE A GOOD CHRISTMAS IN MY ISLAND. MAY
GOD BLESS YOU ALL. LOVE FROM TELENOTI AND ANNA
[sic]

Linda decorated the house with a few snowflakes and garlands she crafted from colored construction paper, but little else marked the holiday besides a series of loud parties at the China Club. Yet another soiree rang in the New Year as 1974 turned into 1975, with a decent band for once—except for the tone-deaf trumpeter. Awoken so many nights by crowds demanding one more song at two a.m. and the clanging of pots and pans until three a.m. kept the Wilcoxes in a perpetual state of exhaustion. The days blended together as the work stretched on and on.

Linda relished her new routine in Fiji, when she had the house to herself and could shape her days as she pleased. She worked ahead on schoolwork, followed the *National Quiz* on the English radio station, and closely monitored the bus schedule, getting to recognize the buses and drivers that rumbled past the house. She met the mailman each day and arranged for lawn mowing. For spending money (ten cents per load) Linda did the family's laundry—no small task by hand, using an eighteen-inch-long blue bar of lye soap and trying to dry the wet clothes in the humid weather between rain squalls.

With the arrival of summer came cyclone season, starting with one named Val. As Val approached in late January, warnings were broadcast every thirty minutes in three languages, cricket matches were canceled, and villagers in outer islands sheltered in caves. The Wilcoxes scurried to protect their boat, worried that after months of hard work, they'd lose *Vela* in a hurricane in the boat yard. Chuck, Garth and Dawn worked to add four extra supports under the hull. With line borrowed from a neighbor in the slipway, Garth secured *Vela* to the bollards on the pier while Dawn collected all the loose wood and tied down the lumber pile.

To reduce windage, Chuck hired a crane to haul out the mast, which had a large vertical crack and needed to be repaired anyway. In pouring rain, the crane attempted to pull the mast but they discovered the crane was too short. So Chuck hopped on the rusty bicycle, eager to find another crane before the hurricane hit. At four thirty, less than two hours before sunset, they finally got the mast out as the sky darkened and the wind started to howl.

Rain fell heavily all night Friday and Saturday and the winds shrieked. At the China Club, the usual Friday night bingo carried on as usual, except their huge woks had lids on them so the bean sprouts wouldn't blow away. From January 30 through February 2, Val hovered over Fiji, whipping up one hundred and thirty-knot winds in some areas and leaving many people homeless, mostly those living in the thatch-roof villages in the eastern and southern parts of the country.

Once heavy rains and winds abated and the barometer began to rise, the Wilcoxes were relieved that *Vela* had been spared from the worst of it.

Despite horrendous weather, Fiji wasn't the worst place to be shipwrecked. On the plus side, it offered inexpensive skilled laborers, local industries and decent shipping options. Yet repairing a boat in a third-world country did pose its challenges: frequent delays that came with "island time" and the difficulty of acquiring the parts they needed. When they could find parts locally, materials were often inferior. With the help of Chuck's father and Joe Gurr, a Sequioa Yacht Club member in the San Francisco Bay Area, the family secured marine parts that were unavailable in Fiji by mail, often losing weeks to postal delays and holidays. Chuck wrote directly to Thomas Foukes of Leytonshire, England for chain and alternator parts and a new Avon dinghy, and balked at the steep prices. He and Dawn cursed their shortsighted sale of specialty marine items to voyagers who'd left the country. Replacing those parts at new prices—if they could find them at all—hit their budget hard. They'd replace what they could and the rest they would have to live without as best as possible.

With the shipwreck, their fortunes had changed dramatically; their financial cushion was now a distant memory. To find ways to pay for their huge setback, Chuck reviewed IRS literature his father had sent to see if he could declare *Vela* a total loss and subtract it from his previous tax bills. Noting that a casualty loss could be carried back three years, he decided to give it a try. That decision, though it offered some financial assistance, would create new headaches that would haunt them for years.

22

In March, Garth and Chuck developed dengue fever, a mosquito-borne virus that had raged into an epidemic in Fiji. The weedy trenches surrounding their house offered ideal breeding ground for the mosquitoes that caused it. With Chuck and Garth waylaid by a deep ache that earns the illness its nickname "break-bone fever," progress on *Vela* ground to a halt. Garth and Chuck spent innumerable hours suffering to the sounds of vegetable chopping, the sizzle and clatter of stir-fry utensils against metal woks, and the annoying calls of "G-58" from over the fence at the China Club from eight p.m. until the wee hours. When the China Club wasn't blaring music, the cooing of doves and the incessant cackling of Kookaburra birds taunted them instead. Days on the calendar clicked by. Sailing season would come to an end whether they were ready or not.

Dawn scoured Suva to find glass to replace the windows that thieves had broken while *Vela* was on the reef. With the help of the military band, she found someone who offered to fix her clarinet, but rescued it when she saw him whack it with a hammer and a chisel. After much searching, Dawn found a new propane-powered camping-style cooler/fridge to replace the unit that had only worked on port tack.

Once Garth recovered, he and Dawn set off one morning for Vatuwaqa on the bus to buy foam and fabric to replace the cushions they'd sold to other sailors before deciding to salvage *Vela*. Dawn was armed with full-sized patterns of the bunks and cockpit seats, after noticing that the Indian shopkeepers didn't know what to make of her drawings and dimensions. The foam factory offered an overwhelming array of foam choices. Ever budget-conscious, Dawn chose the cheapest option. What she didn't realize was the difference between closed-cell and open-cell foam when it comes to the moist environment on a boat. She bought a layer of plastic to create a barrier between the fabric and the foam, thinking that would be enough to keep the cushions from soaking up moisture. That choice would be one Garth and the rest of the family would curse for years—once air and water got in, it couldn't get out, rendering it into a squishy balloon until the plastic ripped and then scrunched into lumps that felt like solidified plastic and were painful to sit upon.

Without a delivery service, Garth and Dawn were faced with the challenge of ferrying the foam home on a crowded bus at rush hour. Walking to the bus, Garth carried the bulk of the long pieces of foam on top of his head, bobbing and weaving through the packed streets. Fortunately Garth was tall enough to clear the heads of most pedestrians. What didn't work as well was crossing the street or changing direction, which involved looking sideways. One false move and he could destroy signage for an entire storefront or a display rack of wares. Dawn scurried ahead, trying to direct him to the safest route and warn unsuspecting pedestrians out of his way as best she could. She rolled the remaining foam into a tight bundle, but every time she relaxed her grip on the springy material, it would quadruple in size and leap out of her arms. Garth would stop until she tamed it once again.

The bulky foam wouldn't fit into the racks below the open buses, so Dawn and Garth slid them through the open windows, over the heads of schoolchildren in their prim uniforms and women in saris, taking care not to bonk the afros of Fijian women or rain ceiling dust down on the babies, pigs or chickens the women carried on their laps.

Amid the pandemonium at the bus station, where they needed to change buses, Dawn climbed off the bus, stepping carefully to the pavement with her unruly bundle. Expanding foam knocked her glasses from her face, sending them flying into the road and popping out a lens. She scrambled to retrieve them before they got run over, launching the foam like a projectile onto the same roadway. Trying not to laugh, Garth patiently waited for her to regroup, with half the foam in his arms, the other still sticking out the bus windows. The bus driver helped by beeping the horn, sending Dawn into an even more flustered state.

At their stop in Nasese, the bus came to a wheezing halt. They didn't even need to ring the bell anymore, since the driver recognized their usual stop. Once they arrived home, Dawn spent days huddled behind her rusty Necchi sewing machine, assembling the foam, mattress ticking, and plastic into five bunk-bottom cushions. Then it was on to seat backs and cockpit cushions.

As the calendar flipped from March to April, Easter and Mohammedan's Birthday (and the associated holidays) caused delays in the mail and days when businesses closed and little got done. Anything sent surface mail after January risked arriving too late for them to sail away that season. Chuck worried that parts he'd ordered, including the Avon dinghy, wouldn't arrive in time. Neither would the kids' new coursework. School administrators wouldn't send new coursework until they'd received the final tests proctored by a local "official," a policy that made homeschooling-while-traveling more difficult given the change of address and mail delays.

More days were lost to what Chuck described as "shenanigans working around an over-abundance of Customs agents and bureaucracy." And an inability to obtain the epoxy they needed to repair the water tanks after the Burns Philp department store burned while a security guard slept. Every delay weighed heavily on the Wilcoxes, and they wondered if they'd ever sail away from Fiji.

Dawn kept their California family apprised of their progress—or lack of it. In early April, she wrote:

> As for leaving in April, we won't be ready since Chuck hasn't been able to build any bunks yet. We will just keep on working and hope to at least move on the boat by May. We have to launch it before moving or the crane can't lift it. But we can't launch until the parts come from England and the engine and the anchor are ready and the Avon dinghy comes. (I'm not good at walking on water.)

As April turned into May, pressure mounted. Their visas were running out and they were desperate to move aboard before they had to pay yet another month's house rent. But the boat was still uninhabitable. Chuck, Garth and Dawn worked feverishly, through thunderous rain squalls so loud they had to shout to hear one another. Frustrated by their slow progress, they spent nearly every waking moment in the yard, until darkness and exhaustion rendered work impossible.

23

Keeping a work party productive under immense time pressure, while working nonstop himself, took a heavy toll on Chuck. Each time he reached a milestone with some monumental task in the rearview mirror, a new task loomed for which he had to figure out what needed to be done and how best to go about it, given the constraints he faced. Working seven days a week nonstop for months in blistering conditions or heavy rain pushed him to a breaking point. After his bout with dengue fever slowed their progress even more, Chuck felt physically and emotionally drained.

When part of the hydraulic system broke, Chuck had to request and wait for a replacement by post from England before he could install the repaired engine. That held up rebuilding the engine enclosure. Then, the family spent countless hours repairing the water tanks. After epoxying and screwing in more than fifty screws, they tested the tank and discovered that it gushed water. Evidently the epoxy hadn't set properly. So with a chisel and a crowbar, Dawn and Garth pried it apart once again, only to spend more money on expensive epoxy and plywood to begin all over again. Heavy rain kept them from working on it for a week, which meant they couldn't install the water tank and subsequently the bunk that sat above it. Every project, it seemed, involved two steps back for every step forward.

Chuck did his best to endure the inevitable lack of materials, the holidays and Customs delays that frustrated every attempt at progress. When he saw Fijian workers sit down to a bowl of kava after a lunch of Roti's and curry, the knowledge of the work remaining gnawed at him, robbing him of patience. He had no "Man Friday" to share his burden.

On May 7th, on the back of paper Garth had used to sketch various rigging scenarios, a weary Chuck wrote to his parents:

Dear Mom and Dad, We are working feverishly to be able to move out of this house before we have to pay another rent. I hope we make it. It gets very frustrating trying to do things in this country because of widespread incompetence and stupidity and lack of materials. It got so bad last week that I would have blown up the boat. I felt that I needed a day off so I took one and the next day I was ready to continue. It is amazing how your system reacts against 7 day week stuff no matter what you're doing. Sometimes I wish I'd taken up some other hobby.

With little choice, Chuck toiled on. Between supervising the man working on the mast and installing the stove and the head, Chuck built the galley counter, the dinette, then the settee bunks, and Dawn followed along behind him, sanding and slapping on a coat of paint as soon as construction was complete. With painful blisters on his hands from swinging the hammer and twisting screws, he still had more to build. It was a staggering regimen.

Sometimes it was hard to remember why they were doing this. Their charming visits to French Polynesia, Suwarrow and Tonga seemed like something that had happened to other people. Chuck longed for nothing more than to lie prone beneath a slow-moving ceiling fan.

With time running out, they had no choice but to leave with some things undone or miss another season. A delay would burn through the rest of their voyaging budget. The Wilcoxes secured a visa extension, hoping they wouldn't need all the time left. But as work dragged on, their hopes to reach Darwin in time to cross the Indian Ocean that season were crushed. They revised their plans, aiming to pass cyclone season in Brisbane, Australia, if they could get that far.

Finally, on May 20th, they launched the boat. Chuck described the process to his parents in a letter.

> Yesterday Vela took to the water exactly eight months to the day that it crashed on the reef. It was sure a struggle getting all the preparations done for the hoisting. Except for actually lifting by the crane I did the job myself inasmuch as I acted as my own contractor.

What should have been a joyous occasion for Chuck was more one of relief. His exhaustion bled onto the page.

> I got down there right at 8 o'clock since a guy with the rigging wire and spreader bars said he would bring them over then. I didn't really believe he would so only waited a half hour for him until I went and found him. He wouldn't admit it but it was obvious he had forgotten it. Then all the wires, shackles, spreader bars were delivered and Garth and I got to wrapping them with used copra sacks (burlap 5 cents each) so they wouldn't scratch the paint. Next the crane showed up early and got set up so that at high water the boat could be lifted in.

Things were pretty hectic when the lifting-gear setup didn't work. The crane was too close to the boat and hit a pair of the spreaders so they had to undo everything and change the setup. On the next try they found the slings were too long and the crane couldn't go any higher. Chuck was exasperated by this time as he had to go in search for longer ones because the hook wouldn't go any lower to the water. He worried they'd miss the tide cycle.

Chuck rushed off to find another pair of spreader bars with shorter wires and hire a truck to deliver them as the crane operator was waiting "on the clock." That did the trick. An hour later than planned, *Vela* finally hit the water without any more hitches. Before letting the slings go, he went below to check for leaks. Finding no major ones, he let the crane go. Eventually the wood would swell and minor gaps would disappear, he hoped.

During those last days in the boat yard, even Linda helped form a chain gang to return the once-rusty pig-iron ballast—now freshly painted—to Dawn's newly painted bilge and to haul all the gear from the house. As soon as the ballast was back in the boat, they moved *Vela* to a mooring, using an old inflatable dinghy they'd picked up for eighty dollars to ferry them, since the one they'd ordered had not arrived yet. By that time it was seven p.m. and everyone was wrung out physically and mentally.

After so many months of back-breaking labor and sleepless nights, Chuck described the relentless challenges he still faced:

When planning an operation like this there comes to mind a whole bunch of possible problems that can occur and I seem to go over it time and again, each time visualizing the worst. That makes me a nervous wreck. The mast went in last Tuesday as scheduled without a hitch. We were lucky, it had been raining every day all day for several days and it stopped while we put the mast in, then resumed. We were sweating it out as we had to put one more coat of antifouling paint on the bottom before launching. As it was, we wanted to do it last Friday but had to settle for Monday and, in Fiji, that is something.

For the next ten days, the family worked nonstop to make *Vela* somewhat livable. Garth and Chuck took turns sleeping on the boat.

On May 30th, just before another month's rent came due for the house, the Wilcoxes moved back aboard, with a bucket under the sink and water from jugs to make up for missing plumbing. At least they'd eliminated the hemorrhage of money that went to rent instead of boat repair. Aboard Vela, they moored near the Tradewinds resort—on the far side of Suva from their rented house—now a dinghy row plus a twelve-cent bus ride into town.

In a letter to his parents, Chuck put their situation into perspective:

It will take some time before we set sail for new places as there are a million details to take care of. Don't forget it took us a year and a half to outfit what we thought was a fully found boat. Here we are doing it in less time but on a far grander scale as we need many more things before it is fully found.

At the start of June, the tasks that still stretched before them would tax most mortals who began with a fresh start and proper materials. The Wilcoxes faced them after eight months of hard labor, accompanied by constant rain and an often inefficient, rumor-fueled chase for supplies. The project list went on and on: hook up the fridge and the stove; connect the engine and start it up; sew the remaining cushions; install lights; lay the canvas decks and coat them with paint; pump the hundred gallons of diesel siphoned from *Vela* before she was salvaged back into her tanks; rebuild the table, shelves, drawers and storage cabinets; lay linoleum; install winches; repack the life raft; and more. Days raced by, and still the project list seemed no shorter. Sometimes they wondered if it could even be done.

It seemed hard to believe there had been a time before the shipwreck, a time when they had only a few minor maintenance tasks between lazy snorkels in aqua water gazing at brightly colored tropical fish and hikes ashore to explore new cultures.

But the Wilcoxes kept at it. The rains abated briefly, giving them better working conditions. Little by little they made progress. In mid-June they celebrated Linda's twelfth birthday and in July they celebrated Garth's fifteenth—modestly now that money was so tight.

Linda kept trying to win money on the *Punja and Sons Hit Parade* on the radio. After she guessed the seven songs correctly one week, Yaminiasi, the announcer, said no one had won. Linda marched down to the station to complain. Two weeks later she won the twenty-dollar prize. It was obviously a fraud, but it was fun for her because they announced her name three times. Her family was impressed.

Dawn's pluck carried them through an endless slog of work. She was grateful for every inch of progress. After Chuck made the mast watertight, she wrote in a letter home:

> It is nice not having a bucket by the mast -- when it rained hard, Chuck and I got up twice to empty same. Handy for getting washing water, though.

In early July Dawn still wrote to her family by the dim light of a kerosene lamp with updates:

> Garth and I laid the linoleum this morning. Your grandson is becoming a fellow of numerous talents, (if only he had time for English.) Chuck filled in the area around the mast. After I did the day's painting on the navigation locker, we rowed over to Mosquito Island to swim, look for shells and loaf for 2 whole hours! Still have to do cockpit, cabin teak floor, and the boom is still not attached. We might get done yet.
>
> And yes, shopping for anything here is complicated. One does get tired of having an adventure every time you need something, but that's how life is here. They sell the lanterns at 10 stores in Suva, but no one sells the wicks.

Back among other world-voyaging sailors, the Wilcoxes traded their Hawaiian charts for ones of Australia and were grateful they'd been able to pick up a used dinghy just in case. They still awaited the Avon replacement, engine parts and the next season's schoolwork. With the arrival of each supply ship, the family waited anxiously for three days while dock workers unloaded at a sluggish pace. Finally their long-awaited packages arrived.

They did their best to muddle through the most critical items on the list and assumed they'd be able to address the rest once they reached Australia.

Yet many choices they had to make would plague them for the rest of their journey.

24

On August 9, 1975, the Wilcox family finally sailed away from Fiji. Everyone was excited for a change. With the sails up and drawing, Chuck pointed the bow toward the opening in the reef that had nearly ended of their voyage almost a year before. He could hardly believe this day had finally come. They'd surmounted obstacles he could never have imagined.

They were truly lucky to be functional within a year of nearly losing the boat, yet an inventory of unfinished work weighed heavily on their minds. They'd been unable to replace the whisker pole so they had no decent way to sail downwind. They still didn't have storm sails, and had never fully addressed the problem with one of the water tanks. Scant wind the day of their test sail left Chuck wondering what other issues they might yet discover. But with sailing season coming to an end, they had to leave now or miss another season. By October, Chuck hoped to be safely moored in Australia, three thousand miles away. There they hoped to address some of these issues during the off-season.

Dawn was keen to visit New Hebrides (now the island nation of Vanuatu) and New Caledonia before passing the hurricane season in the relative safety of Brisbane. They'd already missed so much. Though they'd lived in Fiji for nearly a year, they'd seen little outside the boat yard. Their curiosity about Fijian culture had been curbed by the endless slog to finish the boat. Dawn's primary motivation for voyaging had been to see the world, not the inner workings of boat repair. She looked forward to having nothing on her agenda but to simply navigate and explore. Of course, she knew better than to think their work was done.

For Garth, preparing the boat, sailing, navigating and finding solutions to obstacles along the way were as engaging as exploring other cultures, a reward more valuable because of the effort required to reach them. Linda would just as soon have skipped the whole business altogether, instead preferring to return to their old life in California. She stated her opinion loudly and often, but with little effect. They were setting off again, and that was that.

Chuck motor-sailed for the reef pass out of the city, steering carefully for the center. As the wind freshened and he adjusted course to stay in the channel, he pulled in the mainsail to keep it from flogging. Garth trimmed the jib. The low throb of the engine accompanied the creak in the sails as the wind filled them. Outside the protection of the inner bay, puffs of wind skittered across the water, a good sign they'd have enough wind to sail. A gust sent a shudder across the leech of the mainsail and *Vela* responded, heeling for the first time in nearly a year—from wind, anyway. Chuck felt the tension of the last few months dissipate and relaxed his grip on the wheel. He wasn't clear of the reef yet, but he was close. Free from the tyranny of boat work, he was finally able to resume sailing around the world.

The engine sputtered, then quit. The sudden absence of the steady rumble that accompanied the motor caught everyone's attention immediately. They all looked at Chuck.

Chuck felt a flash of anger, remembering his showdown with the engine mechanics when they'd held his engine hostage and demanded twice their quoted payment. Every inch of progress had come with a battle that had tested his patience and pushed him to the brink of exhaustion.

But the boat's gentle motion and the peacefulness of being under sail lulled him back to a feeling of calm he hadn't felt for months.

"Oh, the hell with it," Chuck said. "Let's just go."

As *Vela* cleared the reef pass, they spotted the glass-bottom tour boat, the *Olooloo*, crashing against the outer reef. Four other yachts had wrecked on reefs in the area during their time in Fiji. Only fifteen days before the Wilcoxes raised anchor to leave the country, a Ferro-cement yacht from New Zealand had smashed into a reef at two a.m. and sunk before its crew could recover emergency gear or money. The Wilcoxes had been lucky to be able to sail away.

2 5

Being underway again was exhilarating. The family felt the thrill of charging along at top speed, overjoyed by such easily measureable progress. *Vela* sailed a record one hundred and thirty-five miles that first day, almost as though the boat was eager to get far from the scene of her near-fatal encounter. They settled into the routine of life at sea, getting used to the motion once again, and standing watches—this time with greater vigilance.

Garth suggested changes to the watch schedules, which they implemented. Now, each person filled three-hour watches twice a day. Twelve-year-old Linda was now on watch from six to nine both mornings and evenings, when most of the family was also on deck. Dawn did the nine-to-twelve shift morning and night, which left her free to prepare meals and calculate their position on her "off-watch." Fifteen-year-old Garth, who had no trouble sleeping at odd hours, took watch from noon until three p.m. and midnight to three a.m. This left Chuck with the late afternoon shift, when he was inclined to be on deck anyway to take star shots. He also took the dreaded three-to-six a.m. shift, those deadly hours when no one wanted to be awake.

As before, Chuck and Dawn worked together on navigation—though fresh from their narrow escape, with more acute anxiety.

Besides navigating, Chuck worked on the smaller, unfinished projects he could tackle while underway, such as rewiring the last of the cabin lights and the compass light. Mostly he was relieved that so much was going right for a change.

Dawn kept busy planning and preparing meals, baking fresh bread and overseeing schoolwork. During their layover in Fiji, Garth had barely completed his coursework to finish the ninth grade, while Linda had doubled up on lessons to complete both sixth and seventh grades. To Garth's chagrin, his mother was more determined than ever to make sure he didn't get behind. But her harping often made it worse, tempting him to procrastinate all the more.

Days passed quickly, their sea-going routine highlighted by the wonders of nature: meteor showers and dolphins frolicking in their bow wave, storm petrels and albatross as they soared overhead and dipped into the waves, and bioluminescence that trailed behind the boat as though *Vela* were a rocket shooting through an inky black sky. They offered immeasurable relief after the constant work in Fiji.

They were so much more experienced now than they'd been when they'd left San Francisco two years earlier, but their boat now lacked many of its fancy amenities and their monthly budget was now half of what it once was. Still they were grateful *Vela* was sailable and they were once again in pursuit of their goal.

Five days after leaving Suva, they were within sight of Efate Island, home of Port Vila, the capital of New Hebrides. They'd traveled six hundred miles. At four thirty in the afternoon on Friday, August 15th, *Vela* neared Pango Point at the entrance to Meli Bay. Port Vila, their destination lay only a few miles beyond. The sky grew dark, with visibility so poor they could barely see into the bay. Unsure of their engine, it seemed unwise to attempt landfall. This would be their first landfall after crashing on a reef and nearly losing the boat, and they were naturally skittish. But they were also in desperate need of a small victory.

Being forced to turn away so close to their destination felt like a personal blow. Instead of a snug night at anchor as they'd envisioned, they had little choice but to find a safer distance from unseen dangers. For Dawn, it was crushing to head back out to sea. To make things worse, the wind came up and began to howl through the rigging. With their destination now behind them, they now had too much wind pushing them away from shore.

Garth and Chuck dropped the mainsail as the seas grew rough. It was the start of a miserable night that grew worse as the hours wore on. In the cockpit, Dawn huddled with her eyes locked on the light on Pango Point until the gloom masked it from view. She fell into despair. They had worked so hard to get to this point, but the strain hadn't let up. Is this how it would always be? She was so weary of the discomfort and the fear. The endless struggle. That evening on watch alone, Dawn considered slipping over the side. It would be so easy to just disappear beneath the waves.

The night wore on and on. At two a.m., Dawn gave Chuck a reciprocal course, allowing for ten degrees of drift downwind. After beating thirty miserable miles out of the bay, at least they'd have a nice downwind sail back, they thought. But the wind shifted, and the trip back in was just as hard-fought as the sail out. They were making only three knots under the jib, surrounded by the froth and chaos of crashing waves. Everyone was seasick. Had they worked so hard to repair *Vela* for this?

At six a.m., Dawn spotted a light through the haze, then the conspicuous hill that marked Pango Point, that same light she'd regarded with such despondency hours before. She sighed with relief, grateful for the tiniest sign of progress. The wind mellowed and the seas flattened.

By eleven a.m., Dawn had sailed *Vela* into the calm waters of the outer bay, with Garth acting as navigator. Chuck hovered over the engine, trying to diagnose the problem.

Eventually, Chuck emerged from below, saying, "It's a bigger problem than I thought. I'll work on it later. Let's just try to sail in."

Dawn was apprehensive, but the sky had begun to clear and the winds were moderate. The bay looked even calmer farther in.

"We can do it." Garth said with confidence. His gaze was steady and sure. "Just like we did on our T-Bird." Well, not exactly. The tubby *Vela* was hardly comparable. Chuck knew how much harder it would be to maneuver *Vela*. This was his first post-shipwreck landfall, and he felt like a nervous wreck. Working together, they drew on their racing skills and tacked their way into the bay like professionals. Their confidence soared. Again it was short-lived.

The Wilcoxes dropped anchor in the quarantine area near the concrete pier. Unfortunately, since it was now Saturday, they couldn't clear into the country or go ashore until Monday. Still, they could stop, get a full night of sleep like a regular family and think about something besides sailing and navigation.

Sunday night the wind swung to the northwest, turning their anchorage into a dangerous lee shore. High winds and seas rolled in from the ocean. Miles of fetch whipped up a nasty froth. *Vela* yanked at her anchor chain, snapping the snubber line. The force of the wind and waves pushed them unnervingly close to the concrete pier. Blanketed by darkness with the engine still not functional, they saw that moving was out of the question. Before they could raise the sails, *Vela* would crash against the sea wall. Chuck worried whether the anchor chain would hold until daylight. Dawn's stomach churned with anxiety. The family endured yet another tense and uncomfortable night.

Their first post-shipwreck landfall had produced yet another trial before they'd recovered from the last one.

In the morning, once he checked into New Hebrides, Chuck was finally able to repair the engine so they could move to a more protected location. They nestled into the narrow slot between Iririki Island and the mainland among the other yachts. Among them were their Australian friends from *Karloo*, who had urged them to salvage *Vela*. When Chuck took apart the engine, he realized *Vela*'s fuel tank hadn't been designed correctly: the intake tube was at the bottom of the tank so that any debris in the tank would flow directly into the engine fuel line and clog it. He cursed all the non-standard ways that *Vela* had been built that he hadn't noticed when they'd bought her, but soon got to work crafting a day tank from an oil can and copper tubing. That seemed to solve the problem— a solution that could have prevented significant heartache only the day before.

The charm of Port Vila helped make up for their traumatic arrival. New Hebrides offered a new geography, people and culture. Before their arrival, the family had read about the way the people lived in the Kastum way, wearing grass skirts or penis sheaths and living in grass houses. Most intriguing was the traditional yam ceremony, in which men and boys would leap from great heights with vines tied around their ankles and hang up-side down with their heads nearly brushing the ground. Unless the Wilcoxes visited outer islands outside of Port Vila, they could not witness the culture in its pure form, but they'd spent most of the sailing season rebuilding *Vela*. Dawn was disappointed, but, with the threat of hurricane season approaching, they could not afford the detour.

Still, there was plenty in Port Vila to contrast it with Fiji or anywhere else they'd been. As Dawn wandered among the few storefronts that lined the narrow wooden sidewalks running along the waterfront and gazed up the steep slopes dotted with colonial buildings, houses and flowering bougainvillea, she noticed a variety of physical characteristics among the people she passed, evidence of the diversity in the islands and different from the other cultures they'd seen in the South Pacific. Before colonialism, the New Hebrideans had never been a united people, so the population spoke forty different languages with little travel between islands. To bridge the language gap, the people spoke Pidgin English learned from black birders. Generally, New Hebrideans were smaller than indigenous Fijians or Polynesians, with darker skin and more closely shorn nappy hair.

A "condominium-style" or divided colonial government run jointly by the English and the French produced endless amusing inefficiencies. For the delight of the coin-collecting philatelists, it offered two sets of collectibles. The duality created a perplexing duplication in medical services, police forces and judicial services, public works and education. The country even honored two different flags, though outside the city villagers' subsistence lives remained largely unaffected by such nonsense.

The French influence naturally produced a ready supply of wine—French, of course—and baguettes. And high prices. Once again, French subsidies produced inflation in French-controlled Port Vila. After the bargains of Fiji, Dawn was shocked at how much more everything cost. With Chuck and basket in tow, Dawn headed for the six-thirty a.m. market. She was delighted to find pamplemousse, citron, pawpaw (what the natives called papaya) and cabbage, but at prices nearly double what they'd been in Fiji. At least the cost of each item was clearly marked, so Dawn didn't have to ask the prices like she did in Fiji and French Polynesia.

While the Wilcoxes were in the colonial territory, locals voted for city officials for the first time. A local political party pushed for independence as they'd witnessed other nearby nations do, but the French resisted this move. The family wondered about the future of New Hebrides as they listened to election results on the radio.

After two relaxing weeks in Port Vila, provisioning and working on boat projects, the family prepared to sail on.

26

The family's second post-shipwreck landfall wasn't much easier than the first. Chuck and Dawn considered skipping New Caledonia, partially in fear of its reefs. Plus they aimed to be in Australia—still more than a thousand miles away—by the end of September, which meant they couldn't linger. But their friends on *Karloo* had gushed over New Caledonia's scenery and waxed poetic about its Melanesian culture with a touch of *la vie Françoise*. Ruth and Geoffrey encouraged the Wilcoxes to visit, showering them with tips for navigating through the reef that surrounds the country. Curiosity about this French territory, combined with information from people they trusted, overcame their wariness.

Just before leaving Vila, Dawn checked the mail and discovered a bonanza. Along with two letters from her mother was news of a $6,000 refund from the IRS. While rebuilding *Vela* had cost them nearly $17,000, half their savings for the rest of the voyage, Chuck and Dawn hoped this modest compensation would ease the financial strain they'd felt since the shipwreck.

On September 2nd, they pulled up the anchor and sailed for Nouméa. Chuck estimated a three-day sail between the capital of New Hebrides and that of New Caledonia, but lack of wind rendered his estimate inaccurate. Two days out of Efate, the wind died. *Vela* bobbed, making little progress. Another frustrating sail, but for a completely different reason. Hours passed and their position relative to the lush high islands of New Hebrides hardly changed. A glass float covered with barnacles bobbed by, hinting that they were moving, though barely. It was easy to retrieve and offered an affordable souvenir to their voyage.

At midnight their second day, Garth stepped into the cockpit to relieve his mother. The night was cloudy, the moon little more than a vaguely bright spot to port. With the green army blanket layered over her shoulders, Dawn studied the dimly lit compass, her lips pursed in concentration. Both her hands gripped the wheel. Garth slid in next to her and she peered up at him, startled by his sudden appearance.

"Thank God you're here." She sighed. "I'm pooped. I can't get the wind vane to steer tonight."

Garth took a quick glance around. The wind was light, which often posed a challenge for wind-vane steering. Then he noticed the backwinded sails. "Ha!" he blurted. His mother never ceased to amaze him; her determination combined with her impatience and eagerness to take action, often before thinking things through, produced the oddest predicaments. "Of course it's hard to steer. You're sailing backwards!"

"Oh." She shrugged. "Humph." She was too tired to care.

• • •

On the third afternoon, Chuck noticed the brass spinner log behaving strangely. Normally it trailed steadily behind the boat, tracking the sea miles they'd traveled in revolutions per hour. Now it was zipping across their stern wave like a comet, swinging wide arcs, diving below the surface and re-emerging. When Chuck pulled it in to investigate, he discovered it was bent, with deep teeth marks. Evidently some sea creature had attempted to dine on it, only to find it bland and excessively crunchy.

Fortunately a spare spinner had survived the shipwreck, so Chuck replaced it. He could pound out the dents on this one later, but in the meantime, he was glad for the spare. If they wanted to avoid reefs, it helped to know where they were.

· · ·

Chuck had learned from other sailors and the sailing directions how important it was to properly time the entrance to Havannah Pass. After six days of sailing, the Wilcoxes reached the pass early. So once again they tacked back and forth until daylight, this time under more pleasant conditions. When daylight arrived, they aimed for what they thought was the pass. That's when things turned ugly.

Seas grew unexpectedly steep. Anxiety crept back into Dawn's mind like an old nemesis she hoped she'd shaken. Her stomach churned. The roar of waves reminded her of the last time she heard something similar. The memory made her shudder. *Not again!* She gripped the lifelines and peered at the colossal waves over Chuck's shoulder.

"Let's put on life jackets," Dawn suggested. Garth, who was right next to her, didn't seem to hear. He'd complained about his ear and had seemed lethargic most of the passage. Suspecting an infection, Nurse Dawn had started him on a dose of antibiotics, but they hadn't helped. She reached for her life jacket and then Garth's, nudged him and handed it to him before putting on her own. Chuck and Linda each donned their life jackets without a word. *Vela*'s motion was still unnervingly erratic, but knowing everyone was wearing a life jacket eased Dawn's worries slightly.

Chuck bit his lip and wrestled with the wheel to keep *Vela* pointing straight despite the uneven pressure of water rushing against the hull as she surfed down the waves. *Vela* had never moved so fast. It felt exciting to Garth, but he knew a boat this size had no business surfing, especially since they weren't sure they'd found the pass. After several more tense moments, a local freighter appeared behind them, reassuring them that they had indeed found the pass. It motored past effortlessly on *Vela's* starboard side, as she struggled in the waves.

As they neared the calmer, protected waters inside the pass, the waves should have gradually lessened. Instead they rose up like a rearing horse, untamed and in a temper. It was then that Chuck realized his mistake. Instead of timing their arrival for slack water, he had mistakenly chosen max ebb, the time when the water flowing out of the pass would be *strongest*. Oops. He worried about the consequences of his mistake. Unlike the powerful ship's engines, *Vela's* could not overcome an adverse current.

With the wind against the waves, the seas had formed into mountainous peaks, as though possessed by a demonic force. *Vela's* stern rose up to meet them, but each successive wave posed a new threat. The chart showed the water shallowed quickly from two hundred and fifty feet to fifty feet at the pass, but these crests seemed gigantic. Humbled again, Chuck fought the forces against the rudder, correcting his course time and again to keep the boat in the center of the pass. Though the log indicated *Vela* was sailing and motoring at seven knots, their actual speed was more like one knot. They fought their way forward.

The strain of navigating the pass in such boisterous conditions came to a quick end once they made it through, though by then both Chuck and Dawn were unnerved. Yet the sudden absence of waves was remarkable. Inside the protected waters, the seas lay down with no evidence of the hazards they'd just endured. Chuck uncurled his fingers from the wheel. He rubbed his temples, suddenly aware how tense he'd been. Dawn nearly skipped below to make a notation in the ship's log: *Havannah Pass - My goodness me o' my, such waves!*

Nouméa, the capital city, was a thirty-mile sail from the pass, more than they could cover that afternoon, especially given how essential good light would be in an area full of reefs. So Chuck identified the nearest possible anchorage and they sailed fifteen miles along the Havannah Canal on piercingly luminescent blue water to the first inlet. There they rounded Pointe Mehoue and anchored inside Rade de l'Este within the larger Baie de Prony. Inside the bay, the water was calm as a millpond.

Dawn was glad they'd come. The spindly pines were unlike the lush vegetation of Fiji or New Hebrides. Once anchored, Dawn and Linda inflated the Avon dinghy and ventured ashore toward the burnt-orange striated rocks, a startling contrast to the milky aquamarine water. The red soil, rich in nickel deposits that drove New Caledonia's economy, was unlike anything they'd seen before.

Dawn hoped to spot the rare birds found only in New Caledonia, including the red-furred fruit bat and the *Cagou*, the flightless national bird. Linda was more excited about the selection of sea shells that would be the envy of any conchologist.

Together, the two tackled Linda's science-class lesson, which, ironically, covered survival. Now, nearly a year after *Vela* hit the reef, in the shallows off the point, they scoured for plants and sea life that might sustain them in a survival situation. As if ….

After several hours, the two returned with a collection of "edibles," including pandanus fruit—too hard to eat, they concluded—loads of limpets, clams, black and bright pink sea cucumbers, two red-and-yellow-striped star fish, a coconut, a few crabs and several spider conches. Hardly an appetizing meal, but instructive, in case they needed survival skills again.

After weeks of cleaning and soaking the shells they'd collected in bleach, Dawn would send them home in the Christmas package. Their recipients wouldn't be as overjoyed as they envisioned. A letter they received months later said: *Thanks so much for your gifts. We put the smelly ones outside.*

After a two-day respite in Baie de Prony, they sailed on through the Canal Woodin. They passed Porc Epic—which spawned jokes about the beloved cartoon character Porky Pig—as they made their way into the city of Nouméa. The blue skies and moderate temperatures were a relief after the moist heat of Fiji and New Hebrides. The cooler weather, along with the bristling pines, reminded them of San Francisco, though it forced Dawn into long pants for the first time since they'd left Hawaii.

By 1:28 in the afternoon, *Vela*'s anchor was down in the Baie de l'Orphelinat yacht basin. Within minutes of clearing into the country, Dawn and Garth headed ashore in search of medical facilities to find out why Garth couldn't hear and to do something about it.

Unfortunately, the two-mile hike into town seemed especially long under the circumstances. As much as Dawn wanted to carry her ailing boy to the hospital, he was by now far taller and heavier than she. And so, at every park bench they encountered, they sat for a spell so Garth could rest. Dawn started to worry whether they'd make it to medical facilities before they closed.

After asking around, Dawn located a French ear-nose-and-throat doctor who'd escaped from Cambodia after two of his partners had been killed and his clinic destroyed. Dawn chatted happily with her fellow medical professional while a woozy Garth numbly waited for the man to inspect his ear.

In a thick French accent, the doctor said, "Ah, it's an abscess just outside the ear drum." He grabbed a tool and leaned over Garth. "I'll incise it and then we'll follow up with hot compresses and antibiotics."

Before Garth could figure out what that gibberish meant, he was crumpled in a heap staring at the doctor's feet. The sudden absence of pressure against his ear drum threw off his balance, and he hit the floor in an instant.

A few minutes later a weak Garth, followed by his mother, still suffering from sticker shock after paying the bill, stumbled out the door. After that kind of fee—a good chunk of the month's budget—hiring a taxi was out of the question. They slowly made their way back to the boat, visiting most of the same benches along the way.

• • •

This French colony, officially named Nouvelle-Caledonie, differed from the fellow colony of French Polynesia and the French influence in Nouméa was far more evident than it had been in the subdivided English/French culture of Port Vila in the New Hebrides. Dawn appreciated the subtle differences that made each location unique.

Dawn described her perceptions in a letter home:

> Greetings from the land of the Frenchys. The tourist maps says Nouméa is like the south of France. Having never been there I don't know, but there are lots of little shops here. To shop one goes to the butchery for meat and eggs, the bakery for bread (it's good but not as sour as San Francisco bread) the alimentary shop for cans, the market for fruit and patisserie for pastry.

Dawn wandered from shop to shop, past colonial houses with shutters and tin roofs, surrounded by purple and magenta bougainvillea and flame trees with reddish-orange flowers shaped like a torch. She marveled at the inefficiency of stocking up for a voyage in boutique-style shops while charmed by the unique experience of it.

Unfortunately, like New Hebrides, this French colony suffered from the inflated prices that often came with expatriate living. While the locals may have adjusted to a higher standard of living, fueled by subsidies from the French government, the Wilcoxes were living on a fixed amount. Dawn felt the acute pressure of their tighter budget. At this rate of spending, they would run out before they made it all the way home.

At the butcher's, Dawn stared at the prices in a stupefied silence. Next to her, her teenaged son hovered over the glass case, practically salivating at the thought of a fresh steak. At the bottom of the sign, she saw a cut of meat for two hundred francs per kilo. She pointed and nodded, holding up a single finger to indicate she wanted one kilo.

The butcher smiled at her and shook his head.

"Non, non, madam." She cocked her head at him. Why wouldn't he sell it to her? She hadn't even spoken, so it couldn't be her terrible accent as it had been in Tahiti. "C'est pour le chien." She looked at him blankly. Then he imitated a dog's bark and she understood. Yikes, she couldn't even afford dog food!

While she dreamed of croissant and *patisserie*, their staggering prices kept her wallet closed. She kept purchases of staple items to a minimum, figuring they could replenish in Australia anything they could live without over the next few weeks.

In an attempt to expand the kids' cultural horizons, she took them to explore the museum. Upon discovering their visit would be free, she vowed to splurge for a croissant on their way back to the boat. Inside the museum, they inspected an example of a traditional local Melanesian hut, a round structure built of grass with low walls and a conical grass roof that gave it the look of a beehive. Dawn wished she could stay longer to explore the outer islands and indigenous culture that produced this unusual structure. Still she was grateful for at least a glimpse.

At the end of each day, Dawn would try to convey the richness of what they were seeing in letters to family back home. She'd encountered things she could scarcely have imagined before they left California two years earlier. The kids weren't just reading about these far-flung places but getting to experience them in a way that would remain with them for the rest of their lives. Perhaps there were easier ways to see the world, but none this memorable.

27

D awn's rosy perspective would again be tested on their passage to
Australia. Less than ten days later all but Garth were ready to re-
evaluate their commitment to the sailing life.

On September 16th, the family hauled up the anchor and sailed away
from the pleasures of the Nouméa Yacht Club. That first day was bouncy,
but soon *Vela* sat becalmed. Even with all the sails up, they made little
headway, so they passed the time spotting jellyfish in the still water and
watching dolphins leaping from its glassy surface.

On the 23rd, Dawn noted in the ship's log that they jibed "*après le
petit dejeuner*" (after breakfast). By three p.m. that afternoon, she noted
the appearance of albatross and then storm petrels. Storm petrels were
supposed to forecast a coming storm. She ground her teeth with worry
as thick clouds gathered on the horizon. With clouds came wind, ideal
for making progress. Only ninety miles from Australia, she hoped they
could make it in before it hit.

After two years in the islands away from the modern world, the family imagined their stop in Australia as a return to "civilization." Dawn
planned to restock the boat's staples, which had dwindled while she kept

purchases to a minimum in expensive island stores where everything had to be imported.

The Wilcoxes needed to finish addressing problems caused by hitting the reef and selling so much sailing gear before deciding to rebuild *Vela*. Chuck steadily worked away at the project list, but he lacked the materials to address many important issues. They had to replace the hand-bearing compass, fenders and lines and the storm sails they'd sold. They needed a whisker pole to pole out the jib for better sailing downwind. They needed to buy charts, not only of the next areas they intended to explore like the Indian Ocean and beyond, but of Australia since the single chart they had for Australia was barely adequate to get them there.

Rebuilding *Vela* had cost them half the money they'd saved to get the rest of the way around the world. Now they would have to live the next three years on what they'd planned to spend in a year and a half. Still, what they had achieved rebuilding *Vela* was nothing short of miraculous with the challenges they'd faced. Plus they'd gotten to spend the last two months sailing to two remarkable island nations.

On September 24th, it rained in torrents and the sky blackened. A gale shrieked in the rigging and rain lashed the decks. They had to shout to be heard above the howl of the wind. A strong current along the Australian coast battled against gale-force winds, creating steep seas that crashed down upon them. What Dawn had thought scary at Havannah Pass seemed like nothing compared to this. Through her salt-sprayed glasses, Dawn saw waves the size of a two-story house.

Chuck suggested they turn north and run before the seas. The maneuver might keep them off the coast until the storm abated, yet it put them at risk of running off the edge of the best chart they had.

Once they turned, *Vela* would run down a wave, wallow as the huge swells blocked the wind, then, just as everyone worried *Vela* would dive into the wave in front and pitchpole, she would rise up and over the storm-tossed sea as though she were riding an elevator. Each wave set them on edge; the next could be the ambush they feared.

It made sense to reduce sail, but the family had sold all the storm sails after the wreck. Without storm sails, Garth and Chuck took the sails down to bare poles, lashing the boom so it wouldn't kill anybody.

Still, waves rocketed them forward, then would build to devastating heights until they looked as though they would crush *Vela*. As the twenty-ton vessel surfed down a steep wave into a trough, Garth was stunned to spot dolphins swimming above them in a nearly transparent wave.

The motion was so violent that it was tough to hang on. Saltwater swirled around them, caught in opposing air currents sparked by crashing waves and driving winds. The wind vane could not handle such forces, so they had to steer by hand. Chuck, Dawn and Garth took turns steering in two-hour shifts, strapped into life vests and tied to the boat. The forces were too intense to put twelve-year-old Linda on the helm. Below, she cinched the lee cloth as tight as she could to keep from flying out of her bunk while *Vela* careened between waves.

The galley was officially closed and they grabbed crackers to stave off hunger as they devoted their full attention to surviving the storm.

Without a decent sight for several days, their exact position was a riddle they desperately needed to solve. Land lay to the west of them. The Great Barrier Reef lay dead ahead. Without a fix, they didn't know exactly how far. Less than forty miles, according to the last estimate. Once they sailed beyond the area covered on their current chart, they would be unable to anticipate or dodge any dangers that lay ahead. Chuck agonized that *Vela* would reach rocks or reefs during the blow. One shipwreck had been more than enough.

To make matters worse, it was getting dark.

Chuck suggested dragging a warp to slow the boat, as he'd read about in Adlard Cole's *Heavy Weather Sailing*. He fished the details of this storm tactic from the depths of his brain as he talked Dawn and Garth through the steps. He worried the line would be too short, but it was all they had. It was worth a try. Garth dragged the heavy line on deck.

"OK. Now tie the end of the line to the aft cleat," Chuck shouted as he wrestled with the wheel. After each wave, the boat would wallow and pull sideways. He knew the danger of broaching if *Vela* was caught beam to the seas.

Garth tied the line to the cleat on the transom.

"Now, bring it around behind the pushpit to the opposite cleat." Dawn held the clump of line and handed it around to Garth, who finished pulling it around the stern to the cleat on the opposite side, a challenge as the motion repeatedly jostled them. Chuck tried to follow their progress while still concentrating on keeping *Vela* aligned with the following seas.

"Careful now," Chuck continued. "We only have one crack at this. Make sure the line is clear, then ease it out as slowly as you can. If the line catches on anything, the force could rip it right off . . . the log, the pushpit, the wind vane, your hands." Garth paid out the line on deck to make sure there were no tangles and that it could run free. He looked up at his father, signaling that he was ready. Heavy raindrops drove at them sideways, and felt like needles on the exposed skin of his hands.

"OK." Chuck gave the command. Garth fed line out, careful to keep his fingers from getting caught or being pulled over with the line as it leapt over the side.

Once the line ran to its end, it snapped, flinging a spray of water upward and sending a groan through the cleats. The loop of line rose in the wall of water behind them, then skipped along the uneven surface, its middle whipping back and forth like a snake possessed.

Dawn and Garth watched, mesmerized by the line's demonic dance in the waves. Dawn's glasses fogged as the hood of her foul-weather jacket trapped the moist air of her breath. Chuck wrestled the wheel as the line caught, then had to compensate when it skipped out of the water. If anything, the line made it harder to steer as it periodically caught, then leapt out of a wave, yanking first to port and then to starboard. After a couple of minutes, Chuck said, "Forget it. This isn't helping." Shaking his head, he added, "Hand me the knife. Let's cut it free." As Dawn handed Chuck the knife in the darkness, it nicked him.

"Ack!" He pulled his hand away. At the same moment, Garth lost his footing.

"Whoa!" Garth yelped, slipping downward at an alarming speed. He recovered himself before he reached the low side of the cockpit. In these conditions, a sobering shock. If anyone went overboard now, they would be invisible within seconds.

This, on top of everything else, spooked Chuck. He was hungry and exhausted beyond belief. It took all his concentration to keep *Vela's* transom aligned with the waves. He worried about the strain on the steering. He was anxious to build a new emergency tiller that worked in case they needed it, but it might already be too late. What if the steering failed during the storm?

Knowing that he was racing toward the Great Barrier Reef without an adequate chart added to the pressure. It had been only two months since he'd driven himself to near madness trying to finish repairs so they could leave Fiji before the sailing season ended. Once again they faced grave danger. He felt light-headed and his head began to pound.

"I can't take this anymore." Chuck said. "As soon as we get to a city, we're selling this boat!" He seemed incredibly agitated, almost irrational to Dawn.

"Calm down," Dawn said.

"I can't calm down! I have to keep this boat together no matter what happens. I just can't do it anymore."

It was then that Dawn thought a tranquilizer that Chuck's dentist friend, Dr. Buddenbaum, had given them might help his frayed nerves. She ducked below to get one.

"Here. Take this," Nurse Dawn said with authority when she returned, with a cup and a pill in hand. Chuck popped the Equanil in his mouth and swallowed a gulp of water. He focused on steering the boat straight in the crazy waves, trying to stay on the edge of control. Gradually he mellowed. A half hour later, Garth took over the watch and Chuck went below to rest. Chuck climbed into his bunk near Linda, who had wedged herself in, just trying to survive these terrible forces and keep from getting injured.

As Garth grasped the wheel he noticed it was sticky. In the glow of the compass light, he realized everything was coated in blood. He recoiled, sickened by the thought, until a whoosh behind him snapped him back to the demands of the moment.

Garth relished the challenge of keeping *Vela* straight in the swell. He would hear a roar behind him and feel a wave pick up *Vela* and shove her along, sending white water swirling around them as they rode up, up . . . and over the crest of the wave and down into hellish troughs until they were surrounded by walls of dark water. Sometimes the boat would ride atop a wave and hang for an instant before screaming downward like a sled on an icy slope. For Garth it was exhilarating. For Dawn it felt like falling into a bottomless void. Her insides churned with worry.

A few hours later, when Chuck next took the wheel, he was perhaps too calm. With the waves as big as they were, it was critical to keep the boat aligned with the waves so they wouldn't get rolled. He had to steer while peering backwards into the darkness, watching for towering peaks that threatened them from behind. This required tremendous concentration and quick reactions. At that moment, concentrating probably wasn't Chuck's strongest suit. His attention lapsed and a wave caught *Vela* off center and tossed her violently onto her side.

Broadside to the waves, *Vela* heeled farther than she ever had before—mast nearly horizontal to the waves, jettisoning anything loose below. Linda screamed from her bunk as things flew off shelves around her. They heard an ominous crash as *Vela* wallowed on her side.

Garth, who lay awake on the port pilot berth, felt a sudden gush of icy cold water and a crush of debris hit his face. When he opened his eyes, the port window above his head was smashed. Shards of shattered safety glass surrounded him. Water sloshed back and forth across the floorboards. *Vela* regained her footing, but the damage was done. The cabin looked like a tornado had torn through it.

Where the port-side window had been, there was now a gaping hole the size of a serving platter near where they'd repaired the hull after the shipwreck only a few short months ago. For the second time in a year, they faced a triage situation.

Water several inches deep ran across the cabin sole. Spray from the deck gushed through the hole. Linda yelled, "My pillow is wet!"

"We've got worse things than that to worry about, Linda," Garth told her and rushed to the companionway to make sure his father was still on board.

"Dad, are you OK?"

His dad looked at him with an eerie calm. "Did the window break?" Chuck called through the hatch, seeming not to comprehend the seriousness of the situation. In the glow of the compass light, he appeared bewildered.

Dawn went to retrieve her purse with the passports. "Get the life raft!" she yelled over her shoulder, without pausing to think what it might be like *inside* a lifeboat in those waves.

"Mom, it isn't that bad." Garth said, in as soothing a voice as he could muster. "All we have to do is put up the storm boards."

Dawn stared at her son for a moment. "Oh... right." She looked to her fifteen-year-old son for direction.

Garth retrieved the storm boards, which they might have already put in if it had been as easy as just placing them over top of what was there. But the way the storm boards had been designed, the windows needed to be removed *before* the boards could be slid into place. And who would do that in a storm?

For the next several hours, Garth and Dawn nailed the boards over top of the glass windows. Water crystals pelted them mercilessly. The two struggled to hang on while needing both hands for their task as the boat pitched and rolled over a hilly sea. If *Vela* had broached then, Garth and Dawn might have been tossed over the side. Linda began pumping out the many gallons of saltwater they'd taken on. All worked steadily while Chuck—now extra-alert—steered. Once the storm windows were in place, they took turns pumping the remaining water.

As soon as it grew light enough to see, they did their best to make sense of the soggy mess below. Water still sloshed above the floor boards; blankets and pillows, books and papers were drenched with saltwater; dishes and utensils were strewn about the cabin in disarray; water dripped inside the kitchen drawers and inside cabinets.

Once things seemed mildly under control, Dawn tried to figure out where they were. Without sights, the best she could do was estimate their position using dead reckoning. With a margin of error to accommodate for drift from current during the night, she ran through her calculations, hoping to discover they were still on the chart they had. After a few minutes, she plotted them to be in the vicinity of Waddy Point, at the north end of Fraser Island. Right next to the edge of their chart. *What a relief,* she thought, hoping she was right.

"We should be able to see Indian Head in the next couple of hours at a compass course of about 310 degrees. We might be able to tuck in there and wait until the waves calm down."

The wind and waves gradually abated. Garth and Chuck put up the staysail and scanned the horizon as daylight brightened the sky. They spotted something that looked like the north end of Fraser Island. Though Dawn had little confidence in her abilities, it was a remarkable feat of navigation.

When Dawn limped away from the navigation table, she realized, that somehow during all of this mayhem that she'd broken a bone in her foot.

After the trauma the family was relieved to drop the anchor behind the point. They spent the next two days in the most God-awful anchorage imaginable. Whenever they weren't sleeping or reading in their enclosed bunks, they had to brace their bodies so they wouldn't go flying. It was tiring, but at least they weren't at sea. They knew conditions were still rough when two plates—supposedly unbreakable Corelware—flew off the counter and smashed.

During their waking hours, they deliberated their future. Dawn and Linda were in favor of flying home. Garth was adamantly against giving up. Fueled by the adrenaline that had helped them survive the storm, he was more excited about the voyage and his role in it than ever. Chuck, who'd sparked the discussion with his mid-storm rant, remained silent.

In the end, since they were in a remote anchorage far from civilization, momentum carried them onward. That, combined with perfect sailing conditions all the way to Mooloolaba, tabled discussions about ending the cruise.

At least for the moment.

28

Vela sailed along a low bluff with ideal winds under bright sunshine. Linda even took the wheel for much of the afternoon as they sliced through the water past the Glasshouse Mountains.

In the late afternoon, as they entered the harbor of Mooloolaba, they spotted a post with a sign. The sign was turned away from them, so they sailed to the opposite side to see what it said. NOT TO SAIL BEYOND, they read just as *Vela* came to a stop in soft mud. Within a few minutes, a prawn boat crew pulled them off and they were on their way again.

After their brief embarrassment on the mud bank, Dawn expertly lassoed a bollard in front of the yacht club in Mooloolaba and "tied it to one of those pokey things," as she called a cleat. It was September 29, 1975, a year after crashing on the reef.

The resort town of Mooloolaba on Australia's east coast offered just the tonic they needed to forget about the storm, their recent stressful landfalls, and the burden of rebuilding the boat in Fiji. This beach town reminded them of Santa Cruz, California during the off-season, with miles of golden sand, camper parks, tents, and take-out food stores. The air smelled of pine trees with pine cones, oleander and hibiscus. The club offered showers and the first glimpse of television they'd seen in years—or "telly," in the Australian vernacular. A yacht provision service let the family order food and gas, and get it delivered. Such a luxury. No hauling heavy loads under a blisteringly hot sun. And to their delight, prices compared favorably to Fiji's—affordable once again. After a steady diet of boat food—various types of stew meat, tuna or corned beef with whatever vegetables they could find, the sudden variety in Australia offered welcome relief. Dawn splurged on scallops and prawns, even lettuce.

A Customs man came all the way from Brisbane to clear them in. Filling out the forms took two hours but cost nothing. After a brief stay in Mooloolaba, the family planned to make the sixty-mile trip south to Brisbane. Chuck and Dawn figured that a bigger city would offer a more convenient and safe venue for passing the cyclone season and finish fixing the boat, so they had their mail sent there.

Chuck caught a Greyhound bus to Brisbane to collect the mail and do what the Aussies call a "recky," or scouting mission. He found what seemed to be a reasonable place to pass the off-season and prepare for the next leg of the journey around the northeast coast of Australia to Darwin, their jumping off point for the Indian Ocean and beyond. He arranged to moor *Vela* up the Brisbane River, across from the Botanical Gardens. After two weeks in Mooloolaba, the family sailed for the city, where they expected to pass the next five months. Since they planned to stay put, they didn't anticipate any boating challenges. But other issues would pose new threats to their voyage.

Vela in Brisbane

29

By the middle of October, *Vela* was tied between a pair of pilings in the Brisbane River in the heart of the city. What Chuck thought would be a convenient location turned out not to be. The Wilcoxes soon discovered that the nearby buildings were government offices and the city so sprawling they had to go miles to run most errands. Often they just walked because the transit system was so inefficient. And with no yachting community, they found fewer resources for boat repair than they might have in Mooloolaba. The Brisbane sun was intense and the humidity suffocating, yet swimming in the muddy river wasn't an option. Since they'd had all their mail sent there, they were stuck.

Their first priority was to make repairs. Dawn and Garth hiked for miles to find safety glass to replace the broken window, and Chuck found a sail loft to repair their battered sails. He also worked on building a new emergency tiller and rebuilding the storm boards so they'd be easier to use the next time they encountered a storm—if there were a next time. Next, Chuck turned to repairing the refrigeration and electronic steering, which had taken a saltwater bath during the storm. Now that he was finally in a place long enough to receive them, he ordered parts as well as a storm sail that would have been so helpful a few weeks earlier.

Living off savings, Chuck became acutely aware of how hyper-inflation eroded their ability to replace parts they'd lost in Fiji. He was shocked at the taxes of 15 to 25 percent on goods in Australia. When he received an equipment catalogue from his father, he replied: *Got the Heath catalogue and am quite depressed at the prices of things.* He tried everything he could to cut costs. When his father told of an increase in their health insurance costs, Chuck replied:

> Considering the fact that they accepted payment after I told them about the trip, I don't think they had a right to raise the premium like that. I think it is silly for a company to advertise worldwide coverage and then to raise the premium if you are on a trip around the world. Yes, the more I think about it, the madder I get. I feel I had been low ball-high balled and I resent it. Please do call up Mr. Eng and tell him my feelings and I'll offer him 150 bux a year and no more. If he says no, then please cancel the policy. The coverage is free here in Brisbane, and since we will be here 6 months or so, there will be no problem with major medical. We will cross that bridge when we come to it.

The family, and Dawn in particular, maintained a steady correspondence with folks back home. Her chatty letters informed relatives about their adventures and kept them connected though they were thousands of miles apart. She sent home undeveloped film (along with a list tracking the photos they took), so the rolls wouldn't mildew aboard. Her mother sent packages filled with magazines, newspaper clippings and clothes and never failed to celebrate everyone's birthday and half birthday and every Hallmark-named holiday with a card. Chuck joked that his mother-in-law single-handedly financed the company. Cards for Valentine's Day, St.

Patrick's Day, and Halloween, all holidays that went unnoticed outside of America, reminded them of the growing divide between them and their fellow citizens. They'd read with befuddlement about a popular craze of streaking and now learned about the pet rock and the mood ring. Hearing reports of such things outside the context of popular culture left them feeling out of touch.

Mail offered a welcome relief from the loneliness of being away from friends and family, but it was expensive, especially sending in the completed school lessons. An air-mail envelope stamp cost forty cents, more than twice what it would be in the U.S. Linda and Garth coveted stamps that depicted Australian pioneer society but the prices were a little too *dear*, as the Australians would say. Dawn tried to find light souvenirs that were easy to mail but found sometimes the price of postage exceeded the cost of the original gift, as with an Aboriginal bark painting she mailed her mother. She apologized for the Christmas package she was assembling: *Chuck is keeping tight reigns [sic] on spending and I feel embarrassed sending you so little but we have to buy sails and charts, so it's all I can manage.*

Less welcome correspondence came from the IRS, requesting that Chuck appear within ten days to explain the deduction for the shipwreck. Chuck marveled at the idiocy of a bureaucracy that would question a deduction *after* granting a refund. In a letter, Chuck expressed his "regret" that he would be unable to attend because he was out of the country and his records were in storage and inaccessible. He hoped that would satisfy them until the family finished sailing around the world.

Though Linda still harbored hopes of returning to the predictability of life back home, all talk of ending the voyage had vanished. In a family for whom finishing what you started was a guiding principle, it was nearly unthinkable to give up, especially after all they'd invested in bringing *Vela* back from her near-fatal encounter. They assumed the sailing would get easier, especially if they could avoid areas where violent storms were likely. They had no intention of subjecting themselves to another one of those if they could help it. Thanks to Henry Kissinger's "shuttle diplomacy," the Suez Canal had recently reopened, offering another option to the storm-ravaged Cape of Good Hope for getting around the globe under sail. Traveling through Europe via the Mediterranean excited Dawn.

The problem with this plan was that no voyagers had passed through the Suez Canal for more than a decade, so no information was available. Dawn and Chuck spent days studying pilot charts page by page to plan their route, then preparing a list of charts and sailing directions to order. At Brisbane's Carnegie Library, Dawn attempted to research the countries en route, but found sparse pickings.

She informed the family at home of their intentions:

Our current plan is to visit Bali and maybe a few other Indonesian ports after Darwin. We'll leave the Brisbane area in Mar-April, go up the Great Barrier Reef in the right weather. Leave Darwin around September or so. Indonesia, Christmas Island, Cocos Island, Diego Garcia (if possible), Seychelles then wait there until January and go up the Red Sea to Suez (unless there's a new war). Will take as long as going around the Cape but should be more interesting, especially seeing a bit of the Med. This is the latest, but cruising people are notorious for changing plans.

In November, for Chuck's thirty-ninth birthday, Dawn baked a cherry pie with her last rusty cans of sour cherries. It was a big improvement over his previous one, which he'd spent removing the patch and clearing the coral from *Vela*'s hull. Linda joked that he was now "as old as Jack Benny," the comedian who'd been "thirty-nine" for decades. The family also looked forward to celebrating Thanksgiving and Christmas, which had gotten lost the previous year in their efforts to rebuild *Vela* after the shipwreck.

Unfortunately, the family's holiday plans took a different turn.

30

Nurse Dawn was always curious about medical care in the countries they visited. After graduating from the University of California-Berkeley, Dawn began caring for "real" patients, while Chuck settled in with an electronics firm in what would become Silicon Valley. Once Garth was born, Dawn quit nursing professionally to nurture her young son and then daughter, but her passion for nursing never waned.

In Tahiti, she'd bicycled around Papeete and was pleased to discover a modern hospital and public health department. In New Hebrides, she couldn't even *find* a hospital. In Tonga, Dawn was amused to discover the forty-bed, two-nurse hospital filled with family members of the patients sleeping on mats and providing meals for their loved ones.

In Fiji, Dawn had a cyst in her breast checked by a New Zealand doctor, and he offered her a job after telling her it was nothing to worry about. So soon after their shipwreck, Dawn was anxious to earn money for their boat repair, so she visited the Fiji Ministry of Health and submitted the fourteen-page work application and twenty-five-cent fee but dropped it once she realized she wouldn't qualify as a resident and it became clear how much work rebuilding the boat would require.

In New Caledonia, her fascination with the French doctor from Cambodia made Garth wonder about their real purpose for the visit. *Was it to check out local medical care or to cure his ear infection?*

In Australia, Dawn soon had an excuse to get an up-close-and-personal look at medical care—on multiple occasions. She hadn't been surprised to find island facilities to be primitive, but in a large country like Australia, she expected more.

The foot that she'd hurt during the storm had swollen and turned purple. She hopped on the bus then limped across the river to the Royal Brisbane Hospital, only to be told they "don't do feet." So she limped on to Princess Alexandria Hospital in Woolloongabba. After a two-hour wait, a doctor concluded it was a fracture without taking an X-ray and suggested that taping it would work. She hobbled on, in search of adhesive tape. Dawn taped up her foot as recommended but was not impressed.

Still drained from rebuilding *Vela* and subsequent trials, Dawn also worried about being anemic and showed signs of a gnawing ulcer. Soon she had even more to worry about.

During a routine pap smear, Dawn discovered that the lump the doctor in Fiji had dismissed was of concern to the Australian doctor. The woman referred Dawn to a specialist.

Dawn described the situation in a letter home to her mother, saying:

I visited a specialist for $18 and he decided it should be removed, along with 1/4 of my left bosum (which wasn't much to start with anyway). He gave me a referral to the Royal Brisbane Hospital and I hiked there on Monday and they put me on the OR schedule for Tuesday of the following week. I have to go in at 10am. They will do a frozen section to check for malignancy but he doesn't think it is. If it is, I'll get a simple Mastectomy and I'll have a lot more to worry about since it's been so long. I was so unconcerned about it, I went to the dentist first.

It was a lonely time for Dawn, yet her first thoughts were still of others. Afraid to alarm her mother, she waited to mail the letter she drafted until she could also divulge the outcome. Not knowing how long she might be gone, she took pains to prepare food and design easy menus for Chuck and the kids to eat during her absence. Since her surgery was scheduled to fall over Thanksgiving, she even reordered a turkey for December 12th, when she hoped to have a delayed celebration. She shielded the worst of her concerns from the children and even Chuck, but such a diagnosis brought everything into question.

Chuck and Dawn had met their freshman year of college in a ballroom dance class. Chuck was looking for a mate and figured a dance class was a likely place to find one. The same was true for Dawn, though neither had any interest in dancing. For the five women in a class with thirty-five men, the odds were better than for the men. Unlike the pharmacist in the class who also asked her out for coffee, Dawn found in Chuck not only a smart engineer—qualities her mother suggested she seek in a husband—but also a man who was unconventional. And persistent.

While she liked the idea of living unconventionally, she couldn't have guessed she would end up attempting to sail around the world—although one of their first dates, a sailing trip, might have been an early clue. Despite the mast falling down when Chuck took Dawn and some other students out sailing, Dawn hadn't panicked—they'd quickly re-stepped the mast and carried on. She'd even found sailing interesting, maybe not enough to sail around the world, but it was a way to explore beyond California's borders with a man who seemed to be mostly a homebody. For her it was the places along the way that appealed, while she had come to accept that, for him, it was in reaching the goal.

Dawn feared what it might do to Chuck and their relationship if he were forced to return to California without completing his dream of circumnavigating. Especially after their sacrifice to rebuild *Vela*. She also worried he might try to complete the voyage without her. Just because he was driven didn't mean he could do it alone. Or even with Garth's help. That would split her family into two, something she didn't want to consider. Besides, without her aboard, who would do the cooking, cleaning, shopping, sewing, and supervise the homeschooling?

On long walks in the Botanical Gardens, Dawn and Chuck discussed what they might do if the tumor were malignant. These walks reminded her of their early days walking hand in hand, when they would communicate through hand squeezes in Morse code. As parents of adolescents aboard a boat, they had few opportunities for time alone though neither was a romantic. She just hoped the tumor wasn't malignant, so she wouldn't have to face such a choice.

Now without insurance, she also worried how they would pay for her care. Though Australia had socialized medicine, they were visiting Americans. Her insides churned from the added stress and she worried herself through more nights of insomnia.

Through friends, the Wilcoxes met another sailing family who'd returned home to Australia after voyaging. The family had invited them to tea. To the Wilcoxes, tea meant sipping a hot beverage after dinner with cookies while listening to Radio Australia air one of a thousand renditions of "Waltzing Mathilda" or indulging Linda's love of Top Forty music on "Friendly 4BK" with Kasey Kasem's countdown of hits from ABBA, the Eagles, Olivia Newton-John, and an emerging Australian group called the Little River Band. Instead that Sunday, after a long drive past a grove of aromatic eucalyptus trees, the Wilcoxes discovered that, to their hosts, "tea" meant piklets and honey then a light supper of cold meat and salads. And no tea, after all. Knowing someone local meant that the family had a Nambour address to use on the health forms. Dawn hoped the local address would be sufficient to secure the free care she needed.

On the day of her scheduled surgery, Dawn put on a brave face and left for the hospital. Chuck assured her they'd be fine and even promised to bake bread while she was gone. Garth rowed her to shore and she rode the bus to the hospital alone. There was no sense wasting bus fare for the others to go, only to come right back.

Without Dawn aboard, everyone attempted to go on with their usual tasks and forget what was happening a few miles away and the uncertainty it entailed. While Linda worked on schoolwork, Garth sprung planking around the frame of his latest model boat. Chuck announced he would bake bread as promised. He soon grew frustrated as he tried to work the thick, floury mixture.

"This is really hard to stir," he said. "It's too dry." Garth and Linda looked up so see him add a little more water.

"That's not how Mom does it," Linda said in a warning voice.

"I don't think that's going to work," Garth confirmed, shaking his head.

Chuck shrugged and kept stirring, more easily folding in the flour now. "Don't worry. It'll be fine."

The yeasty smell soon filled the boat and hinted of future deliciousness. But it was fool's gold. When Chuck pulled the "bread" out of the oven, they saw the dough hadn't risen at all. At one-fourth the thickness of the usual "mom bread," it was as firm as a hardbound book. Garth knocked on it and smirked. "Humph."

It took Chuck ten minutes to pry it out of the bread pan. To prove it was edible, Chuck carved off a piece, popped it in his mouth and began to chew.

"See, it's fine," he said, pausing mid-chew to take a gulp of water. But he ingested only a single piece. The kids wouldn't touch it.

Chuck bicycled to the hospital to see his wife during limited visiting hours. He took along a stack of new letters he'd picked up from the post office on his way. With apprehension, he found his way to her bedside in a sort of enclosed porch. The large main room housed nearly forty beds in a large group of concentric circles around several dinky tables that formed a nurses' station. It seemed almost like a large, yet somber slumber party, with IV bags hovering above the beds.

Dawn's demeanor put him at ease. Her usual chipper self, she appeared unfazed. She regaled him with tales of her adventures since she'd seen him last, babbling about how she'd helped out by comforting patients, doing dishes and calling nurses' attention to empty IV bags. In a hushed voice, she whispered of the shocking shortcomings she'd noticed in the medical care. She sent Chuck home with the now-complete letter for her mother, including the update on her condition so her mother wouldn't have the chance to worry:

Later: Well it all turned out fine & it's not malignant, thank heavens. I went to the theater (no surgery here) about 10 and woke up back here (I never do get to see the recovery room) with a sore, dry throat from the air way, I imagine. Was very woozy and sort of nauseous till 6 or so. I'm sore but haven't needed any pain pills.

But Dawn didn't dwell long on herself. She launched into observations about the care.

I ate a regular diet for breakfast: curry rice and poridge [sic] and I was all set for eggs. No menus in a place like this and the chief sister (graduate nurse) dishes up the food from a heated cart they bring up. The students (called nurses) have to do the dishes in the evening. The place is run by a perfect top sargeant [sic] sister who bellows at the nurses and even at the patients. I've had fun talking to a Canadian sister here who thinks Australian nursing is archaic and we've compared notes. I'll be here a couple more days until they remove the drain. Lost 1/4 of me bosom and it looks like a half deflated balloon as the Canadian Nurse put it. As the Aussies say "She'll be right, mate."

On Saturday, the hospital released her—fortunately without requiring any payment.

An ingrained habit of self-sacrifice kept Dawn from dwelling on her problems, but on the bus ride back to the boat, the magnitude of what she'd been through began to seep into her consciousness. She became self-conscious of how the knit top she was wearing clung to her lopsided chest and called attention to where her missing breast had once been. She pushed the thought away and hugged her purse close.

When Dawn arrived back on the boat, she saw Chuck's attempt at bread. With a laugh she said, "I can see that you missed me." She picked up the "bread," walked to the cockpit and dropped it over the side. It sunk like a stone.

To Chuck and the kids, Dawn seemed to recover well from the incision. She told them that the time she spent in the hospital off her feet gave her foot a better chance to heal and that even her ulcer seemed better. Because Dawn often ignored her own needs, it was hard to be sure, but they took her word for it. The ulcer doctor had suggested "no more oceans," which wasn't a prescription she was likely to follow. When she refused to take barbiturates, he prescribed a mild dose of valium ("mother's little helper") to help make her worries less acute. Since it cost her nothing under the Australian healthcare system, she gave it a try.

As December approached, Christmas decorations pervaded every street and store that surrounded them—incongruous in the intense Brisbane summer heat, especially when Santa visited the Gardens by speedboat wearing nothing but a hat and a red Speedo, nearly hidden under his big belly.

But before the family could celebrate their delayed Thanksgiving, it was Chuck's turn for a health scare. After he had experienced acute intestinal discomfort, Dawn dragged Chuck to the Royal Brisbane Hospital outpatient clinic. There they sat in a crowded waiting room for two and a half hours without even a crusty, decade-old magazine to offer a diversion. With no clues as to whether they were making any progress in line, Chuck reached the end of his patience and marched out of the clinic, fuming. Dawn was nearly as mad at him as he was at the inefficiency of Australia's socialized medicine.

Two days later at four a.m., Chuck awoke with severe abdominal pains. A spooked Garth rowed his parents ashore in the darkness and helped his doubled-over father out of the dinghy.

As Garth rowed, he sensed the strain on his mother and the load that she alone bore. If they were to finish this voyage, she needed an ally. He vowed to fill that role. He wanted to finish this trip. Hopefully his father would be OK.

Dawn secured ten cents from one of the Aborigines hanging around the landing to call a taxi. She pushed Chuck into the back seat, and they zoomed to the hospital across the river.

At the Casualty Department service was quicker. After an X-ray—once the department opened at eight thirty—and three blood tests, the doctor scheduled a follow-up appointment and sent Chuck home. Uncertainty again cast a shadow over their plans. They worried he might have gallstones, which might require surgery, or hepatitis, though the symptoms and tests did not confirm their suspicions.

Tests continued through December and January but never proved anything. By Christmas, Chuck felt fine.

Over the next few months, while the family passed the cyclone season in Brisbane without any further issues, concerns about health faded.

Worry shifted to the cyclones that bore down on them.

• • •

Summer weather in Brisbane was strange, with two or three days of blisteringly hot, sunny weather and oppressive humidity, followed by three or four days of thick clouds and cold rain, with nights chilly enough to require a blanket. A pesky mosquito problem made life unpleasant despite the flypaper that hung from the overhead and the mosquito coils they burned every evening. And then there were the five-inch-long cockroaches that flew aboard on top of the infestation they already had.

Cockroach eggs had made their way aboard *Vela*, nestled inside cardboard packaging, and had transformed into a fleet with a scheduled nightly parade at midnight. Garth quickly learned that when getting a cup of water in the night, it was advisable to waste the first few drops of fresh water, lest they come with a surprise. It was a manifestation so entrenched that the beasts would not be easily deterred, but it wasn't for a lack of trying. Time and again Dawn would close all the hatches and detonate a bug bomb after everyone vacated. But in the moist tropical heat, it was a never-ending battle. No matter what they did, stowaways remained.

Flooding was a continual problem in the region. Roads washed away, leaving Brisbane completely cut off from the rest of the country. Goods became scarce, shelves emptied, and prices skyrocketed. With alarm, Dawn had already noticed a huge jump in prices and rushed to buy provisions before costs rose even more.

Hurricanes, or cyclones as the Aussies called them, brought heavy rain and high winds. This worried Chuck and Dawn. They'd heard about a flood in 1974 when several boats were wrecked because the pilings gave way—pilings like the ones *Vela* was tied to.

During a single week, a warbling siren warned of three separate hurricanes. Amid incessant rain and driving winds, the tea-colored river kept rising. The family was on high alert as the tide flowed out for four days, the river a turbid brown soup thick with clumps of bush, trees, and plastic foam floating past. Garth spent hours one day fending off trees that threatened to gouge the side of *Vela*. Another day Garth fished out a Styrofoam piece that he later crafted into a float for the man-overboard pole he was building. Cyclone Beth and Cyclone David posed the greatest threat, though Cyclone Dawn fizzled unimpressively.

Fortunately, despite torrential rains and flooding, nothing punctured *Vela*'s topsides and the pilings stayed put.

• • •

In response to Chuck's letters to the IRS explaining his inability to appear for a hearing, he received only forms. In January, a frustrated Chuck wrote to his parents:

> I think the IRS employs illiterate fools that have entirely too much power. I am not going to answer the last one they sent until I receive an answer to the other two as I think they are sending them out of order.

In early March, Chuck came down with a fever and the chills, accompanied by aches and pains. The family had been exposed to malaria, dengue and filarisis, so he returned to the hospital for tests. Any of those diseases from tropical parasites could pose a threat to their ability to carry on.

By the second week of March doctors concluded it wasn't malaria and conducted more tests. Again, nothing conclusive. Chuck eventually recovered and their plans to circumnavigate seemed safe once again.

In mid-March, they received a personal letter from the IRS, giving Dawn something new to worry about. Again, Chuck wrote the IRS a reply explaining the entire saga of the shipwreck.

• • •

Instead of doing schoolwork, Garth spent most of his time building things. For the model boat Garth was making, he was going to need a keel. When no one was looking he furtively pulled out one of the dive weights his parents had never used and stuffed it into his drawer. They wouldn't even notice it was missing. He just needed to round what would become the front and taper it aft so it would be hydro-dynamic.

One night, as the others were reading in their bunks, he grabbed a hammer and the dive weight with a plan to row ashore where he could pound it into shape. It was after dark, when he preferred to work after Brisbane's smothering heat had dissipated.

"Taking the garbage out," he said over his shoulder as he climbed the companionway ladder. It elicited no more than a distracted grunt from his mother. She was used to his midnight garbage runs by now.

Garth rowed into shore and pulled up to the ferry landing. At the dock he gave a nod to the Aborigines he recognized at their usual stoops, stuffed the garbage into a bin, and headed across the street where he could work on the pavement under the street light. At nine p.m., the streets were mostly deserted. The Botanical Gardens were officially closed. No one toiled at the nearby insurance agencies or government offices at that hour.

He pounded away at the soft metal, forcing it into shape.

Out of the corner of his eye, he saw a police car stop on their usual rounds to check on the local Aborigines. Garth kept working. *Whack, whack, whack.*

"What are you doing?" he heard and looked up. Heading toward him were two policemen, their hairy legs visible between knee-high socks and shorts. The blue and white checks on their official hats reminded him of the Purina Cat Chow logo. The steady tap of metal against metal must have drawn their attention.

"I'm shaping the keel for my model boat." The men looked at each other. On the hunt for nefarious activity, probably the last thing they expected to find at that hour was an industrious teenager boat-building on city streets.

"Where do you live?"

Garth pointed over to the closed botanical gardens. "On a boat in the river."

They stood there a moment, trying to decide what to make of this oddity. Befuddled, they couldn't come up with a law that he was breaking. They soon departed after, saying in thick Aussie accents, "It's late. You should be heading home."

•　•　•

The Wilcoxes aimed to end their dreary stay in Brisbane by the beginning of April. They scurried to complete tasks, like replacing expired medications and getting yellow-fever shots to protect against outbreaks in East Africa on top of repairs and provisioning.

They waited anxiously for a second shipment of charts and sailing directions they'd ordered to navigate them to Athens, Greece; their permit and boat clearance for Indonesia; and, as usual, the next set of school lessons.

Linda had capitalized on the long, boring layover in Brisbane by tripling her daily lessons. She was determined to catch up with Garth. By spring she was beginning ninth grade, way ahead of her peers at home and only a year behind her older brother. Garth made decent strides in math and science but lagged in anything that required writing. He would zoom through the reading portion of any assignment only to get stuck on a long history question like: *Explain in good paragraphs how China was invaded, conquered and exploited by Western powers.* Dawn thought the correspondence courses were overly demanding and bristled at the mailing delays, but concluded her kids were getting a better education than they might have at home. Plus they were experiencing the world directly rather than filtered through textbooks.

Except for health worries and the IRS hassles, their five-month stay in Brisbane was mostly forgettable except for: Dawn's stint as second clarinet with the Brisbane Citizen's Band using Linda's clarinet that she rescued from the reef; the koalas, kangaroos, and emus at the Lone Pine Sanctuary; and Australia's constitutional crisis, when, fifteen months after Nixon's resignation, they witnessed another democracy in crisis as the Queen's representative sacked the prime minister.

Once all the mail arrived, the Wilcoxes were free to sail on.

31

It was a relief to leave the muddy Brisbane River and begin working their way around the sizable continent of Australia. First they revisited the more yacht-friendly town of Mooloolaba for a brief haul-out, then nervously planned their approach to crossing Wide Bay Bar. The terror of Havannah Pass and the storm off Australia had not faded, and they consulted other sailors about timing their arrival there.

The Wilcoxes departed Mooloolaba in the evening of April 19, the first Monday after Easter. Garth stood on the bowsprit and picked out the buoys while Chuck steered in the dark. As soon as Garth and Dawn hoisted the sails, Linda and Dawn deflated the dinghy and dropped it down the forward hatch. By then they were in a swell from the famous Australian current, the start of a bouncy night. After so long parked in the Brisbane River, they were unused to the motion of the swell. Garth got seasick and Dawn helped with his watches until she too felt her insides churn. Luckily Chuck felt fine and navigated through the night.

Vela arrived off Double Island Point at sunrise as planned and aimed for the bar they had worried about for weeks. Chuck quickly spotted the buoys but waves crashed across the channel. *Here we go again*, Dawn thought. She clenched her teeth and made everyone wear life jackets. The new *Cruising the Coral Coast* guide, by Alan Lucas, indicated that channel markers could be incorrect if the sand shifted.

As Chuck wondered how to pass through safely, two fishing trawlers arrived to lead the way. Chuck figured these fishermen had crossed the bar dozens of times, so he followed them. Both vessels cut inside the range markers. Chuck hoped the water would be deep enough for *Vela's* keel. With the engine on full throttle and the sails drawing, *Vela* dodged breaking waves and surfed across the bar as fast as her tonnage allowed. When they didn't bump, Chuck relaxed. Inside, the strait offered flat water dotted with low islets and a complicated channel through mud and sand banks. They anchored in the afternoon at South White Cliffs, everyone exhausted after a long night.

Garth rowed the family toward the sandy island the next morning. As the dinghy reached the shore, Garth and Chuck hopped out to pull it the rest of the way into shore.

"Whoa!" Garth said, sinking in soft sand up to his knees. He looked up in surprise.

"This sand is like oatmeal!" Chuck said at almost the same moment, his legs disappearing into the beige surface. When he moved he sank even further. "Wait, don't get out of the dinghy!" Chuck shouted. "This is like quicksand." He went on, "Garth, don't move. It'll make it worse." He reached for the dinghy and pulled it closer. Then he hauled himself aboard. "Here, give me your hand," he told Garth, and pulled him into the boat.

"Maybe we should row around to the other side," Dawn said. Everyone nodded. When they landed on the other beach, they found firmer footing. Garth and Linda wanted to climb the ridge, but as they grabbed the boulders to pull themselves up the steep slope, the rocks crumbled into dust.

With Wide Bay Bar behind them, the family settled into a routine, trying to cover as many miles as they could, off by seven a.m. with the anchor down in the late afternoon. Sailing was usually pleasant but coastal navigation required careful attention. With reefs and obstacles nearby, they had to keep track of their position at all times, not just once a day as at sea. With the new hand-bearing compass purchased in Brisbane, Garth enjoyed triangulating subtle features on land to confirm their relative position. Even Linda began to enjoy sailing, given a better grasp of geography and interesting stops along the way. But they kept a brisk pace, which left little time for exploring.

For the next three months they were on the move. Sandclifts, Urangan, Gladstone, Seahill, Keppel Island, Percy Island, Scawfell Island, Goldsmith Island, Hook Island, Bowen, Townsville—each night a different stop.

Chuck tried to explain the accelerated pace to his father, who attempted to handle their mail.

We had to wait for Cyclone season to be over and that is why we left Brisbane the 1st of April. (Even at that, there was a cyclone after that while at Gladstone.) That, put together with high winds for 3 weeks at various places and the fact that to cross the Indian Ocean you should leave Darwin by the end of July and that you can't sail too much at night through the reefs, adds up to getting a move on when you can.

Their families back home grew frustrated with the many address changes and gaps in correspondence. The mail was chasing a perpetually moving target. Dawn tried to explain the predicament to her mother in a letter:

The reason you don't get many letters when we are island hopping is there are only 5 post offices in 1500 miles and the rest of the place is uninhabited.

The Wilcoxes did their best to forward mail to their next stop, but were irritated to discover the Australian postal service charged $1.50 to forward mail for a month for each location. With infrequent service between postal centers, the Wilcoxes worried about lost letters, packages and, most importantly school lessons. The family soon adopted a system of numbering packages so everyone would know if a letter or package were missing. That still didn't address the delays the mail posed to their sailing schedule.

Correspondence learning depended upon the postal service, and that required a juggling act between Dawn, Chuck's father and Erika, the administrative coordinator at University of California. The perpetually changing locations confused everyone. Calvert School, which had supplied everything needed for an entire year—down to pencils, rulers, erasers and even glue—had been so much easier. But Calvert's coursework only went through eighth grade. Now with Linda in ninth grade, her studies had graduated to the UC system along with Garth's, which doubled the complications and expense because high school-level courses were more complex and the standards stricter.

Garth and Linda needed to finish all their lessons before they reached Darwin so Dawn could arrange for someone official to proctor their final tests with sufficient time to order and have them arrive. A delay meant leaving Darwin too late for the best weather crossing the Indian Ocean.

Vela sailed north past sand bluffs and rocky promontories and countless low islands covered with grass, scrub, pine trees or fringed with mangroves. Some stops had towns with a few modest storefronts with sparse pickings and occasionally a post office. They subsidized their diet with fish they caught.

Vela traced Captain Cook's route, with the advantage of information about the dangerous reefs along the coast. They sailed past Endeavour Reef, where Cook's *Endeavour* grounded in 1770 and Cooktown, where his crew rebuilt *Endeavour*. Chuck imagined the burden Captain Cook had faced being shipwrecked in such a remote place. Despite the hardship of rebuilding *Vela*, the Wilcoxes had been remarkably lucky. At least they hadn't needed to cut down the trees first. Reading about Cook's misfortune as they passed these famous landmarks reminded them to be extra vigilant.

The sailing was pleasant and anchorages offered variety, but everyone grew weary of the pace. The family had to lay over a day now and then to rest and give Dawn a chance to do laundry by hand in a deep bucket, agitating with a plumber's helper. But because of the weather, layovers weren't always in places they preferred to linger. Often they were cooped up in the small cabin, anxious to either make progress or explore, but unable to do either. Tempers flared.

Life aboard in a cramped space with two teenagers was no treat. In a hot, confined space with strong personalities, they argued about everything, especially radio usage, music choices and chores. The family's practice of verbal banter could quickly descend into full-throated yelling matches. Chuck and Dawn tired of the family power struggles and the intense emotions of adolescence. Linda complained bitterly about not having privacy, TV, or running water, and being away from her friends. Now nearly thirteen, her emotions were volatile, as they often are with teenage girls, and it didn't take much to set her off.

After the shipwreck, *Vela* no longer had pressure water. Instead, the family lined water jugs on deck in the sun so they would get warm. When it came time to showering in port, they moved the jugs to the cabin top just above the shower and ran a hose down into the aft head under the cockpit. They used a siphon to start the water flowing from the jugs. That meant wasting water while lathering up, unless someone reprimed the water for the final rinse. Then Garth devised a bulkhead-mounted shut-off valve so that everyone could shut the siphon valve off without having to reprime it after lathering up. Motivated by a strong desire to avoid having to reprime mid-shower, they tried to limit themselves to the amount of water in the jugs. Linda wasn't as careful about water usage as the others, which annoyed Garth in particular since he lugged each and every jug of fresh water they consumed. When Linda ran out mid-shower she had several options: ask politely for someone to replace the empty jug with a full one and restart the siphon, beg/negotiate a trade, or wrap herself in a towel and do it herself. Yet there was another approach she employed … with mixed results.

"I'm out of water. Fill it up!" she would demand. While Garth had realized that he could get the others to give him what he wanted by convincing them why it was in their best interest, Linda tried to exert direct control to get them to bend to her will. In a family of strong-willed individuals, that approach often backfired, driving a wedge between them and hardening their position against her.

"I'm getting cold!" Linda yelled.

The others shared a pained look. Dawn, usually in the middle of meal preparation, would think, *here we go*.

"Garth…," Dawn would say, hoping to avoid the battle that might ensue. With a grimace came his reply.

"And why is this my problem?" After brushing his teeth with saltwater to save on fresh water, Garth wondered how Linda could get away with wasting so much water. "Why can't she do it herself like the rest of us?"

"Garth, just do it," Dawn urged. But it was too late. By that point, Linda had descended into a full temper tantrum, complaining bitterly at top volume how this was a form of torture because most normal people had running water. But no one was listening.

Getting off the boat offered a pressure release that helped ease the tension. Linda especially liked the towns, which gave her freedom to wander with the excuse that she was scouting for supplies and doing comparison shopping for her mother.

At Lizard Island, Chuck, Dawn and Linda took the dinghy over the reefs. They peered at giant clams and pale green, purple and branched corals from the safety of the dinghy—because a shark lurked on the other side of the bay and Linda was at that body-sensitive age when she was unwilling to wear a swim suit anyway. At Magnetic Island, the three hiked halfway around the island and spotted a peacock along the way. Garth skipped both shore trips. More frequently, he would choose to stay aboard when the rest of the family went exploring, just to get some time alone. One of those times Chuck, Dawn and Linda went shopping in Bowen in the pouring rain.

Bowen had been designed to become a large town with a sprawling grid system, but the bulk sugar loading on which it banked its fortunes went instead to Townsville. With a fraction of the people it was designed for, on a windy, blustery day Bowen appeared eerily abandoned. By the time the three of them returned to the dock burdened with their purchases, the tide had dropped significantly. When Chuck's six-foot-three frame reached the bottom rung of the ladder on the side of the dock, the dinghy was still a five-foot drop.

"Oh, this is going to be fun," Dawn said. She held the dinghy painter while Chuck dropped into the boat. As he hit the flexible dinghy floor, a cascade of water jetted from under the boat, which barreled away from the dock, ripping the line from Dawn's hand. Water dripped down her face as she fumbled to retrieve the line—still tied, fortunately—and pull the dinghy back in. Rain gushed down on the groceries that sat on the dock at Linda's feet.

"Hurry, I'm getting soaked," Linda said, rain streaming down the back of her neck.

Chuck recovered his balance and reached up to grab the ladder and steady the boat.

"OK, I've got it," he said. Linda handed the groceries down to Dawn and she handed them to Chuck. Then it was time for Dawn to get in.

Clinging to the slippery ladder, Dawn hesitated, knowing that she had to free-fall from the bottom rung. It would be a miracle if she didn't fall in or land on the groceries, she thought, but—miracle of miracles—she landed in the center of the boat, though not without creating a mini-tidal wave in the process. She leaned down to clear space for Linda, who dropped in with a bit more grace, and they rowed the two hundred yards back to *Vela*.

When the rest of his family arrived back on board with their clothes glued to their bodies and water dripping from their hair, Garth was glad he had chosen to stay behind.

On other days Garth would set off alone to prowl the beach or climb on the "mountain"—such as they called them in a flat country like Australia. For him life aboard offered a little too much togetherness, especially when the weather was poor.

High-wind warnings kept them in port for four days at Flinders Island around Linda's thirteenth birthday. Two trawlers ventured out one morning but returned within two hours, confirming the forecast though the landlocked bay appeared calm. Everyone was restless, but Linda was delighted that she got to stay put for her big day.

At ten a.m. on Linda's birthday, while Dawn was whipping eggs for Linda's celebratory cheesecake, the tugboat *Gulf Explorer* came in and yelled over to them, "Would you like some ice cream? Our freezer is broken." There was only one answer to that question.

• • •

With the Great Barrier Reef finally behind them, the Wilcoxes reached Thursday Island at the topmost point in Australia. In the bay were brightly painted pearl luggers with Melanesian crews who would sing as they cooked over wood coals at chest-high metal cookhouses on the aft deck and dive for pearls using old-fashioned hard helmets ventilated with an air hose.

To Dawn's horror, prices on Thursday Island were twice that of Brisbane. Stocking up would have to wait until Darwin, their last stop in Australia. From Thursday Island they planned to jump directly across the sizable Gulf of Carpentaria, an eight-to-ten day sail to Darwin.

Before they left port, everyone wrote letters home while they had postal service. Even Garth, who rarely picked up a pen. The family teased him about how he could turn a simple half-page letter into an all-day project or joke about how Grandma and Grandpa would faint upon receiving one of his annual-ten sentence works of art. He wrote:

Dear Grandma and Grandpa, I can't remember the last time I wrote a letter but it was probably in Brisbane. I have finished all my school work except the finals which I will take in Darwin. We had a fast trip up the reef compared to most people but it wasn't so fast if you consider that it would have taken about 18 days if we had sailed direct. My model sail boat (named Zubenelganubi after a star) sails well on most points of sail but the steering system has too much friction to work in low winds. I believe I have finally solved our dinghy problem. I designed a dory which is in two parts and bolts together. The aft part fits inside the forward part so we have a 15 foot boat that only takes 9 feet of the deck. It has 2 sets of oars, high free board and can be sailed. It should be able to take rough seas and would make a good life boat. It is built in one piece and then cut in half with 1/4" plywood bottom and sides. I don't think I can build it for a while because we never stay long enough in one place. I received 2 two dollar bills a while ago and gave one to Linda. Thank you very much. I always thought the US should have them. I don't want anything for my birthday. Love Garth.

In the margins, he sketched top and side views of his boat design.

Dawn, Chuck and Linda had graduated to drafting letters on the 1953 Royal typewriter they'd saved from the reef, discovering they could fit longer letters into less space which also were easier for everyone to read. For fun, Linda had taken to writing letters to family in Morse code, which she taught herself during many hours alone in Fiji. She even taught it to her cousin, Susie, so they could communicate in secret but was annoyed to discover that Susie had taught her brother, Doug. Linda enjoyed coding the mesing the replies. She began:

-. . .- .-. -.. .-. .-. -. -.. -- & -- .-. .-. -. -.. -- .- ,

(Dear Grandpa & Grandma,)

The Wilcoxes planned to depart for Darwin on June 22nd. While it hadn't been easy covering all that distance around the continent of Australia, they were on schedule to reach Darwin by July 1st as they had planned. They hoped they would have enough time to complete finals before their Australian visas ran out.

At the close of his letter that day to his parents, Chuck confided:

Will write again from Darwin if we make it there. I make no promises about anything anymore. Ever since the wreck I have lost most confidence in myself to do almost anything well. I have enough to start out on the trip but whether we make it there or not is not totally under my control.

32

The family dropped anchor on June 30th, shortly before Garth's sixteenth birthday and the 200th birthday of the United States. In honor of his birthday and the Bicentennial, Garth hoisted all the signal flags and the flags of the countries they'd visited so far on the voyage, while Linda put out the ensign. The festive look of the boat stood in marked contrast to the dust bowl that awaited them ashore.

Cyclone Tracy had rolled through Darwin during the Christmas of 1974, when the Wilcoxes were recovering from their own disaster in Fiji. Garth remembered a song he'd heard on the radio in Brisbane called "*Santa Never Made it into Darwin*," which told how on Christmas day a big wind came and blew the town away. The lyrics, while funny, weren't an exaggeration. The debris from Cyclone Tracy had recently been cleared, so while a street grid still existed, there were no trees and few buildings besides temporary structures. Flat barren land stretched for miles.

Garth rowed them into shore through a strong current and big waves. They tied the dinghy to the high stairway on the wharf with as long a painter as they could, remembering the experience in Bowen.

As they tromped inland, they noticed Aborigines, Italians, Greeks, Chinese, and a lot of hippies camping in the park and on the beach. In the year and a half since Cyclone Tracy, federal money had poured into Darwin, but evidently housing fell far short of the need.

The first priority, as usual, was to collect mail—hopefully some of the parcels that had been chasing them since Bowen. They needed to find the post office, or at least something that functioned as some sort of mail center. They located a likely prospect in the form of a temporary building with a long line snaking around the block. As the family joined the hordes shifting listlessly from one foot to another under a blazing afternoon sun, Dawn realized that, with no permanent address, half the town received mail via general delivery.

At just over twelve degrees from the equator, as soon as the morning breeze waned, Darwin would quickly grow unbearably hot though it was winter in the southern hemisphere. The idea of sleeping in the open under such conditions recalled their days on Makaluva.

Once they collected the mail, Dawn left the kids scheming how they might spend the two-dollar bills Grandma and Grandpa had sent. Dawn went in search of someone acceptable to UC standards to administer Garth and Linda's tests. She finally located the "Commissioner for the Northern Territories of the Commonwealth Teaching Service" and got him to agree to proctor the final exams. Given mail delays, it could take weeks for them to arrive. She returned to the unbearably long line at the post office to send away for the tests.

A second priority was to change the dates of their cruising permit for Bali, if they could. Dawn yearned to stop there, but realized shortly after she sent off their application in Brisbane, that to make it across the Indian Ocean during the right weather, *Vela* would need to reach Bali sooner than they'd thought. So she mailed off the information to Jakarta, hoping the revised clearance would arrive before they needed to cross the Indian Ocean in August. This began her hopeful daily visits to the post office.

Late in the day after their errands, the family returned to the wharf to find the dinghy hanging from its painter, nearly vertical. The tide had dropped twenty-seven feet!

"Humph," Dawn said, remembering the episode in Bowen.

"In the nick of time," Garth said with a laugh, realizing that only a few minutes later, the oars would have tumbled out.

The family hovered over letters and magazines from home telling of Bicentennial celebrations and disturbing reports of climbing inflation, taxes and interest rates. They were amused to learn that President Ford's solution was to issue WIN (Whip Inflation Now) buttons. Dawn read with horror about an incident in her tiny hometown of Chowchilla, California in which twenty-six schoolchildren were kidnapped from a school bus and held hostage underground. What was happening to the country they'd left behind?

Reports of tensions in the Middle East and East Africa renewed their apprehension about their chosen route through the Suez Canal. Their families raised questions about traveling through an area in turmoil. Dawn and Chuck's doubts prompted them to send for charts of South Africa, just in case. They decided to head for the Seychelles and make a final decision there, hoping to have more information by then.

Between visits to the post office to see whether the tests or the clearance for Bali had arrived, Linda studied diligently for her finals, while Garth tackled Michener's nine-hundred-page tome *Centennial* and began building a new model boat. Dawn worried as days passed and Garth showed no inclination to study.

They also took care of myriad last-minute details. The family dutifully stood still and gritted their teeth while their arms were injected with cholera, typhoid, and smallpox booster shots. They searched for supplies to restock the boat. One of the few businesses still flourishing was the Woolworth's department store—or Woolies, in Aussie-talk—perfect for buying staples to cross the Indian Ocean. Unfortunately in Darwin, fresh produce was exceptionally "dear."

Though Chuck's sister and brother-in-law had offered once again to let Linda live with them until the end of the voyage, Dawn and Chuck dismissed it out of hand. While it would allow her to return to the world of her peers, Linda was not interested in returning home alone.

After twenty nail-biting days, all but the last two tests arrived. Garth and Linda tromped into town to take a set each day. One week before they hoped to depart Darwin for they-weren't-sure-where, to Dawn's delight, along with the last two tests, came the clearance for Bali.

Weary of Australia's bigness and sameness, the Wilcoxes were more-than-ready to move on. On July 31, 1976, they bid farewell to the vast empty continent of crocodiles, koalas and kangaroos. Next stop, Bali.

33

After ten days of sailing, they arrived just off the south coast of Indonesia at Benoa just before sunset. They turned back out to sea to wait until daylight to make landfall. They sailed back and forth in an attempt to hold position, but in the morning they found the current had swept them forty miles.

Without wind to counter the current, they needed the engine to make headway. But the fuel pump wasn't working, so Chuck took it apart—twice—to get it operational again. Finally he got the engine started, and they worked their way back toward Benoa, fighting a strong easterly current most of the day. They worried that once again they would miss getting anchored before dark.

In the midafternoon, the horizon filled with dozens of multi-colored sails. What at first looked like a regatta turned out to be the fishing fleet's return after the day's catch. Lateen sails, with brilliant panels of blue, red, yellow, and green zipped back and forth behind them. Soon the brightly painted double outrigger canoes raced past them as though *Vela* were parked, though Chuck had the engine at full throttle. They watched with fascination as the fishermen expertly eased the sheet or hauled it in to respond to subtle shifts in the wind, or stood on the bow and pulled the rig around to change tacks. Though Dawn yearned to photograph the fishing fleet as they flashed past, safe navigation required her full attention. The sailing directions had described the entrance as "tricky."

As *Vela* neared the reef pass, a shape on the reef grew progressively more distinct. When Chuck recognized what it was, his confidence faltered. Wordlessly he stared at a yacht resting at an unnatural, hauntingly familiar angle. Memories of the hard-won battle back from the edge of disaster came flooding back. Chuck tightened his grip on the wheel.

Tide rips broke across the channel, sending white froth across their path. He could feel the pull of the current on the rudder. Sweat trickled down his back. His temple throbbed. From the ratlines, Garth scanned the water for reefs, but the hazy light obscured them. *If they could just stay in the channel...*

Dawn barely moved except for the nervous flicker of her eyes from the chart to the water to Chuck and back to the chart again. Her stomach was in knots once again as the minutes ticked by.

"OK, now you need to steer through the dogleg on a course of 027 degrees," she told Chuck. He made a nearly seventy-five-degree turn to starboard. Dawn ran the back of her hand over her forehead and it came away glistening.

Once through the hairy dogleg, the bay widened and she sighed heavily. Dawn's jaw ached and she realized her teeth had been clenched the entire time they'd been in the channel. Chuck took one hand off the wheel and massaged the tight muscles at the back of his neck.

Next, they had to figure out where to anchor. The charts showed Benoa to the left, but Chuck spotted several masts ahead to the right and continued straight toward the other boats. Just then a Balinese male pulled alongside and hopped aboard *Vela* with a quick leap. Within a second he pushed his canoe away with his bare toe and paid out the line connected to his boat like a leash. It slipped gracefully behind them and stopped just behind *Vela*'s stern wave. The canoe skipped along behind *Vela* like a loyal puppy.

"You anchor there," the man said, pointing over toward the other yachts. He shielded his eyes with his hand as he peered at Chuck. Chuck nodded, wondering who he was.

"I am Mardi," he said, smiling and extending his hand. His dark eyes danced with merriment.

"Hello," Dawn said, intrigued. She reached out and gave his hand an awkward shake. Everyone looked at this elfin boy-man, not quite sure what to make of him but disarmed by his friendliness.

"You need laundry, fuel, trips... I help you," he said, nodding with an air of satisfaction. They'd heard about "boat boys" from other sailors. Mardi explained that the village of Benoa was just a fishing village and said they needed to take a mini-bus to Denpasar to clear in and to shop. He answered a few questions about clearing in, but after a couple minutes he moved toward the rail and began to pull in the line that brought his boat skipping alongside.

"You anchor. Whatever you need, you tell me. OK?" The Wilcoxes nodded, knowing it was unlikely. He was very nice, but they had no extra money and only planned to stay a few days. Dawn dismissed the thought.

"How do you say thank you?" Dawn asked him.

"Terima Kaski," Mardi said with a gracious nod.

"Terma Keska," Dawn said back to him. Mardi smiled and shrugged, unwilling to belabor the difference. Within seconds he was back aboard his canoe as deftly as he'd come. The late afternoon sun glistened off the water as he waved and paddled away.

The Wilcoxes continued into the anchorage, glad to see other yachts. They motored to a spot with adequate swinging room and dropped the anchor. The gear shifter wouldn't shift the engine into reverse, so they couldn't set the anchor as they normally would. When Chuck investigated, he found that all the hydraulic fluid had leaked. Another project for the list.

The next morning, Chuck set off to clear into the country, making sure he wore long pants and socks despite the intense tropical heat. Fellow cruisers had informed him that unless he did, he would be unlikely to have a positive interaction with the officials. Given the rumors he'd heard, he didn't have a good feeling about it in any case.

The rest of the family were eager to explore. For seventy-five *rupiahs* (about fifteen cents), which they borrowed from a fellow cruiser, Dawn, Garth and Linda boarded a jitney bound for Denpasar, eight miles away. They sped past a village of grass huts surrounded by rice paddies, frangipani, bougainvillea and other lush tropical vegetation. Reaching the outskirts of this crowded Indonesian city brought immediate sensory overload. After nearly eleven days at sea, months in the expansiveness of Australia and the years before that in tranquil Pacific islands, they were unprepared for the frenzied energy of this Southeast Asian city.

Outside the windows horns blared as hundreds of bikes, motorcycles, pony carts, and man-pulled carts zigzagged across their path. Given the chaos, Dawn was amazed no one was killed in the first ten minutes. They zoomed past temples, statues of Hindu gods with obligatory offerings, and women carrying huge loads on their heads, some while riding a bicycle. They were fascinated. It seemed like a scene from *National Geographic* in motion. Garth's eyes grew wide, trying to take it all in. Indonesian flags flapped atop buildings. Army officials with firearms strutted in the streets, an unsettling presence they'd never experienced.

When they stepped out of the jitney, the three stood stunned by the whirl of activity, a sudden riot of color, noise and motion. The streets pulsated with energy. Peddlers rang bells to capture the attention of shoppers but couldn't be heard over the rock 'n' roll blaring at full volume from the Chinese stores. Dawn put her finger in her ears to dampen the noise, but the thud of bass reverberated through her bones. Even Linda, a keen fan of Top Forty, found it jarring at a thousand decibels. The odors of engine exhaust, rotting garbage, excrement and sweat assaulted their noses and masked the more subtle scent of spices.

They found a bank to change Australian dollars into rupiahs, then searched for a post office to spend it. Garth spent most of his birthday money in Darwin on materials for his model boat and a copy of the Ayn

Rand novel *Atlas Shrugged*, but Linda saved most of hers to buy stamps for her collection. They finally found the post office hidden behind a huge truck. While a frustrated Linda had to yell her stamp selections through the window to be heard over the chaos around them, Dawn anxiously waited in line behind her. She hoped a letter from her mother might be waiting, though she'd discouraged family from sending mail (or at least anything important) to the uncertainty of Bali's postal system. After a quick transaction a smiling Dawn stepped away from the counter and tucked two letters into her purse along with the newly purchased stamps, and they went in search of fresh produce.

A vendor chased them down the street with an ugly wooden carving of a duck-herding fisherman. None of them were interested, but the man was persistent, dropping his prices as they continued to walk away. At a thousand rupiah, Dawn leaned over to Garth and whispered, "You know, that's only two dollars. I think I'll buy it." Garth shrugged. Dawn handed the man the money and nestled the carving inside her purse alongside the letters and stamps.

A pungent whiff of durian—SE Asia's notoriously stinky fruit—led them to the fresh market. Dawn had balked at the high prices of fruit in Darwin and was eager to replenish their supplies. Overwhelmed by the heat, noise, grime, and stench of exhaust, and possibly the durian, Linda felt faint. While Dawn and Garth made a few quick purchases, Linda found a place to rest near a creek. Stunned by filth and an aggressive odor of decay, she soon realized the locals dumped their garbage there. She was eager to retreat to the boat as soon as Dawn and Garth emerged with a stalk of bananas, green tomatoes and four mangosteen.

Dawn anticipated dining out that evening at the little restaurant on the wharf where fellow sailors said they could get dinner for one hundred rupiah, or about twenty cents. At that price, it made no sense to eat their more expensive provisions aboard. A night's rest from cooking and having someone wait upon her sounded heavenly. She could hardly wait.

When they arrived back at the boat, Chuck was fuming. In Australia, Dawn had written in advance to find out the requirements for visiting.

The Indonesian Consulate informed them they would only need visas if their stay didn't exceed five days, but when Chuck reached the offices, he discovered otherwise. It made his blood boil.

"They demanded seventy-nine hundred rupiah for visas and thirty-four hundred for harbor fees." The veins in his neck bulged as he shared the irritating news. "They told me if I didn't pay they'd put me in jail and I'd have to go to court." Dawn realized then that the budget for souvenirs and gifts had just vanished.

"They're a bunch of thieves, just like people warned." Chuck grew even more peeved at the thought. Little angered him more than feeling ripped off. He'd been reluctant to sail here. Now Dawn felt bad that she'd insisted. "And I have to go back to Immigration tomorrow." Eventually he calmed down, and just as darkness fell, they rowed ashore for dinner.

At Casi restaurant that night, the single table was mostly full, so Dawn and Linda squeezed in as best they could while Garth and Chuck perched on a log. Of the three dishes—all made with turtle meat—Dawn chose the Nasi Goreng and savored its complex flavor.

Relaxing in the company of fellow sailors after finishing their meal, they gleaned information about their planned stops. The Wilcoxes were relieved to learn of other yachts that wanted to traverse through the Suez Canal—half via Christmas Island, Cocos Keeling and the Seychelles, and half north via India.

During a lull in the conversation, Dawn noticed the cook fill a bucket with filthy harbor water and begin "cleaning" the dishes. No soap, no rinsing. She nudged Chuck and said quietly, "We're not eating here again."

They were lucky. Fellow sailors did, with predictable results.

• • •

At four a.m. on Friday the 13th, the second day after their arrival, Garth awoke with a sensation that the boat's motion had changed. The rhythmical shift back and forth was odd, almost as though *Vela* were underway.

He got up and went to the companionway. He could see the distant lights of the town, but not where he expected to see them. It wasn't as though the boat had swung around the anchor. They seemed farther away than they had been.

"Something's wrong," he said. In an instant, everyone was awake. Chuck and Dawn rushed to the cockpit and peered into the darkness. Where were the anchor lights of the other boats? They could hear the sound of water lapping against the hull. There was no hint of breeze, yet shadows slipped past.

"It seems like we're moving." Garth said aloud what they were all thinking.

"We must have dragged anchor," Chuck confirmed. "But where are we?"

They squinted into the shadows, trying to decipher shapes that would offer clues. The faint glow of town seemed masked by something in the foreground. A sliver of moon sent a rippled reflection across the surface of the water, offering another point of reference. As their eyes adjusted, a faint silhouette caught Chuck's attention. Its bulk perplexed him before he remembered the boat wreck they'd seen on the way in.

"Look," Chuck said pointing. "There's that wreck."

"Oh dear," Dawn said. They all realized what that meant.

"We dragged out the pass!" Chuck exclaimed in wonderment. "Unbelievable!" He winced, thinking of the reefs they'd missed while they slept, oblivious. Somehow the current had swept them through the dogleg. And yet *Vela* remained intact, untouched. For a second they sat in stunned silence. Then Chuck started the engine.

"Let's see if we can reanchor," he said, then shouted below. "Linda, we're going to need your help." Chuck hadn't fixed the transmission yet—too busy clearing into the country. At least the engine was stuck in forward gear.

Garth and Dawn went forward to see about the anchor. It still seemed attached, though not performing any useful duty. Dawn and Garth hauled in the anchor and chain so it wouldn't snag anything on their way back into the bay, while Chuck had Linda get him a wrench so they could work around the gear-shifter problem.

Chuck slowly drove them back through the channel against a notable current, trying to simulate what they'd done two days earlier. A brightening sky helped make landmarks more distinct as they reached the trickiest part. He could hardly believe they'd dragged through the pass without hitting anything. Once through, he steered for the mast lights, grateful he could still see them.

When they reached the mooring area, Garth and Dawn dropped the anchor again, as Chuck and Linda double-teamed to simulate a fully functioning engine: Chuck had Linda turn off the engine, then he shifted gears using a wrench and had her restart it in reverse so they could back down on the anchor. This time, they hoped the anchor would hold.

They went back to bed, trying to forget how close they'd just come to another disaster.

After breakfast, Dawn and Linda returned to the delights of town while Chuck resumed his attempt to clear into the country. Garth offered to look after the boat and make sure it didn't go on "walkabout," as they would say in Australia. He was glad for a day to himself.

Boarding the mini-bus, Linda and Dawn were again astounded by the noise and mayhem. They headed straight for the food market for a more thorough shopping. As soon as they ducked inside the dim cavernous space, two girls offered in excellent English to guide them and carry their packages—on their heads. Despite Dawn's best efforts to shake them, the girls wouldn't go away. So Dawn let them lead her to vendors for the items they needed. Though she suspected she was paying more, the girls helped them find what they needed.

As soon as the girls vanished, clutching the seventy-five rupiah tip that Dawn had been strong-armed into giving them, Dawn suggested Linda watch the bags at the entrance while she did a tad more shopping. From the steps, Linda watched people and vehicles scurrying about like ants, women balancing impressive loads on their towel-cushioned heads, toothless old women chewing betelnut and spitting a bloody red goo onto the street, women laying concrete, a dizzying flurry. Meanwhile, Dawn deftly made her way through the maze of alleyways past stacks of papayas, yams, green beans, tomatoes, mangosteens and eggs. She bolstered her supplies of fresh produce, then chose between gray, pink, short- and long-grained rice to buy enough staples to get them to the Seychelles.

With their most important errand completed, Dawn and Linda went in search of a carving shop where Linda could buy a souvenir with the rest of her birthday money. Finding an overwhelming selection of choices, Linda stood paralyzed with indecision until she finally settled on a carved wooden gong and a seahorse pendant made of turtle shell. After one last adrenaline-charged jitney tour through snarled traffic, they returned to the tranquility of the boat.

On August 15th, four days after their arrival, *Vela* departed Bali for Christmas Island in the company of two other sailboats. Chuck couldn't wait to leave. Of the four days they'd spent in Bali, he'd spent three of them clearing into and out of the country.

When Chuck sought final clearance, the official failed to ask for the rest of the fee. He wasn't about to call the man's attention to it. Still, by the time the family sailed out of the harbor, Chuck felt like a fleeing fugitive.

34

On the third anniversary of their voyage, after five days at sea, the Wilcoxes spotted Christmas Island jutting abruptly from the ocean. An Australian possession, the island was nothing more than a company outpost tasked with mining phosphate.

By the time Christmas Island interrupted the horizon, the family was in desperate need of variety in their diet after days of eating little besides mackerel; a fishing bonanza produced what they called a "seven-day" Spanish mackerel because it offered enough protein to satisfy four people, three meals a day for seven days. Everyone hoped they could buy fresh beef from the company store.

It certainly wasn't beauty that made it a pleasant stop. Between the phosphate wharf on the Eastern side, the block houses on the south side and the stripped gashes of the mines that resembled open wounds, it was downright ugly. Nor was it an ideal anchorage.

As the sun neared the horizon, they dropped the hook in Flying Fish Cove, below steep cliffs in what turned out to be an uncomfortable shallow exposed to ocean swell. The fourth attempt to set the anchor finally proved successful. (And a good thing, too. A Japanese boat dragged onto the reef that very night, bending its rudder. Fortunately its crew was able to maneuver the boat off the reef before it wrought any further damage, but it was another reminder how easy it would be to hit another reef.)

Too late to check in that evening, the family settled in for dinner—fish again, of course. Curry this time.

"What's phosphate?" Linda asked, between forkfuls.

"Well, it's made from fish and it's flown in fresh every day," Garth explained with a wry smile. His eyes twinkled with mischief.

"Every day? Here?" She was incredulous. When she looked over at her parents, her grinning father gave a confirming nod.

"Yeah," her mother said, with a look of delight on her face, "indeed it is." The chuckles that followed made Linda even more suspicious of her brother—not someone she was inclined to trust in any case. She had the feeling she was being had, but no one said another word about it.

It didn't take her long to figure it out.

After dinner the family heard their arrival announced on the local radio station. "And today we have *Vela* joining us from the USA, which makes fourteen boats—a record." This was just the first hint of the warm welcome that would make their brief stay memorable.

Venturing ashore the next morning, the family picked their way among brightly painted outrigger canoes lining the rocky beach as they pulled the dinghy up.

"Hello! You can bring your dinghy to the yacht club if you want," someone called to them, pointing at a modest pontoon where dinghies were tied up beneath a small building. In front was a large patio filled with plastic deck chairs and tables.

On the horizon, minarets blared a mildly musical chant, a call to prayer. This was their first experience of the Muslim faith, which gave the place a unique flavor that distinguished it from other Australian territories.

Once a policeman stamped their passports, he offered them a ride in his van to the company store, where they could buy subsidized produce and meat. During their brief drive around the tiny island, everyone waved or said hello, lending the place a country-club-like atmosphere, where Australian overlords supervised Malaysian, Chinese and Indian workers. In front of the block houses, Dawn noticed large round pans of pink, blue, green and red disks—what looked like colored potato chips drying in the sun. She learned it was a form of fish paste, made from dry fish, flour and baking soda with food coloring, that the Malays ate raw or cooked in oil.

After requisite stops at the store and the post office—where, to their delight, Garth and Linda could buy Christmas Island stamps with their leftover Aussie dollars—they ventured to the yacht club. There they found a lively gathering place for three hundred Aussies and visiting yachts from all over the world. In this friendly outpost, the Wilcoxes met more Aussies than in six months touring Australia. Clearly local company managers looked to the sailors to bring the variety the island sorely lacked. That evening the yacht club hosted a barbecue for twenty-one visiting sailors featuring all the steak, sausages and salad they could eat along with a potent punch of hard liquor and wine to drink.

During their visit, the Wilcoxes had the opportunity to see two movies the club showed for free. First they saw *The Taming of the Shrew* with Elizabeth Taylor and Richard Burton at the height of their torrid love affair. It was the Wilcoxes' first movie in a year and a half, since they'd seen *Dove* in Fiji under very different circumstances.

The next day, the club showed the thriller *The French Connection II*. After a quick dinner aboard, the family paddled ashore and tromped up two hundred steps to the club to watch Gene Hackman and Roy Scheider play two rough NYPD narcotics cops on the trail of a drug-smuggling ring. In the dark, while watching the flickering image of a needle injecting heroin, Dawn saw Garth go limp. Perhaps it had been the punch—Dawn couldn't be sure—though he'd never been fond of needles. An empty Coke can dropped from his hand and bounced and rattled its way to the front. Garth revived within a second or two and no one else even noticed, because people in front of them were howling for a doctor for a woman who'd fainted in the first row.

Relaxed hours at the yacht club in the company of people from around the world overshadowed the challenges of sailing, for the moment. Dawn mused that she'd just shared dinner with Belgians, Australians, Canadians, and even Japanese, albeit with some pantomime involved. Aussie expatriates who lived on Christmas Island offered to help Chuck find a part to fix the leaking hydraulic system, and to help them obtain propane. Unfortunately, while the spirit was willing, the result was somewhat disappointing. The hydraulic part failed, but they did manage to get propane—at least enough to get them partway to the Seychelles. The discounts and selection at the company store and plentiful supplies of water let them stock up and tackle eight loads of laundry before they carried on ever westward.

On the bulletin board at the yacht club, Chuck noticed a posting from the boat *Galadril* about their experience traversing the Red Sea. Though it reassured them that another boat had chosen that route, it offered little in the way of concrete information. Anyone sailing around the world in that era was a pioneer, and on that route, even more.

Inside the eighteen bags of mail that came by ship—luckily just before their departure—were several letters for the Wilcoxes. *Imagine, two movies and dinner out, all within three days. We'll have to go to sea to rest*, Dawn jotted to her mother before she mailed English and math tests for Linda and two science lessons for Garth.

Soon after, they set sail for Cocos Keeling.

Six days later, as winds climbed to forty knots and rain lashed at the port lights, they reached Cocos Keeling, another Australian territory, 1,600 miles west of Darwin. Though they arrived amid rain squalls, they had just enough visibility to navigate. *Vela* tucked in behind the uninhabited Direction Island, where there would be protection from the ocean swell.

Unlike the steep rocky shores of Christmas Island, Cocos Keeling was a classic atoll that reminded them of Suwarrow, where they'd met Tom Neale, with low, flat sandy shores and sparse palm trees. Despite gloomy skies, the atoll offered a picturesque lagoon with scattered islands around a reef, and crystal clear water with various colors of blue, green and brown according to depth.

Over the next couple of days in squally weather, they all tackled projects aboard: laundry, fixing the Groco head (again), and patching the cockpit cushions because the Fijian fabric had begun to rot. Eventually a Customs man and his wife paddled out to clear them in. For another day they socialized with fellow sailors, bemoaning the fact that the weather wouldn't cooperate for a visit to West Island (the main island) six miles away, where they hoped to retrieve mail and food supplies before leaving.

Eventually the wind eased, but only marginally. Intent on sending off completed school assignments so they wouldn't get wet or lost, the family decided to take *Vela* over. Andy and Elaine from the boat *Rendezvous* joined their expedition.

When *Vela* reached the poor anchorage off West Island, she was pitching and heaving. Chuck decided to stay with *Vela* while everyone else went ashore. That turned out to be a wise decision, since the snubber line broke away from the anchor chain soon after, sending alarming shudders reverberating through the hull until Chuck fixed it.

The rest of them piled into the motorized dinghy from *Rendezvous* and headed for shore. To Garth the dinghy motor appeared to be on its last legs, refusing to run for more than a few minutes before dying. It could only be restarted when someone held a wire to connect the spark plugs—a job that involved regularly getting shocked. As they slowly made their way in, waves frequently swept over them. So much for keeping the schoolwork dry. By the time they reached shore, the dinghy was sitting precariously low in the water and everyone was drenched.

On land the party met the Customs official and begged a ride the four miles into the settlement. He reluctantly agreed and then dropped them off on the empty streets, telling them that everything was closed for the next hour and a half. They'd just have to wait. And so with time to kill, they took in all the sights—the hospital, the ten-foot-by-fifteen-foot store and the post office—through the windows. That took about five minutes.

Unlike the overwhelming friendliness of Christmas Island, no one here smiled nor paid them any attention. Eventually Garth and Linda found a ball to play catch, then rode a teeter-totter in a small playground across from the PO. Finally the store reopened and charged them 150 percent of the regularly marked prices. Fortunately at the post office they mailed off their completed lessons, collected a few letters, and spent the last of their Australian money to buy all twelve Cocos Keeling stamps for their collection.

They headed back toward the dinghy, cutting through a coconut plantation where they were swarmed by locusts. They tried to flag down several passing vehicles but none would slow down. After about two miles of hiking, with sweat dripping down their backs, they forced a Shell oil truck to stop by standing in the middle of the road. Dawn and Elaine hopped in the cab. Everyone else climbed on top of the enormous yellow tank and tried to hang onto the slippery dome as palm fronds overhead threatened to sweep them off.

The blustery return trip by dinghy to *Vela* was no better. When the motor quit and refused to start again, Dawn paddled, while Linda bailed. By the time they reached *Vela*, the expensive groceries were soaked and Garth had lost his shoes.

35

Two days later, on September 8th, they bade goodbye to their friends on *Halcyon* and *Rendezvous*, two boats they'd traveled with since Bali. These boats were heading to South Africa via Mauritius while the Wilcoxes were bound for the Seychelles off the west coast of Kenya and Tanzania. If they were lucky they'd all meet again in Panama. But they knew better than anyone that anything could happen.

The Wilcoxes warned their families not to expect to hear from them for twenty-six days or more, depending on the winds. When they raised the anchor, they were leaving the sphere of Australia's influence. Their next landfall would be oriented toward Africa, a whole different world they knew little about. Also they were facing the wildly unpredictable weather of the Indian Ocean. Still they were unprepared for its volatility and oddities.

Two days out of Cocos Keeling, Dawn could barely stay on the bunk for all the rolling. An exhausted Linda climbed down from the upper bunk, where the motion was worse, and laid her cushions on the floor. It became a favorite sleeping spot. Heavy shipping traffic traversing between Southeast Asia and South Africa rumbled past, keeping them on edge.

Within a week of leaving Cocos Keeling, the metal brace that supported the spreaders failed and the spreaders worked loose, yawing back and forth in the sloppy waves. With them flailing, Chuck worried about losing the rig. *Vela* would be a long way from anywhere if the rig were to fail in this patch of ocean. They had to do something before it was too late.

During the passage from Bali to Christmas Island, Chuck had appointed sixteen-year-old Garth the official "sail master." In case there had been any question before. This made him responsible for selecting the sail combination and put him first in line for repairing both the fixed and running rigging. And so Garth ventured up the rig with a clamp in hand, but the motion was so jarring he could barely hang on. Frustrated but determined, he had another idea. He rigged up a halyard to pull the spreaders up and another line pulling them down to counterbalance. It seemed to work to hold the spreaders stable, though no one knew how long it might last.

Then the alternator stopped working, so they couldn't charge the batteries. To save electricity they used only the kerosene lantern, which everyone complained was "hardly enough to see by and hotter than Hades." It was always something.

Because she didn't have enough propane, Dawn was now cooking on the Primus single-burner kerosene "stove." Just like on Makaluva, but without the blowing sand. Chuck had bought the Primus as a backup, in case propane wasn't available. She was glad to have it, but hoped the situation was temporary. Trying to concoct a meal to satisfy four people on a single burner was a chore. Plus it was safety-wired to the top of the stove, which meant it stood a foot high off the stove. She had to hold onto pots to keep them from flying off the burner, and bread steamed in a pressure cooker just didn't quite work.

She cooked fish, fish and more fish to save on provisions whenever they could catch something. If the *Vela* fisheries caught a thirty-pound fish instead of a more manageably sized ten-pounder, so be it. But it meant fish until no one could bear another bite.

Days passed slowly. Frigate birds circled lazily overhead. Dolphins surfed in their bow wave and sometimes leapt out of the water like Flipper. Clouds heavy with moisture felt oppressive and depressing. Incessant rain poured down on them for days on end, heavy drops stinging their skin like a malevolent assault. In the ship's log they noted the days *without* rain rather than the ones *with* rain. The despised yellow rain suits spent more time on their bodies than off. Their clothes steamed beneath the rubberized fabric as the temperature rose, but instantly grew cold and damp as the air chilled with the coming of another squall line. The pungent odor of mildew permeated everything. On September 19th, the second anniversary of hitting the reef, in the log book Dawn wrote, *Continuing yuk.*

They were grateful for the occasional luminous starlit nights. On those days, they could see the summer, autumn and winter constellations shift as the night wore on, and watch Jupiter chase Pegasus, followed by Taurus and Orion. But overcast skies hid the stars from view more often than not, and taking sights to calculate their position proved difficult. Lightning often accompanied the rain, sudden and intense, with daggers of current stabbing the sea around them. The peculiar weather made Dawn uneasy.

Their days were absorbed by the demands of the sea—keeping watch, eating, sleeping, making repairs, taking sights and calculating their position. They were hardly different from those of early sailors. Nothing but sky and water; stars or squalls to mark the days; the struggle to employ their wits against the elements. Their world grew small and insular, unaffected by anything beyond what they could see. The Voice of America and BBC were the only hints of a world beyond. Debates about the weak economy and "stagflation" between the candidates for the U.S. presidency—hopeful candidate Mr. James Carter vs. the sitting president, Gerald Ford (whose presidency they'd never experienced)—were the only reminder that they were a middle-class American family. Or at least had been. Their old world seemed a million miles away now.

By this point they were nearly halfway around the earth. The long slow months in Hawaii, Fiji and Australia were a phenomenon of the past. By the time the family reached Darwin two months shy of their third anniversary sailing, they'd covered only seven time zones. Yet within the next twelve months they expected to traverse another nine. With little time in any one place, it was easy to feel detached from any world other than the one that required their wits for survival. Their lives were more impacted by eye-stinging rain and clouds that made navigation more difficult, wind that would whip the water into a froth, UV and the motion that tore at the sails and jostled the precariously supported rig.

On September 22, 1976, they learned that newly independent Seychelles—their intended destination—had just been accepted as the 145th member of the United Nations.

On September 28th, the night sky erupted in violent flashes of lightning and thunder that vibrated through their bones. Lightning displays, little more than a visual marvel back home, posed a scary threat when you were the tallest thing around for thousands of miles. Alone on watch, Garth was careful to avoid touching anything metal as electrical current pulsated through the air around him. Flashes of light punctuated the darkness, briefly connecting the sky to the horizon in an eerie fashion reminiscent of horror film clips, those ominous moments when thunderous music sounds as the hero proceeds unsuspectingly to his demise.

A loud crackle made him jump. A mysterious sound of hissing and an odd glow drew his attention up the mast. What he saw there set him on edge. Heat rushed to his face and his heart rate jumped. *Fire!*

"Dad!" he shouted.

Within seconds both his father and mother were in the cockpit alongside him peering up at the mast. Dawn took in a sharp breath as her eyes took in this otherworldly glow. Chuck said nothing, his gaze still directed upward.

"The mast is on fire!" she said. With a hint of doubt in her voice, she added, "It couldn't be, could it?"

"Sure looks like it!" Garth said. Chuck squinted at it another second or two. He'd read about this—in *Bowditch*, maybe. He tried to remember what it was called.

"St. Elmo's Fire?" Garth said, looking at his father for confirmation.

"Yeah, that's what I was thinking," Chuck said.

"What's that?" Dawn peered at him through her glasses, which sat a little cockeyed from her rush to get them on as she hurried to the cockpit.

"Huh,... amazing," Chuck said, shaking his head.

"What's St. Elmo's Fire?" Dawn repeated her question. Garth looked to his father to explain.

"A phenomenon caused by static electricity." Dawn waited for more detail, but he said nothing more. His brain was already muddling over what this might mean for their electrical system. Just when Chuck thought he had a handle on things, it seemed there was a new perplexing challenge. Some considered St. Elmo's Fire a precursor to getting struck. The rig was grounded to the keel and there was nothing they could do about it at the moment. He just had to hope that everything electrical would be spared. Their lives weren't in danger as far as he knew, but it was still unsettling. It seemed odd to just go back to bed, but what else could they do?

Garth wasn't quite sure what to make of this. The strange fire vanished as quickly as it had appeared. When his father relieved him at the end of his watch, they talked about it, glad to confirm they hadn't just imagined it.

At midnight about twenty-four hours later, when Garth relieved Dawn on watch, though the sky overhead was black, the sea around them had turned a milky white. Directly beneath *Vela* the water surface appeared unnaturally smooth and flat while surrounding them were tide rips that usually didn't bring good news.

"Not another reef!" Garth rushed forward and yanked down the sails as fast as he could. Dawn called down to Chuck, "You should come up here. Uh, I think we have a problem."

Chuck ran up to the cockpit. It appeared as though *Vela* was lit from below by a neon light and floating in a sea of glowing green milk. The surrounding water boiled like soup in a cauldron. So odd.

It didn't make any sense. They still were more than three hundred and thirty miles from the Seychelles. The chart indicated water thousands of feet deep for hundreds of miles in every direction. Could it be an unmarked shoal? Or a newly forming island? Such things did occur in areas of underwater volcanic activity. Charts of the Indian Ocean were not known to be detailed or accurate. Soundings were widely dispersed and extrapolated from limited data.

Without wind on the sails, *Vela* slowed and began to drift. Dawn sighed. She'd grown tired of daily emergencies. At least she wasn't bearing the full weight of this mystery on her shoulders.

"Maybe we should take some soundings," Chuck said, unsure what to do.

Garth grabbed the lead line, untied it and hurled it forward as he had so many times. The lead line was simple and reliable. Between him and his mother they had it down to a science: Garth would fling the line, measuring its length once it stopped paying out, with Dawn relaying information back to the helmsman and helping Garth recoil it for another throw. Usually a steady *plunk* of the lead would be followed by the sound of water droplets running off the line as Garth hauled it in, using his wingspan to "guesstimate" its length before recoiling the line for the next check. This time the line ran all the way to its end, but didn't stop. He coiled it and hurled it again. Same result. Nothing. They tied a number of other lines to it to lengthen its reach. Still nothing.

"I'm not finding any bottom," Garth said, looking at his father. With the weather so still, there was no need for Dawn to relay.

"Well, that's what I'd expect to find here, but I don't like the look of this water." Such an odd color in the middle of the ocean.

"It sure looks like a shoal," Dawn said, nodding.

"Or some kind of silty river runoff, though obviously there aren't any rivers here."

Chuck ran his hand over the bristly gray multi-day growth on his chin, his fingers making a rasping sound as though striking the surface of sandpaper. Linda would joke that when he didn't shave he looked like the old man of the sea, which gave him incentive to shave even when he didn't feel like doing it.

He didn't know what to make of this boiling, discolored water. Maybe all they were seeing were temperature differentials that created this sort of upwelling, combined with bioluminescence. The family had seen amazing light shows of bioluminescence—trails of light dancing behind their rudder on many occasions or streaks of white made by dolphins or fish as they cut through the water, stirring invisible microscopic creatures into glittering sparkles. But never like this. Until the Indian Ocean. When they sailed from Bali to Christmas in the Indian Ocean they'd noticed suspended blobs of bright light in the water. Maybe this was something like that, but on a grander scale. Unsettling, but maybe not threatening.

One thing they were sure about was that the Indian Ocean had a litany of unusual phenomena that put them on edge—mercurial, torrential rains and blustery wind, sudden intense lightning and thunderstorms, weird displays of atmospheric ionization and now these unpredictable glowing ocean currents.

They just hoped that *Vela* could get across it without something else going wrong.

36

The oddly lit water vanished soon after, replaced by the usual slate gray that reflected claustrophobically low clouds scudding overhead. The rig managed to stay up and no other strange phenomena visited them. The lack of an alternator to power electricity for reading and the radio (for all but minimal listening) lent the days endless extra hours, which were absorbed only by the extra effort required to cook meals on the single-burner Primus and bailing every four hours or so to keep up with a new leak in the stuffing box. With all the gear failures and strange weather, everyone would be glad to reach the opposite side of the Indian Ocean.

Pilot charts recommended they arrive in the Seychelles before the Northwest Monsoon began around October 1. They were rapidly approaching that date.

Finally, on the first of October, steep granite islands verdant with tropical vegetation offered a welcome invitation—as if they needed one. Chuck steered for Victoria, the capital of the Seychelles, on Mahé Island.

As *Vela* sailed into the harbor long after dark, a UN ship lit the night with festive lights and a neon sign that read SEYCHELLES, confirming their location in case there was any question. The familiar scent of damp earth filled their nostrils once again.

The Wilcoxes sailed over to what looked like an easy spot to anchor for the night. Another consequence of the alternator failure was that they couldn't power the anchor windlass. Once the anchor was down, they fell into bed for their first full night's rest in nearly a month.

Since they'd left Darwin sixty-two days earlier, they had been underway all but twenty-two of them. The exhausting pace the past few months and volatile sailing conditions in the Indian Ocean had worn them down.

In the morning, as usual, Garth raised the yellow quarantine flag to indicate they awaited clearance. Enchanted by lush surroundings, the whole family was impatient to get off the boat to stretch their legs. In the interim, Garth and Linda finished schoolwork, and Chuck and Dawn drafted letters to mail as soon as they had the chance.

To his parents, Chuck wrote:

> During the trip we decided that although we hadn't got halfway [around the world] yet, we were definitely on our way home. I must admit I would like to see all my relatives and friends again . . . A couple of days before we arrived, we passed the halfway point: at a longitude of 58 degrees E. We have covered a quarter of the Earth since April.

To her mother and sister, Dawn confided:

> I am tired of sailing -- we've covered a lot of miles since April and I wouldn't mind if someone offered to buy the boat. Chuck is getting tired, too--at least on the bad days.

Hours ticked by while they waited for someone to check them into the country, but no one did.

Later that morning, a man motored past and suggested they move over to the main harbor near the lighthouse. He urged them to hurry because Customs would close at noon. As fast as they could, Garth and Dawn raised the heavy anchor hand-over-hand, sweat streaming with their shirts stuck to their bodies under a surprisingly strong morning sun. The family moved and re-anchored *Vela*, reversing the laborious process. Within ten minutes of arriving, the Customs people came. While the Wilcoxes panted and dripped from their exertions, four men with skin as dark as midnight in tidy uniforms processed the necessary paperwork, then charged fifty dollars to spray the boat for pests. Not the most thorough of efforts—tantamount to a light misting with a can of Raid. Garth and Linda stifled a snicker. This lame spraying would have no impact.

As the men completed the official business, Dawn apologized that she had not yet sewn a courtesy flag. Since the Seychelles had gained its independence while they were underway, there was no way for her to know what the country's flag looked like.

"If you'll draw it for me and tell me the colors, I'll sew one," she told them. With pride in their newfound country, the men grinned with pleasure. One man grabbed a pen and piece of scratch paper and made a quick sketch. Another pointed out the color panels. Dawn found their African accents charming.

As soon as the Wilcoxes finished clearing Customs and Immigration, they decided to move the boat nearer to the yacht club. Chuck aimed for an open spot in the anchorage, ready to relax and begin tackling his lengthy list of repairs. Just as they closed in on the spot, a fellow yelled over at them.

"Careful, there's a reef close to that spot!" Having no reverse, naturally *Vela* came to a quick stop within seconds. *Thump!* With the help of a barrel-chested Aussie in a dinghy and a Danforth anchor, the family kedged *Vela* off the reef with no serious damage, except to their dignity.

Finally they were in position to drop anchor (again by hand) and stern-tie to a tree alongside a group of boats. Once settled, the family discovered a virtual United Nations of yachts, including the *Julie II* from Swaziland, *Trilogy* from Canada, and *Dragon Lady* from Holland. Two other boats had kids aboard: *Girl Morgan* from Australia and *Borne Free*, another family from the Bay area. Later a Rhodesian boat arrived with two babies on board.

Being in the company of other yachts and especially among other families with kids Garth and Linda's age made their time in the Seychelles fun. Aboard *Borne Free* was a gregarious sixteen-year-old boy named Mike. For the first time on their journey, Garth had a friend to pal around with. While Linda had encountered girls her age during their voyage, Garth had not. Garth loved commiserating with Mike about school assignments, especially having to read Dickens's long, dry tome *Great Expectations*. They would jokingly greet one another: "Pip, Pip, how 'ere you, Pip?"

Aboard the other boats, fancier and newer than *Vela* were microwave ovens, vacuum cleaners, washers and dryers, and other amenities beyond Dawn's imagination. They reminded her just how much she lived without. *Vela* didn't even have a working stove or electricity—at least until they could get propane and fix the alternator. As soon as they were settled, Chuck wrote to his father to ask his help in securing a replacement alternator. Their options were limited until they did. Dawn's letters to her mother revealed that her patience was wearing thin:

> Unfortunately it means we can't go to see the other islands or bays since we can't start the engine or use the anchor without a battery. I hope it comes before we leave. Or we could just sink the ship and be done with the whole thing. I'm getting a bit tired of doing without more and more, and of sailing between distant ports.

They began the lengthy wait, for Chuck's request to reach his father in California, for Chuck's father to locate and send the parts, and then for them to arrive and clear Customs. In the meantime, they turned to securing water, food and propane.

Dawn loved exploring, and provisioning gave her the perfect excuse. She scoured the streets, walking past the banks, post office and library, to search among the Chinese and Indian shops on Market Street where the selection of dry goods was nearly as varied as it had been in Papeete. She made multiple trips to the voluminous, mostly empty fresh market, picking through oddly stunted fruits and vegetables and sausages and slabs of unidentifiable meat on Saturdays when the butchers came, and stocked up on local tomatoes, cucumbers, bananas and papaya when she could find something that looked edible. Once monsoon season began supplies would dwindle, though she found it hard to believe the selection could get worse.

Dawn also hunted for a propane source. Until she found some, she would have to make do, cooking on the single-burner Primus. Since her attempts at pressure-cooker bread were less than satisfying, she tried the local cassava bread but concluded it was no better.

With her family back home, Dawn shared her fascination with the Seychelles' culture and history, some she learned from a book she'd checked out of the library in Brisbane:

Seychelles were discovered uninhabited in 1608 by the English who carried off many tortoises for meat, later turtle meat was called Seychelle beef. In 1770 French planters and 200 or so black slaves came and tried to colonize St. Annes, but later moved to Victoria site to grow cinnamon, vanilla and coconuts. England captured Victoria from the French Governor 8 times. Each time the governor, Quincy, put the tricolor back up. Finally the English came to stay but 90% are still catholic and speak creole (an archaic pigeon French with African words). It's an interesting mix of races and colors, features and hair because of the whites, slaves, passing seamen, English, Indians and exiled prisoners that came here. The president is half Chinese and half African but wants to be "friend to all nations".

One day, Dawn's explorations took her past a group of women washing in the stream, beating clothes against the rocks as they chattered in

Creole. Then they lay the clothes to dry on tombstones in the cemetery across the road. In their cotton shirtdresses and straw hats, they looked as though they were dressed for Sunday church-going instead of laundry day.

Despite the Seychelles's charms, there was no propane to be found in the entire country. Dawn had been counting on being able to use her three-burner stove and oven once again. But she would have to wait—and, in the meantime, continue trying to concoct meals on a single burner. As if that were her only job.

Within the first ten days of arriving, with Linda's help Dawn washed the clothes and the cushion covers, scoured the galley, and scraped and polished the teak floor. Even with help, it seemed her work never ended. Though she took these tasks upon herself, sometimes she grew weary of her never-ending list and felt a flash of resentment, especially when chores kept her from exploring. Rarely did she stop to question whether there was another way.

To a comment her mother made in a letter about how they seemed to always be repairing the boat and "living without," she responded:

You are right, we are used to spare living, but if I were "strong spirited and courageous" I wouldn't get upset and need Valium. I imagine I'll get back to my placid self once we make it back. I wouldn't mind a few comforts and the trip has been too long and much more work than we planned.

Still, she reasoned,

On the other hand, think of all we have seen, experienced and what memories we will all have while rocking in our rockers at age 90.

One day, Dawn hiked up to the hospital to replenish her prescription for Valium, which the Aussie doctor had prescribed for nerves to help treat her ulcer and she'd gotten for free in Australia. She arrived at the clinic at ten a.m. After standing for an hour, she finally graduated to a seat when one opened. She passed the time in conversation with a man who was born in Kenya of Seychellois parents who'd recently returned at independence. She marveled at how adeptly he switched between good English, French and Creole while conversing with three people at once. At noon all activity stopped when a nurse said something in Creole to a patient. Everyone got up and filed out. Dawn was hungry, so she followed them to a Chinese shop where all the patients got lunch. Then they all walked back and Dawn retained her original seat.

Soon afterward, the nurses came in to get the gurney, and everyone got up en masse to see when the police brought in an old lady who had been knocked down by a car. Nurses put the victim on the table and parked her by the wall until the doctor returned from his lunch break. At one p.m. the government workers' clinic started and Dr. Patel saw all of them before the rest of the people who waited alongside Dawn. After a full day of "free entertainment," at three p.m. the receptionist told the remaining patients, including Dawn, to come early the next day.

At five thirty the following morning, Garth rowed Dawn over to the yacht club so she could be the first one there when the doors opened at seven. She got ticket #1 and explained her request to Dr. Patel. As she left, prescription in hand, she recognized ten of the early patients from the day before. By now, they were old friends.

The new alternator arrived nearly a month after the Wilcoxes reached the Seychelles, as fast as Chuck's father could possibly handle such a request via mail. When Chuck arrived at the post office to collect his long-awaited package, a headache awaited him: Customs demanded a duty of 30 percent. At that price they could not afford it. Dawn detailed the saga to her mother:

The PO said to go to customs for a clearance. Chuck did and they told him to see the Finance Minister. He walked

there and was told to submit a letter. He wrote a very
nice one about needing it and stating he was going to take
it out of the country. He hand delivered it but the F.M.
[Finance Minister] wasn't there, so Chuck went back
Sat am to receive our message that our request was
denied. So there sits our alternator in the PO.

Chuck made an appointment to talk with the minister on Monday.
Government bureaucracy again chafed at Chuck. It was just the kind of
annoyance he had hoped to avoid by sailing away. He worried that if he
couldn't convince the man, the PO would send the alternator back. They
certainly weren't going to pay 30 percent duty for their own alternator.

But after a week of worrying, more paperwork and arguing, Chuck
ended up paying thirteen cents. By the following day, he had installed it
and the engine started right up. He convinced the metal shop to let him
make a bracket to support the water pump, then he flushed the saltwater
and put the engine back on freshwater cooling. Finally after months of
trouble and workaround fixes, the engine was working properly. They
even had reverse gear again.

The stove problem didn't work out quite as well. When the Wilcoxes
finally found propane, it was outrageously expensive. Since Dawn had
coped for so long without the luxury of multiple burners or an oven,
it seemed worth the splurge. After Chuck hooked up the tank, Dawn
could hardly wait to cook her first meal and bake bread in the oven. The
kids looked on expectantly for this momentous return to the grandeur of
their earlier life.

Dawn struck a match to light the stove. *Pffftt*, it sizzled as the yellow
flame flickered beyond her fingertips. She gripped the knob to start the
flow of gas, but the knob wouldn't budge. She tightened her grip and
twisted again. But all she could feel were the pads of her fingers scraping
across the uneven surface as her grip gave way. Thwarted by an obstinate
knob. The fiery flame sputtered out in her other hand. She tried again.

"Errrrr," she grunted as she put her weight behind it.

"Ahhhh!" she exclaimed when it gave way, leaving the detached knob in the palm of her hand. The entire family could hear the hiss of escaping gas.

The sweet, onion-like smell of propane filled the cabin. Propane, which sinks and gathers in the deepest places on a boat, like the bilge. An explosion waiting to happen.

Chuck hustled to turn off the master valve. When he returned, he said, "You should have been exercising the knobs." His matter-of-fact tone implied such a thing had been obvious. She stared at him for a moment.

"Exercising the knobs?" she asked, incredulous. Sparks of resentment sizzled up like flares. She felt heat rush to her face. Her face, neck and ears felt hot enough to catch fire. "How was I supposed to know that?"

The kids didn't move a muscle. Tension hung in the air and they waited for an explosion. But it didn't come.

The pent-up frustrations of the last few months came flooding into her mind, sweeping over her like a tidal wave. Dawn would never forget this ill-timed remark... Or forgive it, either.

A pulsing hammered at her temple, the first hint of an oncoming migraine. She, more than anyone, realized what this meant: the end of the new stove they'd bought in Fiji to replace the one that died on the reef. For the foreseeable future, it was back to the despised Primus, safety-wired to the top of the stove; a single burner, no oven, no broiler, no way to keep pots on the stove.

"Ugghhh!" she groaned loud enough to hear from the next cockpit.

Her outburst was nothing compared with the vicious arguments aboard the Dutch boat, which kept everyone awake and wondering if they should fetch the police. In the morning women from several boats discussed it, wondering whether to intervene. The husband said the wife was an alcoholic while the wife claimed he beat her. In either case, it didn't bode well for an extended voyage. The friction aboard *Vela* wasn't *that* bad.

Such a tight community had its advantages. Mike offered welcome diversion for the kids, whisking them off for a day cruise aboard *Borne*

Free that granted Dawn the luxury of an afternoon to herself. Suddenly free from responsibilities for several hours in a row, she took in the new film *Fiddler on the Roof* with Zero Mostel. The respite helped deflect the stress of returning home late to a hungry family. Just when the palpable tension aboard *Vela* had reached a peak, Mike and his parents invited Garth and Linda to explore the outer islands aboard *Borne Free*. Everyone said yes. It was like pennies from heaven. For eight days, Garth and Linda snorkeled, barbecued and collected shells, played card games and were treated to a couple of restaurant meals on the outer islands. For the family on *Borne Free* it was no big deal, but a rarity for Garth and Linda.

With Garth and Linda away, Dawn and Chuck had time to themselves for the first time in ages. It had been so long they hardly knew what to do with themselves. After Chuck finished fixing the engine and installing spreader braces he'd built, the two took a picnic lunch of wine, Gouda, Indian samosas and a papaya to a pristine white sandy beach nearby. Dawn came home with a sunburn in places the sun didn't often see.

• • •

One night Garth, Dawn and Chuck returned to the boat after taking showers at the yacht club. *Vela* was unusually dark and no one was aboard. Odd, because thirteen-year-old Linda rarely left the boat alone. After they climbed aboard, they looked over and noticed that Linda was aboard *Borne Free* talking to Mike. When she returned, Chuck asked, "What were you doing?"

She replied, "Mike invited me over to see his fish lures."

"Ha!" Garth blurted and his parents burst out laughing.

"What?" Linda said, perplexed. Her family continued laughing but no one said another word.

• • •

Mike got an invitation to play rugby and invited Garth to join him. Neither boy had a clue about rugby, so Garth found a book in the library and looked up the rules. There didn't seem to be many. Garth donned his pair of old Keds, and he and Mike headed for the field. Garth soon found himself in the middle of the scrum, with huge African men towering over him. Mike had never run so fast. These two sixteen-year-old American boys gradually realized they were engaged in a vicious game among players from the Seychelles National Rugby Team. None were Seychellois, but rather mercenaries from all over the African continent. Garth's cotton Keds—already rotted from the steady assault of the tropics—shredded mid-game. When Garth had to write a school report about tribal rivalries in Rhodesia and the drive towards independence, he had a ready source of information.

With all the distractions, the kids hadn't gotten much schoolwork done, though Linda was so far ahead it didn't matter much. It was Garth she most worried about. Dawn ordered the set of final exams be delivered to the newly constructed American embassy, but they didn't arrive until just before Christmas and their planned departure. Garth and Linda dripped in the hot sun in front of the bulletproof glass near the entrance, stated their purpose and waited until the secretary pressed a button to unlock the door. Inside the cool interior under a portrait of Gerald R. Ford, who would be replaced by President-elect James Carter only a month later, a proctor administered their exams. Linda took three finals, Garth only one. *Oh well, maybe the rest in Haifa*, Dawn hoped.

Shortly before the Wilcoxes departed the Seychelles, they bought a single-burner Chinese wick stove. Whereas the Primus required pumping to pressurize the kerosene and roared like an airplane about to take off while in use, it used fuel more efficiently than the new wick stove. Plus the wick stove made a black spot on the ceiling within a few short minutes of lighting. Clearly it was junk, crafted—if such a word could even be lent to such crude workmanship—of tin cans with the painted labels still visible on the inside. But the wick stove did have its uses— as a backup for the Primus underway and gave Dawn the luxury of a "two-burner" stove top in port. Chuck safety-wired it to the top of the old stove alongside the Primus, which they called the blast furnace. Regardless of which cooker she used, Dawn still had to hold the pots on top of this towering monstrosity the entire time she cooked. Rube Goldberg would have been proud.

• • •

One afternoon, as Chuck strode through the cool yacht club on his way back to the boat, a member offered him a tuna he'd caught earlier in the day. Fresh fish was a luxury, especially given the cost of fish in the market, and would be a welcome break from a steady diet of canned meats. He felt like a hero as he handed his bounty over to Dawn and watched her eagerly transform it into curry with vegetables with rice.

As soon as Dawn served the fragrant steaming plates, everyone sat down and dug into the feast. About three bites in, Linda looked over at Garth, who was shoveling it into his mouth as fast as he could. "You look like a lobster, Girch."

Garth looked up from his plate and shot back, "Yeah, well so do you, Lynch."

Dawn glanced over at them and noticed they did look quite red. *That's odd*, she thought. Too busy running errands to prepare for departure, they had hardly been out in the sun recently. Then she noticed that Chuck also had a remarkably rosy complexion. Something tugged at the back of her mind.

"You're beet-red, too, Dawn," Chuck said with a grin. Once he said that, something from Dawn's nurse training clicked.

"Oh dear." Dawn dove for the copy of *Dangerous Marine Animals*. It seemed like a histamine reaction. "Stop, don't eat any more!" Frantic, she thumbed through the pages, flipping back and forth, trying to find the right section.

Garth dropped his fork and it clattered against the rim of the Corelware. He sighed. His stomach growled.

"Are you trying to poison us again, Mom?" Linda joked. Everyone thought back to the taro incident in Fiji when their throats nearly closed up in reaction to oxalic acid. Almost in unison they swallowed, remembering the choking sensation.

Dawn's finger traced down the page, then slowed. "Huh," she mumbled as she scanned the text. The frantic expression on her face altered to one of concentration. All eyes were riveted on Nurse Dawn, now deeply immersed in toxicology.

"Well?" Chuck probed, noticing that his head was beginning to pound. Dawn pushed up her glasses and read them the section verbatim. Interrupting, Chuck asked, "So what does that mean in English?" Dawn set the book aside and inserted a bookmark.

"The tuna is probably old and therefore poisonous, so we can't eat any more," she answered. Garth poked at his fish, wishing that weren't so. She went on. "We should be okay since we haven't eaten much, as long as we flush our systems with plenty of liquids." She dug out the first-aid kit for Benadryl and handed it around. Then she reached for the jar of orange Tang. She measured several heaping teaspoons of orange powder and vigorously whisked them into glasses of water. She handed the first glass to Garth and went on. "That fish probably didn't make it into the cooler soon enough. With tuna, Mahi Mahi and mackerel, that can quickly cause histamine poisoning. Facial flushing within minutes of ingesting is the first sign of a problem." Chuck pursed his lips and nodded slowly.

She whipped up a second glass of orange liquid and handed it to Linda. "Drink up." As soon as Garth finished guzzling the Tang, she refilled his empty glass before making ones for herself and Chuck. "Too bad," she added. Garth cast a longing glance at his mostly full plate, then pushed it away.

Chuck said with a smile, "Yeah. Except for poisoning us, the fish was delicious."

• • •

In mid-December, in honor of the Christmas holiday, a scraggly pine decorated with red balloons appeared in front of the post office. Once again, the family laughed at the incongruity of Christmas decorations in tropical surroundings. One by one, the balloons popped in the hot sun, sending frightened pedestrians scurrying into oncoming traffic, among them a truck with an overheated Santa who was collecting money for old folks.

Christmas of 1976 passed quietly for the Wilcoxes, with far more fun than that of 1974 when the family was deeply immersed in rebuilding *Vela* after the shipwreck and in better company than in 1975 in the muddy Brisbane River. Mike's mother had organized a fancy restaurant dinner for all the foreign yachts, but it was too expensive for the Wilcoxes. Instead, Chuck, Dawn, Garth and Linda feasted on sweet potatoes and white potatoes, Chinese cabbage and a Wilson turkey, a tiny bird squeezed whole into a can. Half the family's gifts were held hostage in Customs, but Mike's family had given them a can of Fritos—their first in three years. After polishing off a dessert of Aussie plum pudding topped with South African cream, Garth and Linda argued over the coveted chips.

Just days before leaving the Seychelles, another present arrived in the form of another letter from the IRS. Apparently the Wilcoxes were missed. It was signed by a Mr. P***d*** (illegible), who they referred to as Mr. Poodoo. An exasperated Chuck again drafted a letter explaining their circumstances.

The family could wait no longer for the charts they ordered for the Red Sea. Without detailed charts, they wouldn't be able to make stops. But the season wouldn't wait. They would have to make do. Four days after Christmas, the Wilcoxes set sail for Djibouti.

37

From fellow yachtsmen and *Ocean Voyages of the World*, published by the British Admiralty, Chuck learned they ought to steer a wide course steer clear of trouble along the East African coast and Socotra, a noted pirate base. It was 1,200 miles to Djibouti, the capital of the French Territory of the Afars and Issas, on the shortest route, but carving an arc around the horn of Africa to reach the Gulf of Aden and avoid these risky areas extended the passage to 2,000 miles. They hated to sail extra miles, but sometimes it helped avoid other problems. Before the Wilcoxes departed, they had been told to keep an eye out for the *Julie II*, a vessel that had not been heard from since leaving weeks earlier.

The first few days, the family faced heavy rain and low visibility. Only a day out of the Seychelles, they could not determine their position well enough to turn back. The evening of the second day, as Dawn, who was steering, heard a clank and felt it reverberate through the wheel. The wheel spun free and she lost control of their heading. The boat rounded up to the clutter of sails flapping. Chuck and Garth pulled the sails down and let *Vela* drift while they investigated.

Chuck discovered that the chain connecting the wheel to the rudder had parted. This was the pricey new chain he'd ordered from the U.S. and installed in Fiji. There was no way to fix it now because they carried no extra chain. So Chuck and Garth deployed the new emergency tiller that Chuck built in Brisbane and then a second time in Darwin after the original Aussie wood split. It seemed as soon as they fixed one thing, something else broke.

This meant they had to hand-steer until they reached Djibouti. The rudder was so large that Linda and Dawn could hardly budge the tiller, and the weather-helm exceeded what even Chuck and Garth could manhandle in any wind. So they rigged a block and tackle with four-to-one purchase to give them leverage.

Steering with a tiller instead of the wheel was counterintuitive, requiring the exact opposite action to change direction, a challenge for a bleary-eyed Dawn in the darkness. She felt so weary of these ad-hoc repairs.

As December drew to a close and 1976 turned into 1977, *Vela* faced the brunt of the northerly winds blowing down the Arabian Sea. On January 4th, *Vela* crossed the equator, her first foray into the northern hemisphere since she had sailed for the Marquesas three years earlier. With the northerly, life aboard grew unpleasant and notations in the ship's log included *ROUGH AND CRUMP WEATHER AND MOTION*, *Screamin' rough*, and *bugger*.

On January 8th the engine overheated. Another frost plug had rusted. That meant no engine to generate power, and therefore no lights for the rest of the passage except to work out sights each night. *Oh joy*, Dawn thought. The next day's excitement was a big rip in the genoa when an entire eight-foot-long seam gave way. Dawn spent the next eight days on her off-watch sewing it back together. When she finished, Garth and Chuck told her that since she had pulled one seam edge over to reach the unfrayed fabric it was lopsided and might rip any minute. She wanted to scream. Fortunately it held.

In a letter home, Dawn outlined their latest challenges, adding:

I wish Chuck would get tired of sailing, because I am.

Once again the Indian Ocean offered more strange upwellings and bioluminescence; dolphins and schools of Mahi Mahi to keep them company; birds that rested for hours aboard the dodger or stern rail; squalls and waves in the cockpit that sent everything floating; and ships that told them they were near a shipping lane.

On January 20th, they heard on Voice of America that James Carter had been inaugurated as president, but they missed his speech because they had to limit radio time to preserve battery power.

As they neared the Gulf of Aden, they steered *Vela* through the slot between Socotra and Cape Guardafui in Somalia. At first a strong westerly current in the Gulf of Aden combined with strong winds to push them towards Djibouti. Then, several hundred miles from Djibouti, the wind died to nothing. Since the motor was not working, there *Vela* sat, drifting slowly, awaiting a whisper of good fortune from Poseidon.

In the mid-afternoon of January 21st, Garth spotted a pole that marked a reef. In a panic they tacked away as quickly as they could, relieved to encounter it during daylight hours. With such light winds, they had little control over their course.

Chuck promptly took sights to determine their position. Dawn could barely sit still long enough for him to take a measurement so she could run the calculations. Her heart jumped wildly in her chest and her stomach burned with worry. Garth climbed the rig and studied the water for signs of other reefs. Chuck, too, was jittery. When Dawn finished her calculations, her position indicated they were near islands that were part of Somalia, now loosely held by the Russians, but mostly in the grips of warring bandits. Knowing where they were brought no comfort. Another close call with a reef—this one *not* in the vicinity of the friendly people of Fiji.

Chuck wondered if this was indicative of the fate that might have befallen the *Julie II*. Or would her crew perhaps be waiting in Djibouti with nothing more than radio trouble to explain her silence? Everyone remained on edge during the entire night of light wind, which kept them close to this double danger.

The following morning after the sun rose, *Vela* drifted into the Gulf of Tadjoura with Djibouti in sight but no sign of wind. Seeing Djibouti gave them the sense that the danger had passed and they began to relax.

As they drifted along, the water surrounding them teamed with sea life. Shrimp-like creatures (called "Moreton Bay Bugs" in Australia) floated on the surface along with crabs. Rainbow-colored Mahi Mahi swam just below. Garth and Linda rigged a shrimp net on a long pole and spent the morning catching shrimp and crabs on the port side. Chuck snagged a Mahi Mahi on the starboard. In the ship's log, Dawn recorded, *Vela fisheries in action.* They were eight miles from Djibouti, but without an engine everyone doubted they could arrive that day. At least they'd have some fine eating even if they didn't reach port before nightfall. Hours passed in a flurry of catching, cleaning and shelling. Dawn turned their bounty into a Creole feast, using the Primus and the Chinese wick stove simultaneously.

Late in the day Poseidon delivered favorable wind. They steamed along with a couple of freighters and a *dhow* that hailed from North Yemen to the west end of the Gulf of Aden and into the port of Djibouti. As they neared the port, they could see that the *Julie II* was not anchored there. Among the vessels in the harbor were a Belgian, a Panamanian and an American yacht. The Wilcoxes were under the impression that Djibouti had just gained its independence, but noticed that the ships and yachts all still flew French courtesy flags.

After twenty-four days of sailing, the family dropped the sails and the hook at four p.m. A reedy man named Misha from the other American yacht rowed over and told the Wilcoxes not to bother checking in. While the French were ready to vacate their former colony, the UN requested they remain another two months because of Russian control of Aden and Somalia. Amid the frosty politics of the Cold War, Western countries feared what a political change in Djibouti might mean for the balance of power and a newly reopened Suez Canal. The French authorities remained—in name only—and had little interest in bothering with Customs for yachts. As a red sun hovered over the arid landscape, Misha explained that he planned to sail for the Maldives in the morning. Indeed, shortly after sunrise, his boat was gone.

Djibouti was an unusual place and they'd already seen some unusual places. The flat, dry desert town was dirty in the way such places become when there is insufficient water to wash things clean. But an undercurrent of something else cast a pall. Fearing the uncertainty of impending independence, nearly all the French and other expatriates had left, which lent the place an air of desolation.

Ironically, the area—one of the driest on earth—would receive more than three years' worth of rainfall during the six days the Wilcoxes were there. As Dawn finished a letter to inform her family that they had arrived safely, she remarked:

Sure is nice being able to wash teeth and dishes with fresh water.

Yet it was a little too much of a good thing. While Garth wouldn't need to worry about hauling water for washing, laundry or replenishing the tanks— they could catch more than enough—the wet laundry refused to dry.

On their first foray into town, Dawn, Garth and Linda took in the peculiarities of this former French colony. On the two-mile walk along the grim streets, people with a mixture of Arabic and African features would occasionally greet them with "Salaam" or "Bonjour," but more often than not ignored them. They brushed past women in long dresses with cloth around their head and shoulders but not their faces. Beneath their robes, the women wore modern platform, cork-soled shoes. Some men wore a sulu (a wraparound skirt), while others wore pants. This was their first exposure to Arabic culture, and they were surprised to see people in what looked like pajamas.

At the bank, to change money, they filled out forms, then waited for tellers to call them; they barely recognized the butchered attempts to call their names when their turn came to complete the exchange. The tellers refused to exchange the ten-rand note that another sailor had given Chuck for boat parts, but agreed to take U.S. funds.

With francs in hand, Dawn, Garth and Linda bought ice cream, a special treat. They realized their mistake when a crowd of young boys gathered around them and begged for some. Young girls tried to sell them cigarettes and bon bons from trays that hung around their necks. Garth bought a piece of candy and immediately regretted it when children ran after him screaming, "Bon bon! Bon bon!" The family had never encountered such poverty. Yet farther down the street, in the window of a patisserie shop, they spotted a tarte large enough to feed a family for fifteen dollars.

They had only just begun to explore when the shops closed at eleven thirty for lunch, and they remembered the inefficiencies of Tahiti. On their way back to the boat, they bought French bread from a wooden cart. The extra loaf they bought vanished long before they made it back to the boat, as they shared it piece by piece with little boys who followed them.

The next day Dawn and Linda ventured on muddy streets back into town while Garth stayed aboard to help his father make repairs. Dawn and Linda located the market with quality potatoes and tomatoes from Somalia. They also found the meat stalls, but since Dawn couldn't identify the meat (goat? old camel?) and everything was coated with flies, she decided they could live without. Thank goodness their cholera and typhoid shots were up to date, Dawn thought.

Meanwhile, Chuck worked day after day on the steering and engine problems, never even stepping ashore. While Garth fixed the headstay and the new main sheet, Chuck bent over the engine, grasping for a solution. He epoxied four frost plugs, hoping that once the family reached

Haifa—if they reached Haifa—he could get a mechanic to dismantle the engine and do a proper repair. Chuck worried how long the engine might last. He was weary of the constant repairs and a perpetual inability to do it right. Though he was clever and ingenious at finding work-arounds to the myriad equipment failures they faced, he wasn't a magician.

On January 28th, the Wilcoxes pointed *Vela* northward. They planned to sail nonstop to Suez, an estimated three weeks. But their plans soon changed.

38

Their passage started slow, with light winds as they sailed past reefs and islands up the straits of Bab el Mandeb and into the Red Sea. The Red Sea wasn't red at all, but was named for the algae blooms that occur certain times of the year.

Twenty ships passed them that first night. Though the chart indicated the Afars and Issas, Ethiopia, Yemen and South Yemen were all within sight, nothing distinguished them from one another. All anyone could see were vast stretches of sand dotted with mosques, squat buildings and oil tanks plus the occasional ship anchored off the coast nearby. The wind gradually strengthened, pushing *Vela* northward. This was a relief, since the best wind and current favored traversing the Red Sea south to north between January and March, and it was already nearly February. The Wilcoxes aimed to sail straight to Suez. Ethiopia was in the midst of a bitter civil war, which made stopping there unwise.

Days passed uneventfully. In the ship's log—intermixed with Chuck's pencil marks noting star locations and navigational fixes—the family joked about the ships that passed during each of their watches:

January 30	0900 12 ships, Red Sea at last
	1200 1 ship, Datsun, tuna
January 31	1500 7 shipinos
	2100 5 shipinos
February 1	0900 6 shipinos
	2100 3 shipinosa
February 2	0900 1 measly shipinosa
	2100 5 shipinosans
February 3	0000 Solo una barca
	0300 7 shipinosiums (top that Lynch)
	0600 No shipsatall
	0915 5 Shipisoleoms does Girch
	2100 1 Shipinosoleominigotut
February 4	0000 Nice wind, clear sky, no bateau
	0900 7 ships, 2 airplanes

Glad to be making progress, the family sailed past Port Sudan, anxious to make headway while conditions were favorable. Then the fun ended.

While Linda was on watch, as *Vela* drew parallel to Jiddha (Jeddah), Saudi Arabia, the wind shifted one hundred and eighty degrees. Now the wind came directly from their destination, Suez. Since it was impossible to steer directly into the wind, it nearly doubled the distance they would have to sail.

The family set up *Vela* to beat as close as possible into the wind, but her baggy, blown-out sails and rounded hull kept her from being able to point toward their destination. They tacked back and forth but gained only thirty miles per day, not the one hundred miles per day they'd been used to covering. The Red Sea could be surprisingly calm, but stirred into a steep chop when the wind kicked up. Vertical seas built quickly into obstacles that all but halted *Vela*'s forward momentum. On impact, waves reverberated through the boat and sent spray flying. With six hundred miles or more yet to travel, it could take three weeks or more to reach Suez. And stress everything aboard in the process. Especially the crew.

Now with wind against them, those same ships, which had once offered a pleasant diversion, became obstacles to worry about as *Vela* zigzagged across the waterway working slowly northward. And in such a narrow sea, it didn't take long sailing before it was time to tack again for fear of getting too close to reefs that lined both coasts.

With scarcely a blade of grass to bind the arid soil and keep it from becoming airborne at every gust of wind, the air grew thick with dust that stung their eyes and obliterated any visual references to aid navigation. The sandy, featureless shoreline soon vanished into the haze, along with the distant mountains that formed its backdrop. At sunset, dust and water vapor hung in the air, turning the horizon into a palette of reds and oranges. Because the horizon was so hazy, Chuck couldn't get accurate star, moon or sun sights, which made it impossible to know where they were with any certainty.

Chuck's agitation rose as low visibility rendered navigation progressively more difficult. He could think of nothing but the reefs that lurked close on both sides, waiting for them to make another mistake. He felt the strain of being the captain—the one who decides when it's safe and when it isn't. He'd felt safe off the coast of Fiji and look what that confidence had gotten him: nine months of backbreaking labor to rebuild the boat. Here, one false move might land him in a hostile place, maybe even jail. They'd come close to grief again on their way into Djibouti, and only luck had saved them. The lack of news about the *Julie II* was worrisome. The multi-national crew had left the Seychelles in November and no one had seen nor heard anything of them since. What had befallen them?

Shortly after Chuck got off watch on February 5th the jib halyard broke and the jib came floating down onto the bow. He and Garth rigged a spare halyard and hauled the jib back up again. Then the antenna fell down, leaving them without the radio time signals that helped ensure accuracy in navigation. Last they knew, the watch was a minute and six-teen seconds fast, but at what rate of watch error?

The next day, during Dawn's watch, a big wave crashed over the back deck. A *thunk* followed by erratic steering told her the steering chain had broken again. After all Chuck's hard work, the repair had lasted only ten days. That meant hand steering—something they couldn't imagine do-ing for another three weeks while fighting headwinds with waves thun-dering against the hull. Mountains of water crashed aboard, adding to a feeling of being out of control.

Linda noticed the fresh water had a salty flavor. Were their water tanks now contaminated, too? These repairs would be impossible at sea. Perhaps in port they'd be able to get parts to make a proper repair. So the morning of the 6th, the family decided to head for a port. Because they had no chart for Jeddah, they steered for Port Sudan, which meant a loss of hard-fought miles.

At four forty-five, with the light off Port Sudan in sight, they heard another *bang!* This time it was the spare jib halyard where the tang part-ed. Garth and Chuck sprang into action to rig the staysail. When they were done, they collapsed in the cockpit. Everyone was worn out. The breakdowns were getting to them all—and to Chuck in particular, who had to figure out what to do about them. Even he was ready to be done with this doomed voyage. Linda was skeptical. She'd heard this kind of talk before.

As they neared Bur (Port) Sudan, the waves laid down and sailing turned pleasant. Within sight of port, Chuck's mood lifted. Their voyage seemed possible once again and he began to talk of repairs. He harbored hopes of carrying on once they recovered, just as Linda had predicted.

Entering the harbor, the engine started without any trouble—as though wanting to help them return to port. But just before he turned it off, the exhaust pipe that Chuck had fabricated at great expense in Australia crumbled, spilling fumes into their living space. Chuck and Dawn shared a look.

In the inner harbor, the family anchored and raised the quarantine flag, awaiting clearance. The *Julie II* was not in Port Sudan, either. There were no Western yachts at all. Around *Vela* in this surprisingly busy port were tankers and freighters from Russia, Panama, Europe, plus some with Arabic writing they couldn't read. All flew a Sudanese courtesy flag that Dawn had yet to sew. Sudan hadn't been a planned stop.

Men fished in a *dhow* driven by a baggy, burlap sail while another man ferried people across the harbor deftly pulling on a set of oars. Ashore, barely discernible through the dust, goats wandered past a man in a turban riding a donkey. Nothing Dawn would be likely to see in Palo Alto, but this sailing business was just getting too hard.

The family discussed their options. They could try to sell the boat in Sudan, or move it overland to the Mediterranean, or sail on once they addressed this litany of equipment failures. None of the choices seemed appealing.

Dawn harbored hopes of selling *Vela* here and flying home, though she didn't think Chuck or Garth were ready to take such a drastic step. Dawn was weary of the voyage, yet still keen to visit Greece and trace ancient history in the Mediterranean Sea. Then she'd be ready to fly home for sure. Though worn down by the constant breakages and setbacks, all felt conflicted about giving up—all but Linda, anyway. Her opinion hadn't really changed about the voyage, though she'd begun keeping a journal, which made the experience more interesting—at least the parts on shore.

Dawn penned a letter to her mother telling where they were, their recent saga and outlining their uncertain plans. Repairs could fill a month or more, if indeed it were possible. Chuck wrote a candid letter to his parents while they awaited clearance.

Here we are, bogged down once more with this one horse shay falling apart around us. It seems like everything is wearing out at once and a lot of it can't be repaired without a major job. For example, the fuel tanks are rusting out and full of crud and the stupid design of them makes it impossible to get inside of them to clean them out.

He admitted how seriously they considered giving up:

Now Garth and I are of the opinion that it's marginal whether we can make the next leg. When he gets pessimistic, it is time to worry about it for sure. We are contemplating several options . . . Garth and I would like to finish the trip even though it is getting harder all the time. Of course, Dawn refuses to fly back unless all of us do it at once.

He wrestled with his feelings:

It seems so sad to get two thirds of the way and have to quit. It was really a heart breaking thought while we were coming in the harbor to think that this would be the last time I would ever be doing this.

He put it out of his mind for the moment and set about writing to sail-makers and engine-part suppliers in England, requesting quotes for sails and parts that might allow them to continue at least to the Mediterranean.

Eventually a Sudanese health officer arrived to clear them into the country, bringing a box of syringes with him. *Thank goodness our shots are up to date*, Dawn thought. He sprayed for pests—about as effectively as in the Seychelles—and charged them twenty dollars for it. The cockroaches aboard *Vela* continued to flourish.

• • •

At five the next morning, a call to prayer blared through a speaker on a minaret, waking the family. After breakfast they rowed to shore. Even though the Wilcoxes had seen plenty of developing countries, they were not prepared for the culture shock of Port Sudan.

Not sure exactly where to land the dinghy, they rowed to the nearest beach. As they neared the low beach where men were swimming, many began to yell at them with such hostility, the Wilcoxes hardly knew what to do. While Garth and Chuck pulled the dinghy up the beach, Linda and Dawn noticed the men weren't wearing any clothes at all and politely averted their eyes. On top of the cliff, women in shapeless black garments appeared to be mid-ablution as well, though unlike the men they had to climb down to retrieve water for their efforts. Evidently the Wilcoxes had found the public bathing beach during peak business.

The family left the dinghy and followed the road, a desiccated crust without an inch of shade. Hot air blew across its surface. As soon as they began to wander through the dusty streets, it became clear that flying home from here might be almost as hard as sailing on—maybe harder.

The land was parched and barren: flat, treeless and bald. Around them wandered hundreds of goats, their curly ears twitched to flick away flies while their front hooves held down branches so they could nibble at scrubby brush just beyond reach. Undernourished camels and donkeys hitched to carts expressed their displeasure with snorts or a distinctive *hee-haw*. Men in turbans wore what looked like dresses.

Here they saw poverty more stark than Djibouti: Tribesmen in filthy rags with bushy hair and deep vertical scars cut into their faces sat cross-legged behind piles of twigs alongside the parched road. Others cooked whatever sustenance they could scrape together over hot coals on the sidewalk, doing their best to subsist on this sun-scorched patch of earth. The stench of smoking camel dung hung in the air. For Garth, the word *desolate* took on new meaning.

Every horizontal surface and even vertical ones were coated with a pervasive grime. Dust tickled their throats, spurring a cough and an overwhelming desire for a beverage or an ice cream. But the Wilcoxes remembered their mistake in Djibouti. Besides, there was none. They licked their parched lips at the memory, and hoped they'd at least be able to find water to replenish their tanks.

In such a barren place, Dawn didn't imagine anything would grow. She didn't have high hopes for grocery shopping. To her surprise, she found giant sacs of onions and a large pink grapefruit, tomatoes, and green bell peppers displayed on large burlap sacks on the cracked ground. Vendors sat patiently behind them, though their eyes betrayed a beaten attitude. Everything was imported and, therefore, expensive.

While it was always a challenge to negotiate a fair price in a foreign place without knowing the local language, this time was even harder. While Dawn thought she knew Arabic numbering, these were different, more like squiggly lines than the bold decisive strokes she'd grown up using. From buying stamps they had learned to recognize the equivalences for each of the characters. There were one hundred piasters in a Sudanese pound and ten millium in a piaster, but at the "market," prices were quoted in shillings. She soon realized that one shilling equaled five piasters and made a card with all the conversions. When one vendor asked too much money, she looked at her reference card, shook her head, and moved on to the next. The first vendor followed her, tapped her on the shoulder and made writing motions. She realized that he wanted to see her card. He examined it for a moment, then tapped his head, as though saying "pretty smart." She thought, *Maybe he'll give me a better price next time*.

In the meat market, an actual building with short concrete walls, thick clouds of flies swirled around the bloody carcasses that hung behind the vendors. The sight turned Garth's stomach, as did an overwhelming stench of blood, and he ducked outside. Dawn had grown used to buying meat under such unsanitary conditions. She stood next to a carcass and pointed and gestured the size of the piece she wanted. The vendor whacked at it, sending bone shards flying. As he handed her the hunk of beef, camel, goat—whatever it was—wrapped in a piece of scratch paper, she pulled out her stash of plastic grocery bags. Standards are relative.

A brief glance into the area selling animal innards—the cheap parts of animals that even the burger chains might shun—and goat heads offered more than enough information to deter her from stepping any further in that direction.

On her third trip into town, Dawn still hadn't found flour, but detected the yeasty scent of baking bread. She followed her nose to a "bakery," such as it was: a low, unlit structure, with loaves of round whole-wheat bread lying on the floor. Desperate, she bought one. While Linda found it tasty, the occasional rock dampened her initial enthusiasm.

Finally Dawn located a store that sold flour and tea with a shopkeeper who spoke modest English, so she could replenish her supplies. She made the mistake of buying a dusty box of corn flakes that had probably been on the shelves for ten years.

Dawn searched vain in for peanut butter. She was desperate for sources of protein, especially given her challenges finding edible meat. When she saw something that resembled peanut butter, she asked what it was. The vendor told her the name, *halvah*, but she'd never heard of it. Close enough, she figured, so she requested some. The vendor wrapped it in newspaper and handed the package to her.

Later when Dawn unwrapped it, she was dismayed to find a reverse image of the day's headlines imprinted on its surface. She scraped it off and offered the rest to the kids for their toast.

"This isn't peanut butter!" Linda complained. It didn't quite have the golden brown color they were used to. It seemed too dry.

"It doesn't spread very well," Garth said, his brow furrowed as his knife crumbled a piece into flaky bits that fell off the toast. Dawn shrugged. She had no idea teenagers could be so picky.

"Well, maybe I can buy peanuts from the ladies on the sidewalk and we can make our own peanut butter." The next day she did just that.

It was an experiment that didn't go well. As they attempted to crush the nuts with a hammer, bits of peanut flew off the baking sheet, making a big mess and not much peanut butter. Meanwhile an emboldened cockroach scurried across the counter.

The dried peanut butter that William had devoured in Tonga didn't seem so awful in hindsight.

After visits to six companies, Chuck finally found a source for propane, which they still needed to fuel the camping cooler they used as a fridge. Unfortunately a rule limited the amount of propane anyone could buy. But Chuck convinced the manager to let him buy it in two fifteen-pound batches. As Chuck and Dawn hauled their tank suspended between two oars, they passed huts with conical roofs and a donkey pulling a kerosene tank painted with the Shell logo in English on one side and in Arabic on the other. While workmen filled their tank, the company manager invited Dawn and Chuck in for tea—more like a cup of sugary milk with a splotch of dirty water. But the liquid was hot and hopefully sanitary, and it helped wash away the dust that crawled down their throats. And it masked the stench of burning camel dung.

Despite high hopes and full propane tanks, Dawn still could not bake in her oven because of wrecked valves. Maybe they could find a replacement valve in the Mediterranean. Until then it was back to the Primus and the Chinese wick stove.

Most of the family's time in Sudan went to repairs and waiting for mail that never came. Garth spent an entire day using every drill bit aboard as he tried to make a stainless-steel tang for the jib halyard, but all were too dull. He spent days trying to perfect a wire-to-rope splice with old line and insufficient tools to fix the halyards, while dreaming of a boat with stronger rigging or no rigging at all. Hunting among the dismal collection of shops for better tools, he finally found and purchased a sharp knife with a thick leather sheath. Using leftover Vesi wood from Fiji and the old stainless rails from the stove wrecked on the reef, he constructed his own marlinspike. For hours, he filed the stove metal to a point with a dull file. After a week of work he finally had a spliced jib halyard. They could not have left port without it.

Meanwhile, Chuck worked on repairing the exhaust pipe, the steering chain, and the Groco head, yet again. He hated fixing the same things over and over again, often because he couldn't get the parts to do it properly or because someone didn't do it right in the first place.

While the Wilcoxes weighed their options, it was evident they didn't really have any. Though Dawn had prepared an inventory of everything on board in case they decided to abandon the boat, Sudan didn't seem like a likely place to sell an oceangoing yacht. They would have to do the best they could to carry on.

The steady northerly always blew through the port, a constant reminder of the task that awaited them: beating north directly into it. They had no charts for stops along the way.

Days were blisteringly hot, but the dry desert air immediately lost its heat and the temperature dropped precipitously when the sun vanished at the end of the day. Dawn loved this time of the day, when all the dishes were done and she could relax in the cockpit with a cup of tea and watch all the port activity: the fishermen sailing, the ships coming in and out.

"Brrr, Sudan!" Linda joked as Dawn shivered one evening, invoking the local name of the port, which had struck them as funny. The joke joined family lore; ever afterward, whenever anyone remarked about a chill in the air, *Bur Sudan* came to mind and brought a smile to their lips, though it was a place that symbolized the hardship of the voyage.

Days of work and waiting made Sudan seem drearier. Exotic at first, the hardscrabble life around them wore thin. It offered no relief from their troubles. The flies were as pesky as they'd been in Brisbane, and soon Linda, armed with a fly swatter, amassed a heap of bodies on the floor. Pervasive dust left a layer of dirt everywhere, turning all the lines brown. It invaded their lungs. Miserable colds and mild intestinal distress sapped their energy and depressed them.

After nearly a month, they still had received no mail. Day after day they checked among a weatherbeaten stack of letters at the post office that Linda thought looked like they had come overland from Khartoum by sick camel. But they found no quotes for new sails, no engine parts, no finals, no lessons, and no letters from family. Anything mailed there could easily have been lost, given the disarray they'd witnessed at the post office. Their hopes of doing anything but sailing on seemed naive.

Finally on March 13th, a few letters from home dribbled in. Chuck's parents offered money to repair the boat. Chuck refused their kind offer. There wasn't anything to buy there in any case.

And then a package of textbooks arrived, minus the syllabus that directed their use. Waiting a few more days produced no additional mail and Chuck refused to delay their departure any longer. The season wouldn't wait for letters and tests that might never come. It was already approaching the middle of March, near the end of the period when conditions were supposed to be favorable.

The voyage to the Suez Canal would take about three weeks, *inshallah*.

Port Sudan Market

39

Just before the Wilcoxes prepared to leave Port Sudan, other yachts trickled in. The arrival of *Girl Morgan*, *Borne Free*, and *Nomad* buoyed the family's spirits. Garth and Linda relished brief reunions with other teenagers, playing for a change instead of just doing schoolwork or preparing for the next leg of the journey. They could share the culture shock with others and retreat to a familiar world more typical to American teenagers than poverty in a stark landscape.

The pack of kids headed into town together. Mike's mother had heard there was a movie theater near the market playing *Here Come the Cops* starring Raquel Welch. They all wanted to go, but first they had to change money. Among men walking around wearing daggers over their pajama tops, Mike found a man willing to convert his dollars into Sudanese pounds. It was illegal, but money-changers offered far better rates than the bank. The group ducked beneath the colonnaded overhang of a crumbling colonial building and watched while Mike and the man haggled over the exchange rate. Finally the man agreed to Mike's price. Mike handed over a ten-dollar bill and collected a wad of pounds. About halfway up the street the man realized he'd given Mike twice what he intended, and he ran after them. There was no way a group of ten pale-faced teenagers was going to get lost among Sudanese, so when the angry man demanded his money, Mike immediately handed it over.

The group found the "movie theater" next to the crowded market, paid the ticket price and went in. They passed through a building entrance to an outdoor courtyard lined with benches. When the movie started, the market next door was so loud they couldn't hear the audio track. The rest of the audience didn't care because they could all read the French and Arabic subtitles. Or perhaps because it was a slapstick comedy of no substance and the dialogue was easy to guess.

For Chuck, the opportunity to compare charts and information with other sailors boosted his confidence. Chuck learned of a route inside the reefs for the first one hundred and forty miles up the Red Sea. But he felt it would be better to sail than rely on an engine that had failed them so often in the past. Navigation inside the reefs seemed tricky and would probably take them even longer. Chuck was understandably skittish about reefs.

The other "yachties" also told them what had happened to *Julie II*. The vessel had hit a reef off Hafun in northern Somalia. The boat was seized and the crew taken prisoner for "spying."

"On what, camels?" Linda joked.

The vessel had run aground near Somalia's only nuclear plant. Truly bad luck. With citizens of the Netherlands, South Africa, Swaziland and Switzerland aboard, their imprisonment spawned an international negotiation involving representatives of four nations. Yet the crew still remained in jail. It rattled Chuck to think how close they'd come to doing the same thing on their way to Djibouti.

In the last few days before their departure, a letter from Chuck's parents brought distressing news. His father was now on a diabetic diet and using oxygen at night. Though his parents still talked of meeting them in Spain, he and Dawn thought it doubtful, even if *Vela* could get there. This made Chuck more inclined to push on without delay, using the most direct route.

The week before, *Thetis*, which the family referred to as a French "Gold Plater," had left for Suez on the outside but returned within three days after their self-steering broke. They'd had crummy weather, rendering the captain seasick the entire trip. There had been a dust storm in Port Sudan at the time, but the weather had improved since then and Chuck reasoned that it was a matter of going during the right conditions. Though other boaters chose the inside route, Chuck felt confident in his decision to sail on the outside.

On the 17th of March, after thirty-seven days in port, *Vela* finally left Bur Sudan, bound for Suez. They raised anchor at seven thirty, motored out of the harbor, and hoisted the sails. *Vela* heeled as wind filled the deep bellies of the old sails. On a heading of 060 degrees, *Vela* sailed as high as she could. The sailing was good for a time.

Unfortunately, the light wind was only a tease. The breeze began to build and with hundreds of miles of fetch, the seas soon turned nasty with short steep waves. They drove *Vela* hard to make progress northward, with her rail in the water and waves crashing over the deck. She shook with the impact of each wave. Her motion grew fierce, and everyone's stomachs turned somersaults.

Poor Dawn was stuck below trying to hold the pressure cooker on top of the Primus. Once, when Dawn rushed to the cockpit to heave over the side, the pressure cooker leapt off the Primus. Dawn picked it up and stuck it back on the heating element, grateful for its locking lid, which kept stew inside instead of spilled across the cabin. *Not that anyone cared to eat anyway*, she thought. The thought of cleaning stew from every bouncing surface made Dawn's stomach lurch all over again and she was back to the cockpit in a flash.

Exhausted from the jarring motion and an inability to sleep or keep anything down, everyone was miserable. Their progress was barely perceptible. *Vela* had never been able to point well given her rotund form and full keel, but with such baggy sails against a steep chop, it was debatable whether she was making headway at all.

After more than twenty-four hours of pitching and slamming, a demoralized Chuck said, "The boat can't handle these conditions." In a beaten voice he added, "Something is going to break." A litany of potential casualties rushed to mind as he thought of all his haphazard attempts at repair that took so much effort but didn't address the root problems.

"But nothing's broken yet," Garth pointed out.

"Yes, but it's only a matter of time." Chuck pinched the bridge of his nose. "It's likely to be like this all the way up the Red Sea. I don't see how we can do it." He rubbed his eyes. *Vela* pounded into the waves, and he reached out to brace himself as water cascaded over his head.

"What other choice do we have?" Dawn wondered aloud. Chuck's eyes rested on her for a moment. He was so exhausted, enervated by everything they'd been through, the relentless trials that never ceased. He bent his head and rubbed the back of his neck.

"I don't know." he said, looking up. Exasperation bled through his voice. "We can't just keep bashing like this. The boat can't take it."

"We have to get up the Red Sea somehow," Garth said. "Why don't we just keep going?"

Chuck closed his eyes for a second. What he really meant was, *I can't take it.*

Chuck looked defeated. He let out a long breath and in a burst of energy, he said, "You can be the captain, Garth. And then you can decide whatever you want." With is shoulders hunched, he turned and slunk below. He climbed into his bunk and pulled the cotton blanket up to his chin. He stared at the coach roof above him for a few seconds before rolling over to face the settee cushion.

Garth stood stunned, not quite sure what to think. He was sixteen. While he felt capable enough to lead, this wouldn't work. They still needed Chuck to navigate. He looked at his mother. She pursed her lips.

"Uhhh, I think we'd better turn back," she said quietly.

As the sun began to sink over the horizon, Garth released the wind vane and turned *Vela* around. Immediately the motion of the boat improved. It was as though they'd imagined the punishing conditions.

By three a.m., the Wilcoxes were back where they started, anchored in Port Sudan and thoroughly depressed. How would they ever get up the Red Sea?

They fell into bed and slept the rest of the night. In the morning, no one said a word about Chuck's meltdown.

After breakfast and a visit with the authorities to reenter the country, they made a trip to the post office to retract mail forwarding instructions. Their efforts produced letter #22 from Dawn's mother and a letter from University of California sent February 24th, which evidently arrived in the country's capital of Khartoum on March 7th. It was now March 21st. Where the letter had been since then was a mystery. And letter #20 was still MIA. It would have been a mistake to assume any parts or sails could have made it there.

Though a relief to have news from home, the UC letter added to their sense of futility. It stated that Garth's history test couldn't be sent since they hadn't received half of the semester's work that Dawn had mailed from the Seychelles on November 22nd.

In a reply to her mother later that day, she wrote:

This school-post office business is so frustrating. Poor Garth works so hard on the stuff but he won't get credit unless he does it over and he can't unless UC sends a duplicate of the questions to Gil [Grandpa] so he can [forward] it to us in Haifa.

Given Garth's inclination to shirk his schoolwork, it would be a miracle if that happened.

Being back in Port Sudan was a bitter pill to swallow. It helped that *Thetis* and *Girl Morgan* were still in port. *Thetis*, with a significantly larger budget, considered hiring a coastal boat to tow them north. That hardly seemed plausible. *Girl Morgan* planned to stay close to shore behind the reefs as much as possible all the way to Mohamad Qol and anchor in the marsas (inlets) each evening along the way. Maybe by the time they reached Mohamad Qol the wind would be lighter.

The Wilcoxes borrowed a pilot book from *Girl Morgan* after Chuck discovered theirs was missing four pages that described the coast. When Dawn went to photocopy the pages, she learned it would cost a dollar and twenty-five cents per page. Never mind. She set to hand-copying while Garth attempted to replicate a chart of the coastline he borrowed from the Port Captain's office. With tissue-thin paper stretched over the chart in front of him, Garth bent to his task, his face contorted in concentration as he used colored pencils to trace every sounding, rock, reef, and inlet between latitude and longitudinal bearings. Many hours later the family finally had sufficient information and courage to attempt the inside route.

The family was eager to move on. They were behind schedule. Plus, in the Ethiopian civil war, Sudan had come out on the side of Eritrea against Ethiopia and Ethiopia had been amassing troops at the border.

On April 1st, the family weighed anchor and departed for their third attempt to sail northward in the Red Sea. In the log book, Dawn wrote: *Happy Foolish April.*

The ship's log of their progress northward read much like the trek inside the Great Barrier reef around the continent of Australia, but with an Arabic flavor to the names: Marsa Fijab, Marsa Salek, Khor Inkefail, and so on. They traversed past miles of sepia-toned scenery, a vast coastal no-man's land with nary a detail to distinguish it from any other nearby location. The sailing was more stressful, navigating through reef passes into anchorages when so many of the marsas looked alike—nothing but sand and dirt on a low, flat coast. They would head toward an anchorage with apprehension, wondering, *Was this the one that had the deep inlet after a jog to starboard or the one with the roadstead-style anchorage to port?*

Each day the Wilcoxes attempted to distinguish where they were from blue, lighter blue, milky blue, turquoise and green waters. Garth would pilot them in from up in the rigging to keep them away from the jagged coral. Unfortunately, the seas on the inside weren't exactly as calm as advertised, but calmer than the outer route.

On rare days when they arrived early enough, they could row ashore to hunt for shells or snorkel in aqua water. Dawn found the rubber on her mask had become as brittle as Chuck's, leaving her little time to look before her mask filled with water. Swimming offered welcome relief from the hot, sand-filled air that chapped their lips, left their throats raw, and brought a never-ending thirst. Usually a stop was too brief to do little more than tuck into a quick meal and fall into bed. The next day they would do it all over again.

One evening in Marsa Salek the sky turned hazy and dark, which seemed to portend a sand storm. The next morning they wanted to get an early start to avoid getting stuck there or failing to reach the next marsa north by sunset. At that hour the haze was gone and a blazing eastern sun reflected off the water surface, rendering the reefs nearly impossible to see. In the middle of an S-curve, they'd reached an impasse in which the only way to make progress at an excruciating pace was for Garth to shout course corrections to keep *Vela* pointed toward the center of the channel while he looked backwards from atop the rig. Once *Vela* made it through and the anxiety of navigating blind ceased, they could still feel the knots in their muscles. It would have been so easy to make a mistake.

Using the chartlets that Garth had traced, *Vela* reached Muhammad Qol mid-morning of April 6th. Two men rowed to *Vela* in a leaky dugout canoe and, through gestures and pointing at a soldier on the jetty, indicated that Chuck should come ashore. Though it had been marked on many maps of Sudan, this tiny village consisted of a few mud-brick buildings, unpainted wooden shacks and a small whitewashed fort.

When Chuck and his "friends" reached shore, the men huddled around him, studying his clearance papers. With the hot sun burning the back of his neck, Chuck licked his cracked lips and worried there would be some problem with his papers. Fortunately they found none.

Once the men dispensed with official business, they tried to sell him some goat horns. When Chuck bluntly told them he had no need for goat horns, the men tried to get him to pay them for bringing him ashore, but the Wilcoxes had no more Sudanese money nor the other requested items: whiskey or cigarettes. Finally Chuck offered to serve them coffee (*bon*) when they rowed him back to the boat. They all agreed that would be acceptable. And so they paddled to *Vela*.

The others were surprised when Chuck returned with his entourage and the men climbed aboard. Soon the tension dissipated and they spent the next couple of hours over coffee mugs laughing and trying to communicate without a common language. They taught each other numbers and the words for camels (cam), and donkeys (donks). Eventually they bade goodbye with newfound vocabulary words *chokran* (thank you) and *salaam* (peace).

Then it was on to Khor Shinab and Khor el Marob, where one afternoon they spotted a herd of wild camels grazing on the sparse low bushes that were stubborn enough to make a home in the sand near shore. The camels moved closer to the water's edge, nibbling for thirty seconds then pausing to look around for danger before shifting attention to another bush. Dawn and Linda each snapped a photo, hoping they were close enough to come out on film.

Dawn mused, *How many other homemakers could study a herd of camels while stirring a batch of fudge?*

The protection of the reefs ended at Marsa Halaib, the last anchorage in Sudan. When the Wilcoxes departed Marsa Halaib at seven a.m. on the 10th, they had calm, sunny weather and could see the mountains of Halib twenty-two miles away. Back in the busy Red Sea, now much calmer than before, the family resumed counting ships. Light wind continued for several days, and *Vela* motored northward, clicking off the miles. But the easy gains were short-lived.

The wind came from their destination. As it rose, the motion aboard became less pleasant. Waves crashed over the deck, stressing the boat and drenching her crew.

On the night of April 13th, something hit the wind-vane paddle and broke it. A whale? Though they couldn't see one, they could hear high-pitched calls through the hull. Chuck engaged the electronic autopilot, hoping its drain on the batteries wouldn't exceed their ability to recharge with an unreliable engine. If that happened, they might have to hand-steer again. He dreaded the thought.

While their fellow Americans puzzled over their tax forms, the Wilcoxes had their own frustrations. On the 14[th,] the fuel tanks plugged up once more.

On the 16[th,] the steering broke and they were back to hand-steering—exhausting, especially in these conditions. To make things worse, Linda was doubled over in pain, so the rest had to stand four-hour watches to cover for her. Nurse Dawn put Linda on a liquid diet and monitored her closely between shifts. Soon she improved.

Fortunately by then, *Vela* wasn't far from Ras Mohammed at the bottom of the Sinai Peninsula. The family navigated between reefs into a charted anchorage and dropped the hook. Everyone was glad for a pause to their misery.

They'd finally reached the top of the Red Sea, a milestone for sure, yet they still had another two hundred miles before they reached Suez at the southern point of the Suez Canal. A beat into northerly winds could easily double the distance.

The family's respite at Ras Mohammed was shorter than they'd hoped. Within minutes a war ship steamed into close proximity just outside the reef and deployed an inflatable dinghy with four uniformed soldiers bearing guns. Though Egypt and Israel had ceased hostilities and the Suez Canal had reopened, the peace was tentative at best. Sinai, which Israel had seized during the war, remained hotly contested.

Though unsure which military approached them, one thing was clear: the Wilcoxes were not welcome. What had once been an open anchorage now appeared to be in restricted territory. The family waited anxiously as the soldiers closed the distance. They stared at this coveted patch of disputed territory, which seemed as desolate as any other place they'd seen bordering the Red Sea. What looked like a sand pile reached up and up and up, as far as they could see, until it formed a craggy mountain.

Unable to tell by the uniforms who he was dealing with, Chuck asked, "Are you Egyptian?" Their reaction told him they were not. From that moment, *they* asked the questions, and they asked a lot of them. A flurry of passports, boat papers and clearance papers exchanged hands. With sweat beaded on her forehead, Dawn could barely take her eyes off the machine guns as she awaited a verdict. Once the commanding officer had asked enough questions to satisfy him, he told the family they would have to leave. Chuck showed them that the area was marked as an open anchorage on the chart. The Israeli officer considered the request, then radioed his mother ship, who then radioed another official. After several tense minutes, the man told them they could stay for forty-eight hours, but no longer.

As he handed back their passports and ship's papers, the man informed them he would not stamp their passports or report their presence because if Egypt discovered *Vela* had stopped in enemy territory, she might not be allowed through the canal. The officer pointed out the new border on the chart and commanded them to keep fifteen miles off the coastline. Easier said than done. The Strait of Gubal and the Gulf of Suez—both of which the Wilcoxes had to navigate to reach Suez—were often only fourteen miles across.

As soon as the soldiers departed, Dawn fixed a quick lunch of corned beef and rice. Then Chuck and Garth set to work on repairs. By the time their reprieve was up, Chuck and Garth had found workable solutions, though Chuck was not optimistic they would last. He was correct, but it wasn't the only problem they'd face.

40

Despite all they'd endured to reach the top of the Red Sea, more misery lay in store. Just keeping the boat operating presented a daunting challenge, especially faced with nonstop brutal headwinds and steep chop.

North of Ras Mohammed, the waterway narrowed significantly with countless additional obstacles to navigate. Motor sailing was the only way to make headway against contrary winds, but that meant relying on the engine, an iffy proposition at best. The next two hundred miles would be some of the toughest they ever sailed.

At the north end of the Red Sea, the Strait of Gubal formed a bottleneck at the top of an already skinny stretch of water. What made it worse were the islands and the reefs scattered across its constricted southern entrance. Lighthouses indicated on the chart were unlit (of course!), offering no visual cues about which side to pass and with how much distance. With no guidebooks or recent information, they had nothing but what they could observe. Few traversed this route under sail, and fewer yet since the war had closed vessel traffic ten years earlier.

All of them were on high alert for telltale breakers or the sound of crushing wood. Struggling to read the chart, take readings with the hand-bearing compass and make snap decisions about course corrections as they threaded through this labyrinth of danger frayed Chuck's already raw nerves. Looming large in his mind was his responsibility to keep them from striking another reef.

They were beating to weather, crashing through waves and trying to keep track of where the dangers lay, when an Israeli gunboat stopped in front of them. Though *Vela* had the right of way, it felt like a game of chicken. As *Vela* drew closer, Chuck wondered whether they would move out of her way. The gunboat moved out of their direct path, but stood by, too close for comfort. Through a loudspeaker, an officer ordered the Wilcoxes to turn west over what was marked on the chart as a mine field. Chuck hesitated as the family registered alarm at what he was asking them to do.

The officer assured them that the mines had been removed, but the Wilcoxes weren't anxious to test the accuracy of this information. With her cast-iron keel, the family had no doubt *Vela* would easily detonate any active mine. What if they'd missed one? The word of a soldier charged with deflecting any threats to his border—a man trained to kill—seemed less than reassuring. If the officer were mistaken, what then? Would he simply shrug and say "Oops!"?

With no other choice, the Wilcoxes tacked away, hoping the gunboat would soon vanish and they would be able to turn back before having to cross the area in question. But the officers held firm, as though daring them to disprove the danger indicated on the chart. After all their hard work to rebuild, *Vela* might become nothing more than shrapnel from a bomb in disputed waters.

As they sailed closer, everyone froze as though ceasing movement might prevent catastrophe. When they were long past the danger and nothing had happened, they exhaled almost as one.

"We didn't get blown up," Dawn said aloud. Everyone nodded numbly.

"Good thing," Linda said.

"Yeah," Garth chimed in.

Chuck could scarcely believe the litany of challenges they faced. He eased his grip on the wheel, stretching his fingers out one by one, then rubbed the back of his neck. They tacked back as soon as they could.

Eight hours later, another gunboat ordered them to tack away again. Fortunately no reefs or minefields were marked on the chart, but limiting the distance they could travel on each tack made working their way northward far more difficult.

The temporary repairs Chuck had made in Ras Mohammed didn't last. Not long after Chuck took evening sights with the sextant and Dawn calculated their position, the fuel pump clogged. Then, as the wind rose, the steering went. Chuck rigged lines to steer the boat with the emergency tiller because the wheel was once again inoperable.

It was Dawn's forty-first birthday. In the log book she wrote:

Bloody miserable night; steering broke - using tiller; sea through ventilators

Later that day a freighter—the *Maritime Hibiscus*— motored past with a yacht on deck. Numb with exhaustion, Dawn noted the sighting in the log book and added in all caps: THE ONLY WAY TO GO.

She'd just about had it. So had Linda, who wrote in the log book in capital letters: I'M GOING HOME.

But they were not done yet.

In a near gale—one of those famous winds known as *khamsin*—they faced more trials.

Already exhausted by the strain of navigating through continuous danger, compounded by heat, dust, thirst and the jarring motion of the boat, they yearned for rest. With all the obstacles, two people had to be on watch at all times: one to steer and one to navigate around the ships, the reefs, and the islands. After forty hours with little sleep, poor judgment posed a greater danger with every passing moment. They anchored illegally again. By this point, the idea of being arrested for illegal entry didn't look so bad.

The next surprises were the oil rigs—some lit, some not. The scariest ones were the oil flares, where the oil companies burned off excess natural gas. They looked like enormous blowtorches, visible for many miles. The blinding glow cast the unlit oil rigs into shadow, rendering them more invisible than they already were.

At one point, long after dark on a moonless night, Garth was navigating. The air reeked of dust and burning oil. Something caught his attention. It was a shadow passing in front of a distant flame—disturbingly close to *Vela*. He shivered.

"Did you see that?" he yelled to Chuck.

"What?" Chuck swiveled his head. Garth pointed to the shadow. Chuck peered into the darkness until he spotted what Garth was pointing to.

"Yikes!"

"Yeah. We got lucky on that one!" An unlit oil rig slipped past them, dangerously close. After that, they studied the dark horizon with extra vigilance. But the aftereffects of the brilliant torch flames played tricks on their vision. Black spots danced before their eyes, rendering their efforts to discern potential dangers more difficult.

"I wonder how many more rigs there are," Chuck muttered, rubbing his eyes. As they threaded through a heavy concentration of ships in a narrow slot between two hostile nations, corals reefs, gunboats, and unlit oil rigs, it seemed the stress would never let up.

Eventually it did. For the last few miles, winds were light and shifty for a time, then filled in from behind, giving them a blessed boost north.

At long last they were relieved to spot the city of Suez.

Garth in the Red Sea

41

Finally the Wilcoxes reached the Port of Suez, at the southern end of the Suez Canal, and not a moment too soon. A late afternoon sun cast long shadows as they anchored in Qadal Quala (Suez Bay) at five thirty. Surrounding them were more than thirty anchored ships and the grime of a commercial harbor but they hardly noticed. They were just glad to be stopped. Weary after surmounting nonstop hurdles through a desolate landscape, all dreamed of a full night's sleep and crawled into their bunks.

The next afternoon they moved *Vela* to the basin off the so-called Suez Yacht Club in Suez Creek, where canal traffic traversed within easy view. Oil floated on the water's surface and the boat next to them was coated with a filthy film. The air reeked of dust, oil and exhaust. Not a place they would choose to linger.

Soon after the family tied up to the wharf, a harbor guard with a shifty glance tried to sell Garth a necklace. The bargain he offered was five dollars each or six necklaces for thirty dollars. Neither Garth nor Chuck wanted a necklace. The guard persisted and lowered the price to two dollars each. No sale. The guard would not leave. He finally said he would take a broken watch in trade. Garth did have one of those. So he dove below and grabbed his Timex, its hands frozen since it submerged on the reef in Fiji. At the sight of the watch, the man grew excited and handed Garth a necklace. Garth—no fool—demanded three. The man licked his lips and he traded them without a moment's hesitation.

When Garth told Linda about his trade, she, too, wanted to bargain her broken Timex for a few souvenirs. With her father she stalked the pier, whipping out her watch whenever she saw a prospective buyer. A few short minutes later, she was also in possession of three ugly necklaces—beads of nickel-plated brass and a crude scarab over a Coptic cross. When Linda showed her mother her prize, Chuck teased, "Hey, I never got a commission!"

· · ·

Within a few hours of docking in Suez, an Egyptian named Mohammed (what else?) offered to guide them through the process of preparing to transit the canal. The Wilcoxes were dead set against hiring an agent, but he was persistent and they soon realized they would need his help. Later he referred to himself as Moses. So Mohammed/Moses—or whatever his name was—drove Dawn, Chuck and Linda the four miles into the pockmarked, rubble-strewn town of Suez in his enormous shiny black taxi. Besides checking in and arranging the canal transit, the Wilcoxes needed to replenish food supplies. Garth remained aboard to deter uninvited guests—at least the human kind. The roach infestation was as entrenched as ever.

Moses took Dawn and Linda to all of his friends and relatives—from whom he surely got a cut—so they could stock up on vegetables for the next leg of their journey. Though Dawn worried how much these services would cost, she was relieved to have the help of Moses to carry the load and transport them via his fancy car instead of the usual long hot, dusty walk back to the boat. Or worse: attempting to navigate some form of public transportation with Egypt's requisite parasitic encounters. In the course of their purchases, they'd received change for Egyptian pounds in the form of Syrian piaster and millem coins, which now filled their pockets. But they doubted they'd be able to spend them. The coins would likely join the Egyptian postage stamps of pyramids and the sphinx and ugly necklaces as the only souvenirs of their visit.

While Dawn and Linda stashed their vast food purchases aboard, Chuck set off with Moses to arrange their canal transit and clearance. He girded himself for the headaches that surely awaited him. Chuck's low tolerance for bureaucracy or chicanery could prove a liability in a place notorious for both. After dodging mines in the waters they'd just plied, Chuck now had to dodge the potential landmines of negotiation. As someone who didn't come from a bargaining culture, he had little patience for this time-wasting practice.

Chuck felt compelled to protect the secret that they'd anchored illegally, given potential repercussions. Though the family had regularly deflected Israeli gunboats as they ping-ponged between hostile camps on both sides of the narrow Gulf of Suez, Chuck had to pretend as if *Vela* had defied the laws of nature and geography and arrived magically straight from Sudan.

He also needed to be covert about their next destination: Israel, Egypt's archnemesis. The Wilcoxes planned to sail directly to Haifa—in hopes of reuniting with long-anticipated mail from family and school administrators—but they were keenly aware that this *place-which-must-not-be-named* should never be mentioned for fear it might evoke the wrath of those who held sway over their fate. So Chuck lied on all the forms, indicating they were clearing for Rhodes, Greece. Apprehension about the reception the family might encounter in Israel also gnawed at the back of his mind after all the gunboat encounters, but he would worry about that later.

For the moment, gaining clearance to transit the canal was his first priority. He spent several days with Moses, tromping from office to office in search of the requisite rubber stamp that followed the typical negotiation and cash handover. That was *after* the hassle to secure funds with which to pay everyone off in the first place.

Chuck quickly tired of the bureaucracy. He had thought it bad in Bali, but his experiences in Egypt were worse. The second evening he complained to Dawn as she chopped onions, carrots and spam for a stew.

"These people are experts at ripping people off. If I hear *inshallah* one more time… It appears God does not *will* anything in this country without extra *baksheesh*." He licked his chapped lips, signaling that he was just getting started.

Dawn continued to chop as he talked. *Ca-chunk, ca-chunk.*

He shook his head. "Yesterday, every time I paid what they demanded, the man would give me a receipt for half the amount." They hadn't expected Chuck to be able to read their numbers. When he pointed out the discrepancy, they shrugged and looked at him with flat, dead eyes. An expectant silence followed, as though they dared him to argue so they could find an excuse to jack the price even higher. Their bold corruption made his blood boil.

Onions sizzled in the frying pan on the wick stove, the sweet smell wafting throughout the cabin.

"Everyone seems to get a cut," he went on. "No one actually does any work. Just a bunch of parasites. No wonder these people are still living among rubble as though the sixty-seven war ended yesterday. It's been ten years, for God's sake!" The impatience in him rose like bile as he thought of the frustrations he'd endured trying to pay the canal-transit fees in a place that would not accept U.S. traveler's checks. After a convoluted double-money exchange starting with the bank followed by an eerie backstreet deal in a bombed-out building, he wondered who Moses was working for. He had no doubt he'd been had. Nothing irritated him more than being taken for a fool. But he'd learned quickly that arguing only made things worse. He yearned for the simplicity of a place without haggling.

After a few more minutes of venting, with Dawn throwing in the occasional nod or murmur as she multi-tasked, Chuck had off-gassed sufficiently. He shifted into a discussion of the next day's plan. He'd reconciled himself to relying on Moses to help him navigate the labyrinth of Egyptian bureaucracy and just paying the money demanded so they could get out of there—the sooner the better. If all went well, *Vela* would transit the canal on Tuesday. Then they would be free of these hassles.

But first, Chuck needed to visit the Egyptian Health Office. The officer didn't even glance at their vaccination records. The man was more interested in his fee—the equivalent of two dollars and fifty cents. When the money appeared, he issued health certificates and Chuck was on his way. As he walked out the door, Chuck couldn't help but peek at the receipt. It read $1.50. He cracked a wry smile, but thought the extra dollar well worth paying to avoid invoking an inspection of *Vela*. God knows where that could lead.

The prospect of returning to civilization in the Mediterranean helped Chuck withstand these petty annoyances. His tongue felt swollen from biting back each time he was tempted to point out the inefficiencies and double-dipping. If he could just get them through this, they would be through the canal in a matter of days. *Inshallah*.

Chuck paid fees of one hundred and forty dollars—nearly a month's budget for a family of four. Within a few days, he'd secured a transit appointment.

On April 26, 1977 at eleven thirty a.m., the Wilcoxes left the wharf at Port of Suez with Abdul, the pilot assigned to them, who spoke no English beyond "cake" and "coffee." They anchored *Vela* to await the convoy approaching from the opposite direction. Dawn made Garden Goulash for lunch (without Spam out of respect for Abdul's practice of Islam). The Wilcoxes watched with amusement as Abdul assaulted the salt-and-pepper shaker to add flavor to this bland American cuisine.

Linda monitored vessel traffic through the binoculars, carefully checking the mimeographed list of vessels in transit to keep track of when their turn would come. When the *Amco* passed by, the family knew their turn was coming. At two-ten p.m. they weighed anchor and prepared to join a freighter and three brightly painted fishing vessels in their convoy. The fishing boats fell into line behind a sick gray freighter, which was belching smoke and rumbled as though its engine might quit any second. Evidently *Vela* wasn't the only vessel with a less-than-reliable engine. *Vela* trailed behind until one of the fishing boats circled back and kindly offered to tow them. But after twenty minutes the fishing boat tired of *Vela's* tedious five-knot speed. Soon after it disappeared, blasting at eight knots.

Adbul indicated they would transit to Ismailia, and the family tried to explain that it would be physically impossible to arrive there by dark at a speed of five knots. No sailboat was allowed to move at night; freighters could, but only if they rented powerful projector lamps for the bow. Abdul knew what that meant. He frowned, swore quietly, and lit another cigarette. They were stuck with each other for two days, like it or not. Abdul continued to chain-smoke, but with him steering the boat downwind of them all, they remained free from his incessant smoke and paid him little attention.

Everyone in the family was totally absorbed in the action surrounding them: Japanese dredges lining the narrow canal; women laboring to shift boulders and widen the navigable water; ferries whizzing across the waterway.

Ships traveled in convoys choreographed so the northbound and the southbound traffic would meet in Great Bitter Lake where there would be enough room for them to pass. The family understood this conceptually, but the waterway was far narrower than they'd imagined. To their surprise, the famed Suez Canal, which opened to the grand strains of Verdi's opera *Aida* in 1869, seemed little wider than a ditch in places.

Vela motored past construction, a mosque and an unusual pyramid-like monument spiked with a boat atop it. It marked the spot where the Israelis had built a floating bridge of barges to cross the narrow waterway during the war. Dawn wondered why they commemorated such a humiliating defeat. Maybe it served to stoke anger, lest they forget. The hostilities between the two nations seemed palpable enough without such reminders. (The Camp David Peace Accords were still a year and a half in the future.) Perhaps the monument celebrated finally clearing the causeway so that ships could once again transit the canal after a seven-year hiatus. Without it, the Wilcoxes would have been forced to sail around South Africa. Given all their challenges, Dawn wondered whether they had made the right choice.

In the early afternoon a pontoon bridge blocked their progress, so Chuck relieved Abdul at the wheel and they anchored *Vela*. Abdul demanded cake and coffee—with all the pleasantries that his vast command of English enabled. Dawn scurried below to procure them. After a half hour sipping coffee and munching on cake, Abdul lit yet another cigarette. Eventually a crew of Egyptian soldiers arrived to remove the pontoon.

Underway again, they motored northward for several more hours until they reached Little Bitter Lake, where the canal widened. As the sun cast long shadows in the late afternoon they passed the narrow neck of Al Kabrit that separated Little Bitter Lake from Great Bitter Lake, where the waterway jogged west and widened north of the signal station. At six p.m. they dropped anchor for the night. After a long day under a hot sun they were all spent.

At dinner, Abdul devoured the stock of olives but otherwise picked at his meal—Wetback's Delight, a family favorite made of ground beef plus all the usual Mexican ingredients, or at least the ones Dawn could get at present. After nightfall, Abdul curled up under a blanket Dawn had given him and slept in the cockpit. The Wilcoxes retreated below, relieved for a break from Abdul and his ever-present smoldering cigarette.

By five the next morning, they motored out of the anchorage with the wind on the nose. Abdul reached for the helm and steered them into Great Bitter Lake. They settled in for another long day. A little later the shadows began to shift abruptly and the family noticed Adbul had wandered off course. They stared at him in surprise. His face remained impassive as though he hadn't realized anything was amiss. Chuck came up next to him and checked the compass.

"You're going southeast!" Chuck said, incredulous. Surely Abdul knew enough to realize that a southeasterly direction would take them back toward Al Kabrit.

"Ha!" Garth barked and everyone else joined him in laughter.

"You're taking us back the way we came!" Thirteen-year-old Linda shouted in amusement. "Some pilot!" A look of surprise crossed Abdul's sweaty face. Then shame. Evidently Abdul had lost sight of the markers and grown disoriented.

Chuck reached for the helm. As soon as Abdul realized the captain was relieving him of command, he looked despondent.

"Abdul no good," he said sadly, shaking his head. Evidently Abdul knew other words besides "cake" and "coffee." He slunk over to sit atop the Avon dinghy which was perched on deck. It wheezed as his weight compressed the air inside. Abdul quickly resumed chain-smoking and sulked the remainder of the trip to Ismailia.

At Ismailia, they dropped off Abdul, as happy to be rid of him as he was to be off duty. The following morning they took on a new pilot who would take them the rest of the way to Port Said on the northern end of the canal. The rest of the transit passed uneventfully, the new pilot being better versed in geography, charts and compass courses, though his belligerent demand for a "gift" upon completion of his duty was less than endearing. The Wilcoxes abandoned him on the end of the first pier they came across and hurried to the anchorage outside the harbor, dropping anchor beyond the machine guns on the breakwater. When an incensed Chuck calmed down, he wondered whether repercussions lay in store. He passed an uneasy though uneventful night.

Exhausted from their arduous battle up the Red Sea and Gulf of Suez and the endless equipment failures along with bureaucracy and bribery that kept them on guard, they were weary of Egypt and anxious to move on. Nothing they could see in the bustling, grimy industrial port on the low, featureless delta north of the canal changed their minds. Though Garth was sick with fever and could be of no help on the passage, they weighed anchor at seven fifteen the following morning, secretly bound for Haifa.

Part III

42

They'd finally reached the Mediterranean, nearly four months after leaving Djibouti and five since they'd celebrated a relaxed and happy Christmas in the Seychelles in the company of other yachts. Since then, almost every moment had felt like a struggle. These last few months of sailing had tested the family to the utmost. Worn down after months—years—of trials, the family was long overdue for a respite.

They had high hopes for the Mediterranean. As they sailed northward, Dawn marveled that the waters were a startling Mediterranean Blue, just like the Crayola crayon. The air smelled so fresh and clean. It was a relief to be away from the tickle of dust in their nostrils and throats and the stench of excrement, diesel exhaust and burning oil.

The fresh breeze blowing south from Europe brought with it a surprising chill after the tropics and the blistering heat of Africa. Everyone shivered in the cockpit during the two-day passage north from Port Said, except for Garth, who burned with a fever below decks. They wrapped the old wool army blanket tightly around their shoulders as they doubled up on the watch schedule to work around Garth's illness.

Forty miles from Haifa, in the late evening, they heard a powerful rumble. A sudden, brilliant spotlight seared everyone's eyeballs.

"Destination?" a voice shouted from the darkness. Though officially Linda's watch, everyone but Garth was on deck. Stunned, they failed to answer.

"What is your destination?" The low voice repeated with a clipped hostility. The accent was difficult to discern. Chuck hesitated, wondering if he should answer. They were between two hostile territories and he had just lied on his clearance papers. He was still on edge after dumping their Egyptian pilot on the nearest pier rather than the official drop off point. Blinded by the spotlight, it was impossible to see the outline of the vessel or its crew.

Who's asking? he wondered.

"For the last time, what is your destination?" The ominous tone of that prompted Chuck into blurting, "Haifa." He hoped his answer wouldn't spark more ire from the inquisitors.

"Your home port?" Chuck relaxed a moment. He'd chosen the right answer.

"Ah, … Honolulu," he said after a brief pause. Since Chuck had re-registered *Vela* in Honolulu to avoid California state taxes, they'd painted HONOLULU on *Vela*'s hull. He caught himself before accidentally blurting "San Francisco." Honolulu was their official home port of record, no matter where their hearts lay.

"Number of people aboard?" the voice demanded.

"Four."

"I only see three."

"Our son is sleeping below," Chuck told him.

"I want to see him."

Dawn tried to explain. "But he is ill with a fever."

"Please bring him on deck," the man commanded, as curt as ever.

Chuck and Dawn shared a quick look. They went below and returned a moment later, dragging a delirious and weak Garth up to the cockpit to prove that indeed *Vela* carried four passengers. When the man seemed satisfied, Garth stumbled below.

Before the boat disappeared into the darkness, one of the officers told them the compass course to Haifa. Startling though the encounter had been, it was a blessing to know the compass course for sure instead of relying on the guesswork that came with their most recent star fix. Still, the low rumble of an engine all night let the Wilcoxes know they were being watched and kept them on edge. They might incur more trouble if their course varied.

The next morning, May 1st, the Wilcoxes finally reached the harbor just outside of Haifa. Customs officials were perplexed as to why the family hadn't stopped at the new marina in Tel Aviv. But the Wilcoxes had no information nor even a chart of Tel Aviv, and their mail had been sent to Haifa, the commercial center.

Clearing into Israel was surprisingly efficient and officials demanded no money, unlike most of their recent bureaucratic experiences. After clearing in, an Israeli yachtsman named Ranny offered to guide them into the fishing harbor where they could anchor for free. He promptly led them aground. Once they motored free, they anchored among trawlers and private fishing vessels in probably the most polluted harbor they had ever seen. The pea-green water reeked of petroleum and chemicals from a factory upstream. A thin layer of oil coated the surface of the water, all the vessels and even the docks and the beach. Over the next few weeks, smoke from a power station upwind would coat *Vela*'s topsides and the family would discover a pesky mosquito problem to rival that of Brisbane. But the price was right, and downtown Haifa was just a bus ride away. Only 1.6 Israeli lire (about twelve cents) on the blue 58 bus.

The Wilcoxes were so relieved to reach Israel, the pollution hardly bothered them. They took comfort in the familiar order of civilization that they hadn't seen in the nearly four years since they left California. Israel offered what the countries they'd recently visited could not: sanitary shops with a selection of fresh foods that Dawn could only dream about, plus, for Chuck, parts and service to address boat issues that had long plagued them.

First the Wilcoxes had to figure out how to change money. Ranny helped them beat the atrocious rates the banks charged without the risk of exchanging through black marketers who, though illegal, were everywhere. Then, Dawn, Garth and Linda visited to the post office to collect their mail and buy stamps after getting their bags searched for bombs at the door. Linda spent nearly everything she had on stamps of biblical images, archeological digs and scenic photographs. She saved a little money for the creamiest ice cream she'd tasted in years. It was heaven compared to the "ice cream" she and her mother had bought in Suez: a filthy bowl of a sticky grayish substance concocted with condensed milk and filled with hair that they'd thrown away because they'd been too afraid to eat it.

Haifa proved ideal for shopping. Once they adjusted to seeing machine-gun-toting soldiers everywhere, Dawn and Linda enjoyed the liveliness of the streets and the cleanliness of the shops—a vacation from the strain of provisioning in fly-infested markets, or from the sparse, dusty shelves inside squat cement block structures, or among displays of rotting produce on bare scorched earth. Narrow, cobbled roads were choked with market stalls filled with every imaginable desire. Their hungry eyes took in watermelon, strawberries, peaches, plums—all at affordable prices.

The 8,000-square-mile territory had a population of three-point-four million people from nearly one hundred countries, who communicated in a mix of languages, mostly Hebrew, Arabic, and Yiddish. Many spoke English, especially bankers and businesspeople—just not all of the shopkeepers. Pantomime once again served Dawn well enough to secure what she needed.

Their culinary discoveries included a blended chickpea paste called *hummus*, another paste made of smoked eggplant called *baba ganoush*, and *pita bread* pockets stuffed with *falafel*, *tahini* sauce, fresh tomatoes and lettuce—which they loved. Dawn bought milk in small plastic bags and fresh strawberries, which leaked or turned into strawberry jam on an overcrowded bus.

Before arriving, the Wilcoxes read as much as they could to learn about the cradle of Western civilization. *Exodus* by Leon Uris and *The Source* by James Michener helped them understand regional history. In search of deeper context, Dawn—as only Dawn would—attempted to speed-read the Bible. Linda's history course probed into ancient Phoenicia and Babylon. More popular reading was Carta's Historical Atlas of Israel, and the family argued over who got to read it first.

The Wilcoxes enjoyed Israel's plethora of museums, especially the Maritime Museum, which featured navigational instruments, models, and ancient charts. The Illegal Immigration Museum detailed the time when Israel was a British Mandate and immigration was restricted. So many people fleeing Europe's wars were turned away—100,000 reportedly came but twenty boatloads, each with four hundred people crammed inside, were caught and refugees deported to Mauritius and Cyprus—that Haifa earned the name "Port of Tears". After Dawn's recent struggle to reach Israel via the Red Sea, she could readily imagine how these people must have felt before journey's end. If she'd been turned away after all their struggles, she might have lost her mind.

While Chuck tackled boat projects, Dawn, Garth, and Linda rode the bus to Akko, one of the world's oldest known city ports. Battled over the centuries by successive invaders, a visit there helped bring the historical periods of the Byzantines, Phoenicians, Greeks, Romans and Arabs into relief and shed light on Israel's place within the Levant. It had long been a dream of Dawn's to see the ancient wonders of the world. Here, what the family had read about in history books took physical form and sparked their curiosity to learn more. The three visited the remains of the Knights Hospital, where pilgrims stopped on their way to the holy land and later evolved into a fortress and Crusader stronghold when the Pope inaugurated a series of raids in the eleventh century. They were so captivated by Akko, the family visited a second time with one of Chuck's former co-workers who had moved to Israel to set up a new plant.

Dawn insisted on visiting Jerusalem, the center of the Holy Land. *Borne Free* had just arrived, and Garth was more interested in spending time with his friend Mike. So while Garth enjoyed a four-day respite from his family aboard *Borne Free* earning money doing splices and boat projects, Dawn and Linda hopped a two-and-a-half-hour bus ride into Jerusalem. As the two bumped along, they saw lush cultivated fields, a marked contrast to the dry rocky ones that weren't, evidence of how irrigation could transform a parched landscape. As the bus climbed toward Jerusalem on roads lined with gum trees, their first sighting of the city on the hill was striking.

When the two reached Jerusalem, they accidentally left the bus too soon and found themselves in Mea Shearim, the Orthodox Jewish section of the city. Dawn gawked at women in long dresses and long sleeves and bearded men with long side curls wearing black hats and suits and prayer garments with fringe at the waist. After Dawn spotted signs imploring visitors to dress properly, she dug into her bag for a long-sleeved blouse.

Dawn and Linda wandered old town streets made of steps and winding lanes so narrow they were barely wider than a hallway, past fruit and vegetable vendors and specialty shops devoted to single items like rubber hoses or motor gears. Using a map Mike had drawn for them, they eventually found sparse lodgings at a hostel for one dollar and fifty cents per night, financed by birthday money Dawn's mother had sent. In the thirty-four-hour trip, the two took in the Church of the Holy Sepulchre, Dome of the Rock, Via Dolorosa, the Wailing Wall, the Room of the Last Supper, the Garden Tomb, Mary's Tomb, the Garden of Gethsemane, the Mount of Olives, all the gates of the old city, and more. At the end of their second day, they hobbled back to the bus on aching feet and collapsed into its comparatively comfy seats.

As the bus chugged north back to Haifa, Dawn flushed with contentment. When she sighted Mount Carmel looming 1,600 feet over the city, she felt like she'd been away a long time. When her eyes rested on *Vela* in the harbor, she felt happy to be home. This was the kind of experience Dawn had dreamed about when she set off on this voyage and just what she needed to whet her appetite to continue voyaging.

Unlike sightseeing, the unnatural act of cramming as many sights into a single day, Dawn loved the chance to experience life in another place. Voyaging and buying supplies—even repairing the boat, though not easy—offered interactions with regular people and gave them a unique glimpse into daily life in the places they stopped.

During the family's stay in Israel, the people elected Menachem Begin to be prime minister. With only ten minutes of news in English, it was hard to grasp the political subtleties until they read news clippings from Dawn's mother. Seeing it with their own eyes gave them a deeper understanding that their fellow Americans missed. Just over a year later, Begin would negotiate the Camp David Peace Accords with Anwar Sadat and President Carter. For this, Sadat would be assassinated in 1981. The family's firsthand experience would inform their view of these historical events when they occurred.

As the calendar flipped to July, Israel's weather turned beastly hot. After nearly two and a half months in Israel enjoying the luxuries of Western civilization, they all felt rested and ready to carry on. Chuck had been able to make many repairs in Israel, including the engine, the steering chain and the sails. They'd shopped for warmer clothes to get them through cooler European weather, obtained replacement parts for the pressure cooker, parts to repair the Groco head (again) and grommets for the flags Dawn sewed for Cyprus, Turkey, Spain, Italy and Portugal (Madeira). They'd also ordered charts for most of the rest of the journey, at least to the Caribbean.

The stove remained an unaddressed annoyance. So close to the end of their voyage, it hardly seemed worth the expense of replacing it when money was so tight. To Chuck, it seemed that Dawn was coping well enough with things as they were. Since she didn't press the point, it dropped off the priority list. "I love being able to buy bread ashore, since pressure-cooker bread isn't so great," she would say, hoping he would take the hint. He didn't. In one of life's cruel ironies, someone disinclined to ask for what she needed was paired with someone who took everything at face value.

Another festering problem was with the IRS. Correspondence continued as the IRS chased the Wilcoxes around the globe. At almost every port, along with chatty letters from loved ones back home, a contrastingly terse one waited from the IRS. No matter what Chuck wrote to explain, it appeared the wheels of bureaucracy ground on unabated as though he were yelling into the wind. Amid their other struggles in the Red Sea, Chuck had nearly forgotten. Unfortunately the IRS had not. In a letter to his father, Chuck responded to reports of further developments:

I will write to the IRS in a day or so, although I doubt very much if they will answer it. They have never answered anything yet so I doubt they will this time. Possibly they can't read my typing.

Dawn mentioned the problem to her mother, but divulged little about the worry it caused her:

The IRS says we have to pay $6,200 but Chuck is still going to fight that when we get back. They say we haven't documented the loss well enough. At least we have the money to cover it. I hope Chuck writes to them here.

Like Dawn, Chuck fretted over the issue endlessly. It ate at him because he knew he was right. Without all their backbreaking labor, *Vela* would have been a total loss. They'd only been able to sail her again because they had worked for free and lived without most of *Vela*'s original equipment, something the IRS didn't figure into their calculations. By equating the pre-shipwreck *Vela* to the post-shipwreck *Vela* and ignoring all they'd paid to replace what they lost and get her sailable again, the agency discounted their loss. But, realizing he wasn't presently in a strong position, Chuck finally told his father:

> On the subject of the IRS, if they send you a bill pay it or as much of it as you can. Then they will owe me interest if I can get it out of them again. Corresponding by mail just doesn't work with them.

Given the costs of rebuilding *Vela*, that $6,200 represented most of the money they needed to finance the rest of the voyage. It would mean the family's budget would be tighter than ever and they would arrive home completely broke.

Still, the family's situation in Israel was a monumental improvement over what they had faced when they left Sudan, Djibouti, or even Australia. They had addressed the most urgent issues and hoped it would prove adequate. Fixing a problem with the stuffing box went so seamlessly Chuck would forever remember Israel as "the place that worked." The kids took final exams in the consul's office, the new semester coursework arrived, and so did the $3,900 worth of traveler's checks they hoped would get them the rest of the way home. On the last day, when he'd run out of money after checking out of the country, someone even gave Chuck two lire for the bus. Though the wife of Chuck's colleague complained about how backward everything seemed in Israel, the Wilcoxes thought the country was wonderful. For Dawn, spending two months in a place with such a rich history and a wealth of food options was a luxury. To have an efficient mail system and public transportation seemed a revelation. She would never take such things for granted again.

The family in Akko, Israel

43

S hortly after Garth's seventeenth birthday and America's Independence Day, which the family celebrated once again with all *Vela's* flags flying, they sailed out of Qishon Harbor. It was eleven a.m. on July 10, 1977. During the time the Wilcoxes were in Israel, daily reports of bombings in Lebanon dampened their interest in visiting the country, so they headed for Cyprus, two hundred miles away. They expected the passage to take about two or three days with steady winds.

For the first time since leaving the Seychelles, they were optimistic they could complete their circumnavigation of the globe. Though home was still nearly half a world away, it felt as though they were on the downhill slope of their epic voyage. If all went well, they would be home within a year.

At three that afternoon, Dawn headed below to start dinner preparations. She immediately noticed water spilling over the floorboards. Linda, only a few feet away and immersed in a novel, apparently hadn't noticed.

"The bilge is full of water!" Dawn announced with alarm. Linda looked up from her book. "How long has the water been rising? Where's it coming from?" Linda shrugged.

"Chuck, we're sinking!" Dawn shouted up the companionway. Garth peered through the hatch with a questioning look.

"We're *always* sinking!" Linda said in an annoyed tone.

Alarmed, Chuck rushed down to investigate. Yanking open cabinets, he pulled out belongings and saw signs of water in multiple compartments. But they hadn't hit anything—at least not that they'd noticed. Soon after Garth, who was on watch, came down to help look for the source of the problem.

"Linda, can you take the wheel?" Dawn asked.

"It isn't my watch," Linda stated and resumed reading.

"Linda …," Dawn said again, but Linda didn't look up. Dawn felt blood surge into the tips of her ears. Linda's reluctance to participate in running the boat had become more pronounced since she'd become a teenager. "We need to pump and find the leak. Someone needs to watch the course and check for ships." Seconds clicked by. Dawn's fingertips tapped anxiously against the bulkhead. *Tap, tap, tap.*

"Linda …." No one could miss the edge in her voice.

"Oh, all right!" Linda huffed, throwing down her book and stomping up to the cockpit.

Chuck dug until he could see all the way to the hull. In the blanket locker, when he pulled wet wool away from the sides of the hull, he could see that water was dribbling downwards *inside* the hull from *above* the waterline. Water appeared to be seeping between planks at a surprising rate.

"No joke, we *are* sinking," Chuck confirmed. "This could get worse in a big wind. We'd better turn around and head back to Israel."

Chuck turned the boat around and started the engine. Linda steered while the others pumped. After seventy-five strokes on the bilge pump they stopped to rest. Sweating and dripping, they switched positions. By four thirty, Dawn had pumped another twelve strokes while Chuck checked whether water was still seeping in. Now, no longer heeled over, *Vela* seemed to be taking on less water.

"I suppose the wood planks and seams above the waterline could have dried out in the time we sat at anchor in that dry harbor," Chuck mused aloud, surprised that something like that could happen so fast. It was a relief that the water flow had slowed. Still, at six p.m. in the ship's log Dawn noted another sixty-four strokes on the bilge pump.

Once again in the distance they heard a rumble. Another Israeli gunboat pulled alongside and an officer shouted over to them.

"Where are you headed?" His words soared over the engine noise.

"We are en route to Haifa with four onboard," Chuck shouted back.

"Where are you coming from?"

"Haifa." The men appeared puzzled.

"We're sinking," Chuck added, but that perplexed them even more. The men talked among themselves in Hebrew.

After a minute or two of deliberation, the soldier said, "Wait here." As if they could do anything else. Chuck interpreted that to mean keep sailing the same course. While Linda steered, Dawn and Garth pumped another forty strokes. Dawn hoped it wouldn't be long. All this pumping was tiring. She was dripping in sweat and worried about things getting wet and ruined. Or sinking. She tried to keep calm but felt a churn in her gut. When the men returned from the wheelhouse they looked suspicious but indicated they would escort *Vela* into port. Dawn unclenched her jaw, which she hadn't realized had been tight.

When the family tied up at the customs dock in Haifa Harbor, soldiers boarded *Vela* with an aggressive stance. One officer demanded to see their passports and ship's papers while another searched through compartments, beginning with Linda's clothes drawer. She stood by anxiously as he rifled through her precious coin collection.

After several tense minutes the head soldier poring over their documentation said, "Ah. I see. You are *Vela* from Honolulu." Everyone nodded. At that moment Chuck realized that the officers had thought "Honolulu" was the boat's name and, not finding it in their list of departed boats, suspected foul play. Once they realized, the soldiers laughed at their mistake. The officer concluded their "interview" with, "Come see me at the office in the morning." It was eight p.m.

Now that *Vela* was upright and stopped, the incoming water had slowed to a trickle.

The next morning the family re-anchored *Vela* in Qishon Harbor. Once they'd completely emptied lockers, Chuck could see daylight through cracks in the seam that were several feet long. It appeared that the topsides had opened up on the starboard side where *Vela* lay on the reef during the salvage process. Probably a stress fracture that had worked loose with all the beating they had been doing.

Over the next few days the Wilcoxes kept pumping while Chuck and Garth stuffed cotton caulking and putty into the gaps to seal the leaks. To reach the cracks along the waterline, they stood alongside on a raft they borrowed from a guy who was rebuilding his speedboat after he'd T-boned a ship during a clandestine refugee run. Now the Wilcoxes better understood the grilling they'd just undergone coming into port. The man was lucky they hadn't thrown him in jail.

Five days later, the Wilcoxes set sail once again for Cyprus. Perhaps this time they would reach their destination.

44

Dawn, in particular, was thrilled to be in the Mediterranean. The Mediterranean Sea was bordered by seventeen countries, with people of multiple faiths speaking over fifty languages. It was the birthplace of ancient civilization, biblical texts, and classical mythology that pervaded modern culture to this day. Her primary motivation for voyaging had been to see these historical places and share them with her children. Being there inspired everyone to read about epic events in the evolution of the world from ancient times to the world wars that reshaped geopolitical boundaries and cultures. Though timing forced the Wilcoxes to sail north past the glow of embattled Beirut, its proximity intrigued them into reading about Lebanon's history to better understand the conflict.

For years the family had sailed in places about which little or no information was available—from books or other sailors. As a result, they'd bumbled into all sorts of frustrating circumstances and challenging situations that they discovered only in hindsight could have been avoided. Here other yachts plied these waters and modern conveniences helped to balance the hardships and made it easier to continue circumnavigating the globe.

While underway, they read about the history of Paphos, the capital of Cyprus during the Roman period and the birthplace of Aphrodite. Though Dawn hadn't finished speed-reading the Bible, by then she had learned about St. Paul's visit to Paphos in AD 45, which brought Christianity to Cyprus. When Paul came to preach he was captured and sentenced to a flogging, but after he'd blinded his accuser, the Roman governor converted to Christianity. *How's that for persuasion?* Dawn mused. She couldn't even get a decent stove.

Named for Kypros, the Greek word for copper, Cyprus's strategic location as well as its copper deposits made it a prize through the ages— conquered by a series of peoples over the centuries, most recently the British. It gained its independence in 1960, though fighting between Greek and Turkish Cypriots culminated in a coup d'etat that ousted the president in July 1974, while the Wilcoxes were blissfully enjoying Fête celebrations in Tahiti. Since then, UN forces had preserved a delicate peace. Dawn was beginning to realize just how eventful the last few years had been while her family had been distracted with sailing across the South Pacific, getting shipwrecked, rebuilding *Vela*, and the struggle to keep voyaging.

As *Vela* sailed past the high cliffs of Cyprus' two mountain ranges and motored into Paphos, Dawn and the kids anticipated exploring its Greek and Roman ruins, monasteries, and castles. The family dropped anchor and stern-tied to the quay alongside other boats and the tidy town and noticed the clean harbor offered a refreshing contrast to the filth of Qishon.

The following day, Dawn, Garth and Linda splurged on a sixty-two-cent taxi ride into town. Shopping, they found cheese and stewed meat imported from Ireland and discovered a new unit of measurement: the *oke*. No one could tell them how much that was but, after playing around with the donut-strapped iron weights and concluding it felt like roughly a kilo, they proceeded to buy half an oke of grapes. The vendors charged them in shillings and they did their best mental gymnastics to execute the purchase without the proper currency.

That day, the hottest day of the year, temperatures reached over 100 degrees Fahrenheit in Cyprus, and they were all overheated and drenched with sweat. After seeing a watermelon in the market, Garth yearned for one. He observed people cutting a small section of fruit before deciding whether to buy. He, too, wanted a sample to be sure it would be tasty. Drawing triangles on its skin, he tried to pantomime what he wanted to the vendor. This quickly evolved into a comedy of errors accompanied by much laughter between the vendor and the family. Finally the woman understood what he was trying to convey and cut a plug piece from the melon he'd selected. Indeed, its flesh was candy-apple red and just as sweet. The problem was that without the plug, both they *and* their juicy watermelon dripped all the way back to the boat.

Though the family had grown used to referring to temperatures in Celsius, they still weren't adept at converting Celsius to Fahrenheit. One thing was all too clear: 32 degrees Centigrade was too hot for comfort. High on their list was finding fabric to make a wind scoop to help funnel the breeze into the boat's interior. They wondered why they hadn't thought of it sooner, but seeing one on another boat gave them the idea.

They went in search of cloth and discovered the Cypriots measured fabric in *piks*. Once again no one knew its Imperial or Metric equivalent. Dawn guessed a pik to be approximately a two-foot increment, or half an *el*, the fabric measure she'd encountered in the Seychelles. With a bundle of cloth in hand, they now could sew a wind scoop.

First they visited Gogos the resident pelican mascot, explored the Crusader castle, and toured the ruins of a first-century-AD Roman villa, destroyed in an earthquake in 1222. Nearby workers were still repairing parts wrecked by Turkish bombs three years earlier. That evening, tied along the Paphos harbor wall as they sipped their after dinner tea, Cypriots came in droves to stare at the yachts. Later, singing from the tavernas serenaded them to sleep. They'd already fit more into a two-day visit than in all the miserable days they'd lingered in Port Sudan.

On July 21, Dawn and Chuck's twentieth anniversary, the family set sail for Greece. There was no chance for romance since they were underway, especially with two teenagers aboard—not that they were so inclined in any case. *Vela* drifted along at two and three knots. On their second day sailing the narrow gap between Greece and Turkey, they were headed toward an inviting bay along Turkey's rugged mountainous coast and they decided to sail in. Since all she could see were a few houses and some tents beyond the beach, Dawn concluded it might be a vacation spot where they could stop briefly without having to clear into Turkey. As they dropped anchor, they were enveloped by the lush scent of pine trees, one they hadn't encountered for years.

Shortly after they anchored, a German rowed out to *Vela* but didn't speak English. Later, two Turks came with two small watermelons. Though they also spoke no English, they were more persistent and far more pleasant. Clearly they wanted to trade. The men showed the Wilcoxes their money and proudly pointed out Turkey's hero and first president, Ataturk—a man who was extremely unpopular less than twenty miles away. Since the Wilcoxes had no Turkish money, nor booze or cigarettes, and the men had no interest in an old jacket with a rusty zipper, they couldn't strike a deal. Still, the men seemed to enjoy their time aboard. It wasn't until three of the Wilcoxes had gone to bed that the men finally realized it was time to leave.

After a sleepless night worrying about gusty winds yanking *Vela*'s anchor off the bottom, the Wilcoxes sailed to the most eastern Greek island of Kastellorizo, just a mile and a half from Turkey. Though the hostility between the two countries remained strong, the narrow distance between them and similar dry, rocky appearance rendered them nearly indistinguishable.

Upon arriving in Kastellorizo, the best natural harbor between Piraeus and Beirut, each of them took in the wide flat waterfront lined with tavernas, the brightly painted buildings with tile roofs that climbed the hills, and the path that led up past four white churches. A ruined fort—named the Red Castle (Kastello Rosso) by the Knights of St. John for its red stone—hovered over it all. Inviting blue water added to its charm.

As they motored closer they spotted familiar boats tied along the quay. Garth and Dawn headed to the bow to ready the anchor and pull out lines for stern-tying to the Quay. But Chuck steered *Vela* over to a remote part of the bay and instructed them to drop anchor. They looked back at him, perplexed.

"Aren't we going to Med-moor?" Dawn asked.

"Why would we want to do that?" Chuck replied.

"Uh, because that's what you do in ports like this," Dawn said. Since they first considered circumnavigating the Wilcoxes had known about Med-mooring, anchoring from the bow and securing the stern to the quay, which was born from a desire to efficiently moor boats in compact ports like the Mediterranean—hence the name. The family had executed the technique flawlessly in many places by this time—Hawaii, Papeete, Maloolaba, Qishon … and Paphos only a few days earlier. Chuck's hesitation couldn't be due to lack of skill. Chuck said nothing.

"There's plenty of room," Dawn ventured in a hopeful voice. The quay was nearly empty with acres of space near their friends. Each of them looked forward to stepping off *Vela* and the casual socializing that came with tying alongside—all but Chuck, anyway. He shrugged. He wondered why they would want to tie to the quay when there was a perfectly good anchorage with adequate swinging room.

Dawn and Garth met each other's eyes. Knowing Chuck, they could imagine what was running through his mind. It occurred to them that he couldn't steer the boat and also pay out the anchor and chain without their help. So there they stood, arms folded, eyeing the master and commander behind the wheel. Their body language and lack of action sent a clear message. For a moment, Chuck gazed back at them in disbelief. Faced with evidence of his eroding authority, he had no choice but to turn the boat toward the quay.

Empowered by their recent "mutiny," Garth and Dawn happily dropped an anchor and tied stern to the village quay among ten other sailing yachts and three motor-sailors. Within minutes they were off the boat and socializing with fellow travelers, who offered as many distractions as the tiny village.

The quay was lined with two-story buildings featuring rounded tops and brightly painted wooden doors, mostly shops or tavernas with living quarters above. Narrow twisty streets of stone rose up and away from the waterfront, though not far. There was no bank or post office and the four modest shops had little but a few melons, onions and canned goods. All the food came from Rhodes by ferry once a week. Looking around, it was clear why. The whole island was rocky and dry.

Once 15,000 people had lived there. But 10,000 left after the British bombed the area to rout out Germans occupiers during World War II. The streets still in use were freshly painted white. But as Dawn explored, she came across many empty houses and a whole section of ruined ones near a minaret. These must have been used by the Turkish people who left when the island was ceded to Greece in 1948. Dawn appreciated the chance to witness this.

Though tension remained high between Turkey and Greece, more onshore diversions helped keep the peace aboard *Vela* between its teen-aged crew. Linda loved being able to get off the boat and explore. When she was happier, everyone was happier. A jostling rivalry had transformed into temporary collegiality as they explored each port and had more opportunity to wander on their own.

Dawn and Garth pored over the charts, estimating distances and making note of places with historical interest along their route. They forged a plan of destinations they wanted to see as *Vela* sailed westward, dictated in large part by books they read about the region and its rich history from ancient times through the two world wars. Though Garth seemed disinterested in his English and history lessons and needed to be coerced into doing them, he was getting an education anyway, just one of his own choosing.

Chuck wasn't as interested in the destinations along their route. His focus was on the sailing and keeping the boat going, something that had gotten more difficult since the shipwreck. With all the damage the shipwreck had inflicted, it took most of his time just to keep up with repairs. In many ports, once he checked into the country and secured parts, he rarely stepped off the boat. More often than not, Dawn, Garth and Linda would go exploring, leaving Chuck alone on board. Dawn was disappointed that Chuck didn't share their encounters. It almost felt as though they were experiencing different voyages. She would return, flush from exploring, and find it frustrating to convey to him the richness of what she'd seen. She poured her enthusiasm into her letters home, to people who couldn't be there. She imagined cherishing these memories in her rocker, but wondered how she and Chuck would reminisce when he'd missed so many of the good parts. For her the shore-side wonders made up for the challenges of sailing.

Sailing in the light air along the Turkish coast produced log entries like "*windus kwitus*" and "*yucky do*." The planned two hundred and forty-mile trip to Rhodes was painfully slow. Fortunately Lindos offered a convenient stop along the way. Tucked behind a castle, the expansive bay offered clear blue water with a beach and high cliffs. Though the resort town was loaded with tourists camped on the beaches and paddling around the bay, the Wilcoxes enjoyed days of swimming in clear blue water and exploring the castle at the top of the steep hill.

Impatient with the tourists who strolled or rode a donkey along the switchback trail up to the castle, Garth climbed straight up, trailing a reluctant mother and sister behind him. Once they reached the top of its thigh-crushing incline and stopped panting, they took in the panoramic view of the whitewashed town, the beach and the stunning azure bay beyond.

They spent hours poking around the impressive Crusader walls with its Byzantine and Hellenistic sections, and noted the secret passageways inside. When tourists started arriving in herds, they sought refuge in a side room. From there they could peer down on the chaotic entry yard choked with donkeys and drivers, women in miniskirts and platform shoes, and men in shorts and sandals with dark socks wearing cameras stretched over enormous bellies. There the three lingered, marveling at the clueless tourists, many of whom would barely poke their noses inside and announce, "There isn't much to see here."

The tourists probably forgot all about the place as soon as they walked out the door, while the Wilcoxes would forever remember their visit partially because of how hard it had been to get there and because of the watercolor of that medieval castle Garth painted and later gave to his grandmother.

The three descended a path of pebble mosaics carved into the barren hill to the immaculate town square, where streets appeared as though they were scrubbed every day and painted once a week. Dawn, Garth and Linda navigated past lanes of women selling lace and embroidery and tourists conned into buying overpriced juice and photos of themselves riding a donkey. In town the three bought crusty loaves of bread for seven drachma, then spent the afternoon swimming, eating grapes and lazing aboard *Vela*.

Such indulgences boosted Dawn's spirits, which had taken a brief but sharp dip after they sailed away from Israel. Having *Vela* threaten to sink a half-day out of Qishon harbor probably hadn't enhanced her enthusiasm for the sailing part of the journey. Nor had spending a night tacking back and forth before they could enter at Paphos after the wind died. One of her telling entries in the log during the passage had been *"hull leaking, high wind, head broken—typical* Vela *day."* Yet, given enough time on shore exploring, those annoyances would recede.

Next the Wilcoxes sailed into Mandraki Harbor, the main town on Rhodes. When *Vela* passed between the bronze doe and stag that guarded the harbor entrance, they saw the imposing Palace of the Grand Master of the Knights of Rhodes. Awed by their castle in Akko, the family had read more about the Knights of St. John, the most famous of the Roman Catholic military orders during the Middle Ages who were charged with the care and defense of the Holy Land. After Islamic forces conquered the Holy Land, the Knights of St. John operated from Rhodes for hundreds of years until they were driven to Malta.

When the family arrived, the kids were delighted to recognize boats they knew, including *Borne Free*, *Quest*, and *Sea Fox*. Garth and Linda rushed ashore as soon as they could. Garth was eager to catch up with his friend Mike once again. With an invitation to stay overnight, Garth didn't hesitate to say yes—glad for a break from his family and another night of variations on canned mackerel, corned beef or Spam. Though he hadn't finished his homework—and neither had Mike—Dawn was happy to grant him play time. Since Garth had finished designing and sewing the windsock, breeze funneled through the boat, making life aboard more comfortable and everyone less cranky. He was earning his keep, even if he wasn't excelling in school. Dawn joked that the windsock created a new problem: now she needed six matches to light the Primus. Linda spent time with Cassie off *Sea Fox* and Lisa from the motor sailor *Quest*. She enjoyed having girlfriends her age with whom she could collect coins, shop in the waterfront arcade, and wander around the ancient walled city.

Poking around of the largest medieval towns in Europe eased the pressures of life aboard. The four scattered in different directions, grateful for time to just play and time to be apart.

One day on their way to the castle, Dawn and Linda cut between two huge stone walls and realized they were lost in the moat, but not until they came across a pile of discarded items under a stone bridge. Curious, they sorted through it and found some postcards that were in decent shape and a half-broken, "authentic" (made-yesterday) ancient Grecian urn with a price tag of two hundred and fifty drachma. (Only $7.50 U.S.). Dawn shrugged and stuffed it and the postcards into her pocketbook.

Finally the two found their way to a grand, lancet-arched doorway tucked between two imposing towers with crenellated turrets—the entrance, no doubt. They learned that the castle, built by the Knights, had been restored as a holiday home for Mussolini. Unfortunately for him, he was executed before he could enjoy the property. But they did.

In the castle's courtyard a blind man played Mozart on a piano. The music seemed fitting as they perused the fancy statues, chandeliers, and marble staircase. Later Dawn spotted a poster advertising a concert by this same man for one hundred drachma. She was pleased she'd heard him for free in a venue superior to any concert hall.

Dawn in Greece

45

While in Mandraki Harbor, Garth and his friend Mike were hired to help deliver three Sudanese crew members to Turkey twenty miles away. Excited about an adventure aboard *Balthazar*, a fifty-foot red ketch, they jumped at the opportunity without question. Besides they could earn a little cash in the process. Garth and Mike set out on *Balthazar* early the following morning with the owner, the Sudanese men, who'd crewed the boat through the Red Sea and Suez Canal, and Kermit, a man from another yacht. With so many aboard, Garth wondered why they'd asked him and Mike to go.

Once they raised the sails for a multi-hour sail, everyone shared their horrors of beating up the Red Sea—the yachtsmen, at least. The three Sudanese men did nothing but sulk on the bow and talk among themselves, leaving Garth wondering if they spoke English at all. No one, it seemed, had a particularly good experience sailing up the Red Sea. Most shared tales of equipment breakdowns, horrible weather conditions, gunboats and corruption. Some spoke of alarming detonations in the harbor designed to "deter potential saboteurs," or even of running onto a reef.

It could have been worse. As lines creaked in their blocks and light wind fluttered across the sails, talk drifted to what had happened to the crew of the *Julie II*. After the four were convicted of illegal entry and sentenced to seventeen years, heavy international news coverage and intense diplomatic pressure—and probably a little "international aid"—swayed officials to reconsider the sentence. The four crew were finally cleared of spy charges and their illegal entry charge was deemed "satisfied" by the eight months they'd served. The crew was released in early July, only a few weeks earlier. Though relieved to hear good news about these people they'd met in the Seychelles, Garth and Mike wondered how the crew had endured grim months in prison fearing for their lives. After "shopping" in Port Sudan, they could only imagine the bleakness of a Somali jail. None of the *Julie II* crew were more than a few years older than Garth and Mike. Just thinking about it made them shudder.

Everyone sat silent for a time, listening to the *whoosh* of the bow wave.

The owner of *Balthazar*, Patrick, had his own frightening story. Off the coast of Socotra, men had forced their way aboard wielding guns. At gunpoint, they demanded he steer for shore. Underway and once anchored, they conducted a thorough search of his boat—which had no shortage of stuff aboard. Upon discovering the liquor cabinet, the men left Patrick quarantined aboard his anchored boat and ventured ashore to celebrate.

When whoops and hollers from shore suggested merrymaking was well underway, Patrick made a break for it. He quietly raised anchor and sailed out of the harbor, thankful for a moonless night. Garth could hardly believe it. Patrick went on, explaining that, not wanting to sail the Red Sea alone, he sought crew along the way. They all nodded in understanding.

After an experience like that, who wouldn't?

In Port Sudan he found these Sudanese men who were willing to sail to the Mediterranean with him. He paused.

With a nod toward the bow and a pained expression, he confirmed what now seemed evident, given the men's lack of assistance raising the sails and getting underway that morning. In the Red Sea, the Sudanese men had been no help at all. They'd lounged in their cabin in the bow like they were passengers aboard the *Queen Mary*.

When *Balthazar* finally reached Greece, the Greek officials wouldn't let them into the country. Anxious to be rid of the Sudanese—lest these Muslim men swim for shore and immigrate into their country—the Greek officials urged Patrick take them to Turkey. With tensions still fresh between Greece and Turkey, they seemed to be saying, *Let the Turks deal with them.*

The breeze picked up as *Balthazar* neared the Turkish coast. The rocks and scrub of the dry hills became more pronounced.

"Where are we headed?" Garth asked.

"Up there," Patrick replied with a vague gesture toward the coast beyond the bow. He paid little attention to the chart, and almost by luck it seemed, they motored into a small nondescript inlet and dropped anchor. The crescent-shaped bay was tiny, dotted with a few weathered houses and modest concrete buildings. Few people moved about. Garth wondered how these men would get back to Sudan from here. He envisioned a long, hot ride on camelback—if they were lucky. Until now, he'd given it little thought. Maybe they had pre-arranged something.

As soon as the anchor settled, Patrick loosened the knots that tied down the dinghy. He barely looked up as he picked at the line's frayed ends. With Kermit's help, he lifted the inflatable and dropped it into the water. Kermit tied it alongside, and Patrick went to fetch oars from below.

When he reappeared on deck, he said, "Garth, you and Mike row these men to shore." The Sudanese crew looked at Patrick, their mouths agape. Their faces darkened. They exchanged a few words with one another in harsh tones, the volume quickly rising. Garth had no idea what their arrangement was, but this clearly wasn't what the men were expecting. He stood there, feeling uneasy. Beads of sweat collected on his upper lip and trickled down his back.

Patrick sensed his hesitation.

"If we are to get back by nightfall, we can't dawdle." Patrick held his gaze.

Kermit nodded. Garth shrugged. He felt sorry for these guys, but what else could he do?

"C'mon, Mike." Garth hopped in the dinghy, followed by Mike. Standing alongside in the dinghy, holding onto the lifelines, Garth and Mike waited for the men to step into the dinghy.

For a moment nothing happened. Then two of the Sudanese went below. The other remained on the bow, his arms crossed. The first one reappeared gripping a couple of plastic shopping bags. The two men exchanged a look.

Just then the third man arrived on deck, wielding a bottle over his head. With a yell, he lunged toward Patrick, who was standing aft. Kermit stepped between them and grabbed the man's wrist. The two wrestled for control of the bottle while the other two Sudanese looked on, their expressions blank and their dark eyes unreadable.

With their feet planted on the floor of the dinghy alongside, Garth and Mike were now eye-level to the action. They watched the scene with disbelief.

This did not look good.

Patrick dived below and returned wielding a meat cleaver. Sunlight glinted off the square metal blade like a signal mirror. Garth's eyebrows shot up and his eyes grew big. He and Mike shared a look of alarm.

They never expected to be caught in something so ugly. Two seventeen-year-old California boys between countries in a battle between a bottle and a meat cleaver in the company of men they barely knew.

For their assistance, Garth and Mike would earn five dollars. This morning that practically looked like free money. Now? Not so much.

The blade flashed a blinding beam. The two locked in battle grunted and grimaced as they struggled for control of the bottle.

Garth wondered what to do. What *could* they do?

Movement from the bow caught Garth's eye as one of the other Sudanese men started aft. A flash of the blade drew their eyes back to Patrick. Then a shout of surprised anguish. The tussle hit a crucial point, and a second later Kermit pulled the bottle, slick with sweat, from the man's dark hands.

Everyone froze, absorbing the sudden change in dynamic. Patrick remained still, meat cleaver raised. For a moment, the other men glared at Patrick with menacing expressions. The tension was palpable. No one moved.

Garth felt sweat dribble down his back. He flexed his fingers around the lifelines. Mike remained still at the bow.

The now-disarmed man hung his head in defeat, his dark features a mask of weariness. Then Patrick flicked the blade in the direction of the dinghy and gave a nod.

The Sudanese shifted their stances subtly. They had lost and they knew it. With slumped shoulders they slinked toward the dinghy. As the first one stepped in with his plastic shopping bag, the bottle-wielding one pressed his lips together and gave a slight nod to Garth.

Once the men sat, they seemed less menacing. Garth and Mike met each other's gaze for a moment. Mike untied the lines as Garth settled into position to row.

Garth curled his fingers around the oars and gave a good long pull. The dinghy surged forward grudgingly. With momentum, the next stroke was easier. Water dripped from the oars until he dug them in again. As they drew closer to shore, the men glared back toward the boat with gloomy expressions, talking quietly among themselves.

The whole affair had a creepy feel. Garth felt like he'd been party to something dirty. As captain, Patrick was responsible for his crew. He seemed to be dropping them off in a foreign country—probably a country for which they had no visa—and left to fend for themselves. Who knows what had been promised? Still, these men had gone after him with a bottle. Who knows what could have transpired?

The dinghy's bow finally nudged onto the sand and the boys wondered what would happen next.

The men stepped out of the boat and gave a nod to the boys.

Wordlessly, Mike pushed the dinghy off the beach and hopped in. As he sat down, his eyes met Garth's for a moment. Garth exhaled loudly and Mike cracked a smile.

With each pull of the oars, Garth increased their distance from the beach. The Sudanese men remained huddled in an uncertain stance, tightly gripping the shopping bags that presumably contained all their belongings.

Mike watched the men grow smaller, then glanced at Garth and gave a small smile. They rolled their eyes. If their mothers only knew.

46

The calendar flipped from July to August, reminding the family how much Mediterranean they had to cover before autumn. From Rhodes, the family continued sailing northwestward through Greece's Dodecanese Islands and on to the Cyclades group as they made their way toward the Greek mainland and Piraeus, their next planned mail stop.

Days passed quickly, at least during the stops. Mediterranean winds were often surprisingly strong or so light that *Vela* would sit bobbing for half a day. Still, compared to the trek up the Red Sea, it was basic sailing—a bit of good and a bit of not-so-good. The highlights of the Mediterranean more than made up for its frustrating winds. For the first time since the South Pacific, each stop brought pleasant experiences.

They sailed past rocky promontories, forts and ruins, and alluring aquamarine water. Frequent stops let them avoid sailing overnight but didn't allow much time to linger. When possible, they steered toward places that intrigued them, but often stops were decided by the wind or lack of it. In some places they never got to venture ashore.

Just north of Rhodes was Symi, another rocky island with brilliant whitewashed houses climbing up the hill. Though they ripped the jib beating in high winds all the way there, the hassle was soon forgotten in port. Med-moored to the Quay—also the main road and the key dining area for local restaurants—the four watched with amusement as tourists, bikes, push carts, donkeys, and even a truck navigated around taverna tables, sending chairs scraping as diners leapt to their feet to make way for them to pass.

In Kos, home of Hippocrates, the father of medicine in the fourth century, Dawn continued her medical pilgrimage. The kids were more interested in the arrival of *Girl Morgan*, the Aussie family with three boys they'd last seen in Port Sudan. Reuniting with other boats helped defuse the tension which naturally arose from differing tastes in music and arguments about schoolwork and chores.

Next came Patmos, the island where St. John wrote the Book of Revelation. Dawn and Linda hiked past donkeys, pomegranates, grape arbors, bright pink hibiscus blossoms, blooming cactus and fragrant eucalyptus to the monastery perched at the top of the mountain. Inside was the dark, depressing Holy Cave of the Apocalypse where St. John saw fire and brimstone in 95 AD.

After a brutal fifteen-mile beat in heavy winds, the Wilcoxes finally reached Fournoi, where they had to re-anchor eight times before the anchor held. Exhausted, they went to bed after dinner, knowing there wasn't time to step ashore. Early the next morning they sailed on, anchoring before nightfall under the steep slopes of Ikaria, where, according to Greek mythology an overreaching Icarus met his end.

On a late mid-August afternoon, the Wilcoxes reached Mykonos. At daybreak, they discovered the pristine sandy beach was covered with thousands of sleeping bags filled with hippies avoiding the high cost of an inn or pension during peak travel season. Dawn and Linda wandered up alleys past gleaming white houses with lush bougainvillea draped over balconies and stairwells to see the town's famous windmills slowly grinding grain. Sightseeing was cut short by the area's famous Meltemi winds that whipped down from the north and kept them bouncing aboard *Vela* in the exposed harbor, another "lost" day. It pained them to miss the exciting stops because of weather.

One afternoon, after sitting under limp sails for nine hours, Chuck finally relented and turned on the engine. Dawn yearned to see the Temple to Poseidon at Cape Sounion, but after all the time they'd lost, they had no time to stop. A grumpy Dawn watched the temple slip past as she peeled potatoes for dinner and harbored mutinous thoughts. She sighed and vowed to return one day, with or without Chuck.

The Wilcoxes celebrated the fourth anniversary of their voyage in Siros. The good days now outweighed the challenging ones, though Chuck still spent most of his time on repairs. All thoughts of abandoning the voyage had vanished, provided their money lasted until they reached home. Chuck hoped that the charts they needed for the rest of the voyage would be waiting in Piraeus.

On August 22nd the family reached Piraeus, Greece, their first big city since they left Haifa over a month earlier. They pulled *Vela* into Zea Marina, their first stay in a slip for years. Their stop needed to be brief to keep costs down and leave enough time to push through the Mediterranean before fall.

Another letter from the IRS welcomed them to Piraeus. Chuck had begun to dread getting mail from his folks, which seemed to always contain bad news. In addition to the IRS demand for yet more information, this batch of letters came bearing news that his father was weak and back in the hospital again. With mail delays, they had no idea what his present condition was. Calling the United States was prohibitively expensive, if they could even find a phone booth. Chuck didn't think they needed to abandon the voyage here. If they just kept sailing they'd be home soon enough.

After loading up on groceries with her trusty—though rusty—grocery cart, Dawn insisted on a quick trip to the Acropolis to show the kids the capital of ancient Greece. Athens had been inhabited for 7,000 years and for a family from California, the depth of the area's history was staggering.

Dawn, Garth and Linda hopped a train into Athens for a marathon day. Navigating the vast, sprawling city full of skyscrapers and shops, they finally found where they could join the stampede of tourists viewing the Acropolis. The tight press of bodies came as a shock after months of wide-open waters and tiny island villages. They could hear "Ma Baker" by Boney M. and Captain and Tennille's "Love Will Keep us Together" blaring from car windows and smell the exhaust swirling between cars jammed in traffic.

In an afternoon, they took in: the Acropolis—where they were frustrated by scaffolding and hordes of tourists who hid the buildings from view; the Ancient Agora, the political and religious heart of ancient Athens and the commercial center of daily life; and hundreds of statues and thousands of ceramic pots and urns in the National Archeological Museum. It had been a free day at the museum, so they got more than their money's worth before their eyes glazed over. They ended the day with the 2,500-year-old temple of Athena, the Parthenon.

In one of the street stalls along the way, Linda picked among the collection of ABBA, Bee Gees and the Eagles, the soundtrack to their European travels and finally bought a cassette tape of the Beatles, who had recently disbanded. Even for her, Donny Osmond was wearing thin. Chuck's reaction upon their return was predictable. "More hippie juice," as Chuck would call any music issued after he and Dawn married in 1957, though Garth had caught him humming along to "easy listening" versions of Beatles' tunes more than once. Though Europe offered more distractions to help keep the peace, the generational divide still sparked arguments aboard—especially when it came to music.

From a Piraeus bookstore, Dawn picked up a copy of *Ulysses Found*, a book written by yachtsman Ernle Bradford, who attempted to determine where Ulysses really went after leaving Troy in Homer's *Odyssey*, the seaborne adventure that has captivated imaginations and scholars since the fifth century BC. Based on years sailing the region and a thorough study of related texts and weather patterns, *Ulysses Found* offered the Wilcoxes a geographical context to this classic tale and enriched their travels in the Mediterranean. While Garth might refuse to read it for English class, he had no problem devouring this classic literature for his own amusement.

After four busy days in Piraeus, they were off again. The family sailed down the Peloponnesian Peninsula, stopping for no more than a night in Aegina, Spetses, Momemvasia, and Pylos. Each day, they discovered more rugged landscape and ruins they might love to explore, but they had to push on.

47

A fter nearly two months the family left Greece on September 5th. They set sail for Malta, three hundred and sixty miles to the southwest. Malta's strategic location at the crossroads of Europe and ideal natural harbors offered refuge to the many peoples who battled for its possession. It also offered the Wilcoxes an excellent place to visit on their way westward. After Akko and Rhodes, the Wilcoxes were already familiar with the Crusades of the eleventh and twelfth centuries and the Knights Hospitaller of St. John. When the Knights of St. John were forced to cede Rhodes to the Ottomans, they fled to Malta in 1522. Just as the Wilcoxes had traced the wanderings of Captain Cook in the Pacific, in the Mediterranean it seemed they were following the Knights, St. Paul, and Ulysses.

The family struggled for five days to cover the miles, first trying to make headway with little or no wind and then beating against strong southerly winds and waves, probably caused by a *sirocco*. These prevailing winds are typically at their worst in September and October when the *Khamsin* winds over Africa create dust storms. Predictably, when the Wilcoxes arrived, the warm, hazy African air made the low island of Malta a challenge to spot.

Because Chuck and Dawn had been unable to obtain a detailed chart of Valletta, Malta's capital, they preferred to wait until daylight to navigate into the busy port. Tired after facing adverse winds and waves for days, the Wilcoxes dropped anchor in huge Marsaxlokk Bay in southeastern Malta. White chalk cliffs, gun emplacements on multiple points and a castle fort above a cave intrigued them, but they did not dare venture ashore before checking in.

That night, as the family settled into bed, a Maltese Army patrol boat arrived and told them they were not allowed to stay there before clearing Customs. After a quick study of the officials' chart of Grand Harbour, they hauled anchor to sail up the coast as the officials demanded.

While they were underway, fireworks commemorated the end of the Great Siege that Malta endured against Turkish invaders in 1565, but the stress of navigating in the dark kept Chuck and Dawn from appreciating the free light show. By the time the Wilcoxes found the harbor entrance, cleared with officials, and found the harbor where the yachts were anchored, it was one a.m. They were exhausted and irritable.

When they awoke, they saw a stunning walled city more impressive than Akko or Rhodes. The island nation is best known for its Crusader fortress built after the Great Siege of 1565. Valletta, Europe's first planned city, was built upon a limestone ridge, but its ambitious construction nearly bankrupted the order before its completion. At first opportunity, Dawn, Garth and Linda changed money and hopped a five-cent bus into Valletta, stepping off at the Triton Fountain in front of the imposing city gate. Wandering was a pleasure on pedestrian-only streets.

They first passed Palazzo Parisio, where Napoleon had evidently stayed during his brief but costly visit in 1798. It also turned out to be the post office. There the young philatelists claimed colorful stamps for their collections: some that highlighted Malta's striking architecture, while others celebrated Queen Elizabeth or her father, who bestowed the George's Cross for Malta's stoicism during World War II. Carved beneath the city were underground tunnels where people sheltered during the bombing. Some stamps celebrated Malta's independence from the British in 1964 and others its role as a neutral meeting place to negotiate international agreements.

As Dawn, Garth, and Linda strolled the narrow streets, they were charmed by the columns and statues throughout the city, horse-drawn carriages decorated with finery, tall townhouses with balconies that hung overhead, and doors with big brass knobs and fancy knockers that opened right onto the street. They were enthralled with the many tiny shops, including one devoted only to buttons. From the steep, stepped streets, peekaboo views revealed the harbors and the blue Mediterranean Sea beyond. The city seemed an homage to stone, with a noticeable lack of greenery.

They headed for the famous St. John's Co-Cathedral and discovered that the building's austere stone exterior belied the lavish interior decor and treasures. Inside the cathedral and along the streets, areas catered to the eight nationalities or langues (tongues) of the Knights: Italy, France, Provence, Auvergne, Castile, Aragon, Germany, and England. The Order consisted of European noblemen who lived like monks and soldiers wore a monk's hooded habit emblazoned with a white Maltese Cross. Among the many languages of tourists, they heard snippets of Malti, a language which sounded Arabic, speckled with Italian, French and English words. Most shopkeepers spoke English.

For eleven days, between the usual boat chores and repairs, the family took in Malta's stunning architecture and history. Delighted though she was, Dawn shared with her mother the frustrations that came with seeing this fascinating place by boat on a tight budget:

We came here partially because we had hopes of hauling out in Malta, but turns out to have been a mistake. The yard couldn't haul us because the keel has a rounded bottom and won't fit the holder. We took the propane tanks in but don't know yet if they can fill our type valve. The food does tend to be cheaper . . . though rice and onions are expensive. In all we lose money due to the outrageous harbor fee of $50, supposedly a month's worth but not pro-rated for a shorter visit. Another big problem is water: They want a $100 deposit then 5 pounds ($11.85) for 1,000 gallons. You get the $100 back the day you leave, but in Maltese pounds so you lose more converting them back to dollars from Monopoly money at the bank. That's the way Malta makes money. Chuck calls it foreign aid. We couldn't afford all that, of course, so it's been a bother. No baths, hair washing, or laundry all week. Today Chuck got permission for taking 100 gal from the bathroom sink in jugs. It will take Garth 5 trips.

Chuck had his own struggles. He lost a day in Pylos and another in Malta filling out forms and writing letters in yet another attempt to pacify the IRS. Between IRS correspondence waiting at every mail stop and never-ending boat repairs, he was robbed of what little enjoyment he took from the places they visited. Their next mail stop would be Gibraltar. There, he imagined would be the next installment in the never-ending tax saga. Aside from exiting the Mediterranean before winter storms set in, the Wilcoxes needed to press on so they could reach home before the family ran out of money or the U.S. tax court held a hearing.

It took three trips rowing into shore before they could pick up their propane tank, because the gas truck needed repairs. When it finally arrived, wonder of wonders, it was full. But because of the delay, the family missed leaving Malta with a nice southerly to push them north.

48

A s the Wilcoxes left Valletta, they sailed past St. Paul's island on Malta's northeast coast, where the saint was shipwrecked in 60 AD. Dawn could relate to Paul finding himself swimming ashore after his ship broke apart, though not to the death sentence that faced him when he returned to Rome. Rebuilding *Vela* for nine months in tropical heat didn't seem so bad in comparison.

At the north end of Malta, *Vela* cut westward through the South Comino Channel, between Gozo and Malta, then sailed close-hauled along Gozo's southerly cliffs, following the coastline carved over millenia by wind and sea. As she held onto a pot on her one-burner Primus, Dawn stared at the aquamarine water and dramatic geographical formations to starboard. Gozo was believed to be the island where the nymph Calypso seduced Ulysses and kept him captive for seven years. Beautiful though it was, Ulysses ached for his home in Ithaca. Dawn, too, yearned for home.

Once past Gozo's off-lying rocks, *Vela* turned northwest. They were bound for the west coast of Sicily, which juts from the toe of Italy's boot into the heart of the Mediterranean, nearly touching Africa at Tunisia and splitting the Mediterranean into two. Though Tunisia was closer than Sicily, the Wilcoxes had no interest in revisiting Africa, even if it were the famed Land of the Lotus Eaters.

A three-day sail north took them to the northwest coast of Sicily, where Ulysses had beached his fleet on the south side of Favignana Island, according to *Ulysses Found*. *Vela* anchored in the north-facing harbor alongside brightly colored fishing boats with the Phoenician-style *Oculus* painted on their bows. Whereas Ulysses and his crew encountered only goats grazing on fertile land and a fresh stream, Dawn found a nice fishing village with an attractive town square where she bought anise-flavored Italian bread, pickled olives, dry salami, and a fragrant Chianti.

While Ulysses ventured east from here into Trapani, where he encountered Cyclops and his deadly cave, the Wilcoxes turned westward.

49

Though the Wilcoxes might have liked to continue tracing Ulysses's voyage from the Odyssey to Circe's Island, it was late September. It seemed sad to miss all of Italy, but they could already feel the chill of fall winds. Instead, the Wilcoxes sailed westward toward the southern tip of Sardinia. Originally they planned to stop at Carloforte in Sardinia but when they neared Cape Spartivento, a patrol boat rushed out to *Vela*.

Lots of arm-waving ensued, accompanied by frenzied Italian.

The officer said, "Balabala balabala balabala, PROHIBIDO, balabala balabala balabala, MILITARIO," or something to that effect, holding up six fingers and pointing emphatically out to sea. His meaning was not crystal clear, but he kept stating over and over again "Prohibido," thereby impressing upon them that they needed to move *Vela* or face unknown consequences. They turned seaward, their hopes dashed of visiting Sardinia's rugged green coast and the watchtowers that looked so interesting.

Amid intermittent puffs and lulls, they headed straight for Palma de Mallorca, the hub of the Balearic Islands fifty miles off Spain's coast. The passage took eight frustratingly calm days. On one windless day, the ship's log seemed stuck on the same mileage number—295.5—for most of the day and the only excitement was when a sunfish came over to check them out. On another, a bird flew inside the cabin, sat on the radio, the bunk, and then on Chuck's foot before flying back out and ingesting a dead-moth lunch in a single gulp. Europe was all around them, yet they were imprisoned on *Vela*, surrounded by a huge moat.

Upon finally arriving at Palma on October 5th, the Wilcoxes were shocked at the ostentatious wealth: walls of high-rise hotels lined the Bay of Palma; villas and country estates climbed the hills behind the beach-front monoliths; and mega-yachts as large as ships sparkled in the bright Mediterranean sunshine. Dominating the skyline was La Seu, a stunning Gothic cathedral built of golden sandstone that towered over the harbor and the town.

The Wilcoxes Med-moored among the fancy superliners that lined the quay. Dwarfed by mammoth displays of wealth, *Vela* appeared shabby and out of place. They hadn't hauled the boat since Mooloolaba and the bottom paint was flaking and covered with barnacles. On the move for so long, they'd had little time for varnish and never-ending upkeep. Though Garth and Linda had scrubbed and polished *Vela*'s bronze winches en route to Malta until they gleamed gold, they were dull once again.

Palma could not have been more different than Sudan—a place so bleak, it seemed as if they'd imagined it. Palma de Mallorca was as lovely as King Jaume the First had declared when he captured Palma in 1229 and pronounced it "the loveliest town that I have ever seen." The Wilcoxes loved it, too, especially the plazas and little parks with benches nestled under the trees, the castle on the hill and the medieval churches decorated with gargoyles.

Only two years after the death of General Francisco Franco, the nation's longtime dictator, the Spanish government was in a state of flux. No clear guidelines for checking into the country meant no paperwork for Chuck. Coins and stamps in circulation featured either Franco or King Juan Carlos and were a collector's delight. After forty years of fascism, the Spanish economy was in shambles. Because of that, Palma was surprisingly affordable, even for the Wilcoxes. The abundance of fresh foods in Palma astounded them and added to their enjoyment of the place, though shopping required navigating across a noisy eight-lane highway and a three-mile walk into town past soulless high-rise hotels. During the family's five-day stay, Dawn stocked up on everything she could—ham, bacon, cheese, milk—though she decided to forego the skinned rabbits, cow's ears, and pig's heads that hung from hooks at the butchers.

While in Palma, Chuck insisted on inspecting the boat's bottom. He worried that *Vela's* bottom paint would fail before they reached home—which, if all went well, would be within eight months. They took *Vela* outside the harbor in search of clearer water to scrape and inspect the hull. Chuck and Dawn struggled into the two-hundred-dollar wet suits salvaged from the reef but never used. By then the aluminum zippers had corroded, rendering both suits useless. Though the growth on *Vela's* bottom cost a knot or more of speed, the frigid water forced them to abort the effort.

And so they carried on at painfully slow speeds, growing increasingly motivated to return to the warmth of the tropics.

50

From Palma de Mallorca the family sailed southwest past the island of Ibiza toward the Iberian Peninsula. They rounded Cabo de Gata, where *Vela* narrowly escaped becoming a "freighter sandwich." After four days underway, they pulled into Almería, Spain at ten-thirty p.m. and dropped anchor. Up on the hill, they could see a lit Moorish castle inviting them to visit.

In the morning, the family discovered an atmosphere much more in line with their middle-class perspective than opulent Palma. Dawn took advantage of Spain's dirt-cheap prices, putting her rusty cart and teen-aged bag-handlers to work hauling two hundred dollars' worth of food, including olives of every sort, cheeses, meats, and six jars of peanut but-ter—at last. Dawn must have single-handedly depleted the town's sup-plies of peanut butter because when she returned to buy a few more jars, she discovered prices had jumped twenty-two cents overnight.

Though all the family did was shop during their weeklong stay, Almería was interesting because of the cave residences carved into the sand-colored, sun-baked cliffs under the castle. Painted or tiled rock around doorways distinguished one home from another. On a walk with

Chuck, Dawn noticed that few streets were paved and rubbish danced across the empty streets. Still, all of the children had shoes, which was more than she could say for her own kids, who had long since outgrown or shredded their closed-toed shoes. Before they left, Dawn was relieved to find sneakers to replace their sandals and green rubber fishermen's boots that—ugly though they were—cost only a dollar. She also found warm-weather clothing to ward off the sudden chill in the air.

As October ticked by, temperatures dipped into the fifties, lower than the family had encountered for years. Everyone shivered not only on night watches, but now during days ashore too. Along the Costa del Sol, there wasn't much *sol...* or wind either. Rain became more frequent, and the family spent progressively more time in their yellow rain suits. The need to press on to the Caribbean became more obvious each day.

The family stopped in Málaga, the birthplace of Picasso, tucked into a bend in the bay and surrounded by lush green mountains. It was a prosperous, touristy town and therefore less affordable. Since there wasn't sufficient room in the marina and winter threatened to descend at any moment, they moved on without delay. They had hopes of hauling *Vela* to repaint the bottom and thereby improve their speed, but once again facilities could not accommodate *Vela's* twenty tons. Nor could they haul at another suggested marina further down the coast—this time due to the outlandish cost. They'd have to hope *Vela's* paint would last long enough.

In a series of day hops, they sailed the remaining sixty-six miles westward along the Alboran Sea, past mountains, villages and beaches. They noted the hotels in pretty Marbella and Torremolinos that Michener had described in *The Drifters*. After stocking up yet again, the Wilcoxes left the Spanish mainland for the last time at the little fishing village of Estepona, where they'd watched fishermen working their nets.

The family reached Gibraltar late afternoon on October 27th. Reaching Gibraltar was an important milestone. It would be their last stop in the Mediterranean and last port of call on the continent of Europe where they had spent some of the most enjoyable months of their voyage exploring the history of Western civilization.

They gaped in awe as they passed close to the famed sentinel rock, which jutted vertically like a limestone shrine from a flat neck of land so low it almost seemed invisible, as though Gibraltar were an island. The sun cast long shadows when *Vela* rounded Europa Point and motored into the harbor. The Wilcoxes tied *Vela* to a large British motor yacht where destroyers had been moored during World War II. Within minutes the sun dropped over the horizon.

This limestone promontory has been fiercely disputed for its strategic location at Europe's southwestern tip, only fifteen miles from Africa. Anyone entering or exiting the Mediterranean travels through this narrow strait, and those who controlled it had tremendous advantages, as the British proved in World War II. It has withstood so many sieges that its name has become synonymous with tenacity: "solid as the Rock of Gibraltar." Its two-and-a-half square miles comprised little more than a British garrison with a few attractions.

Also known as the "Pillars of Hercules" where Ulysses visited at Circe's urging before finding his way back to Ithaca, this natural gate to the Atlantic marked the end of the "known world" in ancient times. For the Wilcoxes, the Pillars of Hercules was also a gateway to the unknown in a sense. Once they passed through, they were truly on their way home, and what the future held *after* the cruise began to infiltrate their thoughts more frequently, at least for Dawn and Linda. Once they passed through this gate, they would begin one of their last ocean passages: crossing the Atlantic. But first they had to check into Gibraltar.

British uniformed Customs and Immigrations officials promptly came to clear them in. The kids were charmed by their British accents and enthralled to learn that one of the officials was a great-grandson of Admiral Nelson of Trafalgar fame, whom they'd recently read about in their history books. Yet another free history lesson.

The Wilcoxes wanted to visit the actual Rock of Gibraltar and see the famous Barbary apes. Three days after they arrived, they split a taxi with a single-handed sailor to the end of the steep road and hiked the rest of the way up as far as they could. After a long, vertical hike through the cloud that hovers over the rock, they could look down on the tiny town and beach perched on the narrow strip of mostly reclaimed land. A hazy view laid out before them and, in the distance lay Africa. In the year since they'd reached the opposite side of the African continent they had seen so many countries.

Eventually they came across a crowd of people hovered around a group of apes. As Linda reached into a bag for her camera, a small ape ran over, climbed to her shoulders and sat on her head. The apes had come to associate bags with food. When the ape's mother tried to join him, Linda became nervous and everyone had a good laugh at her expense. Once free of the apes, she snapped pictures of an ape gorging himself on peanuts he'd stolen from another lady.

After enjoying the view long enough to rest their legs, they began the long, knee-shattering trek down. Their thighs burned in protest, feeling every one of those 1,350 feet after so many days of sailing and limited exercise.

Gibraltar, known as "Gib" by locals, was a mixture of British, Spanish and Moroccan, with a decidedly British flavor: fish-and-chips shops, pubs, Bobbies in smart uniforms, double-decker buses and British coins. The Treaty of Utrecht gave the Brits sovereignty over the rock in 1713. Franco closed the border in 1965 and it had not yet reopened. Because of this, most food was imported from Britain or Morocco and, therefore, *old*. That halted Dawn's frenetic attempts to provision for the coming ocean crossing and she was grateful for the forced break. Dawn confided to her mother:

I'm getting tired of this rush, rush, rush, buy, buy, buy, and stow business, but we spent too long waiting for Garth to finish science in Haifa and must get out of the Mediterranean before winter. It's quite cold now.

Perched on the edge of the Atlantic, Gibraltar was often shrouded in mist, like downtown San Francisco, which could quickly chill them to the bone, even when they wore heavy layers of clothing. The family now had to boil water for bathing, which they began to dread. There could be no doubt that winter was coming. Though sad to leave the Mediterranean, which—except for the frustrating winds—had offered the cruising delights they'd envisioned, they felt drawn to the warmth of the tropics and steady trade winds.

Chuck felt optimistic about finishing the voyage and began to focus his attention on the next challenge—getting out of the strait before the wind turned westerly. A famed *Vendoval* wind would make it difficult to exit the Straits of Gibraltar against a surface current that flows steadily eastward into the Mediterranean. With a four- to five-knot current rushing over the shallow sill of the straits and *Vela*'s tendency to average only four knots, basic math revealed a clear problem if *Vela* didn't get all the way out the strait before a change in the wind. And so, on the advice of a local man, they planned their departure for four a.m.

On November 3, Chuck's forty-first birthday, *Vela* set sail for the Atlantic. First stop: Madeira, six hundred and fifty miles away. By dark that day, they had barely cleared the strait.

51

Eight days after leaving Gibraltar, the fog lifted to reveal the welcome sight of Madeira. The large mountainous islands three hundred and seventy-eight miles off the coast of Morocco were well positioned to offer respite to a weary sailor making his way across the Atlantic between the Mediterranean and the Caribbean.

After a windy passage, Dawn looked forward to relaxing in port, but unfortunately Madeira's capital port offered little rest. Funchal was merely an indentation into the sunny south side of the main island. The bay was open to the east with winds coming from that direction, and the breakwater failed to dampen the violence of the waters off the coast. Rollers swept in from the sea. While the harbor might have been adequate for square riggers when the son of Portugal's king discovered the islands after being blown off course by violent storms in 1418, the Wilcoxes had hoped for better. They ended up having to set two bow anchors and a stern anchor after *Vela* dragged. Then, because yachts were anchored where ships needed to maneuver, they learned they would have to move *Vela* each time a ship arrived. By the second morning they'd already moved *Vela* twice. Given the conditions, Chuck was afraid to leave the boat unattended.

In Madeira, the family encountered a confluence of yachts from Europe. Shortly after anchoring they met people from two Dutch boats who had just begun their voyages. Hungry for advice and reassurance, the novice cruisers hurried over when they noticed *Vela*'s home-port designation of Honolulu. The Dutchman from the trimaran peppered the family with questions until midnight. The next morning, Dawn noticed he'd changed the way he tied his dinghy to mimic what the Wilcoxes did. For the first time, the family realized how much they'd learned in the years they'd struggled to move *Vela* from port to port.

The second Dutch couple owned a steel vessel, built like an old-fashioned schooner, and had just installed a new wind vane a week before. On Sunday, two days after the Wilcoxes arrived, a fishing boat dragged into the Dutch schooner, crushing their brand-new wind vane. The couple spent the following day removing the damaged wind-vane parts to show the harbor master and formally lodge a complaint against the fishing boat that hit them.

That afternoon, Garth and Dawn rowed into the dock to fill water jugs. As Garth was handing a full jug to Dawn in the dinghy, the couple came rowing in. As the couple drew close, a wave broke over them. Their dinghy surged forward, hurtling toward the concrete pier. The lady screamed. Dawn and Garth rushed over to help. Garth reached for the wind-vane parts the woman carried in her hands as Dawn reached for their dinghy painter. Another wave crashed over them and slammed the dinghy sideways. Gushing water from a third wave swept over them and part of their wind vane slipped into the water. The woman cried out in anguish.

Then she and her husband started bewailing their fate in Dutch. Though the language was foreign, its tone was not. The man pounded his fists against the inflatable's air tubes.

Garth yelled over, "How deep is it?" as he made his way toward where their dinghy had ended up. After four years of cruising, it was obvious to Garth that if there were breakers, the water must be shallow. He knew their wind vane wasn't lost forever—yet.

When the man finally looked over, Garth pointed into the water. Gradually the man comprehended that the wind-vane parts might still be retrievable if he acted quickly. Soon, sun glinting off metal caught his eye. And he leapt from the dinghy to reach for the part.

Dawn grabbed the couple's dinghy to help pull it into shore, which left her trying to juggle two dinghies. A wave suddenly ripped her own unsecured dinghy line from her hands and *Vela's* Avon swept onto the rocks. To retrieve it, Dawn had to crawl on her hands and feet over the slimy rocks. When she reached it, she was relieved to find it undamaged. While she regained her footing, a local fisherman helped her lift the Avon up onto the wall. Just then another man in a wooden dinghy capsized, submersing his outboard—potentially ruining it. The fishermen helped him, too. *What a crummy harbor*, Dawn thought, shaking her head at the carnage that had occurred in such a short time.

Garth felt sorry for these people, remembering his own family's struggles to navigate the challenges of life afloat, and spent the next half hour trying to soothe and encourage the upset cruisers. Dawn bit her tongue and mused about how much "fun" *yachting* could be.

While Funchal Harbor was horrible, the town was pleasant. Garth and Dawn strolled all over town together in search of a souvenir from Madeira. What else does one buy in Madeira but … Madeira? This outpost of Portugal garnered fame for wine fortified with brandy that kept well despite exposure to heat and cold aboard ships for months or even years. Garth convinced his mother they needed to conduct a thorough sampling. Linda did not come along. In one of her typical pronouncements, Linda had let it be known that Donny Osmond didn't drink alcohol, so she didn't want to have anything to do with the stuff. (Of course once you make such a pronouncement in the Wilcox clan, no one will let you forget it.) While sampling, shopkeepers first handed a glass of the rich amber liquid to Garth—rather unexpected since he was still only seventeen. But he felt obliged to follow their lead and, once he nodded approval, his mother got a taste, too. In Madeira, meat and vegetables were prohibitively expensive, and not particularly fresh. So was the fancy embroidery the island was known for. A single embroidered piece the size of a placemat cost two hundred escudo or five dollars. The tasty fortified beverage, on the other hand, cost only sixty-five escudo, or a dollar-sixty.

Linda had far more interest in collecting Portuguese stamps and coins and in the flower sellers dressed in their island costume—a red embroidered waistcoat and pleated blouse over a woolen skirt. She was intrigued by the cobbled streets, so narrow that people had to stand in doorways to let vehicles pass. Among those vehicles were ox sleighs—a better solution for cobblestone streets on which wheels wouldn't have worked at all. Along streets of basalt and white marble laid in a pattern the shape of a fan was a statue of Cristobal Colombo, who married the daughter of the first Portuguese Governor in 1478, fourteen years before discovering the islands he called the "West Indies." The Wilcoxes would sail there, too.

Together Dawn and Linda were amazed at the island's lushness—its sunken creeks overgrown with vines, poinsettia, roses, and hibiscus, a marked contrast to the dry Mediterranean. The three rivers that rushed through town from the mountains all around could supply enough water for five Greek islands. The two of them watched graceful black swans with red beaks paddle around a pond in Jardim Botânico, one of the many public parks perched on the hill above town. It helped to compensate for the hassles of the harbor and the discomfort of sailing.

Shortly before the Wilcoxes left Madeira, a dark blue cruise liner proudly flying the British ensign steamed into the harbor with a band playing. Its shiny bronze portholes, Royal coat of arms, gold stripe and crown, along with E II R, announced its importance, in case there were any doubt. It was the *Britannia*, Queen Elizabeth's yacht. The queen wasn't aboard, having flown back from the Caribbean on the Concorde. It could not have been a more different way to travel than aboard *Vela*, with a single-burner Primus still safety-wired to the top of the dead stove and rust streaking down her topsides.

After three full days in Madeira, it was time to move on. Unlike the *Britannia*, the Wilcoxes had no crew to sail their boat to the next port. But Garth didn't mind. On the passage from Gibraltar, Garth studied navigation books and by the time the family left Madeira, he felt prepared to start shooting sights and calculating their positions. With Chuck's encouragement, Garth would navigate alongside his father all the way from Madeira to the Canary Islands, the next stop on their way to the Caribbean.

From Madeira, the Wilcoxes steered almost due south, helped by steady northeast trade winds and a current that swept southwest off the African coast. Each day, they would check the time on the "official ship's chronometer"—Chuck's Seiko self-winding wristwatch—against the time signals on the short-wave radio when they could tune it in. They would note the watch error so they could factor in a correction. Each sunset, Garth and Chuck both measured the angle of the stars with the sextant. Then the two used tables and worksheets to calculate and triangulate their location and compare it against their dead reckoning. As the days passed, Garth's thick pencil marks noting the stars and their locations stood alongside those of his father in the composition notebook the family used for a logbook.

18-22-10 17°33.1' Capella
18-15-00 22°15.5' Aldebaran
18-17-40 41°34.9' Fomalhaut

18-20-45 40°30.1' Deneb
18-22-51 17°48.0' Vega
18-23-50 19°34.5' Capella
18-24-47 24°33.5' Aldebaran
18-25-37 40°59.3' Fomalhaut

FIX 16°50' N
40°06' W

Garth's positions coincided with Chuck's well enough that Chuck agreed to let his son navigate the next leg, from the Canaries to Martinique. Garth was pleased to earn his father's confidence.

After three days underway from Madeira, the family could discern the great height of La Palma, the westernmost island of the Canaries, more than sixty miles away. The shorter islands—Tenerife, Gomera, and Hierro—didn't come into view for another twenty-four hours. The archipelago lay only seventy miles off southern Morocco. Geological formations indicated that the islands had once been part of the African continent, but volcanic activity dramatically altered their features since then—most recently in 1971, only six years before the Wilcoxes arrived.

In the early afternoon of November 19th the family closed the distance to La Palma, a striking island shaped like an inverted cone. Its features slowly came into relief—steep coastal cliffs that rose abruptly toward the world's largest volcanic crater, a once-majestic volcano that had collapsed in on itself. The Wilcoxes dropped anchor off the town of Santa Cruz, in a bight on the east side of the island.

It had once been the third most important harbor in the Spanish Empire, because the Canary Islands possessed an abundance of good wood and fertile soil. Christopher Columbus stopped there to make repairs on his way to the new world, and Dawn was again happy to impart this tidbit of history to her kids. In 1977, it seemed more like a sleepy outpost, a sunny Atlantic Island with a European feel, this one Spanish rather than Portuguese. Franco had led the Nationalist Revolt from here when he was military governor of the islands in 1936, and the aftereffects of his thirty-year rule were still evident in a depressed economy. Like in Palma de Mallorca and the Spanish mainland, that made the Canaries an inexpensive stop.

Shortly after they anchored, the family encountered a single-hander who was sailing on a budget as tight as theirs. The man seemed to always be looking for ways to make a buck or cut costs, much as the Wilcoxes had to, but Garth took an immediate dislike to him. One day when Garth was alone aboard, the man pointed to the spare dinghy that Garth had inherited in Rhodes and said, "You know the American boat *Mustang* lost their dinghy," and paused as though waiting for a reaction. Garth looked at him, wondering why he should care. "You could sell them your dinghy."

Garth looked at the dinghy strapped to *Vela*'s bow. After Garth had helped "deliver" Patrick's Sudanese crew to Turkey, Patrick was clearing out extra stuff from his boat. He offered to pay Garth a few bucks to help him to sort through and get rid of it. A teenager can never have too much spending money and, given the ridiculous allowance Garth's folks were paying him—fifty cents a week for taking out the trash and hauling water and all the miscellaneous repairs he made aboard—it made sense to consider other sources of income. Though understandably wary of doing business with Patrick, Garth thought he might find something useful in the process, so he agreed.

Most of Patrick's stuff was as junky as Garth suspected, but among the detritus was a derelict dinghy with potential. Since the family had sold Garth's beloved sailing dinghy in Fiji after the wreck, he thought this one might be handy as a second dinghy—especially given the challenge of getting a family of four to agree on usage of the family "car." Garth got it to hold air, but the transom was falling off. At some point, he would get around to doing something more with it. In the interim, they'd strapped it to the deck and sailed on.

Garth thought of the fancy American yacht *Mustang* that had just pulled into port with gleaming stainless and bright work and wondered what possible interest they might have in this piece of crap. He shrugged.

The afternoon sun sparkled on the water as Garth waited expectantly for this man to go away. The man studied him for a moment. Then, he offered Garth one hundred dollars for the dinghy. Garth's eyes grew big and without a moment's hesitation, he said "Sure!"

Once the transaction was complete, the man spent the next few days patching the dinghy—as best as one could in a remote place, anyway.

The next time Garth saw the man, he looked smug. Despite the lucrative sale, Garth had tried to avoid him, pegging him as one of those annoying adults who thinks he knows everything and is quick to point it out at every opportunity. He leaned over to Garth and said in a condescending voice, "I sold your dinghy to the people on *Mustang* for twice what I paid you." Garth shrugged.

"You know, young man, with a little hard work you could have made some big bucks off that dinghy," he told Garth with a self-satisfied smile. Garth wondered when his finger would start wagging. "The people on *Mustang* are on a quick trans-Atlantic trip, anxious to replace the dinghy they lost without waiting for a replacement that might never come." He put his hands on his hips and studied Garth, waiting for a reaction. "I only paid you a hundred, but after only a few days' work I sold it to them for two hundred."

Garth gave the man a long look, then said, "I got the dinghy for *free*, didn't do *any* work, and got a hundred bucks for it. I think the return on my investment was pretty good."

That shut the man up.

Though Garth now had a handy sum on top of his birthday money, he couldn't find anything he wanted to spend it on. He'd finished reading *Shōgun*, a book he'd splurged on in Gibraltar, but it had hardly seemed like a gift once the whole family had read it. Unlike Linda, he had little interest in anything the shops had to offer. What he really wanted were books on yacht design, but he was unlikely to find anything like that here. Garth had also searched in vain for months for linseed-oil putty and a bottle big enough to contain his latest effort to build a ship in a bottle. This one was a three-inch scale model of *Vela* he'd carved from leftover Dacua wood from Fiji. He'd carefully reproduced a relatively accurate replica of *Vela*'s bowsprit and pinky stern, mast, boom, and sails. The model even featured hatches, Dorade ventilators and a dodger. Without a bottle to protect it, Garth worried that the delicate model would get wrecked.

Linda strolled the cobbled streets and shady squares, past fine old buildings with ornately carved wooden balconies, and perused the shops. Unfortunately her quest for stamps and coins was frustrated in the Canary Islands because the Spanish colony used the same stamps she'd already obtained on the mainland. Instead, she combed the cassette racks and blew her money on another Beatles album, happy to see one at typically low Spanish prices.

Dawn, of course, bought food. She felt obligated to stock up while prices were cheap, since she didn't know what food might cost in the Caribbean. They took advantage of the clean harbor and warmer water to clean weeds and barnacles off *Vela*'s peeling bottom as best they could to help their speed.

Three days after a Thanksgiving of canned roast pork and mashed potatoes, the Wilcoxes bid adieu to their last European port as they set sail for the French colonial island of Martinique, this time with Garth as navigator. He was proud to have earned his parents' trust as the official navigator. During this passage, he would get to mark their position on the chart, while the rest of the family peered over his shoulder to see how much progress they'd made in the last twenty-four hours.

This 3,000-mile passage the rest of the way across the Atlantic would last nearly as long as the one from Hawaii to the Marquesas. By now the family was accustomed to long passages, and this one didn't seem nearly as daunting. Back in the trade winds, they enjoyed blue days and starlit nights with a gentle breeze from astern. The Canary current gave them a boost to the southwest until the north equatorial current carried them westward.

As *Vela* sailed west, the family passed through a new time zone every week or so. On these longer east/west passages, the sun would rise and set progressively later each day until watch times and mealtimes began to seem illogical. Unlike during Daylight Saving Time, everyone looked forward to changing the clocks at the western edge of the time zone so they could return to normal daylight patterns. On days when it came time to change the clock, each would remain on watch an extra fifteen minutes until they covered the extra hour—usually in the middle of the day so no one would lose sleep.

To pass the time everyone read books and listened to the short-wave radio—whatever they could tune in. They loved BBC programming, especially *BBC News of the World*, game shows, story hour, and even *Top of the Pops*—to varying degrees. They also listened to Voice of America, though they were less enamored with the propaganda and found the over-enunciated "*S P E C I A L   E N G L I S H*" program especially annoying.

They heard Radio Netherlands and Radio Moscow. Through the short wave they learned about an airline crash at Funchal in Madeira and another near La Palma, protests in Malaga, and the resignation of the prime minister of Djibouti—all places they could envision because they'd been to each of them. They listened to debates about handing over the Panama Canal, worrying how it might affect their transit in a few months. Through the radio waves, the world was at their fingertips, though they'd missed the leisure suit and CB-radio craze back home, as well as the sock hops on *Happy Days*, and *Donny & Marie* singing in perfect harmony. While their peers watched *The Jeffersons*, *Chico and the Man*, and *The Six Million Dollar Man*, Linda only learned about them through *Tiger Beat* magazine. Garth would tease her mercilessly about the latest heartthrob-of-the-hour the magazines featured, people famous for reasons neither could completely understand.

As ever, Dawn passed long hours on passage writing letters that described their adventures. Passages were her best time to write, since in port they were usually too busy exploring the country's sites and culture, fixing the boat and provisioning food, water, and fuel. Between cooking, washing, standing watches, navigating, and sewing the flags for the upcoming ports of call, Dawn tried to answer her family's many questions to explain the peculiarities of their lifestyle, even after four and a half years.

Garth is the main water carrier. In Brisbane he got 20 gallons every night at the ferry dock. There are many places where it is too difficult to take the boat to a pier to get water, hence the jugs. In Gibraltar, we could reach the faucet with the 2 hoses and Garth adapted a hose fitting, which are a different size in each country it seems.

Letters offered her an essential link to home and the support system that kept her going through the trials. The correspondence also reminded her how much they'd seen of the world. To those at home these were faraway place names. For her they held memories of direct exposure to a world beyond California that she once had only glimpsed through magazines and newspapers. Letters reminded her of the widening gulf between the person she'd been before and the one she'd become. To her mother, she acknowledged her worries about what would come after the voyage.

I think Chuck and I, but especially Chuck, will have problems with his folks when we get back because we have quite different ideas on how to live and they will not approve. We want to live simply, though I draw the line at living in a tent and I sure want running water and a washing machine. They probably will want us to rush out and buy furniture and a car. You will think we are weird too but you have a more understanding nature.

Though it was a mostly pleasant passage, by December 22, the family was pumping one hundred times per day to keep up with water flooding in through the stuffing box and into the reservoir for the heat exchanger. The Primus had also developed a leak, which took it out of commission. Once again, Dawn worked around the problem as best she could.

The family had hoped to reach Martinique before Christmas and so did little to prepare for a holiday at sea. They couldn't imagine the passage might take that long, but after twenty-nine days of sailing it appeared they would be celebrating underway. When Christmas morning arrived, miles still stretched between them and Martinique. The snowflakes and foil stars that Linda had cut lent the boat a festive air but otherwise the day passed much as any other. For Christmas dinner, while Chuck was still technically on watch, Dawn served a little canned ham she'd bought in Gibraltar, just in case, along with canned French mushrooms, Spanish cauliflower and carrots. For a special treat, they finished the holiday meal with an English pudding topped with an apricot-brandy hard sauce.

The Young Navigator

Garth and shark

52

The day after Christmas, once Garth took sights and finished his calculations, he wrote into the ship's log that a light should be visible
when the taffrail log read 2652. At six a.m. the following morning, when
Chuck got off watch, he penciled into the ship's log book: *Land ho, starboard bow.* After thirty-two days, there was Martinique, just as Garth had
predicted. As the pride of victory washed over Garth when he awoke to
the news, his father joked that he'd secretly taken sights and worked out
their position the evening before to ease his worries.

As the sun rose higher in the sky, their eyes feasted upon the lush
foliage of Martinique and their noses took in the heavy scent of greenery. The welcome sight of terra firma. At three p.m. they passed around
Rocher du Diamant (Diamond Rock) just off the southwestern coast,
and Dawn snapped a photo of the proud navigator as they made landfall.
Like Gibraltar, Diamond Rock had been seized by the British in war,
this time with France in 1804-1805. During the battle British sailors had
hauled the ship's cannons up its steep slopes to blockade Fort-de-France
for nearly a year and a half. According to *National Geographic*, the rock
was still listed as one of Her Majesty's ships and saluted by the British

navy, though their victory was short-lived. In the end, France retained this tropical island. That was fine with the Wilcoxes. Despite language challenges, they always liked French places.

After squalls slowed *Vela*'s progress, they couldn't reach Fort-de-France before dark. As the sun touched the horizon, the Wilcoxes dropped anchor in the lee of Ilet à Ramiers, a little round island across the bay from the capital. As night fell, they heard a sound they hadn't for years: crickets.

In the morning they moved *Vela* to the anchorage off Martinique's new capital city, Fort-de-France. Unlike the La Palma volcano that erupted with ample warning to prevent loss of life, Martinique's former capital, Saint Pierre, had been destroyed when Mount Pelée exploded in 1902, killing all but one of the 30,000 who lived there. Rumor had it the lucky sole survivor had been an inmate in the jail.

Just three days before the end of 1977, the Wilcoxes settled among a large fleet of mostly local yachts and several giant cruise ships. A number of urgent projects demanded immediate attention. During the passage, the Primus leak added to Dawn's cooking frustrations. Yet more worrisome, the heat exchanger on the engine had failed, causing the engine to overheat. Because they had no way to charge the batteries without the engine, they had to ration electricity until they could fix it.

As Dawn wrote to her mother:

> It's boring sitting in the dark at harbor so Garth and I looked around and found a nice little brass lantern that burns kerosene. Garth is figuring a way to hang it up now. We also found a new primus stove. Garth and I have been searching town every day for boat parts.

The chances of finding a new heat exchanger in Martinique were slim to none, and the family could not afford to wait for one to be shipped through a potentially unreliable post. With only another six months of cruising, it made little sense to invest heavily in repairs, especially when money was so tight. Since many diesel engines used raw water cooling,

Chuck figured he could bypass the broken heat exchanger by running saltwater through the system. He knew this wouldn't be good for the engine, but it might get them home. He had done this once before in the Seychelles but had been able to flush the engine with fresh water soon afterward. Maybe he would have that option before they left Panama.

In the meantime, if the Wilcoxes relied less on the engine, they might buy more time. By this point they had successfully sailed into many anchorages when the engine had failed them—Port Vila, several ports in Australia, the Seychelles, Djibouti…, and now Martinique. From here on, the family would make a practice of sailing into and out of anchorages whenever possible and limit engine use to charging the batteries.

As soon as Chuck got the engine running again with a cooling-water bypass, he took advantage of an opportunity to haul *Vela*. If they actually wanted to get all the way home, they had to remove the thousands of gooseneck barnacles that were costing progressively more speed with every mile. Chuck heard that a navy patrol boat was going into a graving dock and yachts could tag along and share the cost based on tonnage. Three other sailboats and a trawler also took this opportunity.

On the morning of January 13, 1978, they motored *Vela* past Baie du Carenage into Bassin de Radoub dry dock—what looked like a large concrete swimming pool with terraced sides and a colossal door at the end. Once all the boats were inside and tied against the wall, the door closed with a clank. As workers pumped the water out, Dawn, Garth and Linda adjusted *Vela*'s lines while she settled and Chuck dove to place block supports in the water under her rounded keel. The crews of the other boats did the same.

The water dropped lower and lower, swirling as it emptied. A little later, amid much shouting and consternation, the Wilcoxes noticed the cause: The full-keeled sailboat in front of them hadn't settled correctly and had fallen over. Workers quickly pumped water back in. They scurried to rebrace it, then resumed emptying the water.

When all the water had finally emptied, the family began work at a furious pace, scraping and recoating *Vela*'s bottom with fresh anti-fouling paint. Using efficient teamwork—with Chuck rolling and the three others "tipping" with brushes to smooth over the paint edges—the Wilcoxes managed to apply two coats with enough spare time to sip tea in the cockpit. While the other crews continued their toil, the Wilcoxes went to bed. Two yacht crews worked through the night to finish before the navy ship was done. No one wanted to be caught half done when the navy ordered the opening and the water flooded back in. When the appointed hour came, everyone was ready.

The total cost of the haul-out was two hundred and ninety francs (around sixty dollars), an incredible deal considering that two days later the government yard transferred to private management and the cost instantly skyrocketed to five times the price they paid. For once the Wilcoxes lucked out.

Though frequent rain squalls made the boat work unpleasant, it explained the island's verdant scenery. Their boat projects left little time for exploring, but the family did appreciate Martinique's French colonial architecture and wrought-iron balconies, narrow roads, the statue of Napoleon's bride Josephine (who grew up in Martinique), and its tantalizing French bread and pastries.

Less endearing were the elevated prices and silly postal restrictions, which forced the Wilcoxes to pay a franc—twenty-two cents—for each letter they received. One of them was from the IRS, informing them their case had been transferred to San Jose. Another irritating regulation kept the family from collecting mail addressed to any one of them not present. Dawn and Linda didn't particularly like the squat toilets with foot pads designating where to crouch, but Garth appreciated how much less water he had to haul thanks to the community showers. One day while Dawn was showering, to her surprise, a "Martican fellow" (as Dawn called them) came in, said something in French, took off his clothes and began to shower. She decided he was safe since she didn't have her glasses on.

While the family was in Martinique, Linda took a final exam, but by this point, Garth had nearly given up all pretense of doing schoolwork.

Dawn worried her son would be destined for a career pumping gas, having no idea that service stations were transforming into self-serve.

During their time in port, they saw the cruise liner *Kunshon* run aground. They all watched with amusement as each day yet another tug boat would arrive from a distant island to try to pull it off. Everyone joked that meanwhile the passengers enjoyed a windfall: parked for a week in the sun with free food, a gorgeous tropical island within view and free entertainment, their cruise extended until they could get into port. When Wilcoxes left Martinique, three tugs were pulling in tandem with a full load of passengers crowded at the rails to watch.

During their three weeks in port, Chuck attempted to call his parents collect several times but had been unable to reach them. He finally reached them shortly before they left. Because of the cost and poor connection, it was a frustratingly brief conversation. Chuck's father was ailing and his condition was unpredictable. He would seem to improve, then take a turn for the worse. The Wilcoxes were less than six months from completing their voyage home. Because of the seasons and the distance, they couldn't sail any faster. Chuck hoped they would make it home in time to see his father again.

53

The sailing directions advised against crossing the Caribbean Sea to Panama between January and March when strong winds and high seas prevailed. The family's plan was to work their way northwest through the Caribbean Islands to the Virgin Islands by March. In St. Thomas, they would prepare for the passage to Panama, their last stop before they sailed directly home to San Francisco. That would give the family two months to explore the tiny islands in the region without too much rushing before their final passages.

From Martinique, *Vela* sailed northwest through the Leeward Islands of the Caribbean archipelago past Dominica and Guadeloupe to the independent nation of Antigua. When the Wilcoxes arrived in English Harbour, Antigua on January 21st, they were surprised at how many international sailboats filled the ideal harbor that had once been a haven for pirates and the British navy. It was no wonder why so many yachts were there. The winds were predictable, the sun nearly always shining. Sailing in the Caribbean felt easy after all they'd been through, almost like an escape from the hardships of moving from place to place by sailboat.

With rust dripping down *Vela*'s topsides and the paint peeling, the family was keenly aware how bedraggled *Vela* appeared. Two days in Martinique's government dock was insufficient to tackle more than the bottom paint. Though Dawn and Linda had been able to prime one side in the anchorage in Martinique, *Vela* looked like she had the measles.

A palpable anxiety fluttered through the fleet as the family sailed their big spotted tub with peeling paint through the anchorage, undoubtedly fueled by worry that this beast might plow into their pristine vessels and wreck their perfect paint and spotless varnish. Within a few days in the harbor, the Wilcoxes witnessed enough demonstrations of inexperience to justify the fears. It became clear to them just how proficient they'd become over the past four and a half years. These yachts looked pristine because they had seen little of the world, whereas *Vela* bore the scars of shipwreck in Fiji, rig failures in the Red Sea, and countless ocean miles—adventures this fleet could scarcely imagine.

Between projects, Garth and Linda poked around Nelson's Dockyard, fondly remembering his relative, the Customs agent from Gibraltar. They loved visiting reproductions of the Dockyard's key buildings, especially the Admiral's House—a free museum containing artifacts from Lord Nelson's time, the Copper and Lumber Store and Officer's Quarters. To Garth, the Spar Loft and the Boat House were most interesting, along with the surrounding battlements and the fortress designed to protect the harbor.

While sailing in the Mediterranean had been difficult, their efforts had been rewarded with multiple layers of history, from ancient civilizations to medieval, renaissance and even 20th century periods. To Dawn, these sixteenth to eighteenth century relics here in the new world seemed recent and unremarkable in comparison.

For the first time, the family was in a place where facilities were devoted to serving the needs of sailors. There were showers, a book swap and wash tubs. Dawn and Linda made use of a line of modern sinks to catch up on laundry without having to pay for and haul wash water. Dawn was amazed how much cleaner the clothes looked when washed and rinsed with fresh water. Everything seemed so much easier. How different their cruise might have been had these conveniences been a part of their voyage sooner.

Yet it seemed odd to be in such a crowded anchorage after so long on their own, just one yacht among many with an American flag flapping from the transom. Many sailors gave them a wide berth but most simply stared as they zoomed past in their dinghies, their outboard engines kicking up a big wake that made scraping and painting *Vela's* topsides more difficult. Few people seemed inclined to talk to them—at least until Dawn and Linda finished painting one side of the boat—perhaps suspecting the paint problems were contagious. The reward after their hard work was a side trip to the Yale archeological dig to see relics of indigenous Arawak Indians. Meanwhile Chuck repaired the Groco head—again—and Garth spent three days copying borrowed charts of the Virgin Islands, which they'd been unable to buy.

After nine days in Antigua, they sailed west to Charleston, Nevis, where Alexander Hamilton was born in 1757. Though it had been some time since any of them had seen one, they remembered his face on the ten-dollar bill to honor his role as father of the U.S. Constitution and the first Secretary of the Treasury. Unfortunately for him, he was probably better remembered for losing a duel and his life to Aaron Burr.

This same tiny island was also where English settlers had anchored in turquoise waters for six days on their way to establish the Jamestown colony in Virginia. In hindsight, given the hardships they would face attempting to settle too late in the season in a malarial swamp, perhaps the settlers might have wished they'd remained in balmy Nevis. Lovely though it was, the Wilcoxes also only stayed for a few days.

When Dawn wasn't shopping or cooking, it seemed she was sewing a courtesy flag for the next microscopic country in the island chain. Linda and Garth would often help and they made a project of learning about the history and culture as they created the flag. As many countries as there were, many lacked the unique flavor of places they'd visited in the

Mediterranean. Rather, to the Wilcoxes, they seemed overrun by tourists and yachtsmen, though not enough to detract from their natural beauty. Still the sailing seemed ideal.

In early February, *Vela* sailed past the lush mountains of St. Kitts, pausing overnight beneath the supposedly "unconquerable" Brimstone Hill Fortress—captured by the French in 1782 only a few years after it was built. *Vela* continued north past the small volcanic islands of Saba and St. Eustatius, where the fledgling United States received its first foreign salute to one of its ships in 1776. If the kids had learned about these details in a classroom among peers, they might have been less likely to retain it, but in the context of their travels it left an impression and added a dimension to their voyage that all but Chuck seemed to relish.

Though several islands loomed invitingly on the horizon, the Wilcoxes pressed on to equally attractive Philipsburg in St. Maarten, the southern Dutch portion of this dry dual-nation island. They anchored in Groot Baie (Great Bay) in front of the town. Here the waters once again shallowed from deep blue to pale aquamarine.

Shortly after dropping anchor, Chuck went to clear in. He returned soon after, announcing that they had less than an hour to get to the bank and post office before both closed for the weekend. The young philatelists had rarely moved so fast. They threw on clothes and grabbed their money. Garth shoved the oars in the sprockets and rowed as fast as he could, while Dawn calculated how many francs to change into guilders and "guesstimated" the exchange rate.

Ashore, they stowed the oars and rushed to the bank only to discover it was packed—it must have been payday. Dawn stood in line while Garth and Linda went in search of another bank. The two came across fellow sailors from New Zealand who pointed them to one with shorter lines. Dawn saw and hurried to follow. The next bank had shorter lines, but lines nonetheless. Garth and Dawn each picked a queue to stand in, while Linda ran interference, double checking that they were in the right place to change francs to guilders. Garth and Dawn inched forward until they both stood two places away from the head of the line. The race was on. Linda closely monitored the hands on the clock, growing more agitated with each minute.

Dawn moved up one spot, and it looked like she would be first. Then her cashier answered the phone. The three groaned audibly. Finally, with ten minutes left—call completed—Dawn surged to the front. But by the time she finished the transaction, a despairing Linda announced the post office was closed. Dawn asked in English if anyone knew of another post office. Someone did. One of the joys since they left Martinique was being able to communicate in English once again. With directions, they flew out the door and tore down the street.

Garth spotted the flag that marked the post office and ducked into the doorway, rushing to the counter. Panting, he ordered one of every stamp. His mistake was not ordering two sets. Transaction complete, Linda stepped in right behind him. As she made her request, the lights flickered. The lady looked at her dispassionately and announced the post office was closed. Linda stared in astonishment.

"But…"

Just then, Dawn stepped in and demanded the lady finish serving her daughter since they would depart on Sunday before the post office reopened. The woman relented, flipping through the stamp binder and sighing heavily as she tore stamps in a frenzied haste. Linda soon had her precious stamps. Dawn worried about being an ugly American, but by God, she'd gotten results.

On Saturday they were free to explore the whole town: Front Street, Back Street and the two tidy streets in between. It took about an hour. Though tiny, the town did have a striking white courthouse built in 1792 on a pleasant brick-paved square. Though "duty free," everything was expensive—especially food. After their efforts to change currency, they discovered that they could have used American currency. All prices were posted in guilders and U.S. dollars, but the vendors seemed to prefer dollars. In an attempt to unload all their guilders, they splurged on a ten-pound wheel of Gouda cheese for fourteen dollars, a t-shirt for Garth, and fresh ice cream, their first in ages. The Gouda was worth every penny and convinced Garth that he liked cheese.

Sunday evening they set sail again, this time for Virgin Gorda. A nighttime departure allowed them to navigate around its reefs after sunrise. The following afternoon they sailed through the reef pass into scenic Virgin Gorda Sound but learned from a Canadian boat that they wouldn't be allowed to enter there, so they couldn't venture ashore.

Instead, Dawn spent the rest of the day writing letters, while Garth patched the jib and spliced a new hook arrangement for the anchor snubber. Linda cleaned conch shells she'd collected in St. Kitts, then worked on the book she'd started about the voyage, which she hoped would earn her extra credit in English or social studies. After noticing several boats flying private flags, Garth decided to make one for *Vela*. Working with his mother, he designed a blue one with a white sail for the Spanish meaning for vela, and the stars in the constellation *Vela*, which lies near the Southern Cross. Soon their flag was flying below the port spreader, while the courtesy flag of the British Virgin Islands flapped below the starboard one. They were starting to realize these would be among their last rare chances to laze at anchor. Once they reached Panama in March, they would be in the last big push for home. Their every moment would be devoted to preparing for their final passage.

The next morning, they up-anchored. Two hours later, they anchored outside a fancy marina off Spanish Town where they could check in. While Chuck handled the paperwork, Dawn and Linda strolled the docks. The two were astounded by the ostentatious display of wealth: the perfectly painted boats with what Dawn described as "some sort of newfangled roll-up sails," and people in new outfits that matched. The two felt self-conscious about the state of their clothes—threadbare, spotted and faded. It made them realize how different things were from when they departed for the South Pacific four years earlier. They were glad they'd at least finished painting the topsides so *Vela* didn't look so awful, at least from a distance.

Vela had once been the fanciest possible boat they could buy. She carried everything one could dream of for comfort aboard. Yet every system had failed by this point, one by one. Gradually they had learned to live without. Here they came face to face with how much had changed since they set out only four and a half years ago. How far their standards had dropped. Though they were now surrounded by Americans and no longer isolated by a language barrier, here the gulf was an economic one of epic proportions.

As soon as Chuck finished clearing in, they moved far from the fancy marina, anchoring in a quiet bay where the family could snorkel the turquoise waters, body surf, collect shells on the white sandy beach, and listen to the palms rustling in the steady breeze. Dawn thought: *This is how cruising should be: countless anchorages to choose from only a few hours apart under ideal sailing conditions.* The only downside was how pricey everything was—that plus the sand fleas that sent her scratching madly. She hoped their money would last to Panama, where she planned to stock up one last time for the final passage home.

The family zipped over to Bellamy Cay, Tortola across Drake Channel, mostly so Garth and Chuck could take a gander at a new boat they'd heard about that had no stays to support the mast. After all the trouble they'd had with *Vela*'s rig, the idea of a mast without stays seemed brilliant. Dawn and Linda had no interest. They were more keen to visit the famous Baths.

As the family reached the southern end of Virgin Gorda the next day, too many boats anchored off the shore made sailing *Vela* through the anchorage too difficult. Garth and Chuck opted to tack back and forth while Dawn and Linda ventured ashore by dinghy to enjoy this natural geographical phenomenon. The two hopped into the Avon and rowed ashore. Big waves crashed against the boulders. They were nervous about landing the dinghy—usually Garth timed the waves and delivered them to shore safe and dry. Eventually they found a sandy spot with less surf and gauged the waves to make a good landing. They quickly hauled the dinghy up the beach and tied it to a tree, though later the tide rose high enough to float it and they had to haul it further ashore. Chuck and Garth would never forgive them if they lost their only dinghy.

Ashore, Dawn and Linda explored the giant granite boulders riddled with caves, tunnels, and crystal-clear water. They paddled around in protected pools and watched geysers spurt through gaps between boulders. Afterward, the two had to figure out how to launch the dinghy in the surf without flipping it, row against the waves out to *Vela*, and gauge the best way to pull alongside a moving sailboat. The idea made Dawn nervous, but the two managed to do it. They felt empowered by their successful independent foray ashore.

When blustery winds and lashing rain kept them aboard at Peter's Island, Linda dug out Robert Louis Stevenson's *Treasure Island*, supposedly based on nearby Norman Island. Dawn drafted a letter to her mother summarizing their recent wanderings, though she wouldn't be able to mail it until they reached St. Thomas. With rain assaulting the deck, her thoughts naturally turned to the chores and sailing that lay ahead.

We have been cruising the British Virgin Islands. Peters on the South Coast was our favorite: reef, shells and no habitations. I got the red and gray stripes painted--first coat. And I made a master provisioning list to fill in St. Thomas. We figure on 115 days--94 sailing here to Panama, Panama to SF plus, plus port days. The Virgin Islands are my favorite spot: beautiful islands, close anchorages, beaches, reefs, greenery and nice wind too. There are a lot of boats but plenty of room. It has been a nice vacation. Now to face a blitz of work and civilization.

The upcoming passages weighed heavily on her mind. So did worry about Chuck's father, as letters from Chuck's parents had grown sparse. They hoped a batch of mail would be waiting in St. Thomas with an update. If not, Chuck would at least have a chance to call.

An additional worry for Dawn was another lump she found in her breast. While it might be a benign cyst like she'd had in Australia, she couldn't be sure. She hoped to get it checked once they reached St. Thomas. Until then she said nothing, reluctant to trouble their families. With Grandpa's ailing health, no doubt, Chuck's parent's already had plenty of worries of their own.

54

In the U.S. Virgin Islands, the Wilcoxes pulled into Cruz Bay to clear into the country, carefully anchoring outside the channel markers. Yet within minutes, a ferry boat rushed by, nearly smashing the wind vane. Soon after, another large vessel came quite close and a man yelled, "You're in the middle of the channel!" But the buoys clearly marked the channel, and *Vela* was not inside them. Regardless, it seemed wise to move so *Vela* wouldn't get smacked. When Chuck rowed ashore to clear in, he learned that the buoys were in the wrong places and "everyone" knew it. Maybe everyone else.

A few days later they moved *Vela* to Lameshur Bay, down the south coast of St. John. After lunch Garth and Dawn hopped into the dinghy to head ashore. Most of the island was a national park, which they wanted to explore. About halfway to the beach, a whaler motored over to them. The insignia on the side of the hull combined with the man's military-style uniform and "Smokey the Bear" hat screamed officialdom. He shouted over to them.

"Where are your life jackets?" They shrugged. The man waited expectantly.

"On the boat," Garth replied, flinging a finger in the direction of *Vela*.

"Per U.S. law, you are required to carry life jackets in your dinghy for each passenger," he said, crossing his arms and leaning back on his heels.

"But they'll just get stolen," Dawn said. Garth and Dawn looked at him, incredulous. They might need those life jackets, but not today. Today they were just going swimming on the beach. They stared at one another.

To that "Ranger Rick" just puffed up his chest and repeated as though they hadn't heard him. "You must carry a life jacket for each person riding in the boat."

What a silly rule, Dawn thought. It was a sunny, calm day and they were headed only another two hundred yards into shore. If their life jackets got stolen from the dinghy, the family wouldn't have them when they might really need them.

"Well, we can work around that," Garth said, his face brightening. Without hesitation, he hopped over the side. "Come on, Mom," he added, grabbing the painter and swimming toward shore with the dinghy in tow. Dawn cracked a smile and slipped into the water to follow, leaving "Ranger Rick" speechless.

A couple of days later the family moved *Vela* on to Trunk Bay on the north side of St. John, touted for its white sand beach and "excellent visibility for snorkelers." The family argued over who got to snorkel first. From the anchorage, Dawn wrote her mother:

> I am waiting for Garth & Linda to return from the snorkel trail here at Trunk Bay, St. Johns [sic], since I get the mask next. We have 2 [masks] left and 3 medium flippers.

Such was the state of affairs aboard *Vela*. When Garth and Linda returned they told her not to bother. They'd swum along the "fantastic" Trunk Bay underwater trail, only to find the coral dead and covered with sand. Seeing a promising area further from shore, they stroked toward it, only to spot a sign that read, THE LIFEGUARD CANNOT SEE YOU BEYOND THIS POINT. TURN BACK. They ignored it, but the lifeguard started blowing his whistle and yelling at them. Annoyed, they headed back to the boat. They'd seen far better snorkeling elsewhere anyway.

So far, not an auspicious return to U.S. territorial waters.

Before the family could head for St. Thomas, they had to return to Cruz Bay to collect water. Evidently there was no water in St. Thomas because the desalinization plant had broken down. They re-anchored—this time outside the mismarked channel. Unfortunately the faucet in Cruz Bay was two blocks from the beach so it turned out to be a chore to fill up, gallon by gallon, jug by jug. When the water brigade had finished, Dawn mused that such challenges kept them from needing to visit a gym. They were all slender and she couldn't help but notice how muscular her seventeen-year-old son's arms had grown from all his rowing and water hauling.

A month after they arrived in Antigua, they reached their last stop in the U.S. Virgin Islands. The sprawling city of Charlotte Amalie on St. Thomas offered little to interest them. The capital of the U.S. Virgin Islands was overrun with cruise liners, noisy, and swarming with tourists. The shopping was good but only if you were looking for French perfume, Swedish crystal, fancy jewelry or booze. After scouring among throngs of pink tourists, Dawn identified two supermarkets—Pueblo and Grand Union—and a drugstore selling wares much more in line with their needs. There was plenty to buy, but at inflated prices. Plus the dinghy dock charged twenty-five cents per hour to tie alongside.

In contrast to steep shop prices, postage was surprisingly cheap. Dawn noticed that a school lesson now cost only twenty-four cents to mail, instead of the dollar-fifty or two dollars it would have cost in Australia. And mailing a letter cost only thirteen cents. They were thrilled to collect a hefty cache of letters (sans delivery fee) and draft multi-page replies.

Faithfully waiting for them as at every port was more hate mail from the IRS. This time it came in the form of a warning from another office. This was worrisome, since a hearing had already been scheduled. Clearly one office didn't know what the other office was doing. It might not be enough to get back in time for a hearing if another office took punitive action first. The family might be out of the country, but their house was not.

More welcome at the post office was the big batch of books Dawn's mother sent, especially considering the lengthy passages to come. The family had read everything aboard and, though the Wilcoxes had traded with other sailboats and visited every English library they could, they always hungered for more good reading material to get them through long days at sea. An unexpected side perk of this pricey American outpost was finding a nice bookstore where Garth discovered a textbook on yacht design. His mother remarked that since Garth rarely parted with his money, it must be a good book. The fact that he barely looked up from it was another sign.

An advantage to being among wealthy Americans was their sudden access to recent American magazines to catch up on news from their country. One afternoon Garth and Dawn fished two yachting magazines, a *Smithsonian* and several issues of *Time* magazine from the garbage. As they read about the U.S. energy crisis and how hyper-inflation was eating away at fixed incomes, Chuck and Dawn worried anew about arriving home broke, without a job.

Though her mother had thoughtfully sent a cashier's check, Dawn found she couldn't cash it in this U.S. territory, though the same bank in the Seychelles and Haifa had done so without a problem. She hoped she'd be able to cash it in Panama. They would need the funds, especially after paying exorbitant prices to provision here. Her mother's generous gift wouldn't be nearly as helpful in San Francisco—though, given the state of the economy, it might.

As soon as he could, Chuck called his parents again and learned his father's health had taken another turn for the worse. His mother offered to send him money to fly home, but Chuck refused. He felt torn. Flying home would take the last money they had—and wouldn't be enough for them all to go. But it wasn't just the money. He knew that if he left, the Wilcoxes would likely miss the season to carry on. It would probably mean abandoning their voyage. After all they'd been through to get this far, he couldn't imagine doing that. They were nearly home. It was *all* of those things and perhaps denial that his father might truly be dying. Dawn felt guilty about not being able to help take care of her ailing father-in-law, but there was only so much she could do at present. Given weather patterns, they were moving as fast as they could. If they just kept sailing, they would be home in a few months and they would *all* get to see him.

Dawn directed her attention to the next pressing concerns.

First Dawn tried to find out whether her lump was something to worry about. She tried to see one doctor but gave up after standing in the rain for an hour outside the locked office. Then she went in search of another, hoping this time for medical care and someone who could give her a diagnosis—preferably a positive one. When she finally got in to see a doctor, he concluded it was fibro cystic disease (lumpy breasts) like she had before. The waiting was the hardest part. Optimistic after two medical opinions that she needn't worry, she and Chuck felt relieved. With that burden lifted, they resumed preparing for the next leg of their journey—their second to last.

Dawn called the College of the Virgin Islands to see if Garth's Advanced Algebra test had arrived. It had, but the "testing officer" told her there would be a fee of twenty-five dollars to administer the exam. After so many other countries had administered them for free, her native country wanted to charge its own citizens to fulfill its *compulsory* education requirement. She was so angry she told the man to send it back. Garth could take it when they got home.

Once she cooled down, her insides churned with worry. As a young mother, Dawn had made every effort to nurture her young son, dutifully recording his first smile, the appearance of his first tooth and progress to solid foods, his first words, first steps, favorite foods, etc. She diligently catered to his intellectual development, zealously consulting Dr. Spock to ensure that her child was on schedule. And the same for Linda when she came along. How had she turned into such a terrible mother, one willing to let her son's education falter like this?

As Dawn scoured the shops for supplies, she noted the produce was old and wrapped in plastic. The cans—though often familiar American brands—came with labels in Spanish, seeming to originate in Puerto Rico. Even in the biggest town of St. Thomas, the cost of fresh meat and eggs exceeded what they could afford. They continued trying to live without—relying on split peas, beans and rice and canned meat to get enough protein. Dawn worried about providing adequate nutrition for her growing children. She bought vitamin and salt tablets to supplement their limited diet. During her shopping trips, she gazed with longing at sirloin three days in a row, and in a moment of weakness splurged the four dollars and seventy-seven cents per pound to buy it. It was their first beef in more than a month. A juicy steak brought back pleasant memories of home.

She envied the carefree tourists stepping off cruise ships or sipping cocktails in the cockpits of the shiny new charter boats that shared their anchorage. How fun it looked to pass the days snorkeling and shopping for souvenirs. Instead she spent hers cooking, washing, mending, supervising schooling, doing watches, navigating, varnishing/painting, and repairing *Vela*. She'd seen so much of the world. And yet... life often looked like the inside of her galley, or hauling a rusty grocery cart full of canned goods wrapped in labels she couldn't read. She was just so tired.

Through the port light something odd caught her eye. She noticed a charter vessel near them had dragged into another and was leaning up against it. The two bobbed in tandem in a way that looked unnatural. In this yachting mecca, countless boats were chartered to people who hadn't a clue about boat handling or anchoring. It looked like another one was in trouble.

"Oh boy. More free entertainment," she said. Garth jumped up and looked out the port light. He laughed.

"The keel is caught on his anchor buoy. This could be interesting." He and Chuck headed out to the cockpit to watch the action. Across the harbor the Coast Guard seemed oblivious. They were busy buzzing around to see if dinghies had life jackets. A second later, they heard a panicked yell.

"Let's go see if we can help," Garth said, and Chuck agreed. They pushed off in the dinghy and were on the scene as the Coasties arrived. From *Vela*, Dawn watched the convention as the delegates from each party put forward their views of potential solutions. Evidently Chuck and Garth made a persuasive case, because within a couple minutes Chuck was aboard *Criterion* and Garth surfaced wearing a borrowed mask and his best (only) shorts. Sweeping gestures from Chuck indicated he was directing the operation, and the seated position of the Coasties indicated they were not. Dawn was impressed that at least these young Coasties seemed smart enough to realize that Chuck and Garth probably had a lot more seamanship experience than they did.

Their final days in St. Thomas passed in a blur, filled with hauling groceries, marking all the cans and coating them with varnish. Dawn and the kids kept busy while Chuck rowed two hours to secure five gallons of kerosene to fuel the primus and the oil lamps and purchase ten jugs so they could carry enough fresh water. Prepping and stowing all the food took days. Exhausted, Dawn hoped this would be enough food to take them all the way home.

Everything had to find a home before they put to sea. Seeing the extra water jugs Chuck had just purchased reminded Dawn that once they reached Panama, they would face the longest passage they'd ever encountered. Their longest one to date had been thirty-two days. The final passage between Panama and San Francisco was likely to be twice as long.

First they needed to get to Panama. Reading in the sailing directions that many experienced sailors considered the passage between the Caribbean and Panama to be one of the roughest of their entire trip was enough to fill Dawn with dread. She'd grown comfortable with the easy sailing of the last few months. Knowing it would be their next-to-last one made it easier to face. Only 1,030 miles to Cristobal, Panama, meant it might only take them a week of misery. The one after that—5,000 miles—was another story altogether.

Their first priority would be to get through the Panama Canal before the U.S. Senate gave it away. Then they could worry about getting home before Chuck's father died, the money ran out, or the IRS seized their house.

55

On March 11th, as early as Chuck felt was safe, the Wilcoxes raised anchor to sail for Panama. *Vela* skirted the south coast of Puerto Rico, leaving Vieques Island to starboard. Once they broke free from the islands, the breeze built. With so much wind, their first twenty-four hours produced a record run. For *Vela*, that meant one hundred and forty-five miles instead of the usual one hundred-mile days. Then record runs the next two days.

On the fifth day, they had to drop the main. Then the best sail—the jib—ripped. Soon *Vela* was down to just the tiny storm jib and still barreling along at six knots or more. In the ship's log Dawn wrote: *As Telenoti would say, 'wave too much'.* The motion was unpleasant—the sort that would make you quit sailing if it were your first time. Conditions remained that way the rest of the trip. Then the toilet broke again and it was back to "bucket and chuck it."

In seven days *Vela* covered the thousand miles. When Chuck laid eyes on Panama, he was relieved, but they weren't there yet. When they reached the entrance to the Panama Canal Zone, he turned on the engine. The needle on the oil pressure gauge dropped precipitously. When he pulled open the engine compartment, oil gushed from the engine, so he shut it down.

They navigated the rest of the way under sail through the well-lit breakwater and dropped anchor in the designated spot for yachts. Barely a minute after the anchor splashed down, a pilot boat dropped off an immigration officer to clear them in. *Now that's service,* Dawn thought. Once they finished a stack of paperwork and the man left, the family fell into bed.

The next morning, Chuck rowed ashore in the pouring rain to visit Customs. Meanwhile Dawn drafted letters to inform their families they'd arrived safely in Panama.

We hadn't intended to sail in, but the engine developed dropping oil pressure and Chuck discovered the lubricating oil was being pumped into the bilge via the cooling system. So that is the end of ye old engine unless he can do a miracle patch. We have the head to fix and the jib to sew, engine to fix and Linda has a final to study for so we have plenty to do. The immig man said part of the treaty was passed by the senate. We couldn't find any English stations on this trip. The broadcast band is jammed with Spanish from C and S America. BBC didn't come in and VoA wasn't to be found. I did get an English broadcast from Radio Moscow, but a little propoganda goes a long way.

A booklet the immigration officer handed them outlined the canal transit process, beginning with someone measuring *Vela* to assess the toll based on tonnage. In the interim, the family began to tackle the tasks on their list. Chuck bent over the engine to see whether it could be saved. It would be the first of many long, frustrating days dissecting the engine and attempting to resurrect it. When the measurer arrived, he pulled out his cloth tape and completed a series of forms. Once the man finished, he handed the Wilcoxes a laminated card with an identification number to use for radio communications while in transit.

After the boat was measured, the Wilcoxes were free to move *Vela* to the Colon Yacht Club, but without an engine they couldn't. The cost of a slip probably would have exceeded their budget in any case. Instead *Vela* remained anchored in "the flats," more than a mile's row to the dinghy dock at Pier 8-9.

The next morning, Garth and Dawn rowed ashore, leaving Chuck bent over the engine and Linda hovering over a textbook to study for her final exams. The two were in search of a sailmaker to repair the ripped jib. They stuffed the torn sail into the rusty metal shopping cart, its axles and wheels so bent that it squeaked along, announcing their presence as they wheeled it past lines of uniform Customs buildings. Heavy machinery rumbled past, hauling heavy containers high overhead and paying them no attention. At the gate, the guard gave them a cursory glance and waved them through into the town of Cristobal, which consisted of little more than government buildings and a post office. When the two exited the Canal Zone into the Panamanian city of Colon, the contrast was striking. Instead of clean, white government buildings, Colon's structures were colorful and dilapidated. The cart rattled and skipped along slum-like streets, past policemen and soldiers stationed on nearly every corner, as they scoured 8 ½ Street in search of the sailmaker they'd heard about. After about three hours, they finally located his house. The man estimated the repair would cost twenty-eight dollars. He seemed competent and his help would save Garth and Dawn weeks of hand sewing. So they left the sail in his care.

By the time they returned to *Vela*, Garth felt achy and tired. Within a few hours, his temperature shot to 103 degrees and, in addition to her other chores, Nurse Dawn had a patient to monitor. There was still propane, kerosene, water and food to get before they'd be ready to move on. Dawn made a list of items for the next day's food shopping with Linda.

After the mile-long row and dodging heavy machinery hauling containers, Linda collected a new batch of Canal Zone stamps before they exited the gate into Cristobal and then Colon. Linda grew wide-eyed as they left the tidy buildings in American territory and were faced with the mayhem and crumbling buildings of Colon. As they trudged along, she stared at numerous policemen and soldiers, brightly colored birds and monkeys in cages in the market, and Cuna Indians who walked in bare feet. The squat women wore colorful, long wraparound skirts and Mola appliqué blouses for which they became famous. Draped over their glossy straight black hair were red-and-yellow cotton shawls. Rings pierced their elongated noses.

When Dawn and Linda found the supermarket among many closed shops, they dragged their rusty cart inside and parked it near the door. Inside were four policemen and four soldiers. One of the policemen told them to put the cart next to him. Linda wondered who would want that rusty old thing, but when she looked back at the cart, a woman already had her hand on it. Once they pried it from her grasp, they parked it next to the policeman as instructed. Several people had warned them away from certain areas and told them to be careful of thieves. It seemed everyone was on edge while the U.S. Congress debated handover of the Canal.

Dawn was relieved to find many locally made products with reasonable prices. Yet, given the hassle of hauling and rowing everything they bought, she didn't buy as much as she should have. Before wheeling the overloaded cart back to the dinghy, she treated Linda to a root beer float at the Dairy Queen.

By Easter Sunday, Chuck concluded he couldn't fix the engine. He'd managed to get it running for about twenty seconds but it developed three other illnesses in the process. Without the right parts and time to take it apart, it seemed pointless to spend more time on it. They had sailed thousands of miles without it already, so he supposed they could live without it. They didn't have much choice. Unfortunately they were still on the wrong side of the canal. They'd have to arrange a tow through the canal and he worried about the expense that might incur.

After lunch a couple days later, Dawn wrote an update to their families, unsure which side of the canal she'd mail it from.

The day after I wrote you last (March 26) Chuck and I went to town and we found a piece of rope for a tow line. It was in a Chinese store underneath a stack of pots and it looked like the watermelon merchant who subleased part of the store would have to move his stock. Thank goodness we finally got it out without all that work. It was $1 a pound and he didn't know how many feet there are in a pound so Chuck had him weigh it and we bought the whole piece. Turned out to be over 200 feet, minus the cockroaches we left in the store. We put it in the cart, bought more vegetables and went to the gas place and put that under the rope. It rained all day so we got plenty wet rowing back home.

Tuesday afternoon, after Garth had recovered and they'd picked up the repaired sail, they were all on board stowing provisions and getting organized. They were nearly ready to transit the canal. Garth shouted from the cockpit, "Ha! Get a load of this!"

The rest of the family rushed outside for a look. Two men were paddling by in an old rubber inner tube covered with netting. It was slow-going, using two planks for oars. One of the men wore a cowboy hat. They looked utterly ridiculous. The Wilcoxes burst into laughter.

Hearing this family laughing at them, the two men paddled over to chat and rest a while. The one in the cowboy hat introduced himself as "Dallas." And yes, he was from Texas. They were crew from *Waterloo*, a Texas shrimper anchored nearby. Evidently, the men had grown tired of paying thirty dollars for the launch service to take them ashore. Since they didn't have a dinghy, they made do.

Chuck asked, "Hey, we could use a tow through the canal. Any chance you guys could tow us?"

Dallas shrugged. "Come an' talk to aur cap'n. Mebbe we can work somethin' aout," he said in a drawl so thick the Wilcoxes shook their heads in wonderment. It had been a long time since they'd heard an accent like that.

After giving the two men a generous head start, Chuck set off in the Avon for the *Waterloo*. The answer to Chuck's request for a tow was "Sure." It would cost *Waterloo* an extra twenty-six dollars to tow a boat through. If the Wilcoxes paid that, he didn't see why they couldn't. Chuck grabbed their papers and he and the captain of the *Waterloo* headed ashore to make arrangements—in *Vela*'s dinghy.

The family had stocked groceries and filled up on water, propane, and kerosene so they would be ready when the right opportunity arose. Still, there was much to do. Dawn and Garth prepared lines and fenders to raft alongside the other boat. Chuck and *Waterloo*'s captain, DJ, returned with an appointment to transit the following morning. After Chuck rowed DJ back to *Waterloo* and returned to *Vela*, the Wilcoxes pulled and stowed the anchor.

DJ brought *Waterloo* alongside *Vela*, but since some of his crew were still in town, he was shorthanded. He smacked *Vela*'s bowsprit, leaving a big dent and bending one of the stanchions. The Wilcoxes couldn't complain. With free help, sometimes you get what you pay for. Once *Vela* was secured alongside *Waterloo*, the rafted boats headed over to where *Waterloo*'s sister ship, the *Debby Wines*, was anchored. Linda's eyes widened at *Waterloo*'s battered appearance. The *Debby Wines* looked equally rough. Both trawlers were on their way to San Diego for an overhaul. One sorely overdue, it appeared.

The three boats hung on a single anchor overnight. The canal pilot was due at five a.m. for their transit, so the family awoke an hour early. At seven a.m. a pilot came for the *Debby Wines*. A little later a Panamanian pilot came for *Waterloo*, but finding two boats tied together, he got upset and left. Finally at nine a.m., an American pilot from Texas arrived. When his handheld radio crackled the go-ahead, they set off. It was Wednesday, March 29th.

For the next eleven hours everyone kept busy. Chuck monitored things aboard *Waterloo* while Dawn and Garth took turns steering *Vela* to keep her bow at the proper angle to help prevent the boats from rubbing together and make it easier for DJ to steer. Dallas snapped picture after picture with his Polaroid camera. He even took a few of the Wilcoxes, which he handed over to them. Without funds to justify the cost of film, these Polaroid shots would be among the few the family had from this part of their voyage.

The *Waterloo-Vela* entourage steered almost due south the four nautical miles from "the flats" to Gatun Locks. Tropical jungle surrounded them, buzzing with insects. It formed a wall of green so dense the sun barely shone through it. The acrid odor of jungle rot filled their noses. The sun quickly stoked the humidity to uncomfortable levels, and they tried to imagine laboring in this heat to build this canal. The banks were muddy, yet every fifteen feet or so lights were cut into the slope to guide vessels that traversed it at night. It was an engineering marvel.

The Panama Canal was built between 1879 and 1914 on the backs of thousands of manual laborers who toiled under an unrelenting sun. On other days, torrents of rain could bring flash floods that turned the jungle into a slippery mess. In an instant, mudslides could negate every inch of hard-won progress, in this place where mosquitoes competed for a pound of flesh and brought deadly malaria, yellow fever or debilitating dengue fever.

When the flotilla reached the Gatun Locks, they had to wait for the vessels that would share the lock with them. First came the *Royal Viking Sky*, a cruise ship that looked like a wall of white. Thousands of camera-toting tourists lined the rail. Then came the tug *George W. Goethals*. They loitered for what seemed like an eternity with idling engines sending noxious plumes of exhaust into the air. Muddy greenish-brown water swirled around them. Linda watched for crocodiles that reportedly lurked in these waters, but was disappointed not to see any. Garth focused his attention on monitoring the lines and fenders.

The entourage motored into the first of the three Gatun Locks that would raise them to the level of Gatun Lake. *Vela* and *Waterloo* tied to the *George W. Goethals*. Aboard *Vela*, no one had to handle any lines. Once the lock chamber was full of boats, a fast tide of water swirled around them as the locks flooded.

When the water stopped rising, the metal doors clanked open and they all proceeded into the second lock. Delays were painful as *Royal Viking Sky* crept forward, pulled along by mules—steel locomotives that ran alongside the lock. By the third lock everyone anticipated the next step. After the top lock, they entered Gatun Lake, the largest man-made lake in the world. It let vessels float over most of what had once been the Isthmus of Panama.

At eight knots they steamed twenty nautical miles past islands, islets, and picnic houses with thatched roofs. Dallas told them that sometimes you could see monkeys. Though Linda looked hard, she couldn't spot any. A rain squall passed over them, but it was brief and hot sunshine soon steamed their clothes dry. In Gamboa, they paused to change pilots so the first one could stop for a hot lunch. Transit clients would have to grab a snack when they could.

Over the next seven miles, the waterway narrowed dramatically and wound through a deep cut, carved through the rock and shale of the Continental Divide. This seven-mile stretch had once been called Culebra (snake) because of its treacherous curves, but was renamed Gaillard Cut after the engineer who had tackled the engineering challenges it posed.

This engineering feat had for many years been the world's largest concrete structure. As they sped past the scenery, each of them wondered how, after such a monumental effort that cost thousands of lives, the U.S. would be willing to give it away. Especially, to entrust its operation to the Panamanians, who could barely keep their own cities running. While anchored in "the Flats" at Cristobal, the family had listened to ongoing Congressional debates on Armed Forces Radio. Flabbergasted, they wondered aloud if any of those debating had even seen the conditions that surrounded one of the most important shipping routes of the world.

When they locked through the Pedro Miguel Locks, Garth helped Chuck and Dallas handle the lines aboard *Waterloo*, leaving Linda and

Dawn in charge of *Vela*. When the locks opened, they traversed the mile and a half across Miraflores Lake to the last two locks.

Dawn was thrilled to pass through the very waterway she had read about in Richard Halliburton's *Book of Marvels* as a girl. She'd been captivated by the adventurer's eight-day swim in the late 1920s through the fifty-mile length of the Panama Canal to the Pacific in alligator-infested waters. On part of his route, current from the emptying locks had been so strong it took him seven hours to swim across the inner channel, escorted by a sniper in case a hungry alligator took a bite. For his passage through the locks, he paid a toll based on his tonnage, just like a ship. Since he weighed one-thirteenth of a ton, it had cost him thirty-six cents.

At last, their flotilla reached the Miraflores Locks that would lower them to the level of the Pacific Ocean. Because of extreme tidal variations of the Pacific Ocean, the Miraflores Lock gates are the canal's tallest. When they reached the front of the lock, Dawn peered over the cliff-like drop-off and felt her stomach lurch.

Dawn watched water churn and tried to ignore the smell of diesel exhaust swirling over the odor of overripe shrimp. As water flowed out of the last lock, she realized that since Chuck had ridden aboard *Waterloo* the whole transit, he couldn't say he'd crossed Panama on *Vela*. It brought a smile to her face.

Once through the Miraflores Locks, the entourage snaked past the Miraflores Bridge, and under the Bridge of the Americas. Near the bridge, a pilot boat drew alongside. A man handed Linda an envelope which said *Vela* on it. She tossed it onto the table below. They motored past the Amador Causeway, which linked a small collection of islands to the mainland, and the pilot station there. They sped to the official anchorage, where *Vela* could easily anchor without an engine. Just as they arrived, *Waterloo* learned that her sister shrimp boat had lost its steering. *Waterloo*'s crew quickly freed *Vela* and went back to tow the *Debby Wines*.

The Wilcoxes had made it through the Panama Canal. One more passage and they'd be home.

By the time *Vela* was anchored, it was seven p.m. Everyone was hungry and tired. After a quick dinner, Chuck opened the clearance envelope and everyone shared a laugh when he realized the clearance was for a Liberian freighter named *Vela*. Since no one ever asked for it, they kept it for a souvenir, having no idea of the consequences to the other *Vela* bound for Los Angeles.

Waterloo never returned to collect the twenty-six-dollar towing fee. Evidently *Waterloo* had other battles to fight.

Though the hassle-filled transit of Suez Canal—little more than a ditch—had cost one hundred and forty dollars, *Vela's* easy transit through the impressively engineered Panama Canal hadn't cost them a penny.

56

The Wilcoxes were now anchored on the Pacific side of the canal in Balboa, in a roadstead anchorage, exposed to whatever winds, waves, and currents Mother Nature might inflict upon them. They hoped to relocate to the Balboa Yacht Club, where they could easily finish the final preparations for their last passage.

The first priority was to pick up mail and check if there was room for *Vela* at the club. Since *Waterloo* hadn't returned, they now had an extra twenty-six dollars for such a luxury.

From the anchorage, it was a two-mile row, just to the end of the causeway where the pilot station was located. Chuck struggled to propel the flat-bottomed inflatable Avon through the chop. Waves splashed over the bow and the wave tops blew off, sending spray through the air. He hoped this would be the only time he'd have to do this. When he reached the pilot station, they said he could leave the dinghy there. The yacht club was still another two-mile walk.

Unfortunately when Chuck reached the yacht club, he discovered the docks were full. "Maybe in a few days," someone said. Chuck hoped that in a few days they'd be on their way north toward home. At least he'd been able to pick up the family's mail. When he arrived back to the dinghy after a blisteringly hot two-mile walk, he slipped on the oily pier and fell in. He returned to *Vela*, bearing wet mail and the grim news that there was no room at the yacht club. Though now difficult to read, everyone was grateful for the waterlogged letters from home.

They still had to buy enough food to carry them home. Unfortunately, the family would have to complete the last provisioning under the current arrangements: a two-mile row in steep chop, plus a two-mile hike along the exposed causeway just to begin the trek into town.

The next day Dawn and Garth set out with the trusty, rusty cart. Since Linda had caught the same fever Garth had suffered and was still feeling poorly, she didn't go along. After an hour-long row—during which Dawn's hat blew away and sank—the two pounded down the two miles of concrete to the yacht club, then caught a bus from there into town.

Like Cristobal on the Caribbean side of the Canal, the American town of Balboa on the Pacific end was clean. Dawn and Garth gazed longingly at all the old familiar American brands as they trudged past stores that were restricted to people who worked for the Panama Canal Commission. Dawn and Garth had to do their shopping in Panama City. Here too, the boundary between the tidy American shops and the old, unpainted buildings on the Panamanian side was striking, and they again questioned the wisdom of turning over the Canal to the Panamanians.

As they made their way along the city streets, members of Panama's military stopped them and advised them that the area was full of thieves. In most places the family had visited, locals all seemed to work for the Chamber of Commerce, making a concerted effort to convince visitors of the charms of their hometown, regardless of what visitors might see. Not so in Panama City. People frequently warned them about "bad boys."

Yet Panama City looked safer than some places the family had visited, though Dawn would never tell her mother that. Still, its center felt like a madhouse, with too many people jostling them. Loudspeakers and hawkers assaulted their ears as they tried to lure customers inside. This elicited the opposite reaction in Garth and Dawn: a strong urge to run away.

Free transit through the canal left more money for food. That became even more critical when Dawn was unable to cash the cashier's check her mother had sent. She would have to make do with the cash they had left.

Chuck had told Dawn to buy provisions for ninety days. None of them could imagine a passage taking three months, and they wondered if Chuck's pessimistic estimate wasn't a bit extreme. When Dawn and Garth finally located a supermarket, they began the arduous process of price comparison, then pulling items off the shelf, and checking them off Dawn's list. They lugged as much as they could carry down Avenida Central, the busiest street in Panama City, and onto the bus, then the rest of the way on foot—the cart now protesting in a high-pitched whine the last two miles along the causeway. They heaped it all into the dinghy and rowed the two miles back to *Vela*, hoping the food wouldn't get soaked by splashes along the way. By the time they arrived back on the boat, they were so tired they could barely move, yet they still had to put everything away.

A couple days later, Linda felt better and the three of them repeated the whole sordid ordeal. This time one of the pilots offered them a ride to the yacht club. Linda groused that a ride *back* when they were loaded with groceries would have been far more helpful.

Before loading up on groceries, first they went to the U.S. Embassy to see if Linda's final had arrived. Located in a nice part of Panama City, Balboa Avenida reminded Dawn of San Francisco's Marina District on the water's edge with well-cared-for houses, some with tile roofs and wrought-iron grillwork on the windows, which she looked forward to seeing once again. Nearby lay a big statue of Balboa pointing out to the ocean he had found. First they would have to cross it to get there.

When the three arrived inside the embassy, the Panamanian woman who "helped" them stated emphatically that it couldn't have possibly been sent to the embassy. She couldn't even be bothered to check. After all her studying, Linda was angry.

A frustrated Dawn shrugged. She was so tired of dealing with the school business and the hassles it entailed. How much simpler life would be when the kids just left the house all day and someone else took care of educating them. They would no longer have to send away multiple times for the books, prospectus, and exams only to wait for them never to arrive. Or to mail them off into the void, never to be seen again, as happened to Garth's coursework they sent from the Seychelles. That as much as anything killed his progress. Imagine requiring someone to redo work he'd already done—especially a seventeen-year-old.

She hated to admit that a part of her was secretly relieved when Garth stopped doing schoolwork, because it eliminated the hassle and the cost. But she worried about the price they would pay for this. Somehow she'd let her smart son become a high-school dropout. She didn't worry about Linda, who had gained two years in school, but Garth had gotten so far behind.

By their second year of voyaging, the kids' knowledge far exceeded hers. Garth had done sophisticated trigonometric calculation to derive their position when he navigated across the Atlantic. But in the society they were returning to, that might not count for much. What good was an impressive understanding of geography and history, literature or even math if you were a high-school dropout?

She hoped the voyage hadn't wrecked her kids' futures, but it was too late to worry about that now. At least they weren't on drugs. The family would deal with the consequences after they arrived home. They had plenty of other things to worry about. Just sailing the rest of the way home would be a challenge.

Dawn treated the kids to lunch at McDonald's—which appeared to be in the slums, though in Panama it was hard to tell. Prices were half those of St. Thomas. Then they took the bus to the supermarket and once again stocked up with as much as they could carry. They stood in a long line marked QUESO. When they arrived at the front, they discovered the queso turned out to be a five-pound block of Velveeta. No resemblance to the Gouda they'd bought in St. Maarten.

By the time they limped on sore feet back to the dinghy at the end of the causeway, Linda thought her arms were going to fall off. Garth still had a two-mile row in front of him.

After spending the next few days unloading and decanting and trying to find places to fit all this food, Dawn stowed the grocery cart for what might be the last time. That rickety old cart had pulled heavier duty than Dawn had ever envisioned when she bought it five years before. She remembered when it was shiny and new. She cracked a smile thinking about the first time she'd overfilled it and bent the wheels and axle in Honolulu, back when Linda was still reading *Pippi Longstocking*. Chuck had epoxied it, and though it never looked as nice, it was far stronger. Then, because the handle was designed for use by someone who stood four-foot-ten, Garth had lashed the flag staff to it to extend its reach so they could trail it behind them without smacking their heels with every step. She smiled when she thought of the time she'd accidentally left the cart at the bus depot in Suva and a Fijian man had brought it back to her. It had hauled so many grocery loads in Greece, Spain and St. Thomas. She closed the door to the hanging locker, happy to think she might never have to use it again. It was hard to imagine they were finally sailing home, that the next time she shopped for groceries would be in California.

After the pilots refused to let them leave the dinghy at the pilot station, their dinghy row would double, so they up-anchored *Vela* to see if a mooring ball had become available at the yacht club. One had. Naturally they'd already finished provisioning. Now it would be far more convenient to shop and haul provisions, but they couldn't afford to buy more. They had no idea how much remained in their bank account back home, but with no more traveler's checks or cash, they were effectively broke. It was time to go.

In one last letter to her mother, Dawn tried to explain the state of affairs aboard. It was an attempt to keep her mother from worrying, though it had the opposite effect.

> My gas stove rusted out in Sudan. I have been cooking on the kerosene Primus at sea and the Chinese wick stove when anchored. The Chinese one is nice and quiet but I have to compromise and use the "blast furnace" too since it uses less fuel. We also use kerosene lanterns since we don't have electricity any more. We still use propane for the fridge. We also have flashlights and a bigger battery torch.

So much had changed since they set out on their first Pacific passage five years earlier. Now hardly anything worked aboard *Vela*, though somehow the propane camping fridge she had bought in Fiji after the shipwreck still hummed away. Soon she would have the luxuries of civilization once again. She could hardly imagine it.

Before departing, Chuck wrote to his parents:

> This hopefully will be the last letter from the Vela as the next communication is supposed to be done by eyeball. That will be nice. Glad you are hanging in there, Dad. We got a letter from Aunt Fan saying how much you seemed to improve while she was there. Shame on you for not informing her of your illness. You would be upset if I were that sick and didn't tell you.

He explained their plans:

> For reference purposes: We plan to go south from here, crossing the equator between the mainland and the Galapagos Islands to a point a few hundred miles to the

west then turn NW to pass just west of Clipperton Island and then NW about 500 miles off the coast till about the latitude of San Jose. Then head for SF. That is the plan. The route is described in British Admiralty "Ocean Passages for the World" for sailing vessels. Of course plans sometimes go awry although not too often. The total distance is just under 5000 miles which I expect to take about 2 months. We are going to take water for 2 and a half times that long just in case we're becalmed etc.

His thoughts turned to the end of the voyage:

The first priority will be to get a job, but if the IRS will come to terms I won't be in such a sweat and I would like to visit relatives and friends first. At any rate, there is nothing to be gained by doing anything before we arrive. There is no hurry. Manana is soon enuff for me, too. Hope to see you all soon. Love, Chuck

At the yacht club, each of them enjoyed hot showers—their last for a *very* long time.

On April 6, 1978, they sailed out of Panama with expired passports and no cash. It was home or bust.

57

The Wilcoxes left with the tide to give them as good a start as possible on what they knew would be a long passage. They just didn't know how long. Chuck told his parents sixty days. Dawn had provisioned for seventy-five.

In fact, it would be far longer than either estimate.

Lack of wind and a strong current swept *Vela* down the coast of South America. A week after leaving Panama, they sighted land: Cape San Francisco in Ecuador—not the San Francisco they were aiming for. A hazy view of the mountains hovered over the horizon and, after dark, they saw the faint glow of Quito. The family realized that, at the rate they were traveling, the passage would last eleven more weeks. At the time that seemed unimaginable.

With no motor, they were at the mercy of the currents and the winds.

Two weeks out, after more drifting they calculated they were close to the Galapagos Islands. They'd read about Darwin, his voyage aboard the *Beagle* and the unusual species he studied there that led to his revolutionary theory of evolution.

On April 21st, in the moonlight, they spotted the silhouette of what they concluded must be San Cristobal. On Garth's midnight watch, amid a haunting stillness, he noticed something odd.

"Hey, I hear goats out here!" Garth yelled from the cockpit.

"I don't hear anything," Dawn said, popping her head through the companionway. She listened another moment as Garth cocked his head.

"There," Garth noted when he heard it again.

"Oh," Dawn agreed. "I hear it now."

"You can't hear goats from this far," Chuck said, incredulous.

"Maybe we're closer than we realize," Garth said. "Maybe we should tack, just in case."

So they tacked. Not that it made much difference. They had no steerageway. Hearing the roar of breakers in the distance, they worried about getting swept onto the rocks. Without any wind and no engine, there was little they could do but worry. The night passed with excruciating slowness.

When the sun rose, they were still within sight of the same island. Somehow being able to see it brought them comfort, though nothing had changed. If the Wilcoxes had wanted to go ashore, they couldn't. They hadn't arranged visas in advance, their passports had expired, and they had no money. The island group taunted them for days.

As *Vela* drifted between the islands, sea lions surfaced, plunged and resurfaced several boat lengths ahead, making it obvious that *Vela* was not moving. They worried *Vela* would be caught in this windless vortex for weeks. The emotional impact struck them first, sending their spirits spiraling downward. Then they realized the implications for their food supply.

Once they finally broke free of the island group, they saw no more land. Days stretched on, one after another, with a featureless horizon, save for the puffy cumulus clouds that floated past, or towering cumulonimbus clouds that dumped heavy rain. The occasional violent squall offered the only interruption to the mind-numbing boredom.

Being adrift in the equatorial Pacific took *Vela* through some of the richest waters on earth. *Vela's* bottom, freshly scraped and recoated only five months earlier in Martinique, was by now host to a thriving ecosystem. The growth cost them what little speed they could eke out of the nonexistent wind. On April 26th and 27th, they hove-to for barnacle-removal detail. Linda watched for sharks while the other three scraped. Since *Vela* had no ladder to the water, the only way to get aboard was to climb up the pipes supporting the poop deck. Linda joked that if sharks *had* appeared while they were scraping, one of them would have "gotten it for sure."

It was hard work, trying to find leverage while treading water. Because the water was more than fifteen degrees cooler than body temperature, even in the tropics, they soon grew chilled. They couldn't work more than an hour at a time but hoped it would shorten the length of time they had to be out here. As they sailed north, the water and air would grow even colder.

Without laundry facilities, they found creative ways to minimize the laundry pile. Garth often towed his shirts, shorts or underwear behind the boat in a lazy attempt to clean them. A few hours dragging through the water behind *Vela* simulated the agitation cycle of a washing machine. But in these rich waters, Garth's "twenty-four-hour laundry" deposited baby barnacles in his undershorts. After picking out thousands of microscopic shells, Garth re-evaluated this strategy.

Since the family was on their way home, Dawn saw no point in saving threadbare clothing. When a piece of clothing was too dirty, she decided they could just toss it overboard and wave it goodbye. One day Dawn threw over an old yellow blouse that was torn. The next morning in the fishing lure, they caught … an old yellow blouse.

Every inch of progress came ever so slowly. Each day as they calculated their position, they were in nearly the same place as the day before. There was so little wind that even the albatross could not take off. For days, the enormous birds bobbed beside them. Some days, something floating in the water would catch their eye. They would struggle to sail up to it, only to discover egg shells or orange peels they'd discarded the day before. Discoveries like these would send their spirits plummeting.

Each glance at the chart reconfirmed their suspicions: they could be out here far longer than they originally anticipated. In late April, after nearly a month of sailing, they'd only sailed 1,300 miles and not all of them toward their destination. *Vela* had covered almost that entire distance in just a week between St. Thomas and Panama. The thought was depressing.

Dawn could not deny what that meant for the food supplies. She began to obsess about food, doing an inventory and employing the old speed-rate-distance formula to estimate supplies required. As the days stretched on with so little progress, Dawn began to reduce the portion sizes to stretch the food a little farther, just in case. It didn't escape notice.

Vela's sails were worn out. The sail cloth was soft and thin, the stitching frayed and weak. It wouldn't take much wind to blow an entire seam, though the shudder of the rig from the swell could do as much damage. Their shapes were now far baggier than in the Red Sea a year ago when Chuck nearly gave up on them. On April 30th, the main ripped several feet across. Dawn and Garth spent the next day painstakingly sewing the main back together while they drifted. It was a terrible patch job, but it would have to do.

A couple of days later the vang broke and they had to pull the main down again. Chuck and Garth spent the next six hours rebuilding the vang. By the time they hoisted the main again, *Vela* had only covered a single mile. Then it was the jib's turn, with a tear in the foot. Without a motor, they were at the mercy of the wind and the sails. If the wind was insufficient to sail, they had no choice but to wait. And wait they did.

Food, once the highlight of the day, now came with an edge, as Dawn served progressively smaller portions. After meals they weren't quite full.

Dawn would announce with forced cheer that they still had ten weeks of food. The reason her numbers hadn't changed was not lost on the crew. As the temperature grew colder, they yearned for more food rather than less, yet portions dwindled in inverse proportion to their desire. Everyone grew grumpy and short tempered.

By May 10th they still had 3,100 miles to go. Dawn calculated that, at fifty miles per day, the trip would last another sixty-two days. Yet their most recent day's run was forty-one miles in twenty-four hours. And the day after, only twenty-eight miles. No matter how she did the math, the numbers revealed the stark reality. They might not have enough food. Dawn's stomach churned with the pressure of keeping the family fed with dwindling supplies. She berated herself for not buying more, yet she had spent all the money they had.

They argued about possibly stopping at Clipperton Island, off the Mexican coast, but Chuck finally convinced Dawn that, since it was un-inhabited, it wouldn't help.

On May 11th, they caught a Mahi Mahi, which extended food supplies another two meals and offered welcome fresh meat. But they generally didn't have much luck fishing despite the sea life that populated *Vela*'s bottom. Why would fish have an interest in a plastic squid lure when there was better eating among the barnacles that clung to *Vela*'s underside? Fresh fish wasn't something they could count on to stretch their meager food supplies. Soon they were back to various renditions of Spam, but now more as a flavoring rather than a core part of the meal. They were hungrier after each meal, especially as they burned through more calories just to stay warm. They would shiver, even in sweaters, long pants, and socks. A lethargy settled over them. No one had the energy to do anything but the minimum. Being late for watch was a capital offense.

They fantasized aloud about food. Once Dawn had dreamed of steak and potatoes, a fresh salad, and apple pie. Now even canned peaches, canned ham, and canned cake seemed like a luxury. Every day at noon, each of them got a piece of hard candy after lunch, a tradition that had grown in importance this passage. As Dawn reached into the canister and handed them out she could not help but notice how few remained rattling around its bottom. One day the inevitable occurred. She reached the last of the treats.

"Uh," she said with an edge to her voice. "This is the last of the candy." Everyone looked up with alarm. The impact of this tiny thing hit them hard. Though they'd all known this day was coming, the advance knowledge couldn't dull the acute sense of lack that it wrought.

After celebrating a ninety-one-mile day, the following day's run was down to a depressing twenty-four miles. Each low mileage day felt like an extension of their sentence in purgatory. Each day seemed more frustrating than the one before.

It seemed they were always tired, ravenous, gloomy, irritable and cold.

Linda tried to keep the fear and depression at bay by planning her days and focusing on schoolwork. But her time on watch stretched on interminably. Without distractions and faced with flapping sails, she felt the futility of their efforts. At the mercy of the wind and fate, which seemed to be against them, she felt the full magnitude of being unable to get off the boat. Sometimes she would sit in the cockpit alone and cry. Would they die out there?

Chuck withdrew, feeling the weight of his responsibility as captain, but powerless to act.

Writing letters home, one of the things that kept Dawn sane during long passages, now made no sense. By the time she could mail them, presumably she'd be home, face-to-face with those to whom she would normally write. If they could get there. Both she and Chuck wondered whether they'd made a mistake assuming they could get home without an engine. Without enough food …

Garth figured they would reach somewhere, eventually. He just hoped it would be *before* the food ran out.

After finishing an insufficient portion of rice with corned beef and canned peas, Garth looked at his empty bowl, as though miraculously more food would appear. He was still hungry. He absently fingered his teeth. He noticed that they wiggled when he pressed against them. He blurted, "Hey, my teeth are loose!"

"So are mine!" Linda exclaimed, reaching up to her mouth. "And my gums hurt."

Dawn moved to where Linda was sitting. Linda pulled her lips apart so her mother could see. Her gums appeared red and irritated, swollen even.

"Oh, my." *Scurvy!* Dawn realized these were symptoms that had plagued sailors for centuries. Without sufficient fresh food, crews of the square riggers had gradually been overcome by lethargy, lost their teeth, and succumbed to wounds that refused to heal and ultimately led to death. It wasn't until Captain Cook ran an experiment, forcing his crew to ingest sauerkraut and bitter limes, that they were able to avert the costly effects of scurvy.

"Scurvy!" Dawn said aloud. The word seeped into everyone's subconscious, evoking images from Anson's disastrous voyage, during which nearly his entire crew died. Overcome by a moment of shock, they all looked at each other in stunned silence, then started to laugh. Imagine that. Scurvy. In 1978.

Dawn was mortified. How she could have failed her family so completely? She'd read in the early days of her nurses training about the debilitating effects of depriving the body of ascorbic acid (Vitamin C), which the body needed for building and repairing connective tissue. She'd bought vitamins in St. Thomas, but had rationed them along with everything else. She pulled out the bottles and distributed a double dose of pellet-shaped pills to her family.

It took days for the malaise that accompanies scurvy to diminish. Still a featureless horizon with no wind wasn't exactly cheery. Nor was the dark interior, dimly lit by kerosene lamps that made it hard to read after sunset. Since they had no way to charge the batteries or power the lights, they had to ration their usage of them and the radio, another morale booster.

May 14th was a dark day aboard, with one disaster following another. They'd been at sea for thirty-nine days. After several squalls that brought lightning and rain, the mainsail ripped again. As Chuck pulled the sail down, his Seiko self-winding wristwatch—the official ship's chronometer—snagged on a loose line and was torn from his wrist. He watched it splash into the ocean and stared in disbelief at his empty wrist.

The magnitude of the loss sunk in slowly. A critical tool for navigation was now gone. The family had briefly discussed whether he should take it off, but he worried this self-winding watch would cease to function without the movement that came with being worn. For Chuck, the memory of that conversation felt like a sharp knife's thrust to the gut.

Garth had picked up a cheap watch in Fiji to replace the one he lost in the shipwreck, but it kept poor time. The accuracy of their navigation would now be unpredictable. They would be more dependent than ever on checking the unreliable watch against time signals from the short wave radio, for which they carried a scarce supply of D cell batteries to power.

A few hours later when Linda was on evening watch, a nut for the backstay plunged into the water with a *thunk*. Linda called her father. When Chuck saw the topping lift trailing in the stern wave, he knew what had occurred. Without the nut, there was now nothing to hold the bolt in place. If the bolt backed out, the backstay would be lost and would no longer be there to support the mast. Without support, who knew how long before the mast came crashing down.

They still had 2,700 miles to sail.

58

The gravity of their situation weighed heavily on Chuck, who was still reeling from losing the timepiece. All that slatting in heavy swells without wind had stressed the rig and worked the nut loose. This might be just one of many things that could give way and jeopardize the rig. If they lost the rig they would be out there bobbing with no hope of reaching land before the food ran out.

Chuck had tried so hard to keep this boat going against all odds. It seemed impossible, beyond what was humanly possible to endure. He felt the added strain of knowing his ailing father hung on to see him again. Now he might not have the chance. The thought was enough to push him over the edge. He buried his head in his hands.

Just then a squall hit. Garth and Dawn sprang into action. They rushed forward to pull down the main, to minimize the pressure on the rig. As soon as the sail was out of the way, Garth reached for the main shackle so it wouldn't wrestle free as it had on their first passage to Hawaii. With the cold metal shackle in his fingers, Garth realized he could use the main halyard to act as the backstay until daylight when they could see what they were doing. With his mother's help he attached it to the boom gallows, a strong part of the boat as far as the halyard would reach. Relying on the main being down and hoping the halyard would hold didn't offer much hope but it was all they had. It struck them just how isolated they were—and how vulnerable.

"If this mast comes down, we're finished," Chuck said, his face clouded, his voice tainted with a pervasive sense of hopelessness.

"What about the emergency beacon?" Dawn asked.

"That'll only bring us help if an airplane is flying within two hundred and fifty miles and can pick up the signal." It wasn't a common flight path. They hadn't heard an airplane for weeks.

Chuck's shoulders drooped with all the doomsday scenarios that swirled through his mind. Too many breakages. Too many unknowns. Too much pressure. The strain of being the captain, of being the one responsible, the one who was supposed to know what to do, overwhelmed him. A painful throbbing started behind his eyes. His head felt like it might explode. He pulled at his lower lip, his eyes far away.

Garth and Dawn shared a look. All they needed was eight hours until morning when they had enough light to see. They had nothing but hope.

Chuck went down to bed. Garth soon followed.

Dawn stayed to keep Linda company while she was on watch. Her father's bleak declaration had frightened her. The two talked about what could happen if the mast came down. Linda wondered aloud what it would be like to die. Dawn tried to reassure her though she felt just as unsure. Eventually their talk turned to what school might be like. Hour by hour they got through the night, with Dawn sending Linda to bed at nine p.m. and Garth relieving her at midnight. By the time Garth's time on watch ended at three a.m., Chuck only had to last a couple hours before the sun peeked over the horizon. It was enough.

As soon as the day seemed bright enough, Garth would go up the rig to try to fix the problem. First they had to find a nut the correct size to fit the bolt. After combing through the tackle boxes of rusty metal parts they finally found a nut that seemed like it would work. A single nut. That meant Garth could not drop it while he was swinging from the bosun's chair sixty feet in the air.

Garth climbed into the bosun's chair and signaled that he was ready. Normally Chuck would crank and Dawn would tail. But Chuck was in no state to help. His brain was on overload, running through a litany of things that could go wrong. Linda stepped in to haul the line while Dawn cranked.

It was slow going. Inch by inch the chair rose. Garth strained to hang on and help ease the load on the halyard by using his arms and legs to climb as *Vela* rode the swell and rolled back and forth. When the bosun's chair reached as high as the halyard could take it, Garth could barely touch the bolt with his hands stretched above his head. Chuck couldn't bear to watch. He envisioned the nut dropping to the deck and bouncing over the side—and with it, any hope of reaching California.

Dawn and Linda stood with their necks craned, trying to see whether Garth was making progress. Watching the mast swinging wildly made them queasy. The motion flung Garth back and forth, and he struggled to keep himself from smacking headfirst into the mast while trying to use both hands for his task. During a lull in the motion, he used his knees to grip the mast and push himself a little higher than the bosun's chair would go. Over and over he tried to maneuver but it was too difficult.

Finally he shimmied up the mast, flung a line over the top of the mast and pulled himself higher. Then he lashed himself and the bosun's chair to the mast above where the halyard would normally reach. Now that he could see what he was doing, he wrapped wire around the threads of the bolt to give him something to hang onto. When he first repositioned the topping lift—which they'd fished from the waves—over the bolt, it felt like a small victory. With an intensity of concentration, he slowly threaded the nut back on, hoping it wouldn't get knocked out of place before he finished. After an hour and a half swinging from the bosun's chair, he'd addressed the problem. But intent on avoiding another potential loss of their only nut, Garth decided to safety-wire it so it could not fall off again.

Finally, after ten more tense minutes, Garth announced, "OK, I'm done." Satisfied the repair might last, he said. "You can let me down now." His mother and sister eased him back down. The moment his feet touched the deck, everyone sighed with relief. Sore from his death grip on the rig, Garth massaged away the kinks in his neck, legs and hands. Another crisis averted. They hoped it would be their last, but knew better.

With Garth back on deck, a jubilant Dawn said, "No matter what your father says, we'll help you pay for college." She hoped he'd have that chance. To celebrate Garth's success, Dawn cooked a generous meal—still canned mackerel and rice, but bigger portions.

Garth's actions rendered him a hero, though no one expected it of him. Once Chuck had recovered, he joked that Garth had earned another year of room and board, but the captain's confidence remained shaken.

Later that same afternoon while Garth stood watch, a dark shadow in the water caught his eye. A manta ray—with what must have been a ten-foot wing span—swooped past *Vela* like a spaceship from another galaxy. Garth watched this pelagic wonder, mesmerized as the creature fell gracefully behind the boat, gliding back and forth across *Vela*'s stern wake. For a moment it hovered just beyond the log spinner that trailed behind *Vela* to click off the miles.

Garth's eyes grew big when he saw the manta ray's cavernous mouth envelop the spinner. A tumble of waves confirmed it had swallowed the spinner. In an instant, Garth's fascination turned to concern. Immediately grasping the consequences of dragging such a huge creature for even a second—not to mention what a whirling brass propeller might do to its digestive system—Garth whipped out his knife and sliced the line.

The Wilcoxes had a spare spinner, but they did not have a spare log. If the log got yanked off the stern rail, navigation would be nearly impossible. Not only would they be missing a reliable chronometer to time their star sights, they would be unable to keep a running DR. To measure their progress—or lack of it—and thereby deduce their relative position, they had to replace the spinner with their one and only spare ... and hope they wouldn't lose that one.

Two hours later they snagged a small fish on the line, but lost it. After such an intense twenty-four hours, once everyone realized their hopes for fresh dinner had vanished, they descended into a funk. In the ship's log, Linda wrote: *I HATE THIS! ! ! !*

On May 18th when the rain stopped mid-morning, Chuck decided they ought to scrape barnacles again. Barnacles on *Vela*'s bottom were costing them what little speed they could wrench from the light winds. He rigged up a line to hang onto with one hand while scraping with the other as the boat rolled in the swell. As Chuck was getting ready to climb in, Dawn shouted, "Wait!" Pointing at the water, she added, "What's that?"

They all peered over the side and saw not one but two brownish-gray dorsal fins. "Shark!" That brought a quick end to plans for going overboard. In truth everyone was relieved. The mere thought of swimming and scraping barnacles in that cold water exhausted them. They had so little energy. Still, *Vela* continued crawling along at an excruciatingly slow pace.

A few hours later the red squid lure snagged a slender five-foot-long blue shark. Knowing it would never work to gaff him, they lassoed him from the tail and dragged him backwards. After much tail-thrashing, he finally tired, and they hauled him aboard and hung him upside-down for several hours, just to be sure he was good and dead. Everyone salivated as Dawn cut him into steaks. She made a tasty shark curry, but by morning the meat emitted such a strong ammonia smell that they had to toss the rest. That day *Vela* made a depressing eight miles.

On May 22nd, after forty-six days of sailing, they still had 2,250 miles to go. In the early afternoon, Dawn calculated that they would need to cover thirty-eight miles per day to make it in the fifty-nine days of food left. Her careful figures thinly veiled an accounting sleight of hand, the truth of which was not lost on her hungry crewmates. The most basic math shows that with seventy-five days' worth of provisions, after forty-six days of eating, you do not have fifty-nine days left. There are only two ways to account for such a discrepancy: creative accounting and diminishing portions. Though it hardly seemed possible, meals became even smaller, leaving vast areas of open real estate in their dinner bowls.

"You call this dinner?" Chuck said with a grin. "This is more like a snack. These portions would emaciate a hamster." He was only half-kidding.

"I'm still hungry," Garth agreed, his eyes staring at his empty bowl. Linda nodded absently, wrapping her arms tightly around herself and shivering. Dawn felt bad, but they would run out of food if she didn't take precautions.

As *Vela* sailed ever northward, skies were often overcast, shrouded in fog or dripping with rain. Cool temperatures forced the family to add sweaters over multiple t-shirts, plus jackets and shoes to their on and off-watch repertoire. After so many years in the tropics, the family wasn't used to temperatures that dipped below seventy-five. Insufficient calories added to their sense of feeling cold all the time.

May 24th sent their spirits tumbling downward once again. The line to "George," the wind vane, broke. As soon as Chuck fixed that, a worse problem appeared.

With a loud crack, the upper port spreader brace snapped. After one of the braces broke in the Indian Ocean, Chuck had replaced the broken crossbeam brace and added vertical braces to reinforce them in the Seychelles, but they'd sailed nearly halfway around the world since then. Just from Panama, *Vela* had been on starboard tack for forty-eight days nonstop. All that time the port shrouds hung slack, swaying and working with the motion of the boat in the swell. The strain had taken its toll and the metal had fatigued. Without the support of the crossbeam brace, the port spreader began yawing back and forth with every wave, pivoting around a single bolt. The remaining vertical brace couldn't keep it from moving. The spreader would eventually break. Could they reach home before it happened?

Even with no wind, the swell rendered a motion so violent, there was no question of going up the mast. With a compromised rig, the danger was even greater. If the spreader failed with Garth aloft, he could get seriously injured or even killed. Garth flinched when he thought of the hour and a half he'd spent up that rig only ten days earlier as the boat rolled from gunwale to gunwale. Besides, they couldn't think of any solution that didn't interfere with the sails, their only means of propulsion.

To reach San Francisco, they would need to tack—to put tension on the port shroud. But without the brace, the spreader would probably not support the mast.

This new development underscored their predicament and sent Chuck to a new low. The decision to press on past Florida to Panama and beyond did not look so smart at the moment. It felt as though they were trapped on a bad-luck vessel, sentenced to breakage after breakage. In the ship's log, he wrote: *I predict dismasting before San Francisco.*

That night in the ship's log, Garth wrote *NUTS*. Dawn wrote at the top of the new page: *Panama to SF or Honolulu.* In faint pencil marks, Chuck added or *DJL*, meaning Davy Jones's Locker. All he could feel was the strong temptation to curl into a fetal position until it was over, whatever *over* turned out to be.

59

A sense of desperation hung over all of them. They were miles from anywhere. There was little they could do.

Yet in the morning the sun came up, just as it had the day before. The spreader still sawed back and forth with *Vela*'s every move. In every other way, life aboard seemed the same as before. More dark, cold rainy days passed with lumpy seas. Then with the help of more breeze, *Vela* had a string of better daily runs. More wind meant progress, though the strain it placed on the rig was worrisome.

Still, nothing had happened. Blue skies appeared, offering mild encouragement.

More days of leaden clouds and erratic wind followed, with nothing but the peaks and valleys that *Vela* rode day after day. The occasional whale, dolphin or flying fish distinguished one day from the next. It lured the family into a sense that they were the only ones on the planet.

On May 29th, their fifty-fourth day since they left Panama, in the mid-afternoon, Chuck was on watch. He sat hunched over, staring off into space. Movement in his peripheral vision prompted him to look up. Then a voice boomed over a loudspeaker.

"Are you all right?"

Chuck sat up and looked around. Several boat-lengths away was an old, white research vessel. On its bow read *Governor Ray*. The encounter caught him unaware.

Without a moment's thought, Chuck waved, then settled back into where he'd been sitting, hand cupped under his chin.

Dawn heard the unexpected sound of voices and felt the thrum of the engine reverberating through the hull. She peeked through the port light. There she saw a vessel lumbering past. She hurried to the cockpit.

"Maybe we should signal them!" she said to Chuck. He pulled at his lip, deep in thought. He looked at her blankly.

But it was already too late. They had but a moment and it was gone.

She bit her lip as she saw *Governor Ray* on the transom and its hailing port, Seattle, blur then disappear. Garth and Linda heard their voices and wondered what was going on.

"Couldn't we have hailed them?" Dawn repeated. Chuck shrugged. "Why not?"

"But we're not in distress," Chuck answered. *Vela* was moving. That seemed like enough. Far from his mind at that moment were the challenges they still faced.

"Maybe we could have gotten food from them or asked them to contact our folks to let them know we are OK."

He looked at her and then in the direction the ship had gone. Since it had been his decision to undertake this voyage, what right did he have to expect help from others?

By then, the vessel had vanished. With no radio, there was no way to signal them. Nothing had changed, but the knowledge of this lost opportunity left Dawn, Linda and Garth feeling more despondent than ever. Chuck just felt numb.

On May 30th, they made "*8 bloody miles*" in twenty-four hours. WWV Radio announced that a tropical depression, now five hundred miles away, had been upgraded to storm status and named *Aleta*. The news of both felt like a personal affront. All they could do was sit and wait. Either the storm would become a problem or it wouldn't.

Without the engine, the Wilcoxes had no way to charge the ship's battery. They powered the short-wave radio with a limited collection of D-cell batteries. Without sufficient power, they had to mostly forego one of their favorite passage pastimes: listening to the radio. Even weather reports from WWV were rationed. They missed BBC and would have even been happy to listen to the "*S P E C I A L E N G L I S H*" program on VoA.

For Linda, radio rationing felt like a sentence to solitary confinement. They were down to a single hour per day. A brief listen one day informed them that the Trans Pac sailboat race had begun. The Wilcoxes counted on the kerosene lanterns they bought in Fiji and Martinique for cabin lights during darkness, but had no way to power the navigation lights that alerted ships to their location. If the usual fog appeared off the coast, they would be even harder to see and in danger of getting run down.

They undertook two more sessions of barnacle-cleaning in bitter cold water until their last two putty knives disintegrated into rust flakes that fell to the bottom.

They still had 1,460 miles to go. The days went on and on.

On June 10ᵗʰ, Linda's fifteenth birthday, instead of celebrating with gifts back home as she'd envisioned, Dawn did her best to make things festive aboard. She served canned ravioli—a respite from corned beef—along with a lopsided chocolate cake made in the pressure cooker that gave it a rubbery texture. Linda enjoyed a brief suspension of radio rationing in honor of her special day and Dawn came up with a pair of socks and a plastic case for gifts. Excitement every teenager dreams about.

The following day they noted that *Vela* had crossed her outbound track, completing their circumnavigation, something that would only matter if they made it to land. In the ship's log that day, Garth wrote,

Don't fall apart yet, boat, though the spreader continued to yaw back and forth. The next day, the Groco toilet broke again. It was back to "bucket and chuck it."

Then came two days with so little wind that a trio of albatross bobbed around them on the oily swell. They nicknamed them Albert, Alberta and Albertson. One of the albatross swam over to check them out.

During the calm, Dawn did laundry on the poop deck and saw tiny pieces of paper floating in the water. Then a floating buoy. Indications they were not alone. Others were out here. Then they hooked a large tuna—a "seven-mealer" by Dawn's estimate. On the 16th, Garth saw a ship, then smoke on the horizon and four airplanes. These offered long-needed encouragement that civilization was near.

On June 17th, after seventy-two straight days at sea, the Wilcoxes finally tacked for San Francisco. Though the spreader wobbled back and forth, it remained attached. Maybe they would make it after all. With six hundred and fifty miles to go, Dawn calculated eleven more days. It was cause for celebration. For the first time they dared to think it might be possible. But they weren't done yet. Alternating fierce squalls packed with wind followed by calms made the next days excruciating. Then the wind shifted and the best compass course they could steer was 100 degrees. The angle wasn't a good heading for San Francisco. So they tacked back onto port to get further north.

Shortly after they tacked back, the spreader broke free from the mast with a BANG! If it had happened when they'd been on port tack, they would have lost the mast.

They'd known it had only been a matter of time. But after three weeks, they'd begun to hope they might make it all the way in before it failed completely. A sudden racket announced this new development. But it was worse than they'd imagined. Chuck, Dawn and Garth stared up at the mast in horror. Though it was hard to see behind the sails in the dark, the spreader, now disconnected from its pivot point on the mast, remained attached to the vertical metal brace Chuck had added to the original brace in the Seychelles. This transformed the spreader into a four-foot-long projectile. Not only would the spreader no longer support the mast, it would wreak havoc on everything in its vicinity for as long as it remained. It felt as though they'd released a madman with a baseball bat. The three cowered in the cockpit wondering how they could get it to stop. The six-foot-long chunk of wood pitched back and forth, a menace to everything in its path.

It slammed against the wooden mast. BAM!

It tore scarring gashes into the mast paint and splintered exposed areas into wood pulp; it flung against the backstay and radio antenna with a twang; it smacked against the worn-out sails, threatening to punch a hole through the thin fabric or tear at its already weakened seams. They cringed in terror. Their trials never seemed to end. How long could they withstand this battering?

Their first priority was to keep from getting killed. They couldn't think of any action that didn't risk that and so they did nothing. There was nothing that could be done but to wait and watch in terror.

"I can't take this anymore," Chuck said finally. Dawn murmured agreement. Garth was officially on watch. Once again, either it fell off or it didn't. Chuck and Dawn headed below, sure this was truly the end.

Near the end of Garth's watch, the spreader fell with splash into the ocean. The noise stopped and it was over. The mast was still up. He shuddered at the memory of the lashing they just survived. The mast could still tumble down at any moment, especially once they tacked, but at least the spreader no longer threatened more damage.

As soon as it was light, Garth and Chuck ran the extra halyards to the toe rail to help support the mast. For the mast to remain standing, they had to reduce the pressure on the rig and find another way to support it until they could reach shore, still five hundred and ninety miles away. They pulled out the toolbox and worked to tighten the upper port shroud. It was the best they could do.

On deck, something shiny caught Garth's eye. He bent down to pick it up. It was the shorn bolt. He rubbed his finger across the blunt edge, awed by the forces that had worked through the metal. When he showed it to his father, Chuck grimaced.

On June 21ˢᵗ, they tacked again for San Francisco, hoping the rig would stay up until they reached land. To minimize the strain on the rig, they dropped the main to the second reef point and used the staysail without the jib. Their speed, already slow, now would be handicapped even more with so little sail area.

While it was frustrating to drift without wind, it was equally maddening to finally have wind but be unable to use it. At least they were moving and they still had a mast. Those once so irksome eight-mile days began to look like an accomplishment. On light-air days, an entire three-hour watch might produce only four miles or two miles or even worse, circles with no discernible progress at all. On and on they sailed. Water and sky. Sky and water. Dawn took another inventory of the food: only three eggs left, no cheese, five onions, but no other fresh food. The next day another albacore tuna provided three meals, but the family members looked lost in their clothes, which hung loosely.

They had pushed themselves far beyond what they thought they could endure. Somehow they had to summon more. At an average speed of just over two knots, they inched their way closer to the coast. Though the horizon looked just the same, they had to have faith that California lay beyond their field of vision. Patience and tenacity was all they had left.

On June 28ᵗʰ, Garth's wristwatch stopped completely. Later in the day, it appeared to be functioning, but it was useless for navigation—or anything, really. Chuck worried about fog the closer they drew to land, when knowing where they were became even more critical.

On the evening of July 1ˢᵗ, the sky cleared. In addition to stars, Dawn detected a faint glow on the horizon. She wondered whether she had imagined it, but later, on watch, Garth spotted a light, which had to be the Farallon Islands. Confirmation came when he heard the steady pulse of the Farallons RDF signal.

It had been eighty-six days since they left Panama. Could they really be almost there? It almost seemed too much to hope for.

At midnight Dawn turned over the watch to Garth. It was his eighteenth birthday. *Happy Man Day, Garth*, she wrote in the ship's log. What better present could there be than to arrive on this monumental day?

At first light, Chuck confirmed sighting the Farrallon Islands. The dry hills of the coast took shape next. Each of them reveled in being the first to spot some familiar feature that confirmed they might reach home at last. Soon they could make out the Golden Gate Bridge, a sight they thought they might never see again. Memories of their naive departure came flooding back.

Dawn found some corn kernels and made popcorn to celebrate as they passed under the Golden Gate at noon. It seemed like a typical windy day on the bay with sailboats tacking back and forth, but so much had happened since they'd passed under this bridge five years before. It was hard to believe they were finally here.

As they sailed into Marina Green at the mouth of the breakwater, someone on another boat yelled over, "Did you sail all the way from Honolulu?"

"Yeah, the long way," Garth shouted back.

They dropped the anchor one last time and raised the yellow quarantine flag. In the ship's log Garth wrote, *Anchor down GG YC Basin.*
LOOKS LIKE WE MADE IT!

Vela at the end of the voyage

60

They had come full circle. The Wilcoxes had set out to sail around the world in four years. Though it had taken them five, by sheer perseverance and hard work, they had done it though it had nearly broken them.

After dropping anchor the Wilcoxes awaited clearance. But no one paid them any attention except to stare at the derelict vessel anchored in their midst. After a little while a Coast Guard auxiliary vessel passed by—probably doing life-jacket inspections. Chuck yelled over to them, "Hey, could you let Customs know we've arrived so we could clear in?" After a few radio calls, the authorities learned that this was the long-overdue *Vela*. After eighty-seven days—more than a month longer than expected—with no reports of a stop in any port along the coast, the family at home had feared the worst.

The volunteer officers towed *Vela* into a berth. Tied alongside posh St. Francis Yacht Club, *Vela* looked out of place among the sleek yachts. Her paint was peeling badly. Rust streaked down her topsides. Barnacles grew well above her bottom paint.

It was hard to imagine they were actually home. That they didn't have to sail on to a new country in a few days. It felt so odd to be back. Home, yet foreign. So much had happened since they'd left five years before. They had worked so hard to get here. Garth raised the courtesy flags of the thirty-four countries they'd visited, plus all their signal flags to commemorate Independence Day and celebrate the completion of their epic voyage.

First they needed to let everyone know they were safe. Instead of writing letters, they could have conversations in person. As soon as Chuck cleared into Customs he went to visit his father. Chuck was shocked to find him shrunken to less than half his former weight, lying in a hospital bed in his parents' living room.

Over the next few days, relatives welcomed them home. Aunts, uncles, cousins, friends and neighbors who'd heard about their return came to visit. One of them, Dawn's cousin Carol Ann, asked if she could let the media know about their story.

On July 7th, a reporter and photographer from the *San Francisco Examiner* came to interview them. The article appeared on page three, under the headline Home are 4 sailors, home from the sea. It featured a photograph of Linda, Garth and Chuck squinting into the camera before a weather-beaten *Vela*. Dawn had been shopping for food at the time, getting yet one more use from her rusty cart. Though they didn't realize it yet, this would be the first of many interviews.

On July 8th, a flotilla of boats from Sequoia Yacht Club escorted *Vela* back to Redwood City, a slow sail in light winds. *Gemini* towed the engineless *Vela* the last quarter mile up the creek and into docks crowded with people. When the now-ragtag *Vela* rounded the last curve, some were shocked at how dramatically *Vela* and the family had been transformed over the last five years. When the family left, *Vela* had been superbly equipped. Now the boat looked neglected. None of the systems she'd departed with were now working. Garth and Linda had grown a head taller. Dawn and Chuck looked skinny, tired, and a little grayer. A chorus of cheers and horns greeted them, a touching, though bewildering welcome-home for weary sailors.

On the dock was a reporter from the *San Jose Mercury News*. The Wilcoxes were soon bewildered by media interest in their story. There were visits from the *San Francisco Chronicle*, the *Palo Alto Times* and the *Stanford Daily*, to follow up on earlier coverage of their shipwreck nearly four years before, when their voyage seemed doomed. CBS Channel 5 news came and filmed aboard *Vela* for hours. The result: thirty seconds on the eleven p.m. news. The Wilcoxes' story went out over the AP and UPI news wire services and was picked up in various publications around the world, including Los Angeles, New York, Toronto and Geneva. They reprinted the same errors and quotes, most focusing on the hardships, of which there were many.

The family visited the set of *San Francisco This Morning* for an interview with Maury Povich. The family waited wide-eyed in the green room among the stars from the *Beach Blanket Babylon* show until they were called out to sit on a couch in front of a bank of cameras. When the cameras lit up, they fielded questions like, *Did you anchor at night in the ocean? Did you encounter any pirates? Were you scared about the Bermuda Triangle?*

The family soon tired of being treated as attractions, like animals at the zoo.

In mid-August, Dawn set up a meeting with the school district to register Garth and Linda for the fall. In a small windowless office school officials were impressed with how far fifteen-year-old Linda had worked ahead. They would start her as a high-school junior, two years ahead of her peers. Garth was another matter. His home-schooling aboard left him far short of a high-school diploma.

It's likely that school officials didn't want an under-challenged eighteen-year-old causing problems; the administrators insisted that even if Garth could make up the academic credits he lacked, he would still need four years of gym to complete his high-school education. A year swinging a hammer and four years sailing, hauling water, and rowing his entire family ashore evidently didn't count as exercise in their book.

The Wilcox family upon their return

Vela in San Francisco Bay post-voyage, July 1978

Postscript

After nearly a month aboard *Vela* in Redwood City, the family moved back into their empty Palo Alto house. That first night, though they were now in a three-bedroom house, everyone slept together on the soggy boat cushions on the floor of the empty living room, much like they'd done in the cement hut on Makaluva. They were grateful for the small things they'd learned to live without.

Over the next few weeks, Chuck and Garth built beds and everyone drifted into separate rooms and then in different directions.

Aboard *Vela*, the cockroaches wouldn't last the first winter. Each weekend, Dawn and Garth bicycled the nine miles to Redwood City where they kept the boat. The two repaired and replaced, scraped and sanded, painted and varnished to restore her to some semblance of respectability. After a brief stint as navigator on a race to Hawaii, Chuck turned his back on sailing. Linda didn't care to step aboard *Vela*—or any sailboat—ever again. As Linda told reporters, "Never again. Once was too much." *Vela*'s days were numbered. For the Wilcoxes she no longer served a purpose and she reminded them of the toughest aspects of their journey. Once *Vela* regained some of her former dignity, Dawn put her up for adoption, and someone was actually willing to pay $14,000. The family was on to other things.

Linda attended high school. Soon after the family's return, she assembled her impressions of places they'd visited into a book-length manuscript, but no publisher she contacted seemed interested. After that Linda took her writing talents into journalism, first with the school newspaper. She went on to become a prize-winning journalist before studying and then practicing law. She tried to forget about sailing around the world or even having a family.

Almost immediately, Chuck had job offers from three companies. Electronics engineers were in high demand, and his former colleagues had learned of his return through the media. Flattering though the offers were, he focused on spending time with his father until his death soon after. And on addressing the pending IRS case. How ironic that the IRS chased him around the globe, when one of Chuck's primary motivators had been to escape the bureaucracy and white noise of contemporary American life. To argue his case, he amassed three grocery sacks full of every receipt related to rebuilding *Vela* after the wreck. Just over a month after the family's return he hopped Caltrain into the city of San Francisco for a hearing. With less than $1,200 in the bank, there was little left to seize, particularly since the family was now living in the only other asset they owned besides *Vela*.

For all Chuck cared, they could have *Vela*. He'd been tempted to sink the boat on many occasions, most recently in the Potato Patch outside the Golden Gate. By the close of the hearing, the IRS agreed to settle the case for nearly every dollar left in their bank account. Once the IRS liquidated the account, Chuck had little choice but to accept one of the job offers with a local electronics company. He had no interest in the comfy, bourgeois existence that his friends had succumbed to, but given his circumstances, what else could he do but go back to work? At least he would now be paid for his ingenuity.

Dawn, with her children now grown and no voyage to prepare for, had to figure out what she wanted in life. Her ulcer seemed to vanish without the stress of sailing. The lump was of no concern. She returned to nursing, caring for geriatric patients, which kept her busy checking blood-sugar levels, administering medications, and monitoring symptoms of dementia and Alzheimer's. In 1986, she finally returned to Cape Sounion to explore the temple they'd sailed past in Greece—without Chuck.

In 1987, she discovered she had low-pressure glaucoma and could expect to gradually go blind. The holes in her vision explained why she'd never been comfortable driving and why using the sextant had been such a challenge. She was glad that because of Chuck's goal she'd gotten to see the world, but twelve years after returning from the voyage, Dawn gathered the courage to go her own way.

After the divorce she focused her indomitable energies on corralling resources for the disabled and visually impaired, transforming into an impassioned crusader, which garnered her awards and press coverage of her own.

Garth, denied the joys of attending high school, never gave it another thought. Since he was eighteen, he took the GED equivalency exam and enrolled in Foothill College, intent on completing the coursework he'd missed. He wanted to apply his experience to a career designing boats. Armed with a few credits and a stellar SAT score, Garth transferred to MIT to study Naval Architecture at one of the few institutions that offered such a program. Upon graduating, he began a career designing tugs, barges, fishing vessels, research vessels, and ferries until love and a yearning to return to sea took him on a seven-year, 34,000-mile voyage with his wife. From 2000 to 2007, he again practiced the fine art of sustaining an ocean-going boat on a tight budget. He eventually built a two-part nesting dinghy similar to the one he designed in Australia as a boy, but Garth still burned with a desire to build and cruise on a vessel of his own design. Using lessons from two voyages totaling 70,000 miles, he designed a thirty-eight-foot boat with simple rigging, inspired by what he'd seen in the Caribbean. With construction underway, he dreams of a third voyage.

Sea trials aboard *Vela* tested everyone in the Wilcox family to their limits. Only Garth seemed to thrive on the challenges they faced. It may come as no surprise that he would be the only one to voyage again.

Vela Glossary

Autopilot/Electronic Autopilot: A device for steering the boat without hands. Chuck designed and built one. The Wilcoxes named theirs "Fred."

Avon inflatable (Dinghy): A rubber coated fabric boat inflated with air to serve as the family's main mode of transportation off the boat.

Backstay: The wire on the back of the boat that runs behind the mainsail and helps to support the mast.

Beating: Sailing as close to the wind as possible. Beating on a sailboat rarely involves eggs.

Boom: The horizontal spar that the main sail attaches to. *Vela*'s was made of wood.

Boom Gallows: A big wooden arch that supports the boom when the sail is furled.

Bowsprit: The pointy beam that sticks out in front of the boat like a prod.

Broach: When a boat rolls onto its sides and turns beam to the seas. When the wind has pushed the boat over to the point where the rudder has come out of the water and the boat will not steer until the wind has spilled off the sails and the boat stands upright again. Not a state to aspire to, nor is it comfortable.

Bunk: Used for sleeping, despite occasional volatile motion.

Celestial Navigation: Measuring your position relative to known positions of celestial bodies through the use of a sextant.

Courtesy Flag: A flag of the country you are currently visiting, flown just below the starboard spreader.

Cockpit: The outside seating area.

Cleat: A fixture for securing lines. The proper name for what Dawn would call "one of those horny things."

Clew: The reinforced corner of the sail that attaches to the sheets to pull the sails.

Cabin sole: The floor of the interior.

Dead Reckoning (DR) or Deduced Reckoning: A calculation of position based on course, speed and time elapsed. As in "I reckon we're here." Not as accurate as celestial navigation, but can be used at night or when cloudy.

Dinghy: Small boat. Can be made of various materials. The Wilcoxes had a hard dinghy, which Garth sailed all over Honolulu and French Polynesia, and an inflatable one the family used for transportation. Also may be referred to as a tender.

Dodger: A spray hood to protect what's down below, much like the pram hood of a carriage.

Fid: A pointy object used to separate strands of line while splicing.

Genoa/Genny: The large sail in the front of the boat.

Gimbal: A metal pivot that allows the stove to remain level (making it the only level surface aboard, in some conditions.)

Groco head: The toilet the family despised because it spent so much time in need of repair. Heads only fail when in use, making for unfortunate timing.

Halyard: The wire or line that pulls or hoists a sail up.

Hand-bearing compass: A hockey-puck-like hand-held compass to use for getting a relative bearing to known landmarks.

Hanks: Metal fittings used to attach the headsails to the forestay.

Hanked on: Attaching sails using hanks.

Head: The toilet and the area where the toilet sits. Area sometimes used for bathing.

Hike/hiking out: Leaning one's weight outboard, to help keep the boat flat. Especially helpful while racing upwind.

Jib: A smaller sail at the front of the boat.

Jibe: Bringing the boom across the boat when the wind is coming from behind.

Lazarette: Cockpit storage locker.

Lead Line: A line with an ingot of lead at the bottom used for swinging ahead of a ship to manually gauge the depth. Once the lead hits the bottom, one can estimate the depth by counting the marks on the line or by guessing the number of arm spans between the lead and the top of the line where measurement begins.

Lifelines: A type of guard rail around the deck of the boat, used to help keep passengers aboard. Can be made of wire, line, or metal braces.

Log Spinner: A metal spinner that twirls behind the boat and measures revolutions to help calculate the speed and distance traveled. Sometimes mistaken for food by aquatic life.

Main/Mainsail: The big sail that attaches directly to the mast and helps drive the boat.

Marlinspike: A pointy object used to force a hole in line while splicing like a small fid used for wire.

Max Ebb: When the current is strongest flowing *out* of an inlet. Not what you want to face if you are trying to venture *into* the inlet. (Also the name of a popular column in *Latitude 38* magazine.)

Moon Shots: Using the sextant, noting the precise angle of the moon at a certain time of day to ascertain current location.

Outboard: The little engine for the dinghy. Also, the area closest to the outside edges of the boat and the opposite of inboard.

Outriggers: On canoes and multi-hull boats, the lighter outboard parts of the boat that help the boat balance.

Painter: The line that attaches to the dinghy's bow for towing or tying it to a dock.

Port: The left side of the boat when facing forward. Or your destination, a safe place to park the boat.

Preventer: A line that keeps the boom from swinging across the boat if the wind catches the back side of the mainsail. Helpful in the event of an accidental jibe.

Ratlines: A type of rope ladder attached to the rigging that helps one climb aloft for sighting rocks or reefs.

Rig/rigging: The mast, wires and lines that support the mast and control the sails.

Round Up: When a boat "rounds up," it heads into the wind.

Rudder: The part of the steering mechanism that moves back and forth in the water with the movement of the tiller or wheel.

Sailing Directions: A description of the shoreline that can be used by ships to help them navigate an ocean, along a coast, or into an inlet.

Sampson Post: Used to tie lines onto the bow.

Settees: The cushioned seating area below deck where the family typically gathered. Also used for sleeping.

Sextant: A device that helps one measure the angle of a celestial body to estimate one's relative location.

Shackle: The metal device that attaches a halyard to the sail so the sails can be raised. Also has other uses.

Sheet: Not just bed linens, sheets are the primary lines that control the angle of the sails.

Slides: provide attachment points on the front of the main sail that help guide it up the mast.

Snubber Line: A shock-absorbing line that eases the tension on the anchor chain in rough anchorages.

Splicing: A way of weaving lines together to form a strong intersection or a loop.

Spreaders: The wooden cross-beams that extend out from the mast and connect to the wires or stays that support the mast. Helpful for keeping the mast up.

Star shots: Using the sextant to note the precise angle of stars at a certain time of day to ascertain one's current location.

Stays: The wires that help hold up the mast.

Staysail: A smaller, second sail just behind the jib sail.

Stormsail: An even smaller sail used in high winds to help steer a boat.

Starboard: The right side of the boat when looking forward.

Steering Quadrant: The connection between wheel and rudder used for steering, tucked inside a cramped compartment.

Tack: Bringing the wind onto the opposite side of the boat when changing direction.

Tang: Metal fitting used to attach the stays to the mast.

Taffrail: the rail around the stern of a ship/boat.

Taffrail Log: the mechanical device that counts the number of miles sailed, based on revolutions of an attached spinner that trails behind the boat.

Tiller (Emergency Tiller): A long, lever-like thing the Wilcoxes used for steering whenever the wheel broke. Barely useable due to the immense force on it caused by severe weather helm.

Topping Lift: A wire or line that holds up the end of the boom.

Vang: The vang connects the boom to the deck to hold it down so the wind doesn't spill out the top of the mainsail.

Whisker Pole: Used to hold out the jib when running downwind so the sail won't flap as much.

Williwaw: A sudden violent wind, usually caused by gusts of cold land air coming down off a mountain.

Acknowledgements

While I spent many hours alone communing with a laptop, I did not write this book without significant input from many others. I am indebted to them for their contribution to this story.

To the Wilcoxes, for living a fascinating adventure worthy of retelling.

To Erika Hublitz, for her hard work gathering material back in 1978, long before I ever laid eyes on my beloved or learned of this amazing story. To Linda Wilcox, for the story she drafted upon their return.

To the reporters, who broke this story as it unfolded, making it easier for me to recreate events using photographs and quotes from the family at the time.

To the Wilcox and DeVaurs families, for keeping the photos and letters the Wilcoxes mailed home which offered more detail than an author has a right to hope for when crafting a story from relatively ancient history. (I am also grateful for the rolltop desk Chuck's father built, which I used to write this book—far roomier than the tiny secretary I used for my last endeavor, *Tightwads on the Loose*, and easier to hide the mess of my creative process.)

To my writing groups: Debra Daniels-Zeller, Kathy Gehrt (in spirit), Elsie Hulsizer, Sheila Kelly, Sharon Morris, Jan Schwert (the Wednesday Writers) and to Mary Curtis, Marilyn Gilbert, Shawn Lowney, Molly Mansker, Jenny Van Aken, and Mary Van Valkenburg (the Tuesday Writers), who read through early drafts for pacing, drama, commas, and wordsmithing and made sure my characters seemed as vivid on the page as they are in real life.

To the fans of my work, whose kind words encouraged me to return to this story, even when I'd grown frustrated or discouraged.

To my friends and family, who listened to me talk ad nauseum about my brain's latest obsession.

To my editor, Jim Thomsen, who helped make sure this manuscript was polished and ready to go. To Lyssa Danehy deHart, who worked her magic to create a clever cover and to the production team who helped turn the final manuscript into something a reader can enjoy.

To Dawn, Garth, and Chuck Wilcox, who endured endless hours of probing questions, and reviewed drafts for inaccuracies and assumptions I made that didn't ring true to their experience.

And especially to my husband, Garth Wilcox, for his unwavering patience and helpful suggestions, for sparking my interest in this story and encouraging me all the way along despite an initial reluctance to be a character in a book—or several. He inspires me in so many ways.

The most interesting people in the world are those who do things because they must, regardless of what others might think. This book is dedicated to the people who have the courage to follow their dreams wherever they might lead.

With gratitude,
Wendy Hinman

About the author

Author Photo by Lee Youngblood

Wendy Hinman is the award-winning author of *Tightwads on the Loose*, about the 34,000-mile seven-year voyage she took aboard a 31-foot boat with her husband, Garth Wilcox, the teenage hero of *Sea Trials*. She is the Editor of the Writers Connection and a sought-after speaker on turning dreams into reality—or succumbing to delusions and the crazy adventures they provoke.

When it comes to choosing a professional speaker for your next event, you can count on Wendy Hinman to deliver humorous and riveting stories that entertain and inspire. Whether for a keynote address or an intimate gathering, she can tailor her life lessons and refreshing perspective to bring you thought-provoking ideas that expand your horizons and bring joy and creativity to life's daily predicaments. She is a polished speaker who has done presentations around the world, is a multi-term president of Toastmasters International and a frequent presenter at yacht clubs, boat shows, book clubs, writing conferences and workshops about reaching your goals one step at a time.

> "Wendy Hinman offers genuine enthusiasm,
> practical noteworthy advice
> and some hilarious tales." *Cruising World Magazine*

Contact her about presenting to your organization today. To listen to interviews with Wendy Hinman, order books in quantity, or for media inquiries, visit www.wendyhinman.com. Or email info@wendyhinman.com.

If you liked this book, please write a review. You may also enjoy *Tightwads on the Loose.*

Reviews for *Tightwads on the Loose*:

"A light-hearted tone and unaffected style make this an entertaining tale." —*San Francisco Book Review*

"Dreams of freedom and adventure: For most people, they remain just that — dreams. For certain others, like Wendy Hinman and Garth Wilcox, such dreams are the stuff life is. In 2000 the couple set sail from Puget Sound for a Pacific Odyssey in their 31-foot cutter, *Velella*. Seven years later, the couple returned home. Along the way, they logged some 34,000 nautical miles, touched 19 countries, endured typhoons, experienced close calls with freighters, potential pirates and phantom night vessels, swam in snake and crocodile infested waters and made do without refrigeration and Internet. A compelling read, "Tightwads on the Loose: a Seven Year Pacific Odyssey" flows as an adventure narrative with a "you are there" flavor. Ms. Hinman had done plenty of professional writing before the voyage: She's as competent with the written word as she is at sea. And she clearly has a sense of humor — a necessary, conjugal survival tool within the confines of a 31-foot boat small enough to prevent her husband from standing straight up." —*Magnolia News*

"Alternately hilarious, exciting and thought provoking, Tightwads on the Loose tells what happens when two people with very disparate personalities set out in a too small boat with a too small budget. Tightwads on the Loose will take you on a glorious romp around the Pacific." —Elsie Hulsizer, author of *Voyages to Windward* and *Glaciers, Bears and Totems*

"It is nice to discover a wordsmith who cares how the words fall upon the page. Wendy Hinman does. She crafts each sentence with care. She is a pleasure to read. I enjoyed this book right from the title. Funny, too!" —*Cap'n Fatty Goodlander, Editor-at-Large of Cruising World magazine.*

"Enjoy a wild ride with Wendy Hinman's *Tightwads on the Loose: A Seven Year Pacific Odyssey*. The pragmatist and the dreamer (at one point Wendy likens herself to Tinker Bell) make entertaining travel companions, and the places they visit capture the imagination." —*Janna Cawrse Esarey, author of The Motion of the Ocean*

"Lively, thoughtful and entertaining, "Tightwads on the Loose" offers a realistic glimpse into the ups and downs of living the cruising dream. Armchair sailors can enjoy the ride, while aspiring voyagers will appreciate Hinman's honesty. She aptly demonstrates that like most worthwhile pursuits, long-distance voyaging is far from easy, and that's a large part of what makes it so satisfying." —*Three Sheets Northwest*

"*Tightwads on the Loose* is the charming true story of a couple whose big dream is to circumnavigate the Pacific Ocean was not deflated by a small budget. Hinman's self-effacing style and eye for the hilarious make the seven-year, 34,000-mile tale a pleasure to read." —*Sailing Magazine*

"Wendy Hinman offers genuine enthusiasm, practical noteworthy advice and some hilarious tales." —*Cruising World Magazine*

Winner of the Journey Award for best true life adventure story, *Chanticleer Book Reviews*

Plus more than 140 positive reviews on Amazon.

47164118R00272

Made in the USA
San Bernardino, CA
24 March 2017